Sum It Up

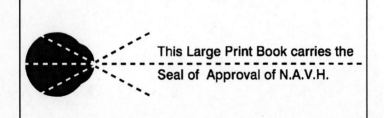

This Large Print Book carries the
Seal of Approval of N.A.V.H.

SUM IT UP

1,098 VICTORIES,
A COUPLE OF IRRELEVANT LOSSES,
AND A LIFE IN PERSPECTIVE

PAT SUMMITT
WITH SALLY JENKINS

LARGE PRINT PRESS
A part of Gale, Cengage Learning

GALE
CENGAGE Learning·

Farmington Hills, Mich • San Francisco • New York • Waterville, Maine
Meriden, Conn • Mason, Ohio • Chicago

GALE
CENGAGE Learning·

LIBRARY OF CONGRESS CATALOGING-IN-PUBLICATION DATA

Summitt, Pat Head, 1952–
    Sum it up : 1,098 victories, a couple of irrelevant losses, and a life in perspective / by Pat Summitt with Sally Jenkins — Large print edition.
        pages cm.
    ISBN 978-1-4104-5820-9 (hardcover) — ISBN 1-4104-5820-2 (hardcover)
    1. Summitt, Pat Head, 1952– 2. Basketball coaches—United States—Biography. 3. Lady Volunteers (Basketball team) 4. Alzheimer's disease—Patients—Biography. I. Jenkins, Sally. II. Title.
GV884.S86A3 2013
796.323092—dc23
[B]   2013001976

ISBN 13: 978-1-59413-712-9 (pbk. : alk. paper)
ISBN 10: 1-59413-712-9 (pbk. : alk. paper)

Published in 2014 by arrangement with Crown Publishers, a division of Random House, Inc.

Printed in the United States of America
2 3 4 5 6   18 17 16 15 14

Dedicated to my families, original and extended: to my son, my mother, my siblings and their families; to my players and their parents and grandparents who made me part of their lives; to the many coaches and coaching mentors I've had the honor to work with who are as close as family; to the many friends who might as well be sisters and brothers; and finally to the family of people who combat Alzheimer's disease

CONTENTS

I know there's something else I'm supposed to be doing. There's something God wants me to do.

Like what?

I'm not sure.

You don't think winning eight national championships and raising a son is enough? You think there's something more you're supposed to be doing?

I know there's something else. I feel it.

— February 23, 2011, on a road trip to Oxford, Mississippi, three months before diagnosis

1
FOOTPRINTS IN THE SAND

I remember a Tennessee field with hay as far as I could see and a tall man standing in it, staring at me with pale blue eyes. Eyes that you wanted to look away from. Daunting eyes. My father had eyes that gave me the feeling he could order up any kind of weather he wanted, just by looking at the sky. If the tobacco crop needed rain, he'd glare upward, until I swore it got cloudy. I gestured at the hay field and said, "Daddy, how long do I have to stay out here?" He said, "You'll be finished when it's done. And it's not done till it's done right."

I remember a leaning gray barn with an iron basketball rim mounted in the hayloft. At night after the chores — after it was done, and done right — my three older brothers and I climbed to the loft for ball games in which they offered no quarter. Just elbows and fists, and the advice "Don't you cry, girl. I better not see you cry." I remember learning to hit back — hard enough to send them through the gallery door into a ten-foot drop to the bales below.

I remember the supper table crammed with bodies, children with clattering forks fighting over the last piece of chicken, and my mild, selfless mother, filling the glasses and plates with a close-lipped smile and a voice soft as a housedress, and then I remember watching her muscle a two-ton truck into gear and roar off to pick up farm supplies.

I remember the searing smell of the ammonia that my college coach waved under my nose, and heavy polyester uniforms with crooked numerals, and the dark hotbox auxiliary gyms with no air-conditioning where they stuck women, one in particular leaking light from holes in the roof, through which birds flapped and splattered their droppings on the floor.

I remember being young and wild with energy, conducting searches for amber liquid refreshments, pulling into joints that sold twenty-cent beer.

"What's your brand?"

"Cold."

I remember standing on a medal podium in the 1976 Montreal Olympics, imbued with a sense that if you won enough basketball games, there was no such thing as poor, or backward, or country, or female, or inferior.

I remember every player — every single one — who wore the Tennessee orange, a shade that our rivals hate, a bold, aggravating color that you can usually find on a roadside crew, "or in a correctional institution," as my friend Wendy Larry jokes. But to us the color is a flag of pride, because it identifies us as Lady Vols and therefore as women of an unmistakable type. Fighters. I remember how many of them fought for a better life for themselves. I just met them halfway.

I remember the faces on the young women who ran suicide drills, flame-lunged and set-jawed, while I drove them on with a stare that burned up the ground between them and me. I remember the sound of my own voice, shouting. "Holdsclaw, sprint *through* the line!" Urgent, determined. "Snow, you're stronger than you think! You don't *ever* let other people tell you who you are!" Exasperated, mocking, baiting. "Holly Warlick, just get out of the drill. Just get out. Put someone in who can throw a pass."

When you see Pat's heartbeat in her neck, you're in trouble. Big trouble. You don't

12

want to look in her eyes, so you try to look someplace else, and then you find her neck — and you see her heartbeat in her neck. Also, you see her teeth gritting. That's not real cool either.

— HOLLY WARLICK

I remember being able to almost read their thoughts. *That lady is crazy; why is she torturing us?* (They embellish.) *I can't ever satisfy her; what does she want from me?* (Only everything.) *Man, I'm getting a bus ticket and going back to New York. Or Indiana. Or Oregon. Or coal country Kentucky.*

"Yeah, I would recommend playing for Pat Summitt," Abby Conklin liked to say, "if a year of counseling comes with it."

Bless their hearts.

I remember chewing the inside of my lower lip over losses, until I had a permanent entrenched scar. I remember asking my friends and family two questions after every NCAA championship game.

"Do you think I was too hard on them?"

"What did Daddy say?"

I remember being so possessed by the job that I coached in my sleep. I'd toss and kick until I woke myself up hollering, "Git down the floor!"

I remember standing on the sideline and

stamping my high heels on the hardwood so furiously it sounded like gunshots, and whacking my hands on the scorer's table until I flattened the gold championship rings on my fingers.

I remember jabbing a finger into an official's face and backing him from midcourt to the baseline.

I remember the sound of certainty in my own voice, lifted over the roar of twenty thousand people and two rivalrous marching bands in a sold-out arena at the NCAA Final Four, as I told our players that though they trailed by eleven points with seven minutes to go, the game was ours. "We're not *leaving* here without a championship!" I shouted hoarsely. "So y'all just go on out there and get it!"

I remember how intensely in the moment I felt in big games. I remember the second-by-second adjustments, the dialing up of players' emotions in the huddles, operating on pure feel, calling plays less by rational process than by some buried sense of rhythm, that *now is the time* for a change of pace. I remember the speed of the decision making — who needs the ball, who needs to be in the game — and how I loved that. *Loved* it.

I remember the laughter that was always

equal to the shouting, great geysers of it that went with victory champagne. Peals of stress-relieving hilarity behind closed doors with assistant coaches who have been more close friends than colleagues, Mickie DeMoss, Holly Warlick, Dean Lockwood, Nikki Caldwell. I remember Mickie, the queen of one-liners, razzing Dean about a date he wouldn't introduce us to. "You know, Dean," she said, "you can always get her teeth fixed," and all of us whooped until we banged our silverware on the table.

I remember their constant teasing about my hair, and my clothes — the outrageous colors, hemlines, and shoulder pads. Once, Holly scanned my light blue suit up and down and said, "No damn Easter egg is going to tell *me* what to do!"

I remember a tiny saloon in the Tennessee hills where the bartender squirted bourbon shots from a squeeze bottle, straight into the customers' mouths. I remember later, when I was older and more sedate, rambling across a vineyard in France with my great friend DeMoss and our former player Caldwell, and deciding to open the bottle of wine we'd just bought, but not having any glasses. "Well, we'll just have to take it to the head," Caldwell said. So we sipped the Bordeaux straight from the bottle.

I remember teaching a clinic to other coaches and opening the floor for questions, and a guy raised his hand and asked if I had any advice when it came to "coaching women." I remember leveling him with a death ray stare and then relaxing and curling up the corner of my mouth and saying, "Don't worry about coaching 'women.' Just go home and coach 'basketball.' "

I remember my wedding day back in Henrietta, Tennessee, to R.B. Summitt, a handsome, deep-chested young banker from Sevierville, Tennessee. My parents against their better judgment ordered a champagne fountain for the reception, and the next morning my mother said softly, "Trisha, I think your guests got too full."

I remember the night my son was born. The doctor placed him on my chest and I said, "Hey, Tyler, I've been waitin' on you." He rolled directly toward the sound of my voice and locked eyes with me and R.B., who was by my shoulder. Holly and Mickie were in the delivery room for reasons too complicated to explain now but that I'll get to later, and Mickie blurted, "He's got kind of a cone head." And Holly said, "Mickie, don't say that!" and they started bickering, and it was true that he did have a little bit of a cone head, but he grew into a fine young baby, and a fine young man, and my greatest achievement.

I remember all this. But there are also things I don't remember; things that I know are important and that I *should* remember. On some days, I feel like a jigsaw with pieces missing. I can put most of the puzzle together, but there are blanks that I can't fill in. It's the middle that's missing. How can I see the whole picture, know what it's supposed to be, when the middle is missing? But then I look at my son, and remember.

It's you, darlin', I think to myself. *It's you.*

Here are some of the things I don't remember.

Sometimes, when I first wake up, I don't remember where I am. For a moment I'm disoriented and uneasy, and I have to lie there until it comes to me.

Occasionally when I'm asked a question, I begin to answer it but then I forget the subject — it slips away like a thread through my fingers.

I struggle to remember directions. There are moments when I'm driving to someplace I should know, and I have to ask, "Do I go left or right here?"

17

I tend not to remember what hotel room I'm in.

I don't remember what time my appointments are for.

I don't remember records, final scores, and statistics. Numbers have a strange slipperiness for me, a lack of specificity; they suggest nothing. If you ask me how many games we won in 1998, or what happened in the 2008 NCAA national championship game, I struggle to remember which one it was.

But if you tell me who was on that team — if you prompt me with names rather than numbers — Shannon Bobbitt, Alexis Hornbuckle, Alberta Auguste, Candace Parker, Nicky Anosike — they bring it all back. Show me a picture of a former player, frozen in an old team photo, and I remember her. "That's Linda Ray," I will say. "She didn't play much but she was a great teammate, and smart. Biochemistry major."

By now, in considering the things I remember and the things I don't, something may have struck you. My memories are not made up so much of information, but rather of episodes and engagements with the people I love. The things I struggle with — times, dates, schedules — are things you could as easily read on a digital watch or calendar. But people and emotions are engraved in me. What this tells me is that facts are only the smallest components of memory. They are elements, but nothing close to the whole.

My birthday (June 14, 1952) is always on Flag Day, but that doesn't begin to sum up the years of my life or the events stamped most deeply on me. Nor do other numbers that are so often used to describe my career. Thirty-eight years as the head coach at Tennessee. Eight national championships. An all-time record of 1,098 victories, and a 100 percent graduation rate, which was the real point of all that winning. Twenty-seven successful years of marriage, followed by one shattering breakup. Six crushing miscarriages compensated for by one matchless, peerless son, for which I'm grateful to God. Two devastating and incurable medical diagnoses.

None of that sums it up.

A memoir is not a documentary. We think we keep an accurate record of ourselves in the bean-counting tablets of our minds, but we don't. None of us sees or remembers everything about one's life; memories are unreliable — they smudge, and fade, like disappearing footprints in the sand. We're too busy standing in the middle of it all to remember everything perfectly, and I was busier than most people.

Always, we rely on others, the people who have known us best, and most intently, to complete the picture of ourselves.

In my case, I'm especially reliant.

In the late spring of 2011, I was diagnosed with early-onset Alzheimer's disease, the progressive neurological illness that attacks the brain. From what I'm told, an unnatural buildup of proteins forms a gluelike plaque in my nerve cells and synapses, interfering with my ability to remember and to reason. So far there is no cure — it's irreversible. It's estimated that about five million Americans suffer from the affliction, and another fifteen million caregivers, spouses, and children are affected by it.

Have you ever walked along a shoreline, only to have your footprints washed away by the surf? That's what Alzheimer's is like. The waves steadily erase the marks we leave in the sand, all the sand castles. Some days are better than others — the waves come in and they recede, bringing a fog with them that sometimes clears.

In my case, symptoms began to appear when I was only fifty-seven. In fact, the doctors believe early-onset Alzheimer's has a strong genetic predictor, and that it may have been progressing hidden in me for some years before I was diagnosed. I'd been walking around with a slow-ticking, slow-exploding bomb in my brain cells, and it only became apparent when it began to seriously interfere with my work.

It's hard to pinpoint the exact day that I first noticed something wrong. Over the course of a year, from 2010 to 2011, I began to experience a troubling series of lapses. I had to ask people to remind me of the same things, over and over. I'd ask three times in the space of an hour, "What time is my meeting again?" — and then be late. In the fall of 2010, one of my college teammates and oldest friends, Esther Hubbard, was supposed to come up for a Tennessee football game. I must have called her four times and said, "Now when are y'all coming?"

It was talk, and repeat. Talk, and repeat. I thought, Something isn't right. Someone is going to have to confront this.
— ESTHER HUBBARD

Close friends noticed that I would forget the most important conversations. Michelle Marciniak, a former point guard with whom I had a long, embattled coach-player relationship that ended with an unforgettable

21

1996 national championship, came up to stay with me that fall. Michelle is an impressively busy young woman, an entrepreneur with her own textile business, but a couple of times a year she visits me in Knoxville and stays over as my houseguest. One night we sat up until about midnight catching up on life. We talked about her family, how her mother and father were doing, over a glass of wine.

The next morning she wandered into the kitchen. There were a few people standing around, as there usually are, friends, neighbors, colleagues — and dogs.

Somebody said, "Michelle, how's your family?"

> Pat had just walked into the kitchen and was pouring herself some coffee. She said, "Yeah, Michelle, how *is* your family?" And it just was like, boom. I froze. I thought, what's going on? And then I started noticing other things from that point on.
>
> — MICHELLE MARCINIAK

I had always struggled to keep track of my car keys and cell phone, but now I lost them three times a day; I could never remember where I had put them last.

At first I thought it was funny, and totally in keeping with my character. I'd always been so hyperfocused on coaching that I didn't even know the weather outside. I'd wear short sleeves in an ice storm. I was a working mother who juggled too many responsibilities and obligations, and it was natural to have moments when I got a little overwhelmed. I'd never known the date, or the name of my hotel — there have been so many of them, and they all look the same, and they are all called Radisson or Clarion or Hyatt or Hilton. Reporters would ask me, "Pat, who's going to win the Super Bowl?" I'd say, "Fellas, who's playing?"

I'd always had too many people in the house and fielded too many phone calls. For as long as I'd worked, I'd been prone to scatteredness. Somehow, I always got it all done and was still standing. "I'm too fast for germs," I joked.

That winter, on the eve of a big game, I pulled up to Tennessee's Thompson-Boling Arena on two wheels as I always did and jumped out to hurry inside to the locker room — leaving the car running, the door partly ajar, and my wallet on the floor. Before tip-off, a security guard had to come in to tell me that my beautiful S-Class Mercedes-Benz was idling like a getaway car, with exhaust pouring from the tailpipe.

I laughed it off. It was a case of having too much on my mind or being technologically challenged. The car had one of those fancy new keyless ignitions, and I had just been in too big of a rush, I thought.

But then I grew confused in the heat of a game. Suddenly, I could not recall a scheme. Normally I would reflexively hold up a hand signal and shout an offensive set to our team, "Horns!" Or a defensive shift, "Charlotte!" But now there were strange empty moments when I couldn't call up the right term.

I would stare at the court unable to track all that I was watching. I'd spent four decades teaching myself to see ten players at once, the whole ninety-four feet of hardwood and all the movement on it, the multiple actions. I was accustomed to analyzing patterns and almost instantaneously ordering up attacks and counters; only now I saw an indistinguishable blur, flashes and bursts.

Friends started asking, "Are you having trouble with your memory?"

Finally I admitted, "Sometimes I draw blanks."

I grew uncertain, and then a little frightened. I began staying in bed until late in the morning, which was unlike me. I'd always been a bolter, the first person up and the most energetic one, too, and I'd always gone to work earlier than anyone on my staff. But I began to dread going into the office.

In bed, there were no challenges. No worrisome situations that required a decision. No conversations in which I feared I might make a telltale slipup. I would lie under the covers, trying to figure out what was wrong in my head. Some mornings I would think to myself, *I don't even want to go in. I'll just stay around here, in a safe place.*

I was late to practice, slipping into the arena while it was already under way and then leaning quietly under one goal. I became increasingly hesitant and withdrawn, to the point that I even avoided meeting with our players one-on-one. I was afraid I might say something wrong.

Finally Mickie DeMoss confronted me. Mickie is a small, dark-eyed, and intense woman who has been a close friend to me for almost forty years. For twenty of those years we had worked together at Tennessee as trusted professional confidantes. Mickie was always truthful with me, even when it was hardest or led to an argument.

"Pat, what is going on with you?" she demanded.

"I don't know," I said. "I don't know."

"You need to be here," she said. "You need to figure it out, so you can be here for this team."

I thought it must be a reaction to medication. Each and every morning, I reluctantly swallowed a handful of prescriptions for various ailments. In 2004, I had developed an irregular heartbeat, and in 2006, I was all but immobilized with crippling pain that was diagnosed as an aggressive case of rheumatoid arthritis. The meds allowed me to get out of bed and keep working, but it wasn't exactly a delightful cocktail.

I went to see my primary care physician, Dr. Amy Bentley, who suggested that I visit the famed Mayo Clinic in Minnesota for a thorough evaluation. But I decided to wait until after the season was over, because altering any of my medications might mean the excruciating pain of arthritis would return. So I went back to work and told myself I would deal with it in the spring.

Things grew worse. Two former Tennessee players happened to be living with me at the time. Shanna Zolman, a great sharp-shooting guard from the class of 2006, was staying in my pool house for a few months while she dealt with a difficult divorce and also rehabbed a knee injury. Another great,

Kara Lawson (class of '03), and her husband, Damien Barling, were staying downstairs while she did some training for the WNBA season. Both of them noticed the same nagging tendencies.

> I remember saying to Damien, "Does Pat tell you the same story twice sometimes?" He said, "Yeah. But just let her tell it again because she's having such a good time telling it." We thought she was just so busy she couldn't remember what she had told you. We talked about how she needed to slow down.
>
> — KARA LAWSON

One afternoon I went with Shanna to downtown Knoxville to meet with a divorce lawyer I had helped her find. I don't go downtown too often, and while we were there, I got turned around on a side street and got lost. "How can you get lost, when you're practically the mayor of this city?" Shanna teased me.

Spring 2011 finally arrived — and with it a disheartening NCAA tournament loss. We were among the favorites to contend for a national championship with a 34-3 record, but by then I was having trouble concentrating and communicating what I wanted to

27

our players in the huddles. I had lost my confidence.

A powerful Notre Dame team upset us in the Elite Eight in Dayton, Ohio, 73–59. Our sideline looked like a fire drill with all our assistants jumping in and out giving instructions, trying to stop the bleeding. When the final buzzer sounded, I stood on the sideline for a long moment, wondering if I had coached my last game. But to be honest, I was so sick with worry over myself that it was almost a relief to able to focus on my health.

That was a very scary time. Because the shoulder that we all leaned on now seemed to be unable to hold us all up like it normally could. And the worst part was not knowing what was wrong. It was like a shadow that nobody wanted to acknowledge.

— TYLER SUMMITT

As soon as we got back to Knoxville, my old friend Kim Mulkey, the Baylor coach, called Mickie. "What's wrong with Pat?" she said. "She isn't herself. I know it." Calls came in from four or five other coaches all saying the same thing, asking concerned, probing questions.

I was about to find out. With the help of my son, Tyler; my longtime personal assistant, LaTina Haynes; my secretary, Katie Wynn; and my close friend Mary Margaret Carter, who is a top nurse anesthetist at the University of Tennessee Medical Center, I booked a series of appointments. I spent that spring occupied with a succession of tedious, alarming visits to doctors. I had heart tests, bone scans, and blood tests.

The doctors are lucky they are still standing. The first one I felt tempted to hit was a fine, much-decorated neurologist at the University of Tennessee Medical Center, Dr. John Dougherty. We went over my medication, and my memory difficulties, and he put me through a series of tests that included a magnetic resonance image of my brain.

After studying the MRI, Dougherty looked grave. He suspected my symptoms were not medication related, he said. In his opinion, I was suffering from a form of "dementia," probably of the Alzheimer's type, and I should prepare to retire.

The word confused me. Dementia? Only elderly people had that. Or battered football players.

I didn't have dementia. How could someone like me have dementia? Hall of Fame coaches did not have dementia. In-demand corporate speakers, motivators, mothers of the year, and holders of all-time records for victories did *not* have dementia. And they did *not* retire.

"You don't know me," I said angrily. "You don't know anything about me."

I was certain that the Mayo Clinic would clear the whole thing up. Mayo was the world-renowned destination for anyone with a difficult or mysterious medical ailment, and surely they would tell me what was really wrong with me, and how to fix it. In late May, I flew out to Minnesota along with Tyler and Mary Margaret and checked into a small hotel next to the clinic.

For three days I underwent a battery of tests. I had another MRI. I had a PET (positron emission tomography) scan, which consists of having radioactive dye shot into your vein to highlight your organs and tissues. Next came a spinal tap — a needle was inserted into my back and fluid collected from my spinal column for analysis. I lay there, with a probe in my backbone. After the needle was removed, the nurse told me to remain lying down for twenty minutes. But sitting still is not something that comes naturally to me. After five minutes, I announced in no uncertain terms, "I feel fine." I jumped off the table. The nurse looked at Tyler and lifted an eyebrow. "I'm not going to be the one to stop her," she said. He just grinned and shook his head.

Then came a neuropsych exam, to evaluate my memory status and problem-solving abilities. In a way, it was the worst part. An attendant led me into a small white room, all alone. The examiner began firing math questions at me. Now, math has always been a sore subject. My college sorority sisters had to do a lot of my math homework for me. Suddenly I felt under pressure.

"Count backward from one hundred by sevens," the examiner said.

Silence.

I was paralyzed.

"Do you know today's date?"

I never know today's date. I deal with dates strictly on a need-to-know basis.

The questions went on and on. Draw the face of a clock. Repeat number sequences. Spell words backward. I felt like I was in a final exam — and failing it. None of the questions seemed relevant; none seemed a test of my real capacities or the way my brain works on a regular basis. Why didn't they test for any of the things I was good at?

At the end of the three days, Tyler and I

met with Dr. Ronald C. Petersen, the Mayo Clinic's leading neurologist and dementia expert, one of the best clinical researchers in the field. He rendered his opinion: I appeared to have "mild" signs of "early-onset dementia, Alzheimer's type."

Alzheimer's type? What did that mean, *type*? My great-grandfather had Alzheimer's. People with Alzheimer's went wandering off into the woods in their pajamas. A bolt of fear shot through me. At the end, my great-grandfather didn't even know his own name. Surely I didn't have that.

There was no 100 percent sure test for Alzheimer's, short of an autopsy, Dr. Petersen explained. But the images of my brain showed small pockmarks, signs of plaque that were hallmarks of the disease. He was still awaiting the result of my spinal tap, but he believed it would show the presence of something called the beta-amyloid protein, which was the closest thing to a clinically certain test for Alzheimer's. If I had beta-amyloid in my cerebrospinal fluid, that meant the protein was building up in my brain, interfering with the nerve cells.

Tyler and I would need to make some decisions, he told us. He discussed the standard drugs for Alzheimer's (more pills), which showed some effectiveness in slowing down the disease. He outlined nonpharmaceutical ways to combat it, such as diet, puzzles and brainteasers, and heavy exercise. He discussed clinical trials and where some of the research stood.

We would need a financial plan, and a long-term plan for my health, he said. Tyler should prepare himself to become "a caregiver." I looked at Tyler — my son was only twenty, a junior at the University of Tennessee. He sat there with his open, flushed young face staring at the doctor, his eyes large and pooling blue, under a shelf of reddish-gold hair. *He needs to be a college boy,* I thought, *not a caregiver.*

The doctor murmured on. As the disease progressed, he said, I would be forced to quit working sooner rather than later. I should make plans to retire.

There was that suggestion again.

"I am *not* ready to retire," I announced.

Dr. Petersen nodded his head. Although Alzheimer's was a dire diagnosis, it didn't mean I had to quit living a productive life. On the contrary, he said, I should work with it for as long as I felt able. But Alzheimer's was hugely unpredictable, he warned. In some people it moved very quickly, while others were able to stay active and engaged for many years. There was no set pattern. I would simply have to wait and see.

I left Mayo in a state of profound denial. "Well, it isn't cancer," I kept saying to Tyler and Mary Margaret. "At least I don't have cancer."

I refused to accept the diagnosis, or any of the advice that went with it. Part of the problem was that I was so highly functional. All my life I'd found that the best way to deal with problems, especially physical ones, was to keep moving. Plunge ahead. "I'm fine," I told Tyler. Once we got home to Knoxville, I would barely discuss it with him. I wouldn't even say the word *Alzheimer's.* I preferred *dementia;* somehow it sounded less severe. Anyway, I was too busy to talk much.

I decided to just go on about my normal business, and for the next several weeks that's what I did. I rushed off to the annual Southeastern Conference meetings in Destin, Florida. Then back to Knoxville for two weeks of annual summer basketball camps. Then I hit the road again for a series of summer league tournaments to evaluate potential recruits. The denial lasted into the following month.

Tyler, meanwhile, was dealing with things in his own way. Which was a lot like mine. He went into action, preferring overdrive to

34

conversation. He met with our accountant. He got himself up to speed on our finances and began to go about reorganizing them. He met with a lawyer. He read about the disease, sorting through the potential therapies and clinics where I might be treated. He downloaded puzzles and brainteasers onto my iPad and encouraged me to play them. He worked out relentlessly in the gym, preparing for his senior season as a walk-on on the Tennessee men's basketball team. He pored over his textbooks; he was an honors student taking an accelerated class load and was on track to graduate in three years instead of four because it was his ambition to be a head coach. He wanted to apply for a job as a graduate assistant and get his master's in education.

But underneath our skins, the diagnosis was wearing on us. Each morning atop Tyler's stack of books was his Bible. Both of us were reading deeply in it. I tended to turn to the Psalms that asked for God's help in staving off enemies. Tyler put a poster of the verse from Isaiah 40:31 over the door to his room in his rented off-campus apartment. "But those who hope in the Lord will renew their strength. They will soar on wings like eagles; they will run and not grow weary, they will walk and not be faint."

When the full blow finally fell, it was heavy. I had an appointment with a psychopharmacologist to check my reactions to the various medications and be sure they didn't conflict. Most of my conversations with doctors by this point were disturbing. But this one was downright traumatic.

The doctor told me that given my diagnosis, frankly, he felt I could no longer work at all. I should step down immediately, because in his opinion the dementia would progress rapidly. I needed to quit, and get myself out of the public eye as quickly as possible, or I would "embarrass" myself and ruin my legacy.

As he spoke, I felt my fist clench. It was all I could do not to lunge across the desk and drop him with one punch. Who did he think he was? Even if I had an irreversible brain disease — even if I did — what right did he have to tell me how to cope with it?

Quit? *Quit?*

"Do you have any idea who you're dealing with?" I said, my voice rising. "You don't know me, and you don't know what I'm capable of."

I emerged from his office in tears. I cried all the way home in the car. In the passenger seat next to me, LaTina also wept. As soon as I walked in the door of my house, I went to my bedroom, climbed into the bed, and curled up in the dark. I didn't get up for hours.

I had always been capable of dealing with any problem, and defeating any opponent, with sheer willpower. I was the resident superhero. Friends, family, and former players struggling physically or emotionally had always come to me for comfort and strong advice on how to push through problems.

"You can't say 'can't' to me," I told our players. "Don't ever say that word; I won't accept it."

I was more than the test numbers on four corners of a piece of paper, I told myself. The brain has an amazing ability to compensate — to transfer tasks. A spinal tap didn't test for leadership, or relationships, or the capacity of my heart.

Alzheimer's might affect other people, but it had never met Pat Summitt, I declared inwardly. My "legacy" was not just an image — a posterized cardboard cutout. I was someone to reckon with. A person of uncompromising substance based on thirty-eight years of unbroken triumph and personified in 161 players who won whole fistfuls of banners and trophies. Mister Al Alzheimer was about to meet Miss Pat.

Quit? *Quit?* I was supposed to walk away

from a Tennessee team that was everything I'd ever worked for, that was inseparable from . . . myself? I might as well try to walk out of my own body or peel off my own shadow. I'd been named head coach of women's basketball at the University of Tennessee when I was just twenty-two years old. I'd hand-built every aspect of the program and handpicked every person associated with it. It wasn't just a job; it was my life, my home, and my family, and the players were the second-deepest love of my life. It wasn't for nothing that my nickname among them was "Mama Pat." Or, when they were feeling especially flip, just "Your Mama." As in, "How'd Your Mama know where we went last night?"

Quit? *Quit?* Coaching isn't social work, but it's more than just a game — it's a heartfelt vocation, in which you are powerfully bonded to students who need you. Often, they need you more than they *know* they need you. It's a job that engages all your mind and muscle and spirit, a job in which you grab kids by the arm and pull them out of their respective emotional fires, whatever that fire is, and show them what real self-worth looks like. Sometimes I almost wanted to say to a kid, "I'm going to save you from yourself, and you don't even realize you need it. It's going to be tough love and you're going to get it in heavy doses, and you won't like me at first, but at the end of the day you will love me. I'm going to show you how to live."

You don't walk away from such a calling just to take care of yourself.

Quit? *Quit?* We keep score in life because it matters. It counts. Too many people opt out and never discover their own abilities, because they fear failure. They don't understand *commitment.* When you learn to keep fighting in the face of potential failure, it gives you a larger skill set to do what you want to do in life. It gives you vision. But you can't acquire it if you're afraid of keeping score.

Basketball is a beautiful game on so many levels, because it creates movement — there is motion within the four lines of the court, and elevation. It's a game that can lift kids out of wretched parks with broken swings and carry them to another plane. But you don't create that beauty without the squeal of sneakers, drenching sweat, and cries of real pain.

This was a different kind of pain, however. And I didn't know how to deal with it. Neither did Tyler. Early one morning, he came in my room and woke me up. My bedroom is a beautiful haven with soft muted beige colors and painted vines on the wall, and it took a moment for my eyes to adjust in the flat, dim light. But when I made out his face, I saw he was weeping. "You're all I've got," he said. "And I need help." He begged me to address the disease with him. I needed to accept it, and help him accept it, too.

I shot upright in bed. "I am right here for you, son," I said. "Let's take care of this right now." It suddenly hit me that in trying to cope with the disease in my own way — with denial — I had actually left my son alone in dealing with it.

Tyler crawled onto the bed, and I put my arms around him. We held each other and had a long talk. We realized that we were both trying to outtough the other. He was trying to be Superman, and I was trying to be Wonder Woman. But as much as we wanted to deny reality, we couldn't. The only way to deal with trouble of this magnitude was to face it — and admit to the fact that I would need a lot of help.

It wasn't easy to reverse roles, to admit that I was struggling and needed care. Surrender didn't come naturally to me, and neither did vulnerability.

All my life, I had preached "taking ownership" to athletes. I insisted they commit to their talent and to themselves, not just by working at the things they were good at, but by admitting the things they weren't good at. It was a difficult, counterintuitive thing to teach — no one feels strong when she examines her own weakness. But in facing weakness, you learn how much there is in you, and you find a blueprint for real strength. Don't look away from the difficult things, I urged our athletes. "Take ownership!"

When you own something, you possess it, live it, act on it.

It was time to take ownership of my diagnosis. The question was, how? What was the best way to confront it? Was it better to retire and concentrate on fighting the Alzheimer's, or was that too much of a concession to the disease? In order to decide, I had to review everything I thought I was about.

I had to remember.

What do you want your players to learn from this? As far as teaching them, what do you want to teach them?

You know, I just want them to understand, "This is what I'm going through. Some of you have gone through knee injuries, you've had other issues, but you don't quit living." You know? You keep going.

How do you feel now that you have a diagnosis? Do you feel better?

I feel better just knowing what I'm dealing with. As far as I'm concerned, it's not going to keep me from living my life. It's not going to keep me from coaching. I'm going to stick my neck out, and do what I always do.

— August 2011, Knoxville, Tennessee, nine weeks after diagnosis

2
COUNTRY GIRL

The Pontiac GTO idled with a low vibration under my seat. Ahead was a two-lane blacktop, a quarter mile of country road in Henrietta, Tennessee, lit by one dim streetlight and the headlamps of the other teenaged drag racers, who had come out in the middle of the night to kill boredom by cheating death in their Dodges and Plymouths. I was sixteen, the only girl at a wheel. Perched on a dormer windowsill of our farmhouse down the road, my sister, Linda, and some of her friends sneaked cigarettes as they gazed at the finish line in the distance, which was just a marker before a blind curve.

Somebody waved a start signal. My wheels bit pavement. Torque pulled at the rear of the car and tires sought traction on black tarmac. I went from 0 to 60 mph in about seven seconds.

Nothing was at stake except bragging

rights. The guys from Ashland City seemed to think they were better drivers, with hotter cars, than folks from Henrietta, an unincorporated little farm community without so much as a caution light or post office, just one little general store. The Ashland City guys would come up in the middle of the night, and our farm boys would leave the feed mill where they drank beer and pull out to the road in their polished muscle cars to take them on.

> Both of us would sneak out that window. There would be guys on the roof of the store too, trying to see who won. It was very, very dangerous. If you met somebody on the road it was a head-on crash.
> — LINDA ATTEBERY

My GTO was a borrowed ride; the only automobiles my family owned were pickup trucks and a dented sedan. But I would beg my boyfriends for their treasured keys. "Come on, let me have a turn at the wheel," I'd say. I was the only girl they ever let drive, maybe because I was taller and stronger than most of the guys. I was the only one who asked, too. It was flat-out scary; even my brothers didn't drag race — and maybe that's why I did it.

45

The car roared through the standing quarter mile, the needle ticking upward.

There wasn't much to Henrietta. The blacktop stretched through meadows and hollows bordered by cornstalks brushed with gold. You could hear the night cicadas and smell the sweet smoke of tobacco curing. There were more barns and sheds than houses.

Parked along the roadside was Howell Foust, in his burnt-orange Dodge Super Bee, which I conned the keys to sometimes. My cousin Ricky Elliott, with his black Chevelle Super Sport, was there too. Rudy Batts in his cream-colored '68 Chevelle with the heel-toe clutch and the four-on-the-floor gearshift tight by your knee. And Phillip Jarrell, in his blue, long-torso, coyote-dusting Plymouth Road Runner.

I hit 100 mph in about fifteen seconds. On the dashboard, the needle of the speedometer shivered at the max point.

The front of the GTO burst across the finish line, just nosing out the other car. I pulled over before the curve and braked, with relief. I had a mixed record as a drag racer. I won some — and sometimes I cleaned out a ditch. But I could not *stand* to lose.

It had something to do, I understood

vaguely, with how I was raised, the fourth of five children and the first girl in a southern farm family. Outside, in the fields, I was treated the same as my older brothers, namely, like a farmhand. I did the same work as a man. But in every other instance, women came in second and had to fight for respect.

I was going to prove I could come in first. I couldn't stand to be second at anything, a bet, a dare, a race, or the nightly games of basketball with my brothers in the hayloft. If I lost, I'd tell them, "We're going to play again after we finish our supper." If I lost again after supper, I'd say, "We're going to stay out here all night." We'd play until I was on a winning side, because I had no intention of going to bed in second place.

The car shuddered to a stop. I switched off the ignition and climbed out. I handed the keys over to their rightful owner and grinned at the boys, who grinned back approvingly. I headed back to the little white farmhouse by the side of the road, where I would slip back through that dormer window silently for fear of waking my parents.

I'm going to bed a winner tonight, I thought. That meant I could sleep.

I drove a tractor long before I ever drove a

car, and I drove it like a fool, too. We were hardscrabble, self-made people. My father had to sell a mule to get the money to marry my mother, that's how little they had starting out. I wish I could say it was a horse, or a cow, or some nobler creature, but it wasn't, it was a mule. The price was a hundred dollars.

Most of the roads were unpaved back then. There was nothing in Henrietta except tobacco fields, cornfields, churches, and the small general store that my parents owned for a while, where we pumped gas and sold sugar to bootleggers. Which caused some comment from the Methodists.

For the first few years of my life we lived in a log cabin in a little place called Oak Plains, with no running water. There was just a pump off the back porch that drew from a well, and an outhouse. Later, when some of the young women who played for me were self-conscious about their lack of wherewithal, I told them it was no excuse for failure to make something out of themselves. "Don't think I'm ignorant as to how you grew up," I said.

The cabin was so small that I slept in a baby bed until I was six, while my three brothers slept heaped together like a wolf pack. The logs seemed to trap every temperature, summer swelter or winter frost. Our only heat came from a fireplace and an old coal stove that my mother cooked on. You could see light coming in from the chinks and cracks between the logs, and the weather would blow right through. You'd get in bed at night, and in the morning have to throw snow off your covers.

Jesse James supposedly laid the cornerstone of the cabin, and although there is no direct proof of that, my daddy believed it and I did too. The area was settled in the early 1800s by rascally fortune hunters from the Carolinas and Kentucky, who littered the surrounding counties with their abandoned chimney stones and named their landmarks things like Half Pone, Raccoon Creek, and Cheap Hill. They lingered invisibly, too, in ghost stories such as the Bell Witch, an invisible specter that slaps children. Our local founder was a pioneer named Abner Gupton, who left an estate of seven thousand acres and three hundred slaves, although by the 1950s, comparatively few people of color were left in the county. I remember an old black man named Blue.

No one ever went to the doctor, couldn't afford it. If you got sick, Daddy just looked at you as if to say, "Get well," and Mama made a potion of Listerine, ground-up aspirin, and salt water. When we got warts, we went to a man who rubbed on them and then made us spit on a stone and throw it over a shoulder and bury a dishrag in the yard.

My mother, Hazel Albright, quit school in the ninth grade and went to work in an Acme boot factory to help support her family. She came from Shady Grove, where her father had a sixty-acre farm and did some sawmilling. She was tiny, just five foot four, with rich brown curls and mild blue eyes, and a light, quick laugh. You'd never have known she didn't have much education and had to scratch for a living, because she's so smart, which you can tell from the way she wins at cards. She never seemed in a bad mood when I was a girl, and I don't ever remember her complaining. She didn't need much to have fun, just good friends around a kitchen table, and some aces and kings to rob them with.

She met my father one afternoon when he came over to talk to her brother about catching a ride to school together. Richard Head was six foot five, with a white-blond head and those sky-blue eyes, and a voice that sounded like it came out from the bottom of a steel drum. He was lovestruck. He said right away he "was going to have her one way or the other." They married when he was twenty and she was still just seventeen.

They were a mismatched pair. My daddy seldom smiled and didn't talk much, but when he did, he *meant* it. People were so intimidated by him they called him Mister Richard, or just Tall Man. Some of his silence was a result of the fact that he was so sore and tired from working all the time. But in retrospect, it must have also been sadness. His mother was ill for much of his life, with rheumatoid arthritis so bad that she became wheelchair-bound, which the family dealt with by lowering the kitchen cabinets and the sink, so that she could continue to keep house. Eventually, she was institutionalized in Nashville. Her illness would be part of my inheritance — it's one thing I got from her, along with a pump organ.

My parents, different as they were, made great partners. They shared a determination to live by their own hands instead of working for others. When they first married, my father took a job as hired farmhand for just $40 a month, but on the side he trapped possums and rabbits to sell for their hides, while my mother cooked hot lunches over at a public school in Ashland City. They raised chickens, and on Saturdays my father would go up to Nashville and peddle them for a dollar apiece. Dollar by dollar, they saved up $100 to buy their first cow. Then they bought another that way, and another, until they had fifteen cows. They would milk them by hand and sell the five-gallon cans to the local schools.

They worked constantly — they didn't know the difference between work and hard work. They had no choice, because the cabin was filling up with kids: my oldest brother, Tommy, was born in June 1945, then came Charles in June of '48, then Kenneth in '50, and me in '52, followed by my sister, Linda, the baby of the family, after a lag of six years, in '58.

We inherited Richard's genes, as you can see in the family pictures that show a row of kids so strapping that it must have taken every dime they had to feed us. When Tommy was thirteen, his head already came to my dad's shoulder, and he would grow to be six foot six. I was scared to death I was going to be as tall as my brother, because by the time I was in third grade I was five foot nine. You can imagine my relief when I stopped at five eleven.

The pictures also show how much pride my parents took in us: I'm invariably in a flouncy little frock with my hair tied by a ribbon, while the boys are in blazers with bow ties, their heads cropped and slick with hair tonic. My mother is always in her best dress — she only had two — a fitted polka-dot one, which she wore with a rope of fake pearls. Next to her is my father, austere in a thin black necktie and crisp white shirt. We are always posed in front of a nice paisley curtain or a neatly trimmed hedge.

My parents put every dollar they earned back into expanding their farm, and by the time I was six, they finally had enough wherewithal to build a one-story brick house on some acreage they bought nearby. We called it the Home Place, an old-fashioned term, but it had modern conveniences including running water and electricity, which meant we could have our first television. My father also installed a large wood heater. The boys would get out of the tub and back up to it, and sometimes the grill would sizzle on their backsides. They'd go to school and change to play ball, and somebody would say, "What happened to your butt?," because they'd have grillwork across it.

But oftentimes the stripes were from Daddy's belt, or whatever else he could reach to whip you with. My father was a good man, but he was also fearsome; there is no other word for him. He was a towering, unsmiling patriarch, and if you disobeyed him, he would come after you with his belt, or a tobacco stick, or a switch, or a milkstrap, or whatever else came to hand. If you misbehaved, you didn't sit in time-out. You got *worn* out.

Kenny was just seven or so when they were building the new house, and one afternoon he went racing through the room while Daddy was laying down flooring. Daddy told him to quit that, but Kenny did it again. Daddy reached out, snatched him up by the collar, and began whacking him on the behind with a piece of hardwood while Kenny's feet still cycled through the air. He was moving so fast when Daddy dropped him that when we tell the story now, we joke he practically left black marks on the floor.

We got switched for missed chores and for forgetting to close a gate and letting the livestock out. If you didn't do something, you got a switch. If you didn't do it on time, you got a switch. You got switched for wrassling over a place on the sofa or for making a racket at Granny's. One minute we'd be quarreling, and the next minute Daddy's belt would fly and we'd scatter like pigeons.

My brothers swear I got off lightly because I was the first daughter. Daddy would whip us in order, Tommy first, then Charles, then Kenneth, and then he'd look for me. One night, my brothers and I got into a pillow fight at bedtime and had a lively contest until we heard Daddy's feet hit the floor. I jumped behind a curtain and hid and then dove headfirst out the window while he laid into the boys.

> She stayed in about as much trouble as we did; she just didn't get as many whippings. Daddy would get on to us, and by the time he'd whip me, then Charles, then Kenneth, she'd be under the bed. He couldn't find her till the next morning and by then he'd forget about it, and everything was fine. I know she got out of whippings at least fifteen, twenty times that way.
> — TOMMY HEAD

But I remember getting my share of his hand. I was no more than five years old when I felt it for the first time. My brothers decided it would be entertaining to teach me a song about beans and bodily functions, and that night I sang it at the dinner table. I had just finished the chorus about "beans, the magical fruit" and was giggling, when his hand rose in the air and I went flying across the room with the imprint of it on my face. He had backhanded me out of my chair — hit me so hard that I did a back-flip. My mother burst into tears as she collected me off the floor.

Dinner when Tall Man was in the house was tense. We would be cutting up and laughing, telling stories and throwing rolls, until Daddy came in the room, and then we'd all go quiet and stock-still. You felt his presence. I don't recall having a lot of sit-down dinners with enjoyable conversation. He might talk a little bit about sports or farming or his hunting dogs, but mostly he grunted or was silent, and we were too.

He was a lot more soft with me than he was with Mom. I remember if they wanted to offer him a glass of wine at dinner, they would pour it and kind of glance over two seats away and then kind of sliiiide it down the table, and look away. If he wanted it, and he took it, they would kind of exhale. I would think, Why are they so scared of this guy? If someone else walked in it would be, "How you doing, *Mister* Head?" And everybody, even my uncles, would say, "Yes, sir. No, sir."

— TYLER SUMMITT

I want to make something clear: my father wasn't an angry man, or unkind, or abusive. He was just weary, and he had a lot on him. The whippings were of the tough love variety; he practiced the generational discipline he had grown up with, of the cut-your-own-switch variety. It was common in our community, and even in our schools, where paddling was regular and widely accepted. To this day, Tennessee is one of nineteen states where disciplinary corporal punishment is still allowed in classrooms.

My father was firm, but he had a giving heart, and he worked himself to the physical breaking point in the fields every day to provide for his family. His hands were brown and stained and the skin was cracked from work, and he limped; he would need two knee replacements by the time he was seventy. He came home at night to a household of five loud, long-limbed, roughhousing kids who at times must have seemed too much to handle. He knew if he didn't teach us to mind, life would have been unbearable for both him and my mother. Obedience was a matter of self-preservation. Eventually, he didn't need a belt; all it took was a word or a look from him. That intimidating man could make us straighten up just by the expression in his eye.

We were a wild, brawling brood when Daddy wasn't looking, and he knew it. The neighbors joked that "hard" should come in front of Head because we were all so stubborn and willful. Tommy was our leader, a young sunburned giant with a shock of blond hair and hands as big and calloused as a man's, who could take two of us on at once. Charles was smaller, the sweetest and most smiling of us, gap-toothed and good-humored, until he got mad. Kenny was the rebel; he had white-blond hair and ice-cube blue eyes and a talent for needling and surprise attacks. Among the things Kenny liked to do was load me on a forklift — and then hit the drop switch. He'd raise me up and then send me to the ground with a clang. Raise me up, and then whang again, until I cried.

The boys and I would start out wrassling, and pretty soon it would turn into a fight. In which I more than held my own. Once, I kicked a three-foot hole in their bedroom door because Charles was in there on the phone and wouldn't get off.

Fighting often got you whipped. "You can play all you want, but no fighting," Daddy said. We fought anyway. We fought with corncobs, firing them at each other like missiles. Kenny and Charles fought so bitterly one afternoon that Kenny threw some hedge clippers at Charles and cut his leg open, leaving a scar. I smacked Kenny with a baseball bat, and he answered by throwing a butcher knife at me that stuck in the kitchen wall.

Smoking got you whipped too, even though we tobacco farmed and it was everywhere. Daddy smoked an occasional cigar, but he told my brothers if he caught them at it, he'd switch them. "Boy, them your cigarettes?" he'd demand. "Naw, sir," Charles would say. But they were.

My father wasn't the only one who could give a whipping — Mama delivered a famous one to Tommy when he was seventeen years old, almost a grown man. It started at the table. Tommy said, "Charles, throw me a biscuit." Charles threw it all right, so hard Tommy couldn't catch it, and it hit him right between the eyes. Tommy picked it up and threw it back, and all of a sudden there was a food fight. Mother got up from the table, grabbed a belt, and whipped big old Tommy, who just stood there and took it, that's how much respect he had for her. More important, he understood how much respect my father had for her. "I knew if I didn't take it, I'd get a worse strap," Tommy said.

Nothing got you punished quicker than not meeting your responsibilities on the farm. The family came first. Putting food on the table was more important than any hobby or any game you had, and the lessons of that — and the punishments — became core values. Daddy taught us that we were all counted on to share the load: before you did anything else, you had to contribute to the family upkeep. We lived from crop to crop, and we didn't think of it as work so much as just necessity.

The only day we didn't work was Sunday; my parents were strict about that. We were in a pew for as long as the doors were open at Mt. Carmel United Methodist Church, where the Heads have attended for over fifty years and my father's parents had gone before us. There, we learned to worship with a simple gratitude to God and affection for Christ. We were taught that you didn't talk about faith; you showed it through kindness to neighbors, and humility, the recognition that none of us was more valuable than another. We read words from Ephesians that would stay with me for the rest of my life:

I have learned in whatever state I am, to be content. I know how to be abased, and I know how to abound. Everywhere and in all things I have learned to be both full and to be hungry, both to abound and to suffer need. I can do all things through Christ who strengthens me (4:11–13).

But even on Sundays the cows still had to be milked, and the chores seemed unending the rest of the week. Tommy was picking up hay by the age of five and earning good money as a hay baler for a combine when he was nine. He got fourteen cents a bale, and three summers in a row he baled at least three thousand bales of hay. Daddy furnished the fuel and the tractor, and Tommy did the work. He earned enough to pay for a new baler and rake in one summer alone. Next, he bought a new cow, and eventually he wound up with four or five of them.

From the time I was small, I wanted to do what my brothers did, so I started setting tobacco at the age of six. I rode with Tommy on the tobacco setter, a machine hooked to a tractor that hauled the young tobacco plants and dug rows for them. Every time it rolled over, we had to place the young plants in holes in the ground. My brother would check my row, and if I didn't set a plant right, he'd catch it.

"Don't tell Daddy I missed one," I whispered.

"You didn't miss it," he said. "I got it."

Tobacco farming was the hardest work I ever did. We'd set from seven in the morning until nine at night. The tobacco plant has deceptively beautiful leaves; in late summer they darken until they're almost blue tinged with a tropical lushness. But they have to be suckered in August, and chopped out in the early fall, and tied in bundles and hung to cure in the barns, which you do by laying down wood and sawdust and lighting a smoldering fire. After that, you never want to see a tobacco plant again.

I learned hard work never killed anyone — but there were a few days when I thought it would. We would get up at three thirty in the morning to chop tobacco before it got too hot. Then we'd go into the garden to pick okra, which you had to wear long sleeves to do because otherwise the prickles would irritate your skin. Then when it got cooler in the late afternoon, we'd go back to the tobacco fields and chop out some more.

My father put any of my friends who came to visit to work — I guess that's why they quit coming. The sooner we got done, the sooner we could go play, so everybody just pitched in. I remember once my best friend, Jane Brown, came over and spent the whole day working in the field with me. Finally she got overheated and went back to the house. She staggered inside and lay down on the kitchen floor, because it was the coolest spot she could find. She was still lying there trying to bring her core temperature back to normal, when the kitchen door opened and my father came stamping through in his boots.

Daddy looked at Jane and grunted. He usually grunted more than he talked.

He said, "What's wrong with you?"

"I'm *tired,* that's what's wrong," she said.

Daddy just stepped right over her and walked on. Then he paused.

"You don't know what tired is, girl," he said. "You haven't followed me around all day. Do that, and then say you're tired."

But all that work went into building something we were proud of. My parents gradually accumulated livestock and land, until we were farming twelve hundred acres of corn, soybeans, and tobacco, which we sold to the big companies, American Brands or Philip Morris. The dairy barn had grown until there were sixty-four cows that needed milking. Then there were the chickens, a herd of beef cattle, and a pen of hogs that had to be tended.

We raised all our own vegetables in a huge garden, enough to feed the family and also to sell in the local markets. We grew butter-beans, peas, squash, okra, and tomatoes that my mother made juice out of, which we drank fresh every morning. All the vegetables had to be frozen or put up for the winter, which meant shucking, shelling, soaking, boiling, bagging, and canning. We had a large outdoor freezer full of corn, beans, beef, and pork.

The cows had to be milked twice a day, seven days a week, at five A.M. and again in the evening. That was some of the most physical work. We started out milking by hand, then we bought a gas-powered milker, and finally an electric one, but it was still a big job. The milk went into tall metal cans that weighed about eighty pounds, and you had to lift them and set them down in an industrial cooler that was full of the coldest water you ever felt. Tommy got too hot one day and started splashing himself with that cold water — and staggered. He almost passed out from it.

Eventually, my parents made so much cash from farming that they were able to buy the small country store in Henrietta, which sold dry goods and gas. We stocked the shelves and ran the register and pumped the gas. Eventually they branched out and also opened a small feed mill across the street and sold farm implements.

There was never a day without some kind of heavy lifting. We got off the school bus and went right into the fields, or vegetable rows, or the barns. Some days I might plow. Others I might get on my pony, Billy, and round up the cattle for feeding. The color of the sky didn't matter; the weather had a lot to do with what needed to be done most urgently. My father would tell us what our job was and then walk away to his own chores. He expected us to get it done without wasting time by standing over us. There was no balking, or dragging, and you knew better than to whine.

We had more responsibilities than other kids, and we knew it. I didn't particularly like it at the time; I thought I was being tortured. My friends only had to do their homework, and they could go play. But we'd work, and work, and then Daddy would look at the sun and say, "I think we can get another hour in."

It was partly out of necessity that we worked, but it was also a matter of philosophy for my parents. They didn't believe kids should be idle, and they thought that farmwork taught a kind of ethics, as well as maturity. You had to take care of things properly so they wouldn't break, find the right tool for a job, and tend the animals and beasts of burden on a farm before you tended to yourself. My father expected us to act responsibly and to make our own decisions in the fields. If you didn't know how to do something, like say change a broken blade on a mower, you studied the machinery or the problem and learned for yourself, without pestering him with questions. If you didn't get it right, he'd say, "Well, Trisha, you know better'n that."

One afternoon when I was about thirteen, my father drove me out to an immense mown field and told me to rake the hay that was lying on the ground. Sitting there was a tractor with a large metal drag attached to the back. I'd never raked hay into bales before, only seen it done by my brothers.

"Daddy, I don't know how to do this," I said.

He just said, "Yeah, you do."

I stared at the field and the machinery doubtfully and looked back at him.

That's when he said, "You won't learn any younger."

Then he wordlessly got back in his truck and drove off, leaving me there. He just expected me to work it out for myself and get it done. For the next six hours, I was alone in the field. I motored back and forth learning to drag the rake so it would work through the hay, and then flipped it over and dragged the other way, until it was in neat piles. I figured out quick that driving in circles didn't get the job done.

When my father finally reappeared, I was terrified of what he'd say or do. But he just looked around, and "Awright." I knew that meant "good job."

I learned to love raking hay. I'd head to the fields with a huge jug of iced tea and ride the tractor for hours and hours, daydreaming — mostly about getting off the farm.

My father didn't praise easily. But he taught his children self-confidence and self-reliance, qualities that so many parents worry about instilling, and even pay good tuition for. He taught us to cope. We could fix complicated machinery, handle livestock, and push through the fatigue of heavy chores. This didn't come from sweet words or laxity. It came from meeting Richard Head's high expectations every single day. It came from knowing that we had to count on one another, and rely on ourselves, without having to turn to others.

I don't recall my father ever telling me, "I love you," or "I'm proud of you," when I was a girl. He didn't say those sorts of things to his children, and he never hugged us either. He reserved his physical affection for my mother. I would be forty-three years old before he actually put his arms around me and kissed me.

But he showed love in his own way. How did he show it? He put it on the table. He put it in the roof over our heads, and in the heat and the running water. He put it into the way he worked for all of us, from before sunup to after dark.

He put it into building us a basketball court in the hayloft. My father loved the game; he had played it in high school, and as a young man one of the few recreations he allowed himself was a weekend game with a local church league, before farm and family responsibilities weighed him down too much. The Mt. Carmel United Methodist Church team was made up mostly of his brothers and cousins, all of whom were as tall and stern looking as he was, and referees thought twice about blowing the whistle against them.

Tired though he was, one afternoon he climbed up a twenty-foot ladder to the loft carrying a stack of wood on his shoulder.

Painstakingly, by hand, with excellent carpentry skills, he built us a wooden backboard that was better than the one we had at school. Then he retrieved an iron rim he had found somewhere and attached it to the backboard. Then he made another trip up and down that ladder and strung lights, so that we could play in the evenings after supper and chores. After it was all done, and done right.

There was no slack in the hayloft. It didn't matter that I was a girl; my brothers needed a fourth, so they said, "Come on, sis." They found out quick that I could elbow just like they could. The barn sat out in a field about fifty yards from our back door, but my parents could hear the racket we made all the way in the house, the high-pitched fussing that went with the thump of the ball, and the thwacking that meant someone had been hip-checked into the planks.

We played year-round. When it was cold, we hung old quilts up to keep the wind out, and we could hear the stabled cows who'd been brought in out of the weather shuffling below us. In the warmer seasons, we made sure to stack all the hay in the back to keep the court clear. It was usually Tommy and me against the middle boys.

I liked it when it was just the four of us, because on weekends when my brothers' friends came over, sometimes I got left out of the game. I didn't appreciate that at all, any more than I appreciated it when they'd go to Rittenbury Pond to swim naked and I couldn't go with them.

"All y'all have to do is put on some shorts," I protested. "Wear your shorts, so I can go with you."

Basketball in the loft was physical; we were big kids and there was a lot of blocking and setting screens that turned into shouldering and shoving. If you drove in for a layup and someone pushed you, you went flying through the gallery door and into the long drop to the hay below. They talked smack, and so did I. When they really wanted to get under my skin, they'd call me Sissy.

"Come on, Sissy, let's see what you got."

We played rough at times but she would hit you just like a guy. It didn't matter. You better hit her, 'cause she was gonna hit you. We played football in the front yard too. Tackle.

— KENNETH HEAD

We played practically every night and my father never stopped us, as long as we'd done our work. It was our one indulgence. Tall Man had been a better-than-average high school basketball player himself — I have a picture of him in shorts, impossibly lanky with old-fashioned ankle-high lace-up black sneakers — and he believed the game was good for us, better than any of the trouble we liked to invent for ourselves.

> We made 'em work, but we did let 'em play ball. We always thought that was better than them running around with these kids that were doing nothing. A lot of them didn't know what work was.
> — HAZEL HEAD

By the time I went from the hayloft to organized basketball I was a confirmed tomboy — a tall, skinny, self-conscious one. I stood a head above every other child in my school except for my cousin Dennis Albright. Almost as humiliating as my height, there was the matter of my weight. I was so thin that my nickname was Bone.

But I was strong enough from lifting hay bales and milk cans that I broke the Roosevelt School's old wooden flagpole by climbing on it. Which got me noticed. I was a third grader sitting on the seesaw in the playground one day when the school princi-

71

pal strolled by and paused. "I'd like you to stay after school and practice with the eighth-grade girls' basketball team," he said. I did as I was told.

My first coach left a large impression. Joe Daves was a six-foot-five disciplinarian along the lines of my father. He kept a large paddle with two holes in it, called Blister II, which he would use on students who acted up. I think he must have broken Blister I on his students. I caught a lick once from Blister II, for chewing gum and talking in class. Daves ordered me to bend over and grab my ankles, and then he blistered me. The paddle picked me up and moved me about a foot in the air.

Back in those days girls' basketball in the state of Tennessee was a strange, inhibited half-court game with six players on a side. Three players stayed on one half of the court, and three on the other, and crossing midcourt was forbidden for fear we might faint. Gym teachers in those days didn't believe girls were capable of running full court — we were capable of heavy farm-work, and of absorbing whippings, but for some reason, they didn't think we could run ninety-four feet without getting the vapors and passing out, or damaging our ovaries. So instead, we practically broke our toes by

72

stopping at the centerline.

There was such concern about whether girls should play the game, in fact, that my basketball career almost came to an abrupt end in eighth grade. Our Home Place sat just inside the Montgomery County line, which meant by residency I was supposed to attend high school in Clarksville. But education officials there had abolished the sport a few years earlier after a young woman ran into the gymnasium wall and died from a head injury.

I sat at dinner one day bemoaning the fact that Clarksville High didn't have basketball for girls, when my dad suddenly spoke. Which he didn't do often.

He said, "Well. We'll just move."

It was an extraordinary statement. We had a comfortable, almost brand-new brick home, which my parents had built with their own hands. Now he intended to walk away from it?

He did. Our grocery store sat on the main street of Henrietta just over the Cheatham County line. Next door to the grocery sat an old white farmhouse, unoccupied and in disrepair. My father bought it and moved us into Henrietta, simply so that I could go to Ashland City High School, which had a very good girls' team.

My parents left their warm, solid, convenient new home for that rickety old place, and they never said a word in protest about it. It was a hardship, but they did it for me. The house was dilapidated, a white two-story clapboard with no insulation, so the wind whipped right through it. I remember standing up against the fireplace and warming my backside while I breathed out frost. Also, the place creaked — the stairs were so old that every other step groaned and squeaked, and we tried to memorize which ones didn't, so that we could sneak up and down them — walk up two, and skip three.

Who back in the 1960s sized up a daughter's jump shot and decided it was important enough to sacrifice for? Almost nobody. In 1968, just sixteen thousand American women played college sports, and most of them did it under a shadow of somebody's disapproval, whether parents who thought it unladylike, or boyfriends who thought it a waste of time. Four decades later, it's commonplace to invest in a young woman's talent: There are now 191,000 women athletes in the NCAA, and if you tell a father that there is no team for his girl to play on, he doesn't just move. He sues. Back then, however, it was virtually unheard of.

But my father valued my talent and had

the instinct and foresight to think that investing in it might do something good for me. And if he hadn't made the sacrifice of moving, we wouldn't be having this conversation. If there was any proof that Richard Head was a loving, committed father, there it was. With that one act, he gave me everything.

> Well, people thought we had lost our minds. But he thought she could be anything, 'cause she was tough and raised up with the boys. He always was right behind her in whatever she did.
>
> — HAZEL HEAD

My father was an engaged and fiercely devoted parent who wanted me to have the same chance as my brothers. He never missed my high school games if he could help it. I remember him sitting in the Ashland City High bleachers, unsmiling and unexpressive as ever, except for his hand: it was beating on the old wooden railing with excitement. He wouldn't yell, but I could hear his fist hammering on the wood, *bang, bang, bang.* I knew without a word what he was saying: "Come on, Trisha."

By the age of fifteen, I was a broad-shouldered, auburn-haired girl with a side part and cheeks reddened from outdoor work. I had reached my full height of five eleven and was so ridiculously strong that I could throw a hay bale higher than most men. My brothers and I would have contests to see who could toss a bale higher into the wagon.

> She could carry a hundred-pound bag of feed on one shoulder, and a sixty-pound bag of dog food under the other arm. I saw her do that seven or eight times. The boys in high school was all scared of her.
> — TOMMY HEAD

My high school coach was a stickler named Mike Jarreau, who taught me the fundamentals of the game with repetition and dedication instead of paddling. He drilled our team for hours in set plays, made us do things over and over until we were as choreographed as a bunch of chorus girls. Sometimes we looked like it. In one drill, you had to sprint to half-court to receive a pass, and jump up in the air ten times, counting aloud, "One! Two! Three! . . ."

It's difficult to explain to someone who has never competed, but a moment arrives in the life of a serious athlete when the game begins to live in you. It so occupies your mind and body that you almost *become* it. You gain a sense of such command over your own arms and legs that it can almost feel like flying, and you begin to crave that sensation daily. Everything else is just an interruption until you can return to it. That was me. I played, quite literally, in my sleep.

My bedroom was so cold in the winter that not even an electric blanket and a plug-in heater made it comfortable. One February night just before the annual state tournament, my best friend, Jane, and I decided we needed to sleep warmly if we were going to play well, so we dragged my mattress down the stairs and laid it in front of the woodstove in the living room. In the middle of the night, Jane felt something whack her on the head. It was my arm. The mattress was jumping, and she heard, "One! Two! Three!" I was practicing the jump drill in my dreams.

In summer, my little room was suffocating. The bed sat right under the window, and when it got hot, I'd throw my legs around as I played in my sleep, and every now and then, I'd kick out the panes. I busted several windows by tossing and thrashing. I'd wake up to a cracking sound and know I'd shattered a piece of glass again by sprinting in my dreams.

I played in hot and cold; the Ashland City gym had no air-conditioning, just some large fans mounted high up in the windows. I played hurt. One season as we were getting ready for the state tournament, I broke my arm practicing my superheroine jumping skills. Our gym doubled as the school auditorium, with a stage at one end, and you could jump from the stage and almost grab the net if you hurled yourself far enough. I got onstage and leaped at the net — and fell on my arm, breaking it.

I tolerated the cast for about forty-eight hours before I soaked it in the bathtub, softening the plaster, and then chipped away with a knife to loosen it until I could move my arm enough to keep shooting.

Playing ball was all I really had. There wasn't much else to do; life on the farm was rigid, strict, and sheltered. I wasn't allowed to go on an actual date until I was sixteen, and even then I was only permitted to venture with my sometime boyfriend Mack as far as Ashland City to see a movie or get something to eat at the Dairy Dip, where we hung out in the parking lot until we spotted the sheriff, who already had us on his radar for drag racing. It was a big deal the first time I ate pizza — I'd never had it before, didn't even know what it was. All we had on the farm was meat and vegetables, which created some culinary adventures. The first time my sister, Linda, went out to a diner, she ordered fried shrimp and ate the tails because she didn't know better.

A big highlight of the week was an episode of *Gunsmoke.* Or we'd sit up on the roof of the grain silo and look at the stars. Sometimes at night for fun my brothers would lead unsuspecting friends through the hog lot and die laughing when they slipped and fell in the mud.

How's this for boredom? We painted the water tower. It started with a haunted house phase; one Saturday night, Jane and I and our friends Ricky and Howell decided to explore some of the abandoned shacks that dotted the countryside. After chasing ghosts with flashlights for an hour or so, we stumbled on an old shed that was full of spray paint cans. All of a sudden we lost interest in ghosts and developed an intense interest in graffiti. The question was, what to paint? One of the guys said, "We need to paint the water tower!" It seemed like the perfect canvas: rising hundreds of feet in the air, it presented a huge bland façade that cried out for paint.

The boys started climbing, and I clambered up the first few rungs after them. But when they announced they intended to paint their initials on it, and they wanted to put mine up there too, I stopped.

My father was the water commissioner for the county, and he had played a major role in getting city water pumped into the tower. In the years since we'd left the log cabin, Richard Head had become a pillar of the community who was involved in every civic issue from road improvements to serving on the Cheatham County court. If he thought I'd had anything to do with defacing the water tower, I would face the wrath of Mister Richard. I said, "You can't put my initials on anything; Daddy will know! You have nothing to lose. But my dad — he'll kill me."

I turned around and said to Jane, "I'm not going all the way up there." She said, "Me neither," and we scrambled back down. But the guys went all the way up and painted "Class of 69" and "Class of 70" in huge letters on the tower.

The next morning, my father sat down to the Sunday breakfast table fuming. He'd been out to check on the cows and had seen the water tower. "I can't believe anybody would do that!" he said. "Whoever did it needs to be punished — and the parents who raised kids to do that ought to be punished just as bad." Jane started choking, and I kicked her under the table. Richard turned on me. "You two know everything that goes on around here," he said. "I want you to find out who did it. I'm not only going after them, I'm going after their parents, too."

I was so scared of Richard Head that I was thirty years old before I told him who painted the tower. Jane and I confessed to him one afternoon when I was home on a visit. He just glared and said, "I guess you young ladies know you aren't too big to spank." And then his shoulders started shaking with laughter.

Wherever I went, I was under strict orders to be home by eleven, and I set some land speed records meeting curfew. One night Jane's car ran out of gas, so we snuck her mother's old Plymouth out of the garage and I drove like I was in the Indy 500 trying to get home. The next morning our local state trooper saw Jane's mother, Sue, and said, "Sue, where in hell were you going last night?" Sue said, "I didn't go nowhere last night."

He said, "You sure did, I clocked you going ninety-five."

"You didn't clock me, I was home in bed."

"Well, it was your car, with your license plate."

Sue just looked at him mystified. Then they both realized what had happened. He said, "You tell that Head girl I know it was her."

My reputation as a speed demon was getting around. But driving fast was the only thing I had to do for excitement, other than compete. I never hunted with my brothers — I couldn't bear to kill things, and I even found it traumatic to do 4-H. There is a picture of me with a calf at a fair, in jeans and a barn jacket, but it pained me to raise small animals and then sell them.

Instead I took up barrel racing. I had a horse named Trigger that was my most beloved friend, and we became intensely competitive in the Ashland City local rodeos. I won a wall full of ribbons doing it, which emboldened me to take up scoop racing, too. In a scoop race, you sit *behind* your horse in a large corn scoop and drag along the ground as he charges around the barrels. One night, I asked my parents to come watch me. Trigger and I went racing out into the arena and swirled around the barrels, then galloped into the final turn for home. But Trigger was towing me so hard that the scoop swung out wide — and headed toward the fence.

I went straight through it. Took out three planks.

When I shook off the splinters and got up, my parents were covering their faces with their hands. My mother said, "I don't think we want to go through this again." And my career as a scoop racer was over. I thought, *It's time to quit.*

Although I loved growing up on the farm, I found it socially isolating. So often I couldn't do the things other kids did, either because I didn't have the money or I had to work. I spent my sixteenth birthday on a tractor. There was no Sweet 16 party, just a long day's work. Some classmates tried to plan a party for me, a small get-together at the Ashland City Country Club, where one of the boys in my class was a member because his father owned a Ford dealership. He arranged for a bunch of us to spend the afternoon swimming, which thrilled me. I'd never been to a country club.

I was set on going — until we got a forecast for rain. My father said, "You've got to drive the tractor and pick up the straw." I looked out at the pasture, and there were a thousand bales of straw on the ground. At first I thought maybe I could get it done in time for the party. I hit the clutch on the tractor and started stacking bales with the automatic lift. Every few minutes I checked my watch, and it got later and later. Finally, I said hesitantly, "Dad, how are we going to get this done in time for the party?"

"There's no way you can go to a party," my father said. "Looks like rain. You've got to help me do this."

I said, "But, Daddy, it's my birthday."

"I don't care whose birthday it is. We can't afford for the rain to come in with this straw on the ground."

I was so upset that I started driving like a crazed woman. At one point, I slammed on the brakes so hard I nearly threw him off the tractor. He looked at me with eyes that had turned radioactive. He didn't say a word, but I knew to be careful and not open my mouth again.

I never made it to the party. It was a sacrifice that my father demanded, and so I made it. I knew better than to cry in front of him about not being able to swim with a bunch of city kids at a country club. *Don't you cry, girl. I better not see you cry.*

When my brothers were thirsty, they held their tea glasses in the air and rattled the ice. Wordlessly, they sat at the table crouched over heaping plates of food, with their glasses upraised and shaking. *Rattle, rattle, rattle.* The sound of ice against glass was a statement. It said, "Serve me."

One of them would drain a glass and then hold it out. *Rattle. Rattle.* "Come fill my glass up." Insistent, unthinking, and demanding, until a female in the house grasped a jug of tea and poured it for him. Then another brother would drain his drink and hold up the glass. *Rattle. Rattle, rattle.* It was the southern way. When men ate, the women served them.

As I got older, the noise began to rile me. It ran up my spine and into my head. *Rattle, rattle, rattle.* Finally one day, it shot up my backbone, into my forehead, and came out of my mouth. *Rattle, rattle.*

"Get it yourself," I snapped.

Grudgingly, those big tall boys might raise calloused hands and pour their own tea. But more often than not they just sat there until my mother came around the table and refilled their glass. It bothered me that she had to wait on my brothers — because as hard as the men in our family worked, nobody could touch my mother for tireless backbreaking labor. She did every bit as much as they did on the farm, and on top of that, she ran the household.

By tradition on a farm in the South, the

men did the outside work, and women did the inside work. But as far as I could tell, my mother worked both inside and outside. After a long day of outdoor farm chores, she did the cooking, cleaning, washing, and ironing. She made most of our clothes herself, because we didn't have a lot of cash to buy them. Late at night she'd pick up dirty clothes after my brothers — who didn't think they should have to do anything in the house because they'd been outside all day — and wash and mend them.

My mother was mild-spoken, but underneath her generous, patient temperament was a tough constitution. She did most of the milking, and would lift those tall eighty-pound milk cans into the cooler by herself, until she eventually ruined her shoulder and needed four surgeries to repair it. After milking, she'd come back and cook breakfast and get us off to school, which was no small job. It was nothing for Tommy to eat a dozen eggs by himself. Along with three sides of bacon *and* sausage, biscuits *and* toast, and a half a jar of jelly.

Next, she'd fix lunch for any of the hired hands Daddy had brought in. After that, she tended her ten-acre vegetable garden, harvesting in her big sun hat. Then she joined my dad in the field to help him with his chores. By the time she came back to the house, the cows had to be done again, and dinner had to be started.

She was never at rest. She could do anything — I remember her saving a wounded baby pig by stitching it up with a needle and thread. She could drive anything too. She got her driver's license in the two-ton truck, which she used to haul wholesale goods for our country store. "Miss Hazel, is Richard gonna make a truck driver out of you?" the local policeman asked her. She just laughed. She'd rumble up to Cumberland Wholesale with my sister, Linda, still a small child, in the cab beside her. She'd load up the truck and then drive it back and unload the goods into the store and stock the shelves.

It was Miss Hazel who made the money to buy our first real car. Our 1952 yellow Plymouth came from her butterbean money, which she grew in that immense vegetable patch behind the house. She drove it faster than anybody in the family, including me. With Miss Hazel at the wheel, you had to worry about whiplash. She'd do eighty on that two-lane blacktop racing from one place to another, and then she'd hit the brake and you'd eat the dashboard.

Mama moved at a faster pace than Dad

did, but then, she had more to do. When my father came home, he would sit down and eat, or relax. She never asked my father to do anything for her that she could do herself — if the trash needed taking out, she did it — because she wanted him to rest. His day was done. But hers was only about half over.

It was a double standard, and I noticed it and thought, *This isn't right.* As a teenager I began volunteering to do more of the housework, simply because I wanted to help my mother. I noticed when the windows in the house needed washing, and I'd do them so she didn't have to. I babysat for Linda and enlisted her in household chores.

I learned to cook and would start supper while Mama was at the store, so that when she came home she could sit down to eat with my father. One by-product was that I learned all her recipes and became almost as good a cook as she is.

MISS HAZEL'S CORNBREAD
20 ounces cornmeal, salted
3 eggs
1 pint sour cream
1 stick butter, melted
1 (16-ounce) can corn niblets, drained
1 (15-ounce) can creamed corn

8 ounces shredded cheddar cheese

Mix ingredients until smooth and pour into a greased iron skillet. Bake at 350°F until golden brown.

Just because a woman worked as hard or harder than a man, I realized, didn't make her an equal in all things, not even in her own family. I'd always labored alongside my brothers because I preferred the outdoors and I'd never felt treated as lesser-than when we were outside. But once we were inside a house, or a school, things were very, very different. I didn't see why they should be, just because I was a female, but they were.

Things were especially different when I began to think about college. At some point the idea of using basketball to get off the farm occurred to me. It occurred to my parents, too, because they began looking for a university where I could continue my playing career.

There had been a time when Daddy would raise cane if we missed farmwork to stay after school for basketball practice. He even made the boys hitchhike to Little League. But then Tommy became a local all-star basketball player, and Kenny started throwing no-hitters on the baseball diamond as an eleven-year-old. Tommy explained to him, "Daddy, I'm gonna get a scholarship to play basketball, and Kenneth's got a good chance to get a baseball scholarship, and it won't cost you a penny for us to go to college. So you need to let us practice a little bit." From then on Daddy didn't fuss. Tommy, true to his word, got a basketball scholarship to Austin Peay, and Kenny followed him there on a baseball scholarship. Both would graduate with honors.

But whatever college I went to, my parents would have to pay my full way. It didn't matter how good an athlete I was — and I was good enough that Ashland City High would eventually name the gym after me — athletic scholarships for women simply didn't exist in 1970. My folks would have to carry my tuition, room, and board and finance my basketball as well, my shoes, my gear.

My father sorted through my college options, the few we could afford, and settled on the University of Tennessee at Martin, a small satellite campus of the state system. It was relatively inexpensive, a plain little campus of red brick and white stone, and we knew a couple of people there. The athletic director, Bettye Giles, was from nearby Clarksville, and the point guard was a good player named Esther Stubblefield whom I had competed against in high school. "Call that Stubblefield girl and talk to her," my father ordered. So I did — I phoned Esther and she said, "I love it. You need to come." That settled it.

The financial commitment would strain my parents, I knew. They had upgraded our house and the store, and they were in the midst of trying to build up Henrietta's main street by adding a small Laundromat, and a one-chair barbershop. We worked as hard as ever; during my senior year, I did shifts behind the counter at the grocery, loaded and unloaded bags of fertilizer, and pumped gas for the cars that pulled up out front. Sinclair gas was our brand, with the green dinosaur sign.

But we were still cash poor. One reason was my father's generosity to our Henrietta neighbors: whenever someone in the community was in need, he carried him on the books for months at a time. If the hired hands ran short of money and needed groceries, my father advanced them. If local farmers needed implements or fertilizer, he'd supply them what they needed and then wait, sometimes forever, to be paid back.

Tobacco farming was high risk because it only paid off as a crop once a year, and there was no telling how many people he helped out when they were shy, or a crop failed. Some of them lived close by and walked over to ask for help. Others came by tractor or car. My brothers and I figured that he gave away close to $100,000 that he never saw again.

Even my mother finally said, "Richard, you just can't keep loaning money out. You're too generous." I agreed. Our own family had to sacrifice while he was carrying people's debts. Since I helped at the family store, I saw the books, and it frustrated me. "All these people that owe y'all money are driving a lot better cars than we are," I said. "If they'd pay you, we might have a better car." Every now and then when we were short of cash, I'd get so irritated that I'd take the initiative and call one of my friends, like Ricky Elliott. "Come over and pick me up," I'd say. "We got to go collect money." We'd jump in his vehicle and call on three or four folks, and I'd collect $500 or $600 to put in the family till. My father wouldn't say anything; he'd just grunt. But my mother would look relieved.

If at times I questioned my father's parenting methods, I never questioned the size of his heart. Beneath that stern veneer, he was a sensitive man. I remember the day that Tommy left home for college. I was upstairs in that tiny bedroom, when I heard a strange sound from the back porch. I peered over the windowsill to see my big strong father sitting in a porch chair choking back sobs. Tears streamed down his face. My father wept, even though Tommy was going to school barely an hour away.

The trouble was, my father would never show it in front of us; he had to sneak off to the back porch and cry in secret. Richard Head just couldn't express himself. As I got ready to go off to college I knew he was proud of me — but he never told me so. I knew he loved me — but he never said so. He took it for granted that everyone would understand he was a kind, loving person. He gave me, and all the rest of us, to understand that when he said something grunting and withered like "Awright," what it really meant was, "You did well." You were supposed to just automatically interpret it as a word of love. We all were. But sometimes it was wearying to do the work of interpreting Richard.

I would spend the coming years driven by a craving for his approval, absolutely determined to show: I am a winner, who deserves love and praise. But there was another consequence too, a certain wounded inwardness. By the time I left for college, I was a shy, socially awkward young woman who covered up her vulnerabilities. *Don't you cry, girl. I better not see you cry.* I had become a little shut off, self-protective; whatever I felt, I learned not to show it to others.

> All that work, all that hardness, beat something out of her. There was always this bit of a safe house inside of her. I think she got hurt emotionally when she was young in that family, and she knew she had to become a strong female to compete, and she learned to fight within the system.
>
> — R.B. SUMMITT

And if that wasn't my father all over. I drew the shades over my eyes, and later, when the young women who played for me cried, I told them champions and leaders and strong women don't cry.

Shortly before I graduated from Ashland City High, my English teacher pulled me aside for a talk. He said, "Trish, have you ever told your parents you love them?" I just stared at him and shook my head. "No,

94

I haven't," I said. We didn't do that in our family, I explained. He told me that he had recently lost his mother and would never have another chance to tell her how much he appreciated her. He wanted me to try to express myself to my parents.

"Whatever you do, tell your mom and dad, before you go off to college, that you love them," he said.

I thought about his advice all that summer but couldn't quite bring myself to do it. Finally, the day of departure arrived and my parents drove me to UT-Martin. We unloaded the car, and then it was time to say good-bye. I turned to my mother, who was sweetness personified to me, the one person in the world who made everything better. Even with her, it was all I could do to say the words aloud. I reached for her and kissed her and said awkwardly, chokingly, "I love you, Mom."

She started crying. We both of us stood there shuddering with tears for a moment. Then I turned to my father. But before I could even get the words out, he spoke first.

"Shut up," he said.

Are you having any symptoms?

There are times when I wake up in the morning and I don't know where I am.

That can't feel good. Does it come to you after a few minutes?

Yes.

What else? Can you tell me any other effects?

Some days are more cloudy and foggy.

I guess you aren't going to get through this thing with no symptoms at all.

I'm doing everything I can. I'm doing my puzzles.

[Later]

Do you have to do them *all* in one day?

You know me. I can't do just one. I've got to

kick its ass.

— November 12, 2011, Knoxville, Tennessee, six months after diagnosis

3
MISS CHI OMEGA

I made a raw impression at the age of eighteen. I was a frank, elbowy girl wearing a home-stitched skirt and cheap shoes, with a rampant mane of hair that ended in a flip. I arrived at UT-Martin carrying one small "soup case," which is how my sorority sisters claim that I said the word *suitcase* in my Tennessee hills accent.

The moment I stepped into Clement Hall, the women's dormitory, I felt backward. My only coloring came from fresh air; I'd never worn mascara or blush. All around me were women in bright cosmetics, their hair teased and sprayed. I'd heard that UT-Martin was a destination for rich girls from Memphis and these must be them, I figured. They seemed impossibly moneyed and made-up. There were prim girls in neat-buttoned cardigans, hip ones in bell-bottom trousers with sash belts, daring ones in miniskirts and knee-high boots that showed off their trim legs.

I shrank when I looked down. The hemline sewn by my mother fell below my knee, to midcalf.

Even the way the other girls spoke seemed well-heeled. They talked with gentle lilts and they didn't say "ain't," whereas I said "yonder," and "reckon," and "done went and gone," and I wondered how Daddy would manage back home in the fields all by "hisself" — judging by their manicured nails, they'd never had dirt on their palms.

Back home, "Trisha" could bale hay and drive a tractor, but at Martin she was inferior, and a figure of fun. I sought out Esther Stubblefield, whom I knew from playing against her in high school. Esther had grown up only twenty miles from me, but she was town reared one county over in Springfield, which had a brick courthouse and sidewalks, so I viewed her as the height of sophistication.

Esther greeted me warmly, but as she gave me the once-over, she realized how country and naive I was. She decided to toy with me.

"You should sign up for Russian," she advised me. "It's an easy A."

It sounds terrible now. But she was just so gullible.

I had never been away from Henrietta before, except for one overnight trip with the 4-H Club. The Martin campus had fewer than five thousand students and sat in a moderate-sized town halfway between Nashville and Memphis, merely a two-hour drive from home. It was hardly cosmopolitan — but to me it felt as foreign as the other side of the globe, and I was scared to death of it. So scared that the very first weekend, I ran back to the farm. I found a ride to Henrietta and walked through the door of our farmhouse with my laundry under my arm.

My father said, "What are you doing here?"

I told him I just felt like coming back for a visit. But we both knew the truth: I was frightened.

"Look, I don't want you on the road every weekend," he said. "And the next time you come, don't bring your dirty clothes with you."

What he meant was, grow up. When I got a little tearful, he said, "I don't want to hear any more about that." So I went back to campus and set about trying somehow to fit in. Slowly, hesitantly, I tried to meet people. One afternoon, I saw a smartly dressed young woman who lived in Clement Hall struggling to lift a heavy old iron typewriter out of the trunk of her car. Now, here was something I knew how to do. I bounded down the stairs. "Hey, hon, let me help you with that," I said. I took the typewriter from her and hauled it up to her room and was rewarded with a bright lipstick smile and a thank-you.

But mostly I stayed on the margin, dreading any conversation that would betray my lack of social skills. I'd never thought about how I sounded before, but now when I heard myself I decided I'd just as soon not speak. I clamped my mouth firmly shut, and I hardly opened it, stayed so quiet that no one knew my correct name. Everyone just assumed that because I was enrolled as Patricia Sue Head, I went by "Pat," and I didn't have the voice to say that no one ever called me that; my name was "Trisha." But rather than speak up and hear the hick from Cheatham County come out, I let it go. So I became Pat. It sounded stronger, I decided.

I was so modest I even dressed in my dorm room closet. But I watched people —

a lot. I studied the girls who tanned themselves on the roof of Clement Hall, lying on aluminum foil. They lathered up with baby oil and iodine, and put Sun-In on their hair, so they would glow at the socials. I mentally cataloged their shoes and their blouses.

Esther Stubblefield rescued me. She was the leader of Martin's basketball team, and she was also a campus social leader, a white-blond streak of energy with a crackling direct honesty, smart mouth, and wicked humor. She was as good-hearted as she was funny, and she felt responsible for helping me adjust to campus life, as both a teammate and an acquaintance from back home. We liked each other instantly, and she took me under her wing. She announced that she wanted to sponsor me for membership with the Chi Omega sorority, the house she belonged to. I looked at her like she was crazy. But Esther insisted. Pledging would help me meet people on campus and force me to get over my shyness, she said. The Chi Os weren't snobs, she assured me; they had a wide-ranging membership, some beauty queens, yes, but also academics and athletes.

"You need to do this," she said.

So I did it. I put on a white dress, agonized over whether my white shoes were right for the season, and went to a social. Esther stayed by my side and walked me through it promising she would back me for membership. But as it turned out, she didn't have to, because unbeknownst to both of us, I had another sponsor. Esther was ready to make her plea on my behalf at the membership meeting, when the refined-looking young woman whose typewriter I had carried stood up. "I want to say something," she said. And she told the story of my hauling the heavy machine up the stairs.

"I don't know Pat personally," she said. "But I want that girl in my sorority."

So that's how I became a sorority girl — I muscled my way in.

Joining a sorority didn't solve all my social problems; I still didn't feel I belonged. Esther invited me to be her roommate on the top floor of Clement Hall where the Chi Os lived. She introduced me around and gave me advice on clothes and makeup, which wasn't easy on my feelings. I'd get ready to go to class, and she'd say, "You aren't wearing those shoes, are you?"

One day, Esther and some of our other sorority sisters decided to go through my closet. My wardrobe either came from Kmart or was sewn by my mother, and I was suddenly ashamed of how limited it was. When they pulled out one of my favorite outfits, a navy blue jumper with a blouse with turtles on it, they all burst into laughter.

> It was a Sunday afternoon and she came in and we were looking at her clothes and I don't know why we were doing it, whether [it was] because she dressed badly. We were pulling things out and there was this blouse with turtles, and we were laughing so hard we were crying. And I know now it hurt her feelings. But she never showed it. She never showed a vulnerable face. She always had that air that everything was in control and fine. It never occurred to me at that time that stuff bothered her. But of course it did.
>
> — ESTHER HUBBARD

I can still hear the high-pitched whooping while I stood there trying to smile. No doubt it was a tacky shirt. But I didn't wear turtle blouses because I had poor taste; I wore them because they were all I had. The laughter wounded me, and it made a lasting impression. I was tired of being made fun of — and determined to not be, ever again. I wanted to change, to fix myself, to acquire some polish. I told myself, *If I ever get a*

105

good job — if I ever make money — I'm gonna dress nice.

I knew I needed help with my grammar. I earned another explosion of Chi Omega hilarity one day when I bounced into the room and flopped down on the bed and said, "My daddy's gonna kill me."

"Why, what did you do?"

"I done blowed four dollars, and I don't know how!"

After the laughter died down, I asked one of my sorority sisters, an English major named Alison Cross, to help me with my speech. Alison, who became a good friend, began to patiently correct me, murmuring the right syntax into my ear, smoothing out my expressions and softening my accent. She had a talent for teaching: she went on to become a dedicated English teacher and guidance counselor in a local school back in Cheatham County.

I wasn't just out of my depth socially at Martin; I was overwhelmed academically. Again, Esther came to my rescue. In the spring of my freshman year, she signed up for all of the same classes, so she could coach me through them. "I need to get in the classroom with you and show you how to do this," she said. "This way we can study together."

Esther tutored me in math and sat with me in geology and taught me how to make decent notes. She showed me how to divide up my reading load in a disciplined way and how to prepare for tests. "Pat, if you will just sit down and really focus, then you can get it all done," she said. It shouldn't surprise you to learn that, like Alison, Esther went on to become a dedicated teacher who served thirty years in the Kentucky public school system, getting kids to love math. Following Esther's lead, I became a decent student — not a great one by any means, but a determined and hardworking one.

She didn't have confidence, but she was smart. When she decided she was going to have good grades, she made good ones. When she set her mind on something, that's what she did. Pat just took advantage of every opportunity to the fullest.

— ESTHER HUBBARD

Step by step, I worked on self-improvement. I lost my shyness and began to enjoy college life, the football games, dates and socials, and the usual dormitory mischief. We got the boys we dated to buy us six-packs of beer, and at night after curfew they would sneak under our windows. We lowered sheets, and they would tie the beer up in a linen knot, and we hauled it four stories up.

Pretty soon there was no trace left of the wallflower. I was a dating fool — there was a boy I was always jumping in the car to go off and see, a desperate commute to the Kentucky border that took me across Paris Landing Bridge. One time, trying to get back to campus for curfew, I got caught speeding and didn't have my driver's license. I was terrified of what my father would say, so I gave my name as Sandra Lee Fields — inspired by the view of nothing but farms. I never lived the name down with the Chi Os.

There wasn't much in the way of entertainment in Martin, just a rough honky-tonk bar named Cadillacs that a sorority girl didn't want to be seen in, so we slipped down to an old trestle bridge to drink our beer. We were so far out in the country that the television reception was poor and you had to bend rabbit-eared antennae to pick up one station in Jackson, Tennessee. Mostly we listened to the radio.

The tumultuous news of those years came to me in short crackling bulletins that I barely remember: the Watergate break-in, Vietnam peace talks, terms like "stagflation" and "price controls," the bouts of Muhammad Ali and Joe Frazier, the exploits of Evel Knievel jumping buses on his motorcycle.

It was the era of streakers, and every now and then some guy would decide to dash nude across campus. Clement Hall sat in a main courtyard, so we were invariably in his path, and the dorm would go into total lockdown, and a curfew was enforced for fear some of us belles might see a naked man.

Though it was the early '70s, we weren't political. Most of the young women I knew at Martin had been sent there specifically because it was out in the country, away from the race and antiwar politics roiling places like Memphis. Vietnam was in our consciousness — but not because we protested it. On the contrary — because our brothers fought in it.

Esther's brother served there in 1968, and my brother Charles went in 1969 as an infantryman in the Big Red One, before coming home with a Purple Heart, shrapnel in his back, and a case of shell shock so bad that he hit the floorboards of our truck one day when it backfired. That was a hard year in our family, and Charles's service in Vietnam was the only thing I ever heard my parents fight about. Charles had saved almost all his army pay, and when he got home he declared his intention of rewarding himself with a red Chevelle Super Sport, the hottest muscle car going. Nobody had ever heard my parents have a cross word, until Daddy forbade Charles to buy that car. "He'll kill himself," he said. Mother turned on him and said, "He went off and fought for his country and almost died! He come home alive, and he deserves to have what he wants." My father shut his mouth and that's all there was to it. Charles got the car.

So we didn't listen to protest songs. When we blasted music on the radio, most of it was Motown, Gladys Knight, or folkie stuff. The Fifth Dimension, or Peter, Paul and Mary's version of "If I Had a Hammer." Or "The Lion Sleeps Tonight," with its introductory chorus, "Wimoweh, wimoweh, wimoweh. . . ." But my favorite was Loretta Lynn, who came out with her autobiographical song, "Coal Miner's Daughter," in a twang that sounded so much like mine.

"The work we done was hard," she crooned, "and at night we'd sleep 'cause we was tarred. . . ."

There was one place I felt completely

comfortable: the gym. I made my way over to the small office where the women's athletic program was in its infancy under the direction of an underfunded physical education teacher. "Are you Miss Bettye Giles?" I asked. When she nodded, I asked, "When does basketball practice start?"

Miss Giles, I learned, had a budget of exactly $500 for three sports: volleyball, basketball, and tennis. And she had just one coach, a small spark of a woman named Nadine Gearin, a volunteer who had never really played any of the above. Nadine was more of a badminton expert.

They not only lacked the funding, they lacked good athletes. Bettye took one look at me and, like Esther, decided I was naive and easily led. She said, "Pat, basketball doesn't start until late fall, and around here we have our athletes play volleyball first, to kind of get in condition."

It was a lie. They just needed a warm body to fill out the roster. But I believed her.

"Volleyball?" I said. "That's what you do to get in condition?"

"Yes," she said firmly. "We want all our basketball players to play volleyball."

"Well, okay. That's fine. Whatever it takes, that's what I'll do, just so I can play basketball."

Did I want to play volleyball? No. It didn't get me in shape, either. But back then I did what I was told and played volleyball until it was basketball season.

Martin's basketball team was barely deserving of the term "varsity" — it had evolved from intramurals only a year earlier, and they still played that silly abbreviated half-court game, with three players on each end of the floor. Our uniforms were plain, school-issued physical education gear that everyone wore to their gym classes, sleeveless blue jerseys of heavy cotton twill, with navy shorts. We passed them out by size, and we put numerals on them with athletic tape, until Miss Nadine got us some real ones.

Nadine had a friend in the fabric department of a local store who gave her a sheet of scrap felt. She cut out the numbers and offered to sew them on, but we said, "No, we can sew 'em on ourselves." But you could tell how few of us took home economics. They were the crookedest bunch of numbers you ever saw. Some girls had their numbers up around the neckline, and some down around the waist. Some had one number lower than the other. Esther was number 21, and hers, of course, were perfect. I was number 55, and mine were pretty straight. My official team photo shows me with my long hair wound in a bun with strands falling out, striped tube socks up to my knee pads, and high-topped Converse.

Nadine was an old-fashioned, old-school, ladies' gym teacher. She was a tiny little thing, no more than about five foot three, with tightly curled hair and narrow spectacles, and a high-pitched, chirruping voice that was inherently comical. She wore high heels to be taller, and one afternoon she broke one off while she was coaching us, and she limped around the court on her lopsided little shoe, her face red with exertion, until we all died laughing.

But we were grateful to her: she was an unpaid volunteer who gave us her time so that we'd have an opportunity to play. She didn't know a lot about basketball — and she told us she didn't know a lot. But she tried; she bought, at her own expense, every book she could find about strategy, and to her credit she asked questions. She'd ask, "Who do you think should play guard?"

Sometimes our input wasn't the most dedicated or useful.

"Miss Gearin," we'd say, "it's fraternity rush this week and we're supposed to be at the Pike house by eight. We need to stop practice at seven fifteen so we can get our

113

makeup on and be ready."

Nadine would just say sweetly, "Well. Okay."

That was the state of women's basketball in 1970, and my starting point. There were no mentors or so-called coaching trees for women, like there were for ambitious young male coaches who grew out of the personality cults around legends like Clair Bee in New York, Frank McGuire in North Carolina, Adolph Rupp in Kentucky, or John Wooden in California. Nor were there rich regional playgrounds for women, like the schoolyard network of Philadelphia. But if Nadine didn't teach us much Xs and Os, she taught us respect and teamwork, and she took us where we wanted to go.

We were so poor we didn't even have a team bus. The Lady Pacers traveled in two borrowed station wagons, with Nadine and a team manager behind the wheels. We'd cram three in the front seat, and four people in back, and the tallest of us suffered the most. Imagine half a dozen girls, a couple of whom stood five foot ten or above, climbing out of a car with cramped legs, and trying to play ball.

Nadine was an endless source of amusement on these trips, with her high-pitched voice and innocent little face. She was so tiny she had to sit on a pillow to see over the steering wheel — but then she'd hit the gas and go roaring down the road at ninety miles per hour. Once, as we were caravanning to a game, she got pulled over by a cop.

He said, "Do you know how fast you were going?"

She said, sweetly, "No, but I couldn't have been speeding."

"Ma'am, you were going over seventy-five miles an hour!"

Nadine said, feigning shock, "That just couldn't be . . . Oh! Wait just a minute! I've got new tires on my car. Could that make me go so fast?"

Our training meals were bologna and cheese sandwiches at a rest stop, or McDonald's. We didn't stay in hotels — no money. Instead we slept on mats on the floor of the gym where we played the next day. Our archrival was Tennessee Tech over in Cookeville, a 215-mile drive, which meant a four-hour trip jammed together in the station wagons. Then we slept stiffly in sleeping bags on the hardwood floor of the Tennessee Tech field house.

What a frumpy, earth-bound, starved, and sleep-deprived little team we were, playing in dank, humid gyms that reeked of industrial cleanser and floor varnish and ointment, with a faint waft of hairspray and perfume underneath female perspiration. But I loved it, treasured the cheap uniform that didn't breathe, the damp jersey that got heavier the more I sweated, and couldn't wait to tie up my clumsy flat-soled sneakers, made of canvas with metal eyelets for laces. We knew nothing about training, or about our own bodies; every day of practice was an exercise in curious self-discovery.

Somehow in my first season we went 16-3 to win the Tennessee state title. At the end of it we went back to Tennessee Tech for a tournament, in which all the women's teams in the state converged for a single weekend. After driving four hours to Cookeville and sleeping on a floor, we played six games in two days — two on Friday night, and then *four* on Saturday. One right after the other.

Without washing our uniforms.

We got about fifteen minutes to rest between games. By late Saturday afternoon, our knees were buckling. Nadine dealt with it by cracking ammonia sticks and waving them under our nostrils. We didn't have conditioning, or weights, but we had ammonia. If she thought I looked a little peaked, she would whip out one of her ammonia packets and break it open and thrust it under my nose until I wrenched my head away, my eyes watering. It actually worked, right up until our sixth game. We lost it to Belmont, and by then we were so weary we didn't care, we were just ready to go home.

Our training was crude, the conditions were awful, and we thought nothing of it. It hardly occurred to us that we were entitled to better, or more. Until, at the end of that season, the UT-Martin athletic department's way of rewarding us for winning the state title was to invite us to an awards banquet — for the men's team, which that season had won just three games. While we went 16-3, the guys had gone 3-20. Yet we sat for hours, watching guys receive plaques and awards and congratulations for their efforts. Finally, they paused the proceedings to briefly introduce us. That was our recognition: we got to stand up for a minute.

The coach of the men's team was an old boy named Floyd Burdette, who had played ball for Martin in the 1930s, and whom we jokingly called Buckethead. Every year Burdette held an open tryout and, for one day, anybody on campus could attempt to make the team. Apparently Floyd heard about how I grew up playing with my brothers and could dribble like a guy, a vision of equality he found alarming. He watched me handle the ball in the gym one day and went to Miss Giles.

"Do *not* let her try out for my basketball team," he said. "Don't you send her over there."

Miss Giles realized Coach Burdette was terrified of a women's movement on campus. Helen Reddy's "I Am Woman" was all over the radio every five minutes. The drum-driven chord changes and "hear me roar" crescendo of the song have become a cliché, but at the time we felt it was an anthem of soul-shaking positivism, and there was a lot of discussion about "liberation." Burdette was worried Miss Giles would try to strike a feminist blow by sending me to the men's tryout, and he might be politically pressured to give me a spot on the team.

Bettye took the opportunity to torment him a little. "I'm not sending her anywhere," Miss Giles said. "But she might decide to come on her own." She suggested I was already better than a couple of his walk-ons. Which maybe I was.

She reminded him, "The sign says, 'Open tryouts.' It does *not* say what sex."

He flushed and said, "I refuse to have a girl on the floor."

At the time he felt that he would probably

have to take her on the team as a walk-on. He didn't want to get into the male-female thing. It was very much what men felt — that as women made progress it was going to detract from their program. I faced that here an awful lot.

— BETTYE GILES

It was an era when sports pages didn't cover women much, and if they did, they used terms like "the sex that burns the toast," a phrase I actually read in an issue of *Sports Illustrated.* The local paper was kind to us and gave us good coverage, but on one occasion it actually referred to me — I promise this is true — as "Pretty Pat Head." Which I actually didn't mind in the slightest.

This may sound odd, but despite everything, those of us who played basketball in the deprived, formative era of the early 1970s wouldn't trade the experience. In all the years afterward it gave us a pride of ownership, a sense that we were the architects of our own game, and that our success was entirely self-earned; we'd never been handed anything. And there was a lot to be said for building yourself from the ground up.

If we got any money from our universities, it was a pittance, usually bestowed by a benevolent, or not so benevolent, male administrator. Athletic departments of that era weren't yet big businesses, but rather fiefdoms ruled by crew-cut former gridiron stars, most of whom thought anything spent on a female in athletics came at the expense of men. At Tennessee Tech, for instance, a twenty-two-year-old coach named Marynell Meadors worked under an athletic director named Flavious Smith, a local football hero from the 1950s. When Marynell launched a women's basketball team at Tech in 1970, he refused to fund it. Nevertheless, she dominated the state.

I said, "Do you think we could possibly start some women's sports?" He said, "Oh yeah, we can do that." I said, "Well, do you think we could have some money to operate on?" He said, "I'll give you a hundred dollars." I said, "Oh, thank you." You learned by watching men practice in their gym. If they'd let you in. Sometimes they were offended if you asked to come in.

— MARYNELL MEADORS

Tennessee Tech could only afford to take day trips, and they traveled in a fifteen-passenger van that was so dilapidated the doors wouldn't always stay shut. Marynell was always fearful that the door would slide open and one of her players would fall out on the highway. Also, the van had bald tires.

Over at Austin Peay, a dynamic young coach named Lin Dunn had to cope with a bulldog-faced athletic director named Dave Aaron, who had coached basketball in the 1950s. When Lin launched the women's varsity, he refused to give her a dime or even a vehicle to travel with. He told her, "You can only use the gym when no one else wants it." Including, he said, every intramural team.

> I remember begging for a van and he said no. So we drove in my big old red Impala. It could only fit eight people in it, so if you didn't have a good week of practice, you didn't go. I would slip into the men's locker room and steal things. I stole a set of warm-ups they didn't want anymore. I was always finagling things to get by.
>
> — LIN DUNN

We got more support from our own fathers. At Martin's games, you'd see our dads sidle up to Bettye Giles and press bills in her hand, to help feed us or pay for our gas. My father was one of them. On more than one occasion, Richard slipped a hundred-dollar bill into the purse of Miss Giles.

What little other money we had, we raised. At UT-Martin, we raked yards and had bake sales. Once, we peddled raffle tickets for a bicycle — I sold my share of chances but forgot to write down the names of the poor folks I sold tickets to. They never knew how they got cheated.

Out at Cal State Fullerton, my future Olympic coach, Billie Moore, organized a Blue Chip Stamp drive to fund her team. She passed out the booklets to her players and they filled them up and exchanged them for merchandise they would auction. Another year Billie got them to sell candy — but that only lasted one season because her players ate it all, and weight became an issue.

Next, Billie tried car washes. She put up a sign and handed out hoses and sponges to her players. Some were more industrious than others.

We'd finish a car, and I'd check it, and one side of the car was washed and the other didn't have a drop of water on it. Also, at the end of the day we had all these extra floor mats. The kids had forgotten to put them back in the cars.

— BILLIE MOORE

But we were modernizing fast. Three events in 1972 changed everything for us. First, a group of dedicated women administrators formed the Association of Intercollegiate Athletics for Women, because the NCAA didn't yet care enough about females to bother with us. The AIAW stepped in to govern women's sports and established championships for us — including a sixteen-team basketball tournament that was eventually replaced by the women's NCAA tournament.

The second big event was the announcement that women's basketball would be an Olympic sport for the first time at the 1976 Summer Games in Montreal. And the third, though we didn't know much about it yet, was the passing of Title IX, the little-noticed portion of the Equal Opportunity in Education Act that stated "no person in the United States shall, on the basis of sex, be excluded from participation in, be denied the benefits of, or be subjected to discrimination under any education program or activity receiving Federal financial assistance." Although it would be several years before it was fully implemented, that legislative phrase led to athletic scholarships for women.

What these developments did was to make

winning *available* to women. Previously, competition was a hobby — not a very socially acceptable one. But now that there were trophies, gold medals, and prestige on the table, interest in women's sports surged. Everyone likes winning, no matter what form it takes — and even older male football administrators had to respect an Olympic gold medal sport. Forty years later, commentators at the 2012 London Olympics would marvel over the fact that American women significantly outmedaled men and attempt to analyze how such a thing happened. It started in 1972. That year triggered stratospheric growth, a boom.

I felt the effects immediately, and personally. Universities abandoned their archaic inhibitions and adopted a standardized full-court game, and at UT-Martin I could at last play five-on-five. I began to tell people, "I want to play in the Olympics."

I spent that summer self-teaching myself the full-court game. I got ahold of a *Fundamentals of Basketball* textbook from our physical education department and studied the diagrams. I went back to Henrietta and into the hay barn with my brothers, and we walked through sets — sometimes using a dog or a bucket as a stand-in. Esther came over from Springfield, and the two of us would go against Charles and Kenneth, while Tommy, who was doing some part-time high school coaching, taught us the old Auburn shuffle, a series of patterns run continuously from either side of the court that emphasized movement to get high-percentage shots. We'd weave around up-turned pails, or Dad's dogs.

In the fall, we took it all back to school. Nadine let us put in our plays and run our own practices and coach each other — Esther would cuss at me to defend, or box out. "Quit passing it; you need to be the one shooting," Esther would snap. We practiced against six and seven defenders to make things more difficult and assigned double-teams so we learned to fight out of them. We came up with our own training regimens and set our own curfew. When other girls were going to the frat socials, we talked over game plans in the dorm and went to bed early.

The result was a huge season for a little team from Tennessee. We went 20-8, and qualified for the inaugural national championship tournament. A review of the box scores shows that I averaged 19 points and 15 rebounds a game, so the plays we designed in the hayloft must have worked. I carried us to the southern regional championship with an upset of North Carolina when I scored 31 of our 54 points.

On March 16, 1972, the sixteen most elite teams in the country gathered for the first AIAW national championship tournament in Normal, Illinois. It was a five-hundred-mile road trip, but somehow, Bettye and Nadine begged and borrowed the money to send us. After we won the state tournament in Knoxville, Bettye went to a drugstore on the main drag and bought a large glass piggy bank and literally carried it around on the street, seeking donations. For a snapshot of the women's game in 1972 imagine a full-grown woman walking around with a piggy bank, panhandling for change.

> At first I was embarrassed, and then I thought, What the heck, I'm not doing this for me.
>
> — BETTYE GILES

Once again, we piled into those station wagons. It was a seven-hour trip to Normal, where we actually got to stay in a motel — sleeping four to a room. We were the only team there without proper uniforms, or warm-ups. In an old photo of the sixteen teams, you can tell which ones we are: we're bare armed in sleeveless jerseys, with no jackets.

We didn't last long. We won our first-round game over Long Beach State, but in the next we were put firmly down by Mississippi State College for Women, 49–25. Still, it was an education to be there, because we got to see different styles of basketball, the best of which was the revelatory up-tempo game of Immaculata University, the "Might Macs," who went on to win the first of their three straight national titles under Hall of Famer Cathy Rush. They were Catholic girls from a little school in Pennsylvania who practically wore pinafores when they played, but they were fast, sharp-eyed, hard-elbowed easterners, and they were backed by a fanatical following of nuns, who made such a huge, gonging racket pounding on pots and pans that their noisemakers would eventually be banned.

It was the high point of my collegiate career; UT-Martin never made it back to the national tournament while I was there. But that brief appearance was enough to crack a door open. I learned later that some eight-millimeter film of my performance made its way, thanks to Bettye and Nadine, to the talent evaluators who would select our Olympic team. Shortly afterward, a letter came in the mail.

It was embossed with the initials "USA" on the top.

"It is my privilege to invite you to trials for the selection of the World University Games team," the letter read.

If women from the USA were going to compete in the Olympics for the first time, they had to get international experience. The World University Games were an important preliminary, to be held in August of 1973 in Moscow, the Soviet Union. Now, I had never even been on an airplane, much less out of the country; the farthest I had ever been was Normal, in the rear of a station wagon. But I was prepared to fly to Mars if I thought it would get me out of my Kmart clothes and into a uniform that said "USA" on it.

Miss Nadine put me in a car, and on her own time and at her own expense she drove me all the way to Fairfield, Iowa, for the USA trials. There, I made the cut to the final eighteen players and was invited to the final stage of the selection process, a month-long training camp in Boston in the summer of '73. If I made the team there, we'd go direct to Moscow for seventeen days of competition.

In June of 1973, I went home to Henrietta to pack a month's worth of clothes and visit my folks for a few days. To a farm kid who had never been airborne, the trip ahead of me felt like sailing to the end of the world without a map. On the morning I left for Boston, my family sat around the kitchen table. I hugged my mother and sister, who were both in tears, and then I put a hand on my father's shoulder. He was, I knew, quietly elated for me.

"Bye, Daddy. I love you," I said.

"Awright," he said.

The American Airlines flight from Nashville to Boston had a row of seats in the front that faced backward, and I was assigned to one of them. I sat there, immobilized with fear, with 150 other passengers staring back at me. As we taxied for takeoff I wondered if they could tell I'd never flown. I could almost see them thinking, *That kid is scared to death.*

I didn't feel a whole lot safer once I landed in Boston. Our training camp was on the campus of Northeastern University in the heart of Boston, and as soon as all eighteen players checked into the dorm, we received an emphatic lecture from the coaches telling us not to go anywhere by ourselves, because just down the street was a red-light district where all the merchant sailors who came into the harbor went to celebrate their shore leave. I looked out the window, petrified. *What am I doing here?* I thought.

But it turned out to be one of the most transforming experiences of my life. I'd never been in a truly elite environment before, but now I was training with the very best college players in the country, under the best coaches, and I loved it.

Our head coach was a warm, encouraging woman named Jill Upton of Mississippi State College for Women. But it was her assistant, Billie Moore of Cal State Fullerton, who handled our daily training and who ultimately made the biggest impression on me. Billie would go on to become the Olympic coach and move to UCLA, where she won a national championship in 1978, earned the respect and friendship of John Wooden, and coached a pretty good multisport athlete named Jackie Joyner.

Billie was the most demanding person I'd met since my father. She had a very alive coaching style; loquacious and high energy, she talked and gestured with her hands, which made her short blond hair bounce up and down. If you didn't do something exactly right, she snapped, "Again." And then she'd stalk down the court after you, with her hair flopping. If you didn't get it right again, you ran. And ran. And ran. "Again!" she would bark.

"We aren't going to be the most talented team in international play," Billie warned. "So we better be in shape."

I'd never in my life had to condition at that level, or to meet such challenges, expressed with such intensity. But I took to Billie instantly, and in retrospect I think I must have known that here was the kind of person I wanted to be. She had no discernible traces of fear or self-consciousness. She was forceful, uncompromising, strong voiced, and she didn't seem to think she had to demand less of us just because we were women. If anything, she suggested that she intended to demand *more* from us because we were women.

"Again!" she would roar, and point at the baseline. We ran until our knees were sore, and when the trainers told her to back off, she put us in a swimming pool and she made us run under water. We spent so much time in the pool we told her, "We're going to be able to qualify as a water polo team."

As I got to know Billie I found out she was a farm girl like me, who'd come from Westmoreland, Kansas, but she had only traces of a flat midwestern accent left and had acquired a California shine, or maybe it was just an aura of professional excellence. She recognized something familiar in me, the small-town girl fighting to improve herself. I told her about competing with my brothers, and described my father, and how he raised me like another son, but that I'd discovered there were different rules for women. Billie replied, "When I coach, I just coach players."

Playing for Billie, I discovered my identity: a physical, hardworking slasher who carried my elbows up around my ears. I'd drive straight through whoever was under the goal — and eventually people learned to move aside. I grew more confident by the day as I realized I could compete with the best and was going to make the team.

There are players who aren't always willing to play the hard parts of the game. But Pat played all the parts of it the way you'd like it to be played, with intensity, and a willingness to make everyone around her better. She would defend, and she was a huge factor on the boards. She was strong, very physical. She was not a finesse player. There were players who were prettier than her, could jump shoot better. But there was no one that competed better.

I'm not saying she wasn't talented. But it was her work ethic that made her special.
— BILLIE MOORE

I lost my fears and insecurities, thanks partly to Billie, and to my eastern teammates, like our six-one center Theresa Shank Grentz from Immaculata, whom I'd meet again years later as a coaching opponent. They taught me to enjoy the strange sights and smells and tastes of the Eastern Seaboard, the thick old brownstones of the South End and my first lobster rolls and clam bakes. We sampled the Boston pubs and met guys on campus, who would come to the dorm and call for us over the PA system.

About two weeks after I got to Boston, a Tennessee contingent arrived to check on me: my mother, Bettye, and Nadine. My mother had boarded an airplane for the first time in her life at the suggestion of my father, who was dying to know how I was doing in camp. Richard stayed home to run the farm and the businesses, reluctantly, but he gave my mother careful instructions to talk to the coaches and find out what my chances were of becoming an Olympian.

For the next three days my mother watched the coaches drive us from baseline

133

to baseline. At first she either couldn't get up the nerve to talk to anybody or wouldn't impose. Each night when she called home my father said, "Did you talk to the coaches yet?" My mother said no and ventured the opinion that she didn't think the coaches particularly *wanted* to talk to her. But Father kept insisting and suggested that she try Billie, since we were becoming friendly. Mother told me later she thought he was "going to die" if she didn't do what he asked her to. Finally my mother caught up with Billie on the steps of the gym and introduced herself.

"Her father sent me up here," she said. "He thinks our daughter is supposed to be in the Olympic Games. He said I have to be sure to talk to you and wants me to ask you, do you think our daughter has a chance of making this team?"

"Oh, yeah," Billie said.

Mother had carefully rehearsed what else Richard told her to say. "He wants you to know that whatever she needs to work on to be Olympic caliber, she'll do it."

My father was campaigning for me, from hundreds of miles away.

Billie said the usual things to my mother about how if I continued to work hard I had a good chance of making it to Montreal, and she suggested a few things I needed to improve on and then said good-bye.

In early August, we flew to the Soviet Union with the USA men's team, which starred a marvelous leaping skywalker of a player from North Carolina State named David Thompson, and checked into a dormitory at the University of Moscow. My main impression was of massive grayness, of towers and onion domes intermingled with industrial rectangles that turned out to be apartments. Red Square was like a sudden blast of color and elaborateness amid all the flat gray, and it seemed like everywhere were dusty-olive-uniformed soldiers with their flat, embossed caps.

Between games there wasn't much to do, so we spent most of our free time at the dorm playing cards. We ate our meals at the University of Moscow cafeteria, which invariably served vats of borscht, as well as a tureen with floating fish heads looking at you. Billie got so sick she needed a shot, and we had to prop her up on the bench. We ate mostly bread and potatoes, and vanilla wafers.

But the food became irrelevant. Halfway through the medal round, in a Sunday night game against a country I can't remember, I took a hard Eastern Bloc elbow to the face

— and it dislocated my jaw. It felt as if my face had cracked in half. It hurt just to blink my eyes. The USA's team doctor examined me and told me I needed to have my jaw reset in a hospital. I looked at Billie and mumbled crookedly, "Please come with me." It sounded like "peas cm wif mm."

They loaded me into a rickety Soviet ambulance that felt like the drive shaft was held together by a bobby pin. Every time we hit a pothole, starbursts of pain lit up in my face. When we got to a local hospital, there were no doctors because it was Sunday. We got back in the ambulance and bounced around to a couple of clinics and hospitals, pain spearing through my face, but found no one who could treat me. Finally, the driver took us back to the University of Moscow.

In the dormitory, the team doctor set my jaw himself. He grabbed my face firmly, reached deep into my mouth, and found my jawbone. I let him do it — didn't have a choice. With a sharp motion, he wrenched my jaw back into place, while from the back of my mouth came a cry like something an animal would make.

For the rest of the trip I was on a diet of liquids. I didn't eat anything I couldn't sip through a straw, except some boiled and mashed Soviet potatoes, which I could barely chew.

I couldn't eat. But I could breathe — that meant I could still play. We made the gold medal game, against a Soviet Union team that was the most dominant on the planet in women's basketball, Billie informed us. The Soviets, with their military-style program, were in the midst of winning *five straight* world championships from 1959 onward. What's more, they had a virtually unstoppable player, a seven-foot-two giantess at center named Uljana Semjonova, who was almost as thick as she was tall. Billie's idea was that since we couldn't outjump her, maybe we could outrun her. It didn't work. Playing against Semjonova was like playing against a towering oak tree — one that moved. We were crushed, not surprisingly, 82–44. But it was hard to be too disappointed. The Soviets finished undefeated at 7-0, but we won the silver medal with a 7-2 record, and I'd been our high scorer in three of those games.

By the time we flew home, I had lost fifteen pounds because I couldn't chew. My face still felt crooked, and when I tried to talk, a cold nail of pain went through my jaw. I wanted to surprise my parents and had a friend pick me up at the Nashville airport and drive me to the farmhouse. My mother threw open the door — and burst into tears at how I looked.

My polyester sweats were hanging off me like I was a clothes hook, and my face was bruised. But I had a gleaming silver medal hanging on a blue ribbon around my neck. And on my jacket it said, "USA Basketball."

I was a changed person when I came back to Martin for my senior year. I'd been somewhere in the world, done something, and won something, and I carried the glow of the medal with me. Plus, there was this new aggressive, sideways thrust to my crooked jaw.

I was no longer a country girl; I'd matured. I was confident and self-assured about who I was and, also, what I wanted to become. And I understood how to get there. I'd gained so much confidence, in fact, that my parents felt obliged to caution me. "Winning doesn't make you better than anyone else," they told me. "Losing doesn't make you a bad person either. What goes around comes around, so you better be humble."

But winning certainly altered how people treated me. Men looked at that silver medal like I'd come home from a war with a battle flag. The university administration even honored me on the field at halftime of a football game. Me, a woman. At a football game. I was asked to speak at a Rotary club. I was invited to give a speech in Memphis on what I'd observed of the Soviet Union.

For the first time, I understood just how much I could gain from basketball, how it could help me in all facets of who I wanted to be as a woman. The example was clear: that medal earned me a respect I couldn't have acquired in any other field. It occurred to me that the winner's podium was a pretty good place from which to conduct a women's movement.

The thing I always marvel about is that Pat and her teammates' experiences as college basketball players was no less important to them than the ones today who go to a Final Four with all the trappings. And in fact I'm not sure it didn't have a greater impression and mean more to people like Pat, because they had to work so hard for it, and today so much is given to them.

— BILLIE MOORE

Up to that point I had complicated, unclear feelings about Feminism with a capital F. I was isolated in a corner of the South, and I was further removed from the so-called sexual politics of the day by my passion for basketball, which feminists didn't seem to have much use for. Feminists were demonstrators in New York City who spoke in hot rhetoric about "revolution," and some of them had a tenor of complaint that I felt uncomfortable with. Dwelling on grievance was not something I cared to do; it wasn't my temperament or how I was raised.

What's more, I didn't feel like some of my own sensibilities were especially "feminist." There were lots of aspects of being a woman I didn't want to be liberated from. I wanted to be equal, certainly. But I liked the word *lady.* To me it connoted a kind of grace. I appreciated the fact that our team was called the Lady Pacers. And I was flattered to be called "Pretty Pat Head" by the local male sportswriter.

This is not to say that I didn't have the most powerful feelings on the subject of womanhood; I did. Fierce ones. And I had friends who were politically active, like Lin Dunn from Austin Peay, who belonged to the National Organization for Women.

But I didn't have the need to make some kind of open declaration. What I had instead was a deep, inarticulate purpose. I wanted to change things in the most solid, demonstrable way for young women like me, help broaden their lives and choices, through athletics. I wanted to help other women be . . . strong. If I had to sum up my feelings at the time, I'm not sure I could have. But the writer Nora Ephron would say it years later for me. "Above all, be the heroine of your life, not the victim," she said. That, right there, was the heart of my conviction.

With Pat, she didn't get into that militant feminism. She was more patient. Maybe it was the background with her family, and the way her dad drilled her, "This is who we are and we don't get out of line." I got out of line. But Pat, I don't think she ever did. I wonder if she ever slammed her foot down and said "By damn!" I think she was more diplomatic and negotiated in a different way, with southern charm. And of course, she got what she wanted.

— Lin Dunn

What spoke to me was the combination of wit, guile, and muscularity of a Billie Jean King, who at the time was the number one tennis player in the world, cutting an indelible figure with her bounding serve-and-volley athleticism and glossy brunette shag.

141

In September of '73, the fall of my senior year, King won her $100,000 Battle of the Sexes challenge match over a baiting male opponent named Bobby Riggs. Before a packed crowd in the Houston Astrodome and a worldwide TV audience, Billie Jean drove him off the court in three straight sets, and then laughingly called him "Roberta." It was a tremendous moment.

If you showed the Battle of the Sexes to college women now, it would seem like a dated stunt. But at the time it was the grandest example of competitive ferocity and performance under pressure I'd ever seen from a woman. Under the most intense spotlight, in a chaotic setting with blaring trumpets and marching bands and fanfare, King didn't wilt. Instead she handled the carnival chaos coolly. "I like bands," she said. She won the respect of men like heavyweight champion George Foreman, who leaped out of his seat to applaud her between points. Like every other woman in the country I pressed close to the television and screamed an exultant "Yes!" when it was over. That match was a springboard — it brought awareness to female athletes and made us relevant. From that point on, the suggestion that there were some things women couldn't do would lose ground.

Did I have grievances as a young woman? You bet. But protesting or sign carrying wasn't me — and wasn't going to get it done. Billie Jean, now there was an influential force. Was there anything more equalizing than her sheer toughness, her combination of smarts and muscle? I wanted to influence, and to change. But there was only one way I could see that changed things: winning. You changed things for women by winning.

The experience of playing internationally had given me a serious purpose, and I wanted my teammates to take the game as seriously as I did. I was majoring in education with the intention of becoming a teacher and a coach. I figured I would find a job where I could support myself while I trained for the Olympics. In the meantime, the Martin team was my version of training wheels.

I imported all the drills I'd learned from Billie Moore to our team, and some of Billie Jean King's full-throatedness as well. I ran our bench as if I was the coach, and, like any fresh convert, I was a little too fervent.

Early in the season we had a young post player named Julia Brundige who I thought was getting physically beaten against Jackson State. I scolded her to play tougher, but she kept getting pushed around by her opposite number. During a time-out I told her, "You better get out there and give her a bloody nose, or your ass is going on the bench!"

Well, that got Julia so fired up that she went right out and committed a hard foul. When the whistle blew, she stood there trembling with frustration and holding the ball. When the ref came over to retrieve it, Julia was still so furious that she said, "You want this ball?"

"Yes," he said.

"Then go get it," she said.

And she chucked it as hard as she could the length of the court.

Whistle. Technical foul.

After I quit staring in amazement, I told Julia, "All I meant was play physical. I didn't mean get a technical foul."

It was the last bit of coaching I would do for a while. Basketball is an inherently humbling game. Anyone who has ever played it or coached it knows that it moves too fast to savor victory for very long — the action is too fluid. One event flows right into another, and the moment you pause to congratulate yourself, the ball flies down the court, and you're on the other end of events.

In January of '74, we went on the road to play a Wednesday night game at Austin Peay, which was an easy drive from Henrietta. My parents and most of my friends from home came to see me play, and they instead witnessed the worst moment of my career. Late in the first half, I crashed the boards for a rebound and started to make a turn up the court to throw an outlet pass. Just as I did so another player clipped me in the left knee. I turned one way, and my knee turned the other.

I crumpled to the court and knew right away it was serious. There was a spear of pain, followed by a spreading sensation as if boiling water had been thrown on my leg. After a minute the burning subsided, but I was left with a sickly hollow feeling in my knee. When my teammates helped me up, I couldn't put any weight on it and had to be half carried to the sideline.

Initially I tried to deny just how badly I was hurt. After halftime I even hobbled onto the floor to warm up, wishfully testing my knee to see if I could go back in the game. But it just buckled like it was made out of sticks.

We lost the game. Afterward, arrangements were made to take me to the local county hospital. But suddenly my father stepped forward.

"I want her to see a specialist," he said.

I couldn't believe my ears. A *specialist*? My father never wanted anyone to see a doctor — it was too expensive. Not even when I'd driven a rusty nail through my foot in the barn as a girl did he want me to see a doctor, which had caused one of the few sharp exchanges between my parents; my mother finally prevailed and called a country doctor who treated me by running a needle with disinfectant through the hole.

But now my father insisted. He didn't want me in a county hospital; he was going to send me to the best orthopedic surgeon he could find. So he put me in the car and we drove to St. Thomas Hospital in Nashville.

There in the examining room an orthopedic surgeon probed my knee and told me I had blown out my "anterior cruciate ligament," the connective tissue in the hinge of the knee joint that keeps it stable. I had also torn my meniscus cartilage. There was nothing left in my knee but a bunch of floating, disconnected shreds. I would need "reconstructive" surgery, the doctor said. I cringed at the word: in the early 1970s, reconstructive surgery was effectively a career ender. These days an ACL can be repaired with the delicate instruments of arthroscopy, a couple of small incisions, and six months of rehab. But the technique back then was a heavy-handed and rudimentary job with a scalpel that left nasty scars, and usually a knee was never the same.

I looked at my collapsed knee and saw my entire life collapsing with it. I might never get to take another athletic step.

"I don't know if you'll play again," the surgeon said.

My father turned those irradiated blue eyes on him.

"Play?" he said. "She's going to be in the Olympics."

"I don't . . ."

"Fix it," my father said firmly. "You go in there and you fix it."

My father's certainty was the only reassuring thing I heard, and I latched on to it. If Daddy said I would play again, that meant I would. Later that night, my old childhood friend Jane Brown came to the hospital to visit. She found my parents in the lobby with Nadine and Bettye, all of them looking like doom. My father had an arm around my mother, whose chin was trembling.

"What's wrong?" Jane asked.

"The doctor says she won't ever play

again," my mother answered.

As Jane headed to my room she tried to think of something comforting to say to me. She came through the door and said, "Trisha . . ." But I cut her off.

"That doctor is crazy as hell if he thinks I won't play again," I said.

I meant it. I was as determined as my father not to view the ACL as career ending — that just wasn't an option. I thought, *There's no way this is stopping me.*

The next morning, the surgeon opened up my entire knee with a foot-long incision and attempted to stitch and graft things back into their proper places. I woke up with my leg heavily swathed in a cast that went from above my knee down to my toes. I was on crutches for weeks. When the bandages came off, there was a winding twelve-inch scar, a long tailing S-curve that started above my knee and stopped at my calf.

When the surgeon came to visit me, he told me he'd heard that the only thing more painful than a torn-up knee was childbirth. I just looked at him.

"I think I'll be adopting all my kids," I said.

After that came months of tedious rehabilitation. Back then there were no fitness centers or personal trainers, and if you wanted physical therapy, you had to go to a clinic. I was on my own in Henrietta and did the best I could; most of my therapy was homemade. I found an old cloth bag with handles on it that belonged to my mother, loaded it up with bricks, and then hoisted myself up on our kitchen counter. I hooked the bag over my foot and did leg lifts with it, trying to strengthen my quadriceps.

I ran the back roads of our farm. Around the same time, my brother Tommy was recovering from a broken leg, so we worked out together, hobbling. It was sort of like the old days in the hayloft; as soon as we both could stand on two feet again, we played one-on-one. I knew I was healing on the day that Tommy had a hard time winning.

Only way I could beat her was to push her out of the way and shoot a layup. I said, "I'm through. I think you're in better shape than I am."

— TOMMY HEAD

I went back to school to continue rehabbing and to enjoy the rest of my senior year. To kill the boredom, we went to drive-ins to see disaster films like *The Poseidon Adventure.* One evening out of sheer mischief I pulled the main electrical breaker in the dorm, plunging us into darkness. They had to call the janitor out of Sunday night church to get the lights back on, and for years afterward he said, "I know it was that Head girl. Everyone loves her, but I know she's nothing but trouble."

It was time to start job hunting. Vietnam wound down, and the Watergate scandal peaked, but I was more preoccupied with my knee and my future. If I couldn't recover, the most realistic scenario was that I'd wind up back in Henrietta standing in front of a blackboard at one of the local high schools.

To finish my degree at UT-Martin I was required to do some student teaching, and that spring I got a taste of what it was to be a high school instructor at a local school in Greenfield, Tennessee. Student teaching was a constant battle against chaos; the kids all thought they could take advantage of me because I was a young substitute. I learned something important about projecting authority: you had to set the tone immediately if you didn't want to be challenged.

I also learned that maybe I didn't want to

spend the rest of my life trying to control classrooms of wild, bored teenagers.

The teacher I was working under asked me to cover a class while he ran an errand downtown. Sitting at a row of desks was a roomful of thirty or so students, including some of the most popular athletes in the school. I turned my back and was looking at the blackboard when a paper wad hit me in the arm. Now, a paper wad expertly done is heavy — it's been soaked in water and then packed into a tight hard ball — and it hurts. I wheeled around and made eye contact with every student in that room, and as soon as I met eyes with the culprit, I knew he did it. He was one of the better-off kids in the school, the son of a prominent doctor. The kids stared at me, to gauge my reaction. His daddy was important, and I was just the female substitute. And I knew that's what they thought.

"I don't want to hear a sound out of anyone," I said. "I will be right back."

I went down to the teacher's lounge and said, "I need a paddle."

There was a large paddle, just like the old Blister II that had been used on me back in Henrietta. When I got back to the classroom, you could hear a pin drop. I stared at the perpetrator with Richard Head's eyes.

"Why'd you do it?" I said.

"I was just messing around," he said. "I didn't mean to hit you, I meant to hit the blackboard."

"You missed it," I said.

"Yes, ma'am," he said.

"Come outside," I said.

In the hallway, I told him to grab his ankles. I hit him hard enough to pick him up off the floor, and then I said, "Go have a seat," and we walked back in the classroom. For the next few days I waited to hear something about it from the teacher, or from the boy's father, but no one ever said a word, and I got an A in student teaching.

Bettye Giles didn't believe I belonged at the high school level and urged me to apply to graduate school, which I did. She was determined to see me become a college coach, and she actually told the local newspaper that spring, "We need people like Pat in our field. The future depends on them." Bettye called the women's athletic directors at the University of Tennessee, Dr. Nancy Lay and Dr. Helen Watson, and personally pushed my application, telling them, "If you don't take her, somebody else will."

That April, a letter arrived from Tennessee offering me a place in the master's program in the physical education department, with a part-time job as an assistant to Tennessee's basketball coach, Margaret Hutson. I was unsure of whether to accept. Tennessee was on the other side of the state, away from my family and my college friends, and it was hardly a force in women's basketball. I wavered, unsure a big state school was where I belonged.

But just two weeks later, Margaret Hutson decided to go on a sabbatical to pursue a doctorate. Tennessee suddenly had an opening for head coach. I was in the UT-Martin gym working out with some of my teammates, when Miss Giles walked in.

"I just got off the phone with the athletic director in Knoxville," she said. "They would like you to be their *head* coach."

I was stunned. I said, "Now why would I want to go there and do that?"

My teammates started chattering at me.

"Because it's a job and you'll be paid to coach basketball," they said. "Go."

So I went.

How disappointed were you when you would lose?

Sick. Just sick at my stomach.

Why does it make you physically ill?

Because I feel like I should be able to do something about it. But you can't always do that.

[Later]

You can't do anything about Alzheimer's, either. But my understanding is, you want to work as much as possible for as long as possible?

Sure.

What's your biggest concern about the diagnosis going forward? What concerns you?

You know, I — the diagnosis is what it is. It's not like I worry about going to bed and not waking up. But at first, man, it just knocked me out of my chair. Why me? We talked about that, went through all that, and now I have a better understanding. You know, I feel like I'm helping other people. That's important.

— May 25, 2012, Alys Beach, Florida, one year after diagnosis

4
OLYMPIAN

I was driving across the Tennessee campus on a fall day in 1974, heading over to my new office, when I spotted a couple of young women bouncing a basketball on the sidewalk. I recognized them as two of Tennessee's returning players, Diane Brady and Sue Thomas, and they had just finished a pickup game with some guys. I pulled over in my light green Cutlass with the vinyl top and rolled down my window.

"What are you girls doing?"

"We just been beatin' these boys in basketball," Diane said.

I liked the sound of that.

"Well, do you know who I am?"

"You must be Pat Head," Diane said.

"I am. Tryouts will be in two weeks."

I was a newly minted twenty-two-year-old coach, and the young woman looking back at me was twenty-one. I was only two or three months older than her, and a season earlier had stood on a court playing against her. Yet now I was supposed to tell her what to do.

I was bluffing.

How did I begin? I just began — put one foot in front of the other. When I view the start of my professional life from the end point, I see that I was just a linear force, on a straight, determined march forward. I had no sense yet of the cycle of things and no deep or ingenious thoughts. All I had was my own impulse to emerge into the professional world, to get going.

My office was in a small attic at the top of a creaking old building called Alumni Gym. I had to climb five flights of stairs to get to it, and, honey, it was hot as the blazes up there. But it was the least of the heat that I was under. I didn't spend much time at my desk, because I was too busy running from one place to another. I was taking four classes toward my master's, and teaching four more to undergraduates as part of the advanced degree program, and whatever I had left after that eight-hour day I was supposed to devote to coaching, while on the side I was trying to rehab my knee and train for the Olympics. So I wasn't thinking, *I'm going to build a national powerhouse at Tennessee and be a trailblazer for women.* My aim that first season was just to survive.

I'd never coached a day in my life. I'd never organized a practice or designed a game plan, never brought a team together. The first thing I had to do was get some players. As I scanned the Tennessee roster, I saw that the average height of the squad was all of five foot five. The senior point guard was Joy Scruggs — a slight little brunette who stood exactly five foot one.

In later years I had a policy with our players: always look me in the eye. That wasn't possible with this group. They weren't tall enough.

I made flyers announcing open tryouts and posted them around campus. There was no such thing as recruiting back then in women's basketball; to make up a team you just walked down dormitory hallways, saying, "You wanna play?"

When I walked into Alumni Gym for those first tryouts, I found forty or so young women, and every one was a short, sweet little white girl who hailed from the state of Tennessee and had come out of the high school system that forbade them from playing full court. They wore their own mismatching practice gear, ragged T-shirts and canvas sneakers, along with earrings and necklaces and hair clips. Then there was Suzanne Barbre, a freshman. She came to tryouts wearing Daisy Duke cutoff jean shorts — and carrying a pocketbook.

I had no basketball "philosophy." All I had was some basic training as a student teacher, which told me, "Go in and start off tough. You can always let up." I walked into the room intending to let them know who was in charge. I surveyed them appraisingly. "You must have had a good summer," I said. "You've probably put on a few pounds. You're going to have to work hard to get back in shape."

For the next three hours, I drilled them at a frenetic pace: fast-break drills, defensive drills, full-court passing drills. A couple of the young ladies were so inexperienced they didn't know to turn around as they went up the court and got hit in the back of the head with the ball.

Then came conditioning: "Hit the stairs!" I ordered. They sprinted up one set of the extremely steep Alumni bleachers and down another. "Again," I ordered. And again.

Forty girls went up one set of bleacher stairs — and half of them quit at the top. They just never came down.

Of the twenty or so remaining players, I noticed four of them running together with their tongues hanging out. After the second suicide sprint, when they got to the end line, they just kept on going. All four of them ran out of the gym door, up the steps, and I never saw them again.

That night I called Billie Moore and wondered aloud if I'd been too demanding. It was only the first day.

"Billie, about forty people came," I said. "But half of them left and didn't come back."

"That's wonderful," Billie said, delighted. "That's just fine."

"It is?" I said.

"Better to have seven or eight who really want to be there," she said.

Actually, I ended up with eleven players. I took them down to a little cubbyhole office in the basement of Alumni and opened up a big brown box. Inside were their new uniforms, bright orange ones that had been bought with money from a doughnut sale. They were made of hot coarse polyester, and not all of them fit, but at least they made us look like a team — until we washed them, when they all bled into slightly different shades.

Next, I had to find some volunteer assistants, because I simply had more work than I could handle. In addition to my classes, and holding practices, I also had to drive the van on road trips, do the team laundry, and tape ankles, since we didn't have trainers. For help I turned to a friend and fellow grad student, Sylvia Rhyne, a sweet bighearted Southern Baptist girl with a spacious grin. Sylvia volunteered to be an assistant coach while another fellow grad student named Judy Rose offered to be our manager. Years later Sylvia Rhyne Hatchell would win a national championship at North Carolina, while Judy Wilkins Rose became athletics director at UNC-Charlotte and a force in the NCAA.

The day of our first game arrived: December 7, 1974, against Mercer University. I got to Alumni Gym early because, in addition to doing the team laundry, it was my responsibility to see that the floor was ready. Our men's team played in Stokely Athletics Center, a modern 12,700-seat arena with a full staff to set it up on game days. But it was up to me to get Alumni, a sagging old redbrick relic of the 1920s that also housed a swimming pool and a stage, ready for a crowd. It seated thirty-two hundred people on shaky pull-out bleachers that closely crowded the sidelines, and the floor was so dim with varnish and had so many black lines on it you could hardly tell where to shoot a free throw from. Also it was dark —

you practically needed a miner's lamp to see.

I turned on the lights and found the game clock and set it up. I swept the floor clean. Next, I had to set up the benches. As I did so, I heard a shuffling noise and turned to find that Alumni's custodian, a gentleman named Doug Pease, was unfolding chairs. Doug could tell how harried and overworked I was and decided to help, and from that moment on he became my chief ally. He'd turn on the breakers in the morning and stay with me until we closed up the gym at night.

Once the floor was set up, I went into the locker room, which was just a lounge area with a couple of vending machines and some straight-backed Naugahyde chairs. I began to tape our players' ankles, which I wasn't very good at — in our first practice, I left ridges in the tape, which rubbed against their feet and blistered them. Thirty years later players still complained that they had scars from my tape job. Finally, a sophomore guard named Jackie Watson said, "Coach, I know how to tape ankles," and I said, "Then you're gonna have to help me out." So Jackie became the official ankle taper.

My pregame instructions were simple, by

necessity. Since so many of our new players had never played full court, I gave everyone specific responsibilities and told them to just concentrate on that. Our point guard was the young woman I'd met on the sidewalk, Diane Brady, a curly-haired senior, five foot two, with a soft-spoken, breathy voice and a wide-eyed, almost angelic face.

I looked down at Diane and said, "Your job is to take care of the ball. Do you understand me?"

Diane talked slow in her breathy little voice and she said, "I got it, Coach. I got it."

Then she said, "Are you nervous?"

"No," I lied. "Why — am I acting like it?"

"Well, your neck's broke out," she said.

I glanced in a mirror and saw that, in fact, my neck was mottled with vivid red splotches, which would continue to appear on every game day for the next thirty-eight years. "Let's just go play," I said hastily.

There were exactly fifty-three spectators in the gym, and most were parents. University president Andy Holt was there, carrying a sack of ham biscuits to snack on. Also in the crowd was Esther Hubbard, who was newly married and had driven over from her home in nearby Johnson City for moral support. Esther was around quite a lot and had gotten to know the players, so well, in fact, that as Diane Brady was dribbling up the court, she spotted Esther. Diane paused in middribble to wave and say, "Heeeeyyyy!" Which Esther thought was "cute," but her coach was less pleased.

We lost the game. By one point, 84–83.

Afterward I called my parents. My mother answered the phone — and, bless her heart, never asked if we won or lost. Never even mentioned it, which was typical of her. She wanted to know if I liked graduate school, and how my classes were, and whether I was getting enough to eat, letting me know in her own way that she loved me no matter what the score was. But finally, after a few minutes of telling her about school, I said, "Mama, you better let me talk to Dad."

He came to the phone, which he didn't particularly like talking on. I never heard my father say hello.

He just picked up the receiver and said, "Awright."

"Hi, Dad," I said.

"How'd you do?"

"We lost."

"How much?

"Uh, one point."

Pause.

"Well," he said, "you don't take donkeys

to the Kentucky Derby."

And then he put the phone down. That was it.

Obviously, my father wasn't going to be a great source of coaching advice. Nevertheless, there was something in what he said. It was lesson number one, the most fundamental fact of coaching: it was all about the players. There were a lot of things I could do as a coach, but I couldn't go out there and make kids taller, or faster.

But of course they weren't donkeys — they were incredibly willing kids who got the most out of what they had, and the season before, under a far more experienced coach in Margaret Hutson, they'd gone 25-2. Logic told me that I was at least as responsible for a one-point loss as they were. One point? That was reversible. I couldn't make them bigger, but I *could* prepare them better, neutralize some weaknesses, and enhance their strengths by becoming a better coach. I hadn't helped them much from the bench, I realized. I wish now that I'd been more knowledgeable, but I wasn't. Before the game started, my brother Tommy asked me, "What kind of defense will Mercer play?" I replied, "I don't know." That's how unprepared I was.

We had almost a month off before our

next game because it was Christmas break, which left me plenty of time to think about what to do. All I had to go on was my instincts, and they told me, "Run, don't walk." We didn't have a lot of basketball knowledge, I reasoned, so we'd have to go on courage. And since we didn't have size, we'd have to go on speed. We'd have to become a running, pressing team. If we couldn't outplay people, maybe we could outrun them.

We went back into Alumni Gym and I instituted a fast-break offense, and to practice it we used something called the Bungle Drill, which we named after a hit song that year, "Bungle in the Jungle." It was a full-court up-tempo weave that the players actually loved. Every time I called it out, our freshman guard Suzanne Barbre would look at little Diane Brady and say, "Brady, let's go bungle in the jungle!" Off they would go, weaving up the court, with my voice driving them.

It was December and freezing outside, and Alumni Gym was barely heated, so the kids practiced in full sweats, blowing plumes of frost out of their mouths. I'd say, "Look at Brady, she's not even sweating," as if I was a prosecutor and her lack of sweat was evidence against them. Then I'd make them run some more.

It worked. When we came back from Christmas break on January 10, 1975, we got our first victory, a 69–32 win over Middle Tennessee State, and from there we went on a six-game winning streak. We ended up posting more than 100 points in eight games, and the kids sprinted so hard and tirelessly that a referee actually said to them, "What do you girls do, run up and down those east Tennessee mountains?" Late in the season, a Tennessee human physiology professor conducted a heart rate experiment on them. He asked guard Jackie Watson and a couple of other players to run on a treadmill, and was amazed at how long they could go without stopping.

"What in the world does she do to you all?" he asked.

Looking back on it, that first team put up with an awful lot from their young, hard-headed coach. I was reluctant to get too friendly with them, or even to laugh, in case it might undermine my authority. I built a wall so they would know that despite our ages I was in charge. My style was intentionally barking and intimidating.

We traveled in a fifteen-passenger van, sometimes for as long as twelve or fourteen hours, and I wasn't a lot of fun on those long, monotonous drives. I'd grip the wheel and zone out, thinking about how we could get better, to the point that I got a crease in my forehead. Periodically, to keep from falling asleep, I'd roll the window down and stick my head out into the cold air. Once, when we were driving in bad weather, I was concentrating so hard that I never noticed when the rain stopped. The wipers kept going. *Screech, screech.* I kept driving. After a few minutes, the windshield got so dry that the wipers began to make that sound that's worse that squeaking. *Rhent, rhent, rhent.* Behind me, the players raised their eyebrows and choked back giggles, but I drove on, oblivious.

It seemed like we drove forever. The tension in the van was getting thick. Finally someone said to no one in particular but loud enough for her to hear, "Is it still raining?" We all thought we'd die for trying not to laugh. It was just enough for Pat to realize the wipers could be turned off.

— JOY SCRUGGS

One big road trip that year was to Western Carolina, in Cullowhee, North Carolina, and it was a trying one. We played horribly, and to compound matters every one of our starters got in foul trouble. We finally pulled the game out in the final seconds, 69–66, which was a relief, but I wasn't happy. I went in the locker room and put my hands on my hips and delivered a tirade as if we'd just lost. They looked back at me in shock; I could see from their expressions what they were thinking: *We've never been yelled at before for winning.*

After the game, we loaded up the team van and set out on the four-hour return trip. Most of the kids fell asleep, while I stewed. But Diane Brady wasn't asleep. Out of the darkness I heard her soft voice say, "I thought we could have played some zone since we were in such foul trouble." All around Diane, players flinched — they were no doubt thinking, *If Brady doesn't shut up, we're going to have to run tomorrow.*

I started talking about what kind of D to play — which was like telling Moses how to part the sea.

— DIANE BRADY

But I was so surprised, I just said, "Why do you say that?" I let Diane explain that the way the refs were blowing the whistle, maybe a more conservative zone would have saved us some fouls. But what little philoso-

170

phy I had at the time, I was stubborn about. I taught strict man-to-man defense, because it was active and aggressive. In my mind a zone was "lazy." It meant sitting back while the other team came at you. A zone was static, stationary. I let Diane argue back, and neither of us conceded the point, and finally the discussion wound down.

I didn't make anybody run — I actually respected Diane for having the spirit to talk basketball with me. But I was a little concerned with whether she'd follow my orders. I found out she was on my side one afternoon during a game against East Tennessee State. There was a dead ball near our bench, and she came over to inbound. She was standing near me on the sideline, so I gave her some instructions on what to do when play restarted. Brady was so intent on doing what I asked that she never made an entry pass — she just dribbled the ball inbounds. The ref blew the whistle — turnover. I didn't have the heart to bark at her for the mistake, because I was so relieved she listened to me. That was what an insecure young coach I was.

I was uneven, not yet sure of my methods, and often as not I sabotaged us. When we fell behind our cross-state rival Union University by five points, I decided to "motivate" them for the second half by making them run wind sprints in the basement during intermission. It was not exactly the recipe for a comeback — we lost. On another occasion, my halftime speech consisted of announcing, "I don't know what to say. You all talk it over, and when you decide that you want to play, you can come back out on the floor." Then I turned and left.

We finished with a 16-8 record, and I wish I could say it was all part of the master plan and I knew what Tennessee would become. But I didn't. I was just a twenty-two-year-old kid fighting through her first job, confused and blind to the future. Someone who didn't know what she was doing yet, except that she loved the game and wanted it to grow. At the end of that season when our women's sports administrator Nancy Lay asked me what I "envisioned" for the future, I answered, "I want to fill the gym."

The better results came off the court. Diane Brady graduated and went off to work for an accountant, but within a few weeks she called me and said she thought she was in the wrong line of work. She wanted to become a teacher and a coach, and could I help her get into the master's program? I was touched: Diane had been such a loyal, diligent player, and the fact that she wanted to be a coach meant I hadn't traumatized her too badly, and even had a little influence. When she came back to campus to enroll in grad school, she stayed in my apartment for a night. It was nice to be at ease with her and to talk like friends instead of player-coach.

That night I gave Diane two books that were important to me at the time, and which show you where my head was. One was Zig Ziglar's *Reaching the Top,* the first of thousands of leadership books I'd collect over the coming years, looking for a clue as to how to do my job. Ziglar was the success guru of the 1970s, and he issued platitudes that rang true to me, like, "Your attitude, not your aptitude, will determine your altitude." But perhaps most influential was this one, which spoke to the aspiring teacher in me: "You can have everything in life you want, if you will just help other people get what they want."

The other book was a thin little volume called *Hope for the Flowers,* by Trina Paulus, a 1972 bestseller that was a work of the consciousness-raising period. It was a story of the transformation of a caterpillar character named Stripe into a butterfly, and it shows you what an idealistic, fresh teacher I was, not too far removed from the country girl who yearned for metamorphosis. The meaning was simple: Stripe the caterpillar wished to be something more, but he learned that transformation didn't come just from striving. You had to go deep inside, where it was dark and frightening, and meet yourself. If you were willing to do that, then you might grow wings.

Diane never gave either one back to me. She kept them both. And that was okay.

I didn't let our players know it, but when I wasn't coaching, I was still as much of a student as they were, and as young at heart, which you could tell if you swung by my little apartment just off the main drag. You'd have heard the clinking of bottles and my stereo blasting the wails of Linda Ronstadt and the Stone Poneys, singing "Different Drum."

Yes, and I ain't saying you ain't pretty
All I'm saying is I'm not ready
For any person place or thing
To try and pull the reins in on me

Soon as I stepped off the basketball court, I'd lose the stern face and slip into some jeans and go looking for as much cheap adventure as you could find on my stipend of $250 a month. The grad students in the phys ed department shared the same office space in that hot attic, and we were bonded by a combination of poverty, hilarity, and overwork. We went to the Scottish Inn for thirty-five-cent cocktails, or ate Lum's hot dogs cooked in beer, or went to Western Sizzlin' because you could get a salad and a baked potato for a dollar.

Since we had no money, we were always trying to sneak our way into things for free. There was an all-girl band in town named the 19th Amendment, which commanded our loyalty, and we found out they were booked to play at a young bankers' convention at a large hotel in town. I put on my most authoritative voice and called the hotel. "I'm with the Pan Hellenic Organization," I said. I was considering whether or not to hire the 19th Amendment for my *own* convention, and could I possibly bring a group of colleagues to hear them? Not only did they let us in; they put us at a table at the very front, and we ate and drank for free.

Pat would do about anything really — she was fearless. She was the ring-leader of everything and the professors all loved her

175

to death; she could win 'em over. There were about six of us. We had cookouts almost every weekend, and her apartment was the gathering place and everybody congregated there. She had a big stereo, and we'd buy the groceries and she'd cook. She had confidence plus, everything was a challenge, and she didn't back down from anybody or anything.

— SYLVIA HATCHELL

We formed our own softball team and entered the Knoxville Recreational Women's League, playing in baseball shirts with big letters on them that said AST, which drove our opponents crazy trying to figure out what it meant. It was our joke: it stood for "A Softball Team," which made us fall around with laughter.

I supplemented my small income by playing cards, at which I was as bold as I was good. I got to know some of the UT faculty and discovered a small, friendly professorial poker group and talked my way into their game. I'd play with the professors into the small hours of the morning and take their money. For some reason they didn't hold it against me.

Nor did one of those professors, Dr. Barbara Meade, hold it against me when I

176

decided it would be hilarious to paper her yard one night. I had the keys to Alumni Gym, and Sylvia and I collected all the toilet rolls from the restrooms and drove out to Dr. Meade's home in west Knoxville and draped her pear trees in so much paper it looked like a Russian blizzard. We must have felt faintly guilty, because we offered to cut her lawn for her. Sylvia would push the mower one lap, and then I'd hand her my beer and take the mower and push it for a lap.

Life then seemed like one huge contest to me, and I met it with what seems to me now like inexhaustible vitality — where did I find the energy to play softball? — and a certain amount of swagger. I was always going a hundred miles an hour in my Cutlass, trying to get to all the places I needed to go and get there first. One afternoon Sylvia and I were driving in traffic when a guy nosed in front of me. I reflexively hit the gas and cut him off. At the next stoplight he started chewing me out. Well, he had met his match. "If you want to pull over, we can settle it right now," I said, and it was all Sylvia could do to stop me from getting out of the car.

Somehow, between all of that, I acquired my master's degree and learned to teach.

For all my mischief, I'd found my calling. The Tennessee program wasn't designed to make a basketball coach out of me, it was to make an educator, and I discovered that I loved the job.

The idea of it was that I should be able to teach more than Xs and Os. I should be able to teach . . . anything. I absorbed the "whole-part-whole method," how to explain an overall concept to students, break it down into smaller pieces, then put it back together again with emphasis, explaining the key concepts that unlocked larger schemes.

I was required to teach phys ed classes in sports I'd never played, like racquetball and badminton. But my favorite was self-defense, which meant I had to learn some rudimentary martial arts techniques. I liked to think I could defend myself, and liked to teach other women to do it. Plus, I enjoyed making all the noises.

I became dedicated. I taught a class in Fundamentals of Basketball, which was immediately popular with all the campus star athletes, who figured it for an easy grade. Among those who signed up was Ernie Grunfeld, a six-foot-six ballplayer with a crooked smile and a flowing game. The Tennessee men's team was in the midst of a fabulous hey-day with Ernie and his fellow New York playground ace Bernard King, nicknamed the "Ernie and Bernie Show," because they lit up the campus with their bright personalities and explosive games. Ernie was on the USA national team, so I knew him a little bit, and I figured I'd enjoy having him in class. Except he never came. He and the rest of the athletes cut it, assuming I'd give them an A.

I couldn't do it. I was too principled in the classroom and too intolerant of laziness. I just couldn't rubber-stamp their transcripts because they were stars on the men's team.

I gave Ernie a D.

He came to my office, incredulous.

"How could you give me a D?" he asked.

"You didn't show up," I said.

"Yeah. But I know all that stuff."

"Ernie, get out of here," I said, laughing, "before I give you an F."

The message got around: don't cut Pat's class.

At the end of the spring semester, the Tennessee administration offered me a full-time job. Well, really, three jobs. At a starting salary of $8,900, I'd be head coach of the women's basketball team, an instructor required to teach three courses, and an administrator in the athletics department. The salary was a relief, but it meant more work than ever. In the 1975–1976 season, Tennessee had a budget of just $5,000 for six women's sports, and I was in charge of administering most of them. I had to order the uniforms, do the scheduling, including travel, and serve as the rules compliance person. I was also still trying to rehabilitate my knee and train as a world-class athlete.

I was overwhelmed. Something was bound to suffer, and it was my knee. I tried to get workouts in, but it was difficult. I'd get up early in the morning and go to a weight room, and try to strengthen my leg, which was still stiff and painful a year after surgery.

There were no women in the weight room at that time; it was only guys. She would go in there and do curls with that leg. She had a major scar. Big-time scar. Let me tell you she went after it. She'd have tears in her eyes because of the pain, trying to get that leg back. You talk about commitment.

— SYLVIA HATCHELL

But I just couldn't keep up with it, and slowly but surely I fell out of shape. In September of 1975, I rejoined the USA national team for the World Championships in Bogotá, Colombia, and the Pan American Games in Mexico City. I was slow and overweight, and I hobbled. In Mexico City when they handed out our USA gear, among the things we got was a dress for official functions. I held my dress up, and I thought: *That thing is huge.* It was a size 16 and it should have swallowed me, but it didn't. There was a little market where we would go trade our international souvenirs, and I decided to trade my dress. When I pulled it out, the lady who ran the market started laughing and said, "Oh, grande, grande, grande!" Well, it was grande. I thought, *This lady right here knows what she's looking at.* And I knew, too. My body had changed since the knee injury.

I got benched. I hardly played, unless it was a twenty-point blowout. I joked that I played end, guard, and tackle: sat on the end of the bench, guarded the water bottles, and tackled anyone who came in there that wasn't supposed to be there.

Our head coach was Cathy Rush from Immaculata, with Billie Moore again serving as an assistant, and they had little use for me in the shape I was in. They had more use for me at the card table, where Cathy had a tendency to win big pots and then quit, so I couldn't get my money back. I lost a lot of my per diem meal money to her.

But I learned a valuable coaching lesson on that trip. By then I was the most senior member of the team, and it was embarrassing and hurtful to be on the end of the bench with a bad knee. All around me were young collegians like Ann Meyers, who was a star at UCLA, and Nancy Lieberman, a phenomenal flame-haired teenaged guard from New York. As the oldest person on the team I knew that their eyes were on me. I had every opportunity to feel sorry for myself and create tension.

What I learned is that how someone accepts being a member of the supporting cast is critical to chemistry: an unhappy role player can be disruptive, create a culture of whining, and undermine the authority of the decision makers. For the first time in my life I was in that position and had to decide how to deal with it. Nancy sat on the bench next to me, though for a different reason: she was too young and inexperienced to get much playing time. It would have been very easy for me to lean over and whisper complaints in her ear.

But I decided if I ever wanted to amount to anything as a professional I had to be an example for Nancy. She and I were invariably the last players to get in the game, and one afternoon it got particularly humiliating. The USA was up by more than 30 points and there were just a couple of minutes left when Cathy Rush finally looked down the bench and pointed at Nancy and me. It was time for the scrubs to mop up.

Nancy was furious. She said, "I'm not going in."

"Why?" I said.

"This is embarrassing," she said. "I'm not going in."

Nancy went on to become a great player and friend of mine, but she was young, and the young are inherently self-absorbed.

"Oh, yes, you are," I said. "And I'll tell you one thing. You better not pass me the ball, because if you do, you'll never get it back."

I spent the rest of the tournament swallowing my pride, and drinking beer with Ernie Grunfeld in the local marketplaces. It wasn't a great trip, and it got worse.

Although we managed to win the gold in the Pan Ams, we finished a lowly eighth out of fourteen teams in the World Championships. It was a huge setback because it denied us an automatic spot in the Montreal Games. We were relegated to a pre-

Olympic qualifying tournament.

One afternoon after practice as I was walking off the court I saw Bill Wall, the executive director of what has now become USA Basketball. Bill was a no-nonsense executive in gray flannel whose commitment to supporting the women's game was critical; he supported us financially when others would have marginalized us. Perhaps just as important, he was genuinely interested in us. Bill knew I was out of shape and that I'd been spending a lot of time sampling Mexican beer.

Bill said, "You're not going to make the Olympic team like this."

"What do you mean?" I said.

"You'll never make it," he said.

I wheeled around and glared at him, and said, "Oh yes I will."

My jaw was thrust halfway back to America. But Bill was just being honest, and trying to motivate me. When I went to Billie Moore and repeated what Bill had said, she was equally honest.

She said, "If you have any desire to make the Olympic team, you better take off at least ten or fifteen pounds. You're going to be older, and you've got a bad knee. If you don't get yourself in the best shape you've ever been in, and become much quicker, you won't have a chance to compete."

It was a low point. I'd fought so hard to come back from the knee, and to learn I might not make it to Montreal shook me to the core. I was going to be devastated if I didn't make that team. I refused to even think about it.

"Well, then, you'd better get a plan," Billie said.

This may come as a surprise, but when I'm challenged, I can be a little excessive. I didn't lose ten pounds, or even fifteen, in the next year. I lost twenty-seven pounds. There were no more barbecues and thirty-five-cent beers. I swore off red meat. I got up every morning and ran for miles, and any day that I didn't get my mileage in, I made myself run double the next. I trained five and six hours a day. After I ran, I went to the weight room and then to the gym to play pickup against guys. I worked with total commitment, determined to be in the shape of my life at the USA Trials.

Looking back on it, I was probably still too much of a player to do a great job as a coach. I crammed in my duties to the team on the side, and the result was that my second season wouldn't go down as Tennessee's finest: we'd lost five seniors and had four rookies. Our starting center was a freshman named Jane Pemberton, who had only played defense in high school. She couldn't shoot a BB in the ocean, which wasn't her fault; Jane had just never shot the ball. Ever.

Naturally, I didn't want her to start now.

"Jane," I said, "I don't want you shooting tonight. Your job is to rebound. Do you understand that?"

"Oh, yes, ma'am," she said.

If there was one thing I had at the end of every game, it was instant feedback, because there was a box score that told me what kind of job we did. That night when I looked at the box, a couple of statistics jumped out at me. Jane Pemberton had only one rebound. But Suzanne Barbre, our shooting guard, had seven.

I looked at Jane and said, "What's the *one* thing I asked you to do?"

She thought for a minute, and kind of scratched her head, and said, "Rebound?"

"That's right. You have one, and you're playing *center*. Suzanne here had *seven*. Does that tell you anything?"

"Yes, ma'am," Jane said. "You oughta think about moving me over to guard."

True story.

Once again, I tried to make up for our

shortcomings with conditioning. Around Thanksgiving, I held one of the most legendary practices in the annals of the program. It was a beautiful football Saturday, the day of the big annual Tennessee-Vanderbilt game. It was noon as we walked onto the court, and the players could hear the pregame bands playing over in Neyland Stadium, which backed up to Alumni Gym. We were still practicing when the halftime ceremonies began.

"Did y'all have dates?" I asked. "Did y'all think you were going to the game?"

Another hour went by in a blur. And another. Next thing they knew, the football game was over. We'd been practicing for more than four hours. When I finally let them leave Alumni, at the same time the football crowd left the stadium, they could barely walk to their cars.

We went 16-11 that season, which would stand for thirty-some years as our worst record. The real force in the state was Tennessee Tech under Marynell Meadors, with whom I had carried over a rivalry from college at UT-Martin. We'd have a lot of antagonists at Tennessee over the years, but none of them were quite as low-down bitter as that early enmity with Tech. Our annual game was dubbed the "Toilet Bowl," thanks to a stunt pulled by the Tech students that season.

They got ahold of a toilet bowl and painted it in school colors of purple and gold and rolled it onto the court, where the mascot started chucking oranges (our color) into it, to the great delight of the students in the crowd, who were equipped with squares of bathroom tissue. The first time Tech scored a basket they made it snow toilet paper, and both teams had to leave the floor so it could be swept.

My family had driven over for the game and didn't take it at all well, especially since we were losing. Some old Tech boy was sitting near my father and figured out who he was and decided to give him a bad time by screaming at me, "Pat Head, you're a bitch!" He kept it up the whole game while my father just sat quietly and never twitched a facial muscle. "I've seen a better Head on a nickel beer!" he'd scream. My little sister, Linda, was there with her boyfriend, Wesley Attebery, a tough tobacco farmer with sharp-toed boots and a handlebar mustache.

Wesley finally turned to the screamer and said, "You need to keep yer damn mouth shut."

The screamer said, "What's it to you?"

Wesley said, "She might be my sister-in-law one day."

The screamer sneered, and said, "I don't give a —"

And that's when Wesley hauled off and hit him, broke his glasses, grabbed him underneath the collar, and said, "Boy, you done —ed up now, I'm fixin' to kill yer ass." By now people on our bench saw the scuffle break out and were about to climb into the stands, so it was a good thing the game ended. My father never moved; he just sat there grinning like a fox.

He must have thought it was a pretty grand thing, because he took everybody to eat at Cracker Barrel after that and bought the damn supper.
                              — WESLEY ATTEBERY

That was pretty much the story of the '76 season.

The end of the Tennessee season was just the beginning of mine. In the summer of 1976, I reported to the USA Trials, which were held in the small town of Warrensburg, Missouri, on the campus of Central Missouri State. For five weeks I fought every day, in a cauldron of a gym cooled only by some giant industrial fans, to make the

Olympic team.

The trials started with twenty-four players, and fourteen of them were forwards — my position. Only a dozen players would make the team, and I was the oldest player there, with a foot-long scar on my knee. Those were my odds.

Billie made us fight for a spot by playing one-on-one, full court. With a gleam in her eye, she ordered me to go against one of the youngest and quickest players on the team, Cindy Brogdon, an eighteen-year-old college freshman from Mercer University. "There's nothing like going one-on-one to find out who wants it the most," Billie said.

Cindy was a sweet kid from Buford, Georgia, with a fair, narrow, triangular young face and springs for legs. She could spot up and shoot from any place inside of half-court, with a smooth stroke and unbelievable range that would hold up among today's players. She was a whole lot better than I was and I had to figure out, quick, how to beat her.

I had two advantages: I was bigger, and I worked harder. Cindy was thin, and like most young players she liked to sell tickets with her shot, but she didn't spend too much energy on other parts of her game.

■ ■ ■ ■

I told myself, *She can't score if she doesn't have the ball.* I made her work so hard to get the ball it demoralized her. Cindy got her first shot off, and it missed — and from then on, I bodied her away from the basket, beat her to the boards, and just wore her out. After five minutes of going full court, I'd won, 5–0.

> Pat was all up in my face, and when my first attempt didn't go in, I never got a second chance because of her aggressive boxing out. She was so strong you could not get around her to follow your shot. She was the most aggressive person I ever met on a basketball court.
> — CINDY BROGDON

It meant more to me than to her; she was sure to make the team because of her scoring ability, whereas my status had been more in doubt. Once Cindy recovered from the shock, which she did quickly, we became good friends, and when we both made the final cut, I invited her to be my roommate. I couldn't help but identify with her: she was a country girl who hadn't traveled much outside of Georgia and was experiencing international play for the first time. I remembered how alone I'd felt at the age of eighteen when I left the farm.

I was the oldest member of the team at twenty-four and became a sort of magnet for all the young players from the South. Another kid who felt out of her element was Trish Roberts, a slightly built, mortally shy girl from Monroe, Georgia. On the court Trish had an almost phantom quickness and one of the smoothest offensive games I've ever seen. But off the court she would hardly look at you and was so bashful she wouldn't speak, which I found affecting. She was terrified of the easterners on the team, with their unfamiliar vowels and smart mouths, and especially intimidated by Billie Moore. If Billie said "boo" to her, she'd flinch and run in the other direction. I spent a lot of time trying to draw Trish out.

I was very shy and really nervous and scared a lot, and I had never been a lot of places and thrown in with girls who were different. I was in awe of their accents and the way they reacted to things. I was used to saying yes ma'am and no ma'am. Pat was very encouraging to others, and she always sat near or was around the coaches. I think she was soaking up and learning everything she could from them. She was so much more mature than the rest of us.

— TRISH ROBERTS

The team that Billie put together was diverse in both talent and geography and reads now like a Hall of Fame induction list. Our anchor was the magnificent Lusia Harris, a rangy center who was in the midst of winning three straight national championships at Delta State and once hung 58 points on Tennessee Tech. Nancy Dunkle was a crafty six-foot-two forward and a three-time all-American for Billie at Cal State Fullerton. Ann Meyers of UCLA was a four-time all-American who looked like California personified with a toothpaste commercial smile. Juliene Simpson of New Jersey was a selfless, scrapping guard who like me was older than the rest at twenty-three. Then there was my young flame-headed friend Nancy Lieberman, of Far Rockaway, New York; a center from Illinois, Charlotte Lewis; and a trio of easterners — Gail Marquis of New York, Mary Anne O'Conner of Connecticut, and Sue Rojcewicz of Worcester, Massachusetts.

I made the team strictly for my veteran

smarts and willingness to defend, an unusual trait on an all-star team. I would take a charge, or whatever else Billie asked of me, and I went to the boards so hard I ended up second in rebounding. One day when we were scrimmaging against some male players, Billie barked at me, "Put a body on that guy!" She claims the next trip down the court, I sent him into the bleachers. I wasn't a great player, but apparently I was a good teammate, because I was elected a cocaptain.

Pat led by example. I mean she was a hard worker. If there was a ball rolling on the floor, she was going to dive. She and I went up for a rebound, and she put her elbow out and it got me right in my hip bone. To this day I still have problems with that bruise.

— TRISH ROBERTS

But making the team was only half the battle. Next, we went to an Olympic prequalifying tournament in Hamilton, Ontario, where we would have to win to get to Montreal. We were considered a vast underdog: the USA team had finished a lowly eighth in the World Championships a year earlier. Once again Billie ran us so hard

194

every muscle in our legs was sore. She didn't just put us through two-a-days, she put us through three-a-days. It was brutal. We worked out morning, noon, and night, six hours a day.

Some players weren't used to Billie's style, and Lusia Harris was one of them. She played a slower-tempo, walk-the-ball-up-the-court style at Delta State, and she was hurting. I ran alongside her, practically pulling her up and down the floor.

Lusia said, "But, Billie, at Delta State they wait for me to get down the floor."

"You aren't in Cleveland, Mississippi, anymore," Billie said. "The Russians aren't going to wait for you."

We scrimmaged against men's teams, and one day the guys got out on too many fast breaks, while our sore-legged players stood and watched them. Billie didn't say much, but I knew her well enough to know she wasn't happy. When the younger players like Cindy Brogdon wanted to go out and find pizza, I said, "I'll tell you right now we better get to bed and get some rest because Billie is going to kill us tomorrow." The next day we went the first hour without ever shooting or even touching a ball. "You're going to play the game right," Billie said, and she made us run until some of us had the dry heaves.

After five weeks of that, we went to Ontario. Billie withheld from us just how little faith USA Basketball had in us: they ticketed us to fly straight home after the tournament, instead of to Montreal, figuring we'd never come through qualifying, and gave us a budget of just $500.

We shocked them by storming through the tournament in first place. My family drove to Hamilton all the way from Henrietta in a yellow Cadillac my brother Tommy bought. It was the heart of tobacco season, which tells you how important it was to Daddy to see me play in a USA uniform, but he got mad because he thought I should be scoring more. Every time I went in the game, he shouted, "Shoot it, Trisha!" And every time he shouted it, Trish Roberts would pull up and shoot it.

Trish said, "I don't know who that man hollering at me is."

Since there were no expectations that we'd get to Montreal, no one had made any provisions for us, and with ten days still remaining to the Opening Ceremonies, we had nowhere to stay, we were homeless. Bill Wall gave Billie his American Express card to tide us over, and Billie got on the phone to an executive at Kodak, one of our sponsors, who found us rooms in an unoccupied dormitory at the University of Rochester that was under renovation. We spent ten days in Rochester sleeping in dormitory bunk beds, listening to hammering, and practicing. Small crowds of twenty or so would gather to watch us sprinting, cursing, and sprinting again as Billie pushed us.

Finally, it was time to go to Montreal, where our quarters weren't much better. All twelve of us were assigned to a two-bedroom apartment in the Olympic village. We crammed five players to a room — who all had to share the same bath — and out of desperation put a couple of cots in the kitchen. If anyone wanted some privacy, she just walked out. I don't know how we lived that way, I only recall being so excited to be there that it didn't matter. We were thankful to have beds, and uniforms that said USA on them.

We just accepted it. We grew up in a generation where we had one pair of shoes to do everything. Today, heaven forbid if their game shoes touch a court that has asphalt on it. But we were very happy to get a pair of shoes.

— ANN MEYERS

More than forty years later, it's difficult to separate my own memories from the snapshots of the Montreal Games on my wall. I remember how vast and full the oval Olympic Stadium seemed during the Opening Ceremonies, and my USA blazer with white blouse and handkerchief in the pocket. I remember the polyester sweat suits with zipper collars and piping that were the fashion then. I remember the jagged modern architecture of the village, Edwin Moses galloping over hurdles, the little valentine face of gymnast Nadia Comaneci, and watching Ernie Grunfeld help win a gold for the U.S. men's team, coached by that kind, philosophic gentleman Dean Smith.

Above all I remember seven-foot-two Uljana Semjonova, against whom I dreaded playing, based on my last encounter with her at the World University Games.

The Olympics was all about whether anyone could upset the Soviets, and we knew we were probably playing for the silver. We were reminded of it every time we saw Semjonova in the village. One night we went to the arena to watch a game and found ourselves sitting right behind her. She was eating an apple, and we couldn't take our eyes off it. It looked like a golf ball in her hand. She ate it in two bites.

But I discovered, through that one-of-a-kind Olympic experience of sharing a village together, that Semjonova was as gentle as she was large. I don't know what possessed me to try to talk to her except sheer curiosity, but one afternoon in the cafeteria I sat down next to her and tried to begin a conversation. She was from Latvia, I gathered that much. We couldn't exchange many words, except *nyet* and *da,* but somehow we communicated well enough to become friendly. I remember being out in the village one afternoon with some teammates and running into her. I introduced my teammates, who gathered around her. She took off one of her rings and showed it to us — it was the size of a fifty-cent piece.

Playing against her was a helpless feeling, however. Billie had a cassette player, and before every game she blasted Natalie Cole's "This Will Be," which became our theme song. On the day that we met the Soviets, she played it one more time. But we knew it was probably *not* to be.

Billie tried to come up with a game plan for Semjonova, but how do you stop seven foot two? I was assigned to defend her, and I remember my head coming up to her armpit. I stood there in my polyester red, white, and blue uniform, as tall as I could make myself seem at five foot eleven — and I was right under her armpit.

Since we couldn't match up with her, the best hope was to get her in foul trouble. The plan was to put one person in front of her, and when she posted up and turned, to have someone else slide over and take a charge. Trish Roberts played down low because she was six foot one, but she was built like a sapling.

> Well, the big girl posted up every single time on the same side, which meant I was usually the one who had to come over. I remember I took the first charge. I belly flopped, and when I looked up, I saw Semjonova falling. I crawled out of that lane fast, because I knew if she fell on me, it was over.
>
> — TRISH ROBERTS

The final score was 112–77. Nevertheless, we clinched silver, which was far more than anyone expected of us, and we became one of the more popular American stories of the Games, a kind of David and Goliath tale. Afterward, when Billie met the American press, a reporter asked her, "What does the U.S. team need in order to catch up with the Soviets?"

Billie answered, "About ten more inches."

Billie knew we'd done all we could, and she was deeply proud of us. She told us to feel a sense of the occasion. "I want you to understand what a moment in time you have," she said. "What an impact you have. There will be many more Olympic teams that follow you. But there will only be one team that was the first."

I can't say that I understood at the time what pioneers we were, or what a tradition we would inaugurate. The USA women's team would become more dominant than the Soviets ever dreamed. From 1976 to 2012 our American women would amass a record of 58-3 and win seven gold medals, including five straight, and Tennessee would be a huge factor in that success.

All I knew then was that four years of work and hardship had paid off. I remember all of us clustered on the medal podium together, and a photographer called out to us, and we turned as one and waved. I remember staying up all night, feeling a sense of the moment, though perhaps not quite in the way Billie expected us to, sitting on a curb in the Olympic village sharing beers with my teammates.

I remember feeling that an Olympic medal was a mountainous achievement for a girl from Henrietta, Tennessee. Just as it was for a girl from Monroe, Georgia, or from Cleveland, Mississippi, or Far Rockaway, New York. And I remember the understanding that came with it; when you set a goal of such distant possibility and reach it, you gain an insight into *what it takes* that lasts the rest of your life. It felt utterly life altering. To summon the competitiveness to work every single day for a goal that was months and even years ahead was the most invaluable lesson I'd ever learn. I thought I could accomplish anything. And I thought I could teach it to others.

It was time to hang up my sneakers and jersey and go back to Tennessee to continue the work I had started, putting sneakers and jerseys on other women. Before I left Montreal, I had a conversation with Trish Roberts. She was in the midst of a checkerboard college career: she had played a season at North Georgia State College and then transferred to Emporia State College out in Kansas. But she didn't like being at a small college in the Midwest and wanted to move closer to home, preferably to a larger school, where she could play on a bigger stage.

Trish didn't realize I was a college coach until she was sitting on the team bus going to practice one day, and she mentioned to

Lusia Harris, "I don't want to go back to Emporia. I think I should transfer." Lusia told her, "Maybe you ought to go to Tennessee and play for Pat." When Trish looked surprised, Lusia explained that I wasn't a college player like the rest of them, I was a coach, which accounted for how much more serious I was.

Trish came to my seat and said, "What's your team like?"

I happened to keep a folder of coaching notes and other Tennessee material in my equipment bag, including a team picture. I pulled it out and showed it to Trish. She turned to Lusia and raised a skeptical eyebrow.

"Can you see me standing in the back row with all them white girls?" she said.

Maybe she couldn't. But I sure could.

If someone says what does Alzheimer's feel like, what do you say?

Well, it's an opponent for me. I know what I'm dealing with. I think I've got a pretty good game plan, with all the doctors and everything. But like I said, probably the one thing, it's like waking up in a strange place.

It seems like there are symptoms inside, and then ones from the outside that are imposed on you. Like, "We think you should consider whether to retire."

Exactly.

So the diagnosis brings things from outside that are as difficult to deal with as anything happening inside your body? You don't have as much control?

Well, I don't really feel that. I feel like I still have control of who I am. . . . And I think people have good intentions. But sometimes I'm like, "Leave me alone." I don't feel that anymore. But for a while I was like "Leave me fricking alone."

[Later]

I'm not going to let it take everything from me.

And you haven't.

No. I don't intend to.

— June 21, 2012, driving from Knoxville to Nashville

5

BRIDESMAID AND BRIDE

A lot of people are afraid of commitment because it means they'll have to say, "That's the best I can do." They *elect* to be average. When you compete, you decide to find out what your real limits are, not just what you think they are. I wasn't afraid of that commitment, or of demanding it from others. But when it came to emotional commitment, the off-a-cliff peril of grasping another hand and saying, "I do," I was more hesitant. The problem was, I understood the word too well.

At the University of Tennessee in 1976–1977, we committed. Gave it everything we had — and lost. There were no trophies or glittering rings, and little applause in those years. But we laid down the foundational values of Lady Vols basketball on which everything that came after was built: effort, discipline, and intensity. There was something else, too, that was another foundational value, though I had trouble expressing it: love. That was there. Underneath all the yelling.

Trish Roberts committed to Tennessee. At the time there were no restrictions under the AIAW rules governing women's sports, so she came to Knoxville and enrolled for the start of the 1976 school year. She wanted to see how good she could be, even though I warned her, "Our roles have changed now. I'm going to be hard on you."

"Pat, I don't have a problem with that," she said. "I just want to play ball."

I was hard on her, hard on all of them, harder than I would ever be again on any team. So hard that in retrospect I don't know how they didn't break, or quit. I couldn't have played for me then. I was so committed, so unsmiling and intent on building the program, that I must have seemed like a scowl with lipstick.

Winning an Olympic medal made me hungry to repeat the experience of achieving something. I was done as a player, but I was just beginning as a coach, and there were other prizes out there. I came roaring home from Montreal ready to shout to our players the secrets I'd learned about what it takes to win something big, starting with the most crucial one: You had to be willing

to physically outwork and outtough everyone in your path.

I recruited guys to practice against and
made Trish and our other players go against
them every day. I borrowed an old lesson
from my brothers about arm wrestling
against someone stronger than you: that too
was all about commitment; you had to
survive the first jolt, and then dig in. I
wanted our players to learn to hold their
ground, and when they didn't, I sneered.

"Babies," I said. "Sissies. *Nice* girls."

The Xs and Os were way basic. You just
did it harder. You went faster. If there was
an obstacle, you did it anyway. It was, "I
don't care if they're standing there waiting
for you. Run into them."
— NANCY DARSCH

I was hardest of all on an effervescent freshman named Frances Hollingsworth "Holly"
Warlick, a freshman guard from Knoxville.
Holly had a golden head and gray-green
eyes, and two big white chips for front teeth,
which she showed all the time. She had a
habit of smiling even wider when she was
mad than she did when she was laughing,
which was an interesting quality, and one I
liked. On the outside she was adorable, but

on the inside she had the heart of a boxer battling out of a corner.

Holly had lost her father, Bill, to a cerebral hemorrhage just two years earlier when she was a junior in high school, cutting her girlhood short. His death plunged the family into not only an emotional crisis but a financial one, and Holly ended up sharing a room with her mother, Fran, who had to go to work as a hotel clerk. Holly turned her sorrow into competitive fuel, trying to solve all her problems by running right through them. She had a straight-ahead approach that I admired; nothing ever seemed to get her down or defeat her. She was one of the most contagiously high-energy athletes I ever saw, with a magical ability to lift others with her own inspired, streaking effort.

She was a state champion in the 400, and she'd go hurtling toward the basket at such a velocity that sometimes she couldn't make a layup. She'd charge in at full speed and whang the ball off the backboard. "The bricklayer," we called her.

Trish and Holly arrived on campus at a fortunate moment. The days of punch and cookies were over. President Gerald R. Ford had signed Title IX regulations into law in 1975, and schools hurriedly poured money into women's basketball in an effort to comply. The University of Texas shelled out $17,000 in 1976 to hire a coach named Jody Conradt, shocking a local newspaper into printing this headline: "Woman Hired at Man's Salary."

After all the years of bad uniforms and bake sales, I was suddenly in the middle of a gold rush. Tennessee's president, Dr. Ed Boling, set up an independent women's athletic department and funded us to the tune of $126,000 for seven sports, and we had our own athletic director, a talented executive named Gloria Ray. I no longer had to be a jack-of-all-trades administrator, no more making out schedules for the tennis team, no more ankle taping. I had a recruiting budget and was allowed to hire an assistant. My first hire was a tiny fireball of a grad student named Elizabeth Jackson, but eventually I chose as my permanent assistant a clipped, deadpan but drily funny young woman from Massachusetts named Nancy Darsch who had a quality I lacked: patience.

For the first time, there was scholarship money. It was only enough for three full rides at $3,000 apiece, but it was something. I split one of them into three partials so I could spread it around: Sue Thomas got money for books, Suzanne Barbre got room

211

and board, while Lisa McGill got tuition.

Best of all, as a concession to Title IX compliance, we got to move out of Alumni Gym and into the newly renovated arena where our men's team played, the Stokely Athletics Center. We weren't equal, but it was a good start, and it gave us newfound, respectable status. To go with it I decided we needed a new identity, a break from the dingy, underfunded past. I called a team meeting.

"We need a new name," I said. "What do you want to be called?"

The team stared back at me, not entirely sure what I was getting at, quite possibly because they were hungover. More about that in a moment.

"A name," I said. "We need to choose a name."

Up until then we were the "Volettes," somebody's idea of a feminized version of the Tennessee Volunteers. But to me it sounded too much like a chorus line of dancing girls. It was our choice what to call ourselves, I told them. We could remain the Volettes, or we could pick something else, something new.

"Who do you want to be?" I said. "Do you just want to be the Volunteers, like the guys? Or how about the Lady Volunteers?"

"Lady sounds classy," someone said.

"Yeah, 'cause we're so good-lookin'," Lisa McGill said.

They voted, and Lady Vols we became. We debuted in Stokely on November 13, 1976, against Kentucky, just after a home football game, and got a spillover crowd. We gave them their money's worth. Our players swayed and loosened up to Rod Stewart's "Hot Legs," which they considered their theme song. Then the ball went up, and all I saw for the next forty minutes was a streak of color — a great detonating burst of orange.

Holly and Trish together were like a match touching dynamite. Trish would fling the ball ahead and Holly would chase it, outrunning everybody. Then Holly would charge to the basket — miss the layup — and Trish would rise up in the air and softly field the rebound and lay it in. Holly kidded her that she missed on purpose, put the ball on the backboard to get the assist.

All of a sudden, it was an easy game. I didn't have to say anything in the huddles; what was there to say, except, "Keep doing what you're doing"? I was just a bystander, enjoying the view from the best seat in the house as we beat Kentucky 107–53. Trish scored 51 points and had 20 rebounds that day, to break the scoring record for Stokely. Which may have had something to do with our halftime snack: orange slices and Coca-Cola — as if we needed any more octane.

By the next morning it was all over town that there was an electric new brand of basketball worth watching at Tennessee, and it wasn't played by guys. The phone rang off the hook from people who wanted season tickets or to give us a donation. Overnight we started drawing crowds of six thousand, who roared appreciatively at our headlong style. They were such darling kids, and on top of it they expended so much energy, that audiences found them irresistible. The newspapers started covering us and named Holly "the Secretary of Defense," for her combative style. The Lady Vols got so much attention they started putting on makeup and nail polish for games.

When you played that team, you saw all their players giving everything they had — they had absolutely nothing left when they left the court. They played hard every second of every minute they were in the game. You couldn't beat 'em because they gave so much. I remember Warlick, I mean this kid, she would go up eighteen rows in the stands to save a ball and get it

214

back in. And not only that, there were people standing there waiting to catch it.
— MARYNELL MEADORS

The most surprising thing about that team was that they could play the way they did, while being so wild off the court. I had to be hard on them, because with the exception of Trish, who didn't drink, they were as hard partying as they were hard charging. The drinking age in Tennessee back then was just eighteen, and it was perfectly legal for them to go to bars, but it was against our training rules. They tried to hide their beer-foamed frolics from me, but they'd come into practice reeking, and it only got worse as I sweated it out of them.

Lisa McGill was a ringleader. She was a garrulous young lady with wide brown eyes and a bawling laugh, who came from enough money in Gatlinburg, Tennessee, to own a fur coat, which she infamously wore one night to the supermarket along with her flip-flops, to buy more beer. Her apartment was headquarters, which was something of a relief; at least indoors and out of the public eye our players couldn't get in too much trouble. I assigned our student manager, Donna Fielden, to keep an eye on them. Donna would go over to Lisa's apartment carrying stacks of practice gear and leave tidy piles of shirts, shorts, bras, and sneakers for each player, with name cards on top. Next, she would set four alarm clocks. Then she'd walk out the door, saying, "If y'all don't make it to practice, it's not *my* fault."

Shortly after Christmas, I got the word that they had pulled an all-nighter. I decided, "I'm going to run 'em until they can't puke anymore." When they arrived for practice that day, bleary-eyed and rank, I awaited them with four garbage cans, placed strategically on each corner of the court. "Get on the line," I said.

After fifteen suicides, there was a player in every corner, heaving. One of the trash cans got so unpleasant that players took a left and veered over to the opposite corner. Nobody was left standing except for Trish, who didn't drink, and Holly, who wasn't going to give in. She just stood there grinning that overbroad grin that told you how mad she was inside.

No amount of disciplining could tame them — they just went right back to living it up. Pretty soon I'd hear another story of them strutting around town in their 501 jeans carrying beer bottles. I'd work them until they crawled out of the gym, and they'd just pop back up ready for more. They had no quit in them.

It was a trait that came straight from Holly. It was a constant challenge to control all that high energy, channel it in the right direction, and finally, I arrived at a more clever approach. Rather than just running Holly to death, I baited her. I instituted a drill just for her: I'd put twenty minutes on the clock and keep track of her misses and turnovers. She had to make ten straight layups, or the whole team had to run *for* her. Holly would make eight — and then chunk it and groan. I'd yell, "Everybody on the line for Holly!," and make her feel responsible for the collective pain. She would stand there flushed and radiating fury through her huge grin. But it taught her to be a more responsible leader and to play under control.

We were scared of her. And we loved her. I would walk out going, "She's crazy as hell." Then I'd come back the next day and she'd challenge me again, and I would respond and throw it back in her face. She knew that. I'd be like, "I'll show her!" Yeah, you'll show her. That's what she wanted.
— HOLLY WARLICK

Our steadying influence was Trish Roberts, who set Tennessee records with 29.9 points and 14.2 rebounds a game that season, and they've never been matched. She was sweet, churchy, and conscientious in the way she went about all of her business. At the end of every semester I made a big point of reading the names aloud of anyone who made above a 3.0 grade point average. After the first semester, Trish said, "I want to be one of those people whose name you call." Next thing I knew, she made the honor roll.

> Pat pushed me and saw something in me I didn't see in myself. When she believes strongly in something, then she is going to hound you, and hound you, until you see it. Eventually.
>
> — TRISH ROBERTS

The whole team fed off the energy that Trish and Holly created. We steadily climbed the rankings until we were fifth in the country and made it to the AIAW National Championships in Minneapolis. It was the farthest a Tennessee women's team had ever been from home, and here's how nervous and inexperienced we were: when we got to the airport, I said to our manager, Donna, "Where is your equipment trunk?" She'd

218

left it, packed with our uniforms, behind in the locker room. I tossed my car keys to Lisa McGill and said, "Go. Go as fast as you can, and don't wreck, and don't stop."

But our run ended in the national semifinals, where we met Delta State and center Lusia Harris, my Olympic teammate. Delta State was a small school in cotton country, and its coach was the legendary Margaret Wade, an elegant Mississippian who wore her silvery hair teased and helmetlike, and a rope of pearls. Margaret was the picture of a lady, until she opened her blazer and showed a tag she kept pinned inside. It said, "Give Them Hell."

Which they proceeded to do. Lusia was the first truly dominant player of modern women's basketball, six foot three and 185 hard-muscled pounds of pivoting, to-the-rim force, so much that a few months later the New Orleans Jazz would draft her, making her the first woman ever taken by an NBA team. She would be inducted into the Naismith Basketball Hall of Fame in 1992 with a class that included Connie Hawkins and Bob Lanier. In three seasons, Lusia and Delta State racked up three straight titles and a record of 109-6. We were just too small for her. We had no business being in that game, but we fought valiantly. At one point Holly was trapped by the defense and had nowhere to go — so she whipped a half-court pass under her legs up to Trish for a layup. I missed the play. I was looking down at some stats and heard the crowd erupt.

"What happened?" I asked Nancy.

"You don't want to know," Nancy said.

We got within four points that day, 72–68. But we just couldn't stop Lusia.

The trouble with commitment is that you can give it everything, and fail. When your utmost is not quite good enough, what then? Here's what you do. You say a few choked, hoarse words to a bunch of kids whose heads are so low that you can see the backs of their pale, curved necks, and you can't find their faces behind the curtains of their hair, damp with sweat and crying. Then you walk out and find some private corner where your own head drops into your hands.

> I remember very clearly after the game I had gone into the restroom. And Pat must have gone in there. I remember hearing her, crying. To be so close, you know?
> — TRISH ROBERTS

If I had met R.B. Summitt any earlier in life, I wouldn't have had time for him. I'd already lost a couple of relationships to my ambition. There was a fellow coach who seemed so enamored, until he began to complain about my hectic schedule and started seeing someone on the side. Right before I went to the 1976 Olympics, he had given me an ultimatum. I went over to my friend Jane Brown's house in tears. "I need to talk to you," I said. My boyfriend had told me it was the Olympics or him. "What am I going to do?" I cried.

Jane said, "Trish, you don't put conditions on love. If he loves you, he backs you. He supports you. Why doesn't he want you to go? You've worked too hard for this. You have to go."

I wanted her to go for her, but I also selfishly wanted her to go for me, for all of us, because if she was on that floor playing, a part of me was on that floor playing. A part of a lot of us was on that floor playing: her family, my family, her coaches and teammates and sorority sisters and friends. She was living the dream for all of us.
— JANE BROWN CLARK

After Montreal I was wounded and on the defensive, wrapped up in my career and waiting for the guy who didn't think it came at his expense. When I finally did meet R.B. in April of 1977, I made him wait four long, patient years, because I wanted to be sure he knew what he was getting into. He came over to my apartment one night at the invitation of my roommate, Marsha McGregor, a state bank examiner, who was hosting a barbecue for a banking convention in town. Several leisure-suited guys filled up the room, and one of them drifted in my direction, a stocky, muscular sort with dark hair and a smile-creased face and spectacles that made him look athletic and smart at the same time. I was hardly dressed for socializing; I'd just gotten back from a basketball camp and had on a tank top and shorts. But this guy seemed to appreciate the view and introduced himself as R.B. I thought, *What kind of silly name is that?,* and for the rest of the night and some time afterward insisted on calling him "C.B.," as in citizens band radio.

The initials stood for Ross Barnes, and it was a fine old southern name from Sevier County, Tennessee, where his father, Ross, owned a bank, and his mother, Mae, was a schoolteacher who'd made a name as a local feminist pioneer for getting her pilot's license. I'd actually heard of R.B. around campus: as a student at Tennessee he had been a fraternity council leader who won the "torchbearer" award, the highest prize for academic achievement and activism given by the university.

For the rest of the night, "C.B." tried to block out the other guys who swirled around. At some point someone asked to see my Olympic medal, and R.B. marveled over it and listened to my stories of playing in Montreal against the Soviets. At the end of the evening he was the last guy left in the apartment, and we sat up talking until well past midnight. Finally I said, hesitantly, "So is it basketball you're interested in, or is it me?"

"It's you," he said. "I don't know anything about basketball."

We just seemed to fall into easy step together. We had a formal date that weekend — I tested him by taking him to hear the 19th Amendment — and the next, and the next, until we were seeing each other constantly. He was a southern charm boy, a door opener and an arch-persuader. He called me "Patricia" and made me feel elegant; no one else had ever done that.

After only four months of seeing each other, I took him to meet my family, an experience he survived despite the best efforts of my brothers to drown him. We all went out waterskiing on the Cumberland River, which R.B. had never done much of. It was R.B.'s turn to retrieve the ski, and just as he leaned over to get it, Kenneth gunned the engine and R.B. almost fell overboard, and got a river-water shampoo, which made my brothers laugh until they cried. Then when he tried to stand up on the ski, he submerged, but refused to let go of the rope. After about ten minutes of being dragged underwater, he popped back up — skiing. He was that stubborn; he wouldn't let go of the line. R.B. always said afterward that it was the story of our courtship.

A lot of people weren't sure they liked them together. He was the fraternity boy, and he always dated blondes. Pat was a challenge, now. She was so different from all the other women he had been going out with.

— SYLVIA RHYNE HATCHELL

R.B. didn't complain when I had to travel twenty-six thousand miles in the summer coaching the junior national team in the Pan American Games in Mexico City and we couldn't talk because the phones were too expensive. He just said he missed me. He didn't complain when, instead of going out to dinner, I had to work late writing letters to recruits. He would come over and hang out, and I'd put Linda Ronstadt on the stereo and gaze at him speculatively.

> Yes, and I ain't saying you ain't pretty
> All I'm saying is I'm not ready
> For any person place or thing
> To try and pull the reins in on me

I waited for him to make an irritated remark about how time-consuming my job was, but he never did. Instead, to my amazement, he dove headfirst into it. I had to run around town to Rotary clubs and civic groups, begging for support, but I hated and feared public speaking. R.B. would help me write remarks and listen to me rehearse them, then would drive me to the event and wait patiently in the car, because I was too nervous to let him sit in the audience.

He encouraged and defended me when I got my first negative press, for entering into a controversial campaign to overturn the antiquated rules of girls' basketball in Tennessee's middle schools and high schools. Our state was one of just five left in the entire country that forced girls to play half-court (with Oklahoma, Texas, New York, and Iowa), and I wanted to change it. When a local girl named Victoria Cape sued in U.S. District Court, arguing that the rules were an "arbitrary, capricious, and unreasonable distinction," I testified on her behalf.

I declared that the Tennessee schools forced "a mental and physical handicap" on girls, and stumped all around the state, begging parents and other coaches to testify similarly and support a rule change. Women weren't pushed physically, I said; we hadn't tapped into an iota of what we were capable of. "Don't tell *me* we're not strong enough to run full court," I said.

It was a highly divisive stance that earned outrage across the state from high school coaches, who considered six-on-six a rich tradition. Some never spoke to me again. They argued all kinds of nonsense. They said the rules were necessary to "prevent girls from straining themselves" or to "aid the clumsy girls." Jim Smiddy of Bradley County High, one of the winningest coaches in the state, insisted that the split-court game was "the prettiest thing about girls' basketball." Bill "Pusher" Howell from Murfreesboro declared that if girls tried to play full court, "the scores would be in the 20s and 30s and it would be the dullest thing you ever witnessed."

So here she comes, trying to tell all these country guys to change. They did not like Pat Head. Thought she was disrupting the game. "It's not broke, why you gonna fix it?" She was not a popular coach at the beginning.

— HOLLY WARLICK

I replied that I couldn't keep taking players who had never crossed the half-court line and put the University of Tennessee at a total competitive disadvantage. "If you don't change, I can't recruit Tennessee players to our *state* school," I said. We needed to catch up to the rest of the country.

We won the campaign. A wonderful sports columnist for the *Nashville Tennessean* named F.M. Williams, a gentleman in a plaid sports coat with black-rimmed glasses, helped swing public opinion. F.M. made it a point to come to our games and to drop mentions of us into his columns along with Tennessee football. "The barrier to change has been built by old coaches, who don't like learning new techniques at this late date in their careers," he declared.

Finally, District Court Judge Robert Taylor ruled that the "weak and awkward girls" rationale was indeed discriminatory. "When a state chooses to deny a significant education experience to a class of its citizens and no rational justification for such different treatment can be found, the Constitution requires that such distinction be voided," he ordered. It ended an era. Tennessee high schools went to the full-court game for the 1979–80 season, and Oklahoma and Iowa soon followed.

But the acrimony of the campaign reaffirmed something I knew instinctively: sports for women still smacked of revolution to a lot of men, especially in the South. There was deep resistance to Title IX. I saw and felt it every day. When I took the junior national team to Mexico City for the Pan Am Games, the men stayed in a comfortable hotel, while we were assigned to a dilapidated old dormitory from the 1968 Olympic Games that was so filthy our players wouldn't get under the bedsheets, and the showers had standing water in them.

The next morning we went to breakfast, and somebody said, "Look at all those cats."

Bill Wall, who'd come over to visit us, said, "Those aren't cats, those are rats."

I said, "You've got to get us out of here, right now." And he did. But when we went to practice, there were no lights, and no nets on the rim, and we had one flat ball.

For all our comparative luxuries at Tennessee, we were still slighted. Although we played in Stokely, our locker room was in the basement and we shared it with male wrestlers. When we went on the road for doubleheaders with the men's team, we packed into our fifteen-passenger van, while they flew. Scheduling court time was a constant headache. We were told that we couldn't set foot on the court until the men had finished practicing. But when *we* practiced, the guys would come out while we were still working and warm up and shoot. There were days when we couldn't get into our locker room because it was being used for a visiting men's team in one sport or another. We didn't have anything that we could point to and say, "Wait a minute, that's ours."

In 1977, the AIAW convention came to Memphis, and the main topic of conversation was the open hostility women faced regarding Title IX. Elma Roane of Memphis State complained that the NCAA wanted women's basketball "to remain a club sport." Bettye Giles said, "It's been difficult to maintain a working relationship. Eventually we're going to have to get together. Everyone needs to get rid of this male-female thing and start working on what's best for everybody."

There were two ways to approach the problem: I could go right at it, or I could try to finesse it. I chose finesse. The fact was that we couldn't fight these battles by ourselves: it was important for women to lead women, but we needed powerful male allies too, men like Bill Wall and Dr. Ed Boling. Even Victoria Cape had a man behind her: it was really her father, James, who brought the lawsuit against Tennessee high schools. Especially in the South, a woman didn't make male allies by ranting or picking needless fights. There was an old saying, "You don't cut what you can untie."

I found a softer presentation worked better. I felt I understood guys' sensibilities and knew how to talk to them, having grown up with three brothers. I also liked their company and wasn't easily offended. There was so much apprehension about what Title IX would mean for men's sports that it was important to reassure them. When our women's athletic director, Gloria Ray, and I lobbied for donations, we made a point of saying, "We are not a substitute for men's sports. We're an addition to them."

I envied my male counterparts their marketing budgets, large staffs, and air travel; they had it easy. But I bit my tongue. Nancy Darsch became my full-time assistant in

1979, and she was much more outspoken than I was. When we faced an eight-hour trip in a van while the men flew to the same city, she wanted me to take it up with the university authorities. But I knew it was important to be flexible. I told Nancy, "It doesn't do any good to criticize. Let's find some solutions or alternatives."

> I would get her all fired up, and then she'd have to calm herself before she went into a meeting. There is the old saying that you catch more flies with honey than vinegar. She had a knack for how to present things and how to reason with people and do it calmly. She had a way with the men in decision-making positions.
>
> — NANCY DARSCH

When the men's team got ten pairs of sneakers, I didn't storm in and demand ten pairs for us. We didn't need ten. I would ask for two pairs. When I looked at the men's recruiting budget, I didn't demand that we have matching funds. I just gasped and said, "We couldn't spend that in two years. We don't need that much." Emulating the excesses of the men's teams and the way they overspent wasn't my recipe for fiscal success.

I won one small issue at a time: an upgrade from motels to Hiltons; a small budget for air travel. There was the memorable day when we moved upstairs in Stokely to a real dressing room. When I walked our kids into their new quarters and they saw their sleek wooden lockers, with doors that closed and their own nameplates, they were so overwhelmed they actually got tears in their eyes.

But I also knew that no matter how soft my approach, some in the men's department resented me, an uncomfortable sensation that would persist for decades, and it was important and reassuring to have someone like R.B. at my side. When I felt exposed and criticized during the high school controversy, R.B. didn't just support me, he told me he was *proud* of me. When I came home from work frustrated and wearily observed, "It's a man's world," he just looked back at me sympathetically and said, "You're right."

He didn't act self-conscious about the fact that his girlfriend was a better athlete than he was. Instead he let me teach him racquetball, and we played until we were drenched with sweat. Then we'd walk up on "The Hill," a peak at the center of campus, and sit on a lawn amid the old redbrick and white stone citadel-like buildings, with a view of the surrounding hills and the lazy brown Tennessee River. We'd open beers and talk while we cooled off and watched the sun set.

When R.B. got to be a decent enough player to start beating me, I got edgy about it and had trouble cooking his dinner cheerfully. He understood what a competitor I was, and he quietly announced he didn't think it was "good for our relationship," and instead we entered local tournaments and played other people instead of each other.

We went to Tennessee football games together every weekend, and I would look around at the tremendous, rabid support from the huge crowds that filled Neyland Stadium. When I told R.B. I dreamed of filling up an arena to see the Lady Vols play, he didn't laugh. He told me that he believed I was capable of it one day.

He came to every one of our home games and began making occasional road trips with me, offering to help drive. In those days he owned a Ford window van with captain's chairs, a cooler, curtains, and fold-down backbench seats. He would haul the luggage for the team, so we had more room to stretch out our long legs in our fifteen-passenger vehicle. Sometimes I'd leave Nancy with the team van and ride with R.B., but more often than not I didn't feel I should ride separately from the team, so he'd play lead dog for us and drive ahead because he had a CB and a radar detector. On those long drives, I'd loan R.B. one of our players, to help keep him awake.

The kids teased me that they were relieved when R.B. and I met, because there were so many days when I came to practice happy. R.B. had a way of getting me to relent, of reminding me they were just kids. He would laugh at everything they did and talk about how silly they were, just teenagers, and tell me how much he enjoyed being part of the team and what I did for a living.

> I could handle it. To me her work was challenging and different and fun, and I could see what a great opportunity it was for her. I just had this sense that women should have the same opportunities, and that was a thing we talked about a lot, how the game built so much social character.
>
> — R.B. SUMMITT

R.B. helped me through the first serious crisis I faced with a player. Lisa McGill's wildness finally got the better of her. In the summer of '77 she went to a boating and waterskiing party and she was in the river carving up the water on a competition ski,

234

when she jumped a wake and lost control and went into a cartwheel. She catapulted across the water, and the ski caught, and the force of it almost took her leg off. She ripped every muscle and tendon she had, and some veins and arteries as well.

I rushed to the emergency room, to find Lisa in shock, on an IV, and being prepped for emergency surgery. "I'm really sick," she said. I knew her well enough to ask, "What have you been drinking today?" She answered, "Scotch and water." I said plaintively, "Well, you oughta be sick."

I walked into an anteroom to talk to the orthopedic surgeon, Dr. Bill Youmans, who would operate on Lady Vols throughout my career. I asked him how bad it was. His face told me it was not good, but I wasn't prepared for his answer: He'd never seen a worse leg injury. The worst-case scenario was that she could actually lose her leg.

"Pat, I don't know if she'll ever play again," he said. "I don't know if she'll walk. I don't know if I can fix it."

I had a flashback of lying in a hospital in Nashville, as a surgeon said similar words. I stared at Dr. Youmans with Richard Head's eyes. "I guess this is where the rubber meets the road," I said.

He fixed it, but Lisa was in a cast from

hip to toe and we wouldn't know if she could play again for months. Two days after the surgery, I told Lisa's mother she needed to get some rest and offered to stay the night at the hospital. I slept on a cot by Lisa's bedside, and in the middle of the night I woke up to hear her calling, "Pat, Pat, help me." I jumped up and found that she had sweated through her nightclothes. "I'm freezing to death," she said. I found some dry things and propped her up and gingerly helped her change, trying not to cause too much pain. It was about three A.M. when I finally got her settled back to sleep. As she was drifting off, I blurted awkwardly, "I love you, Lise." She said, "I love you, too."

The first person to show up at the hospital the next morning was R.B. Summitt. He came with coffee, juice, and doughnuts. For the rest of the summer he was my emotional support, which I'd never had before; previously, when things went badly, I was on my own, because my family was back in Henrietta. R.B. became the person I confided in about the sickening worry during the long afternoons at the hospital, and then the 5:30 A.M. workouts in the swimming pool when she started to rehabilitate. Lisa swam so much that when Dr. Youmans told her she couldn't even think about playing for a year, she decided to try out for the Lady Vol swimming team and made it. It helped strengthen her leg, and she eventually rejoined us.

Lisa's accident uncovered something in me. The kind of commitment we had on our team put all kinds of emotions at stake. When you worked, played, and fought as hard as we did together, we couldn't help loving one another. But the thing about love and commitment was that it could also wound.

After just a few months of being together, R.B. bought a diamond ring and showed it to me. It was probably a mistake — it scared me. For all his support, I told R.B. I wasn't convinced that he really knew what he was getting into with me, or with my work, which I had no intention of giving up. I saw better than he did what was ahead: marriage to me wouldn't be easy, and it certainly wouldn't be conventional. I was a highly unusual choice for a traditional southern man — even my own brother Tommy shook his head and told him, "I don't know how you put up with Sis." How would R.B. feel when the novelty of my basketball passion wore off? Would he pressure me to quit? I declined the proposal — for now. I wasn't refusing him, I said, but I felt it was premature.

"I want to be sure," I said. "I need more time."

He agreed to wait.

I loved our players and wanted a closer relationship with them, but up to that point, I didn't know how to have it. I was so consumed with their performance on the court that I had trouble talking to them about other things. It was pretty obvious *they* didn't want to talk to *me,* when they'd all try to pack into the equipment van driven by Nancy Darsch instead of riding with me. At the time, I convinced myself it was a compliment.

When we lost, my van was a miserable place to be. It had a double gas tank, and when it ran low I could flip a switch to the other tank. That meant we could drive for hours without pulling over for a bathroom break or a bite of food.

"I'll never push you more than I'll push myself," I said. It never occurred to me to ask what demon was pushing *me* so hard in the back. I'd push and push — and then walk out of the gym and leave Nancy to bind up their emotional wounds, soothe their feelings, and listen to their woes.

Even for me sometimes observing, I would feel pain for them. I would try to smooth it over, put an arm around a shoulder and say, "You're okay." She was fierce, no question about it, but those players got pushed beyond their comfort zone and that was not a bad thing. She wanted them to go at it with her. Pat wanted them to fight.

— NANCY DARSCH

It was the Richard in me, I guess. I visited Henrietta and sat on the sofa and watched my father play checkers with my little nephew, Derrick, one of Tommy's sons. Daddy wouldn't let him take a single piece. They'd play, and Daddy would sweep the board, and Derrick would cry.

"Let him win!" I said.

"No," Daddy said. "He won't get better."

That was how I was with our players. It was all in the name of making them stronger. Feel bullied? Do something about it. Suffer a setback? Handle it. The one thing I hated, the one thing I couldn't stand, was when they acted weak, or hurt, or intimidated.

"Don't *wilt*!" I shouted. "Be assertive!"

I thought I could will them to a championship. But no matter how hard I worked

239

them, we couldn't quite get to the top. In three of Holly Warlick's four years at Tennessee, we finished either second or third in the country. I have patchwork memories of how desperately hard they played, and how I burned after each season-ending loss:

• In 1978, climbing all the way to number one in the country, only to be torpedoed by a media firestorm when a scathing *Sports Illustrated* article called us "the University of Transfer," because Cindy Brogdon had decided to follow Trish Roberts to Tennessee, angering coaches around the country who felt I'd used my Olympic relationship to influence them into switching schools. We were knocked off by a bigger, stronger number six Maryland in the regionals of the AIAW tournament, and afterward our players sobbed. "I can't believe we weren't tall enough," they wailed.

• In 1979, flying with the men's team to a doubleheader at Louisiana State University in turbulence so bad that heads were hitting the ceiling of the plane, and everyone was nauseated. The players thought I would cancel practice; instead I made us go right to the arena and told anyone who was still sick to "throw up, and get on the court." We fought to overtime only to have the LSU men's coach, Dale Brown, order us off the floor so the men could start on time. Dale became a friend to women's basketball, but he wasn't that night. I said, "No way are we getting off this court. We're not leaving," and we argued eye to eye until we compromised and played the overtime on a running clock.

• At the end of that season, making it to the AIAW tournament at Fordham in New York City, and our center Kathy O'Neil was so country that when we drove into Manhattan she said, "Look, y'all, there's the Golden Gate Bridge!" Nancy had to tell her no, that one was in California. At every stoplight the window washers came out and Miss Hazel of Henrietta tried to tip each one of them. We played in Rose Hill Arena in the Bronx, where there were holes in the ceiling and pigeons nesting behind the backboard. The birds flapped in the rafters and dropped bombs along the sidelines, and periodically I had to relocate to avoid getting my suit ruined. We won there, only to get killed by Louisiana Tech in the Final Four in Greensboro, North Carolina, 102–84. It was the second time in three years we finished third in the country.

"The harder you work," I told them, "the harder it is to surrender." But too often they

241

interpreted it as intimidation or punishment. Holly would stare back at me with that bright, implacable grin of hers, and then go to her room and blast Johnny Paycheck's "Take This Job and Shove It" on her stereo, and scream the words: "I ain't WORK-ING here no more!"

But eventually, I changed. And if I hadn't, we wouldn't be having this conversation. You'd be talking to someone else, because the kids would have all quit and I'd have burned out, fast. What changed me? Jill Rankin, partly. Also R.B. Summitt.

I tried to help with team chemistry because my minor in college was psychology. But of course, I had to try to figure out Pat first.
— R.B. SUMMITT

Jill was another transfer. Nothing in the rules prohibited transfers, despite the anger of my fellow coaches, and players from other schools were ringing my phone off the hook for a good reason: we were the hot, rising program, and Stokely was the biggest stage for women in the game. I actually could have taken more transfers than I did; even Nancy Lieberman wanted to be a Lady Vol, but I felt it wasn't a good mix and told her to stay at Old Dominion. But when Jill

242

called, I jumped at her: she was a six-foot-three center and a three-time all-American at tiny Wayland Baptist College out in Texas, with great presence around the basket. When Jill's coach, Dean Weese, left the school for a pro league, she no longer wanted to stay at Wayland and called me to ask if she could finish out her career as a Lady Vol. "Come on," I said. There would be no more crying about height.

I had coached Jill on the USA national team in competitions like the Pam Am Games, so I knew the kind of player we were getting. If the ball touched her fingers, it was going in, but that wasn't the best thing about her. It was how she lightened me up that made her such a valuable addition. On top of that strong body Jill had a pixie haircut, and the soul of one, too. She was a deadly funny, self-secure young woman who wasn't the least bit afraid of me; in fact, she seemed to think I was good material. I let her get away with murder. She would stroll into my office and sit in my chair and put her feet up on my desk.

In years to come, I always introduced Jill by saying, "She's the first player who ever made fun of me." Pause. "To my face."

Jill had heard from other players how intense I was. "You don't jack with her," they said. But that just convinced Jill that it was her role in life to loosen me up. She was a great mimic, and she studied the way I walked. Once I was walking through the parking lot on my way into the arena for a game, in a dapper outfit of burgundy vest, gauchos, and wine-colored boots, when here comes Rankin after me, copying the walk perfectly. She went long-striding into the gym, fast and businesslike, with one arm swinging wide and the other held close to her body. The kids shrieked and I turned around, just in time to catch her. She never missed a beat.

Or she'd get right up close and set her jaw and peck them on the chest with her finger, then growl at them in my voice, "You WILL rebound!"

Life was a comedy with Jill around. That season we went to UT-Martin to play, and it was important to me that we look good in front of my alma mater. I was so wired up that when Holly and Jill were a little late leaving the motel for the team bus, I threw rocks at their doors. When we got to the gym, it seemed like everyone I ever knew was in the stands. I was pleased at how glamorous we looked as we took the floor: I had ordered us fancy new warm-ups, very trendy long bell-bottoms with twenty-four-inch-diameter cuffs like the NBA guys wore. The Lady Vols ran on the floor and started a three-man weave, with Jill leading off. Well, somehow her feet got tangled in her bell-bottoms, and she tripped. Fell flat. And started sliding. She dusted at least six feet of the court.

Everyone wanted to laugh. But I gave her one of those "I can't believe that just happened" looks and signaled her to get up, keep going. Well, two minutes later another player, Jerilynn Harper, tripped on her big bell-bottoms. Fell flat. I hissed, "Get those things off!" But by then the kids, led by Jill, were cackling uncontrollably, and so was the audience, and so was I.

Jill taught me that I could be demanding and still have fun; the two weren't mutually exclusive. Even when I was angriest, Jill had a way of breaking me down. Late that season we took a bad loss at South Carolina. We were up by 18 points at the half, but it was a terrible environment, with a rock band behind our bench that made it impossible to hear, and in the second half we came out flat, didn't score until the nine-minute mark. Ended up losing the game. I was furious, and it provoked one of my more ingenious motivational techniques.

When we got back to our Town & Country

Hotel, I told the kids to pack their own uniforms instead of giving them to the managers for laundering. The next day we drove home, and as I pulled into the parking lot, I said, "Don't go back to your dorms. We're going straight to the locker room. Get your uniforms out. We're going to finish those twenty minutes you didn't play in them. They aren't ready for the laundry yet — you didn't play hard enough to get 'em dirty." I made them dig their sweaty, cold uniforms out of the laundry bag and put them on.

> Pat could make you hate losing as bad as she did by putting consequences on it. If you didn't hate it for all the right reasons, she was going to *teach* you to hate it.
>
> — JILL RANKIN

Holly was so mad, she said, "I'll show her. I'm even putting my sweaty socks back on." She decided to try to stink me out. Not only did she pull on her damp wet, reeking socks, she even put her sweaty sports bra back on. That gave Jill an idea.

"If we've got to play in these uniforms again, then we should have player introductions again," she said.

Holly brightened up at that. She, Jill, and

246

Kathy O'Neil walked out into the Stokely tunnel and did the Tennessee cheer: "T-E-Double N-E-Double S-Double E!" Then Jill put her hands around her mouth like a megaphone and said, "And now, ladies and gentlemen, starting for the Lady Vols at point guard, number 22, HOOOOOLLLLLLY WARRRRRRLICK!" and mimicked crowd noise. Holly went running out to midcourt pumping her fists high above her head. Then Jill introduced herself, "JIIILLLLLL RAAAANKINNN!!!!!" And she ran out and high-fived Holly.

They both turned back to look at Kathy who was waiting her turn in that tunnel. She said, excitedly, "Introduce me!" But all of a sudden Jill and Holly saw me striding down the tunnel. Holly shook her head at Kathy, like uh-uh. Kathy said, "What's wrong?" By then Holly and Jill had frozen.

I said, "You think this is *funny*?"

"No, ma'am."

"You do, don't you? You think this is funny."

"No, ma'am."

But it was funny, of course. It got even funnier when people started wandering into the gym and saw our players in their uniforms and said, "Hey, is there a game tonight?" They were embarrassed — mortified. But it made an impression.

We didn't win a championship that year either, but the laughter lessened the pain. Holly and Jill led us right to the brink of one: we made the AIAW title game, for a televised matchup on NBC against the number one team in the country, Old Dominion, led by a six-foot-eight center named Anne Donovan, and my old teammate Nancy Lieberman. Who proceeded to play as if her sole intent was to make me sorry I hadn't let her transfer. It was all in place for us to take the final step to a championship — and we just couldn't get it done. Maybe it was nerves, or we tried too hard, but our guards made just two of fourteen shots. Old Dominion won, 68–53.

It was another wrenching loss, and it was compounded on March 21, when President Jimmy Carter announced the American boycott of the 1980 Olympics in Moscow, to protest the 1979 Soviet invasion of Afghanistan. There was nothing abstract about the boycott for us. Holly, Jill, and our six-five center Cindy Noble had been selected to be on the Olympic team, and I was scheduled to be there as an assistant coach to my friend Sue Gunter. The kids couldn't get over the loss of such an opportunity — and never would.

The only good thing about the boycott was that it gave me the summer off and allowed me to plan my wedding. One night that May over dinner at my apartment, R.B. gave me an ultimatum: "I'm calling the question," he said. It was a parliamentary term meaning it was time for me to make a decision. I had to marry him or release him and let him move on. "This is dragging out and we both want children, and we aren't getting younger," he said.

By this time we had been dating for almost four years, more than long enough for me to decide whether we were right together. He had not always been patient, occasionally breaking off with me to date others, to my misery. I had no intention of losing him again and had been waiting for him to propose.

If R.B. was braced for disappointment when he issued his ultimatum, this time I surprised him.

I smiled and said, "I've been thinking that August 23 would be a good date."

Just then R.B. glanced over at my digital clock — which was beaming 8:23 P.M. We took it as a sign, a blessing on the date.

We were tremendously different. He was a big reader who loved science fiction, and I barely cracked a book unless it was a how-to-succeed tract. He loved the Smoky Mountains and I liked the Florida beaches. He was patient and slow talking, sentimental and wide open with his feelings. I was fast and furious and kept my deeper feelings under cover. I liked Elvis, Loretta, and Dolly. He liked John Denver and ABBA.

But he smoothed my edges, took me out of basketball, opened life up, and taught me to be more expressive, made it easier to say the words that my father never could, "I love you."

I got married in the first and only wedding dress I tried on — that's how decisive I was. Once I wanted to be married, I didn't second-guess. At the rehearsal dinner my father looked at R.B. and said, "Ain't gonna be no divorce." R.B. reached over and shook his hand and said, "You're right."

There would be no more "separating" the personal and the professional for me. From then on, they began to merge. Jill Rankin tied most of the rice bags, and Nancy Darsch was a bridesmaid. Holly, Cindy Noble, Suzanne Barbre, and the rest of the Lady Vols "decorated" our car with tin cans.

The ceremony was conducted by our pastor at Mt. Carmel United Methodist Church, although my father suggested he could have done as well, because he had become a justice of the peace. We were standing in the hall waiting to walk down the aisle, when my old friend Jane Brown, who was a bridesmaid, reached over and hugged me and said, "I've been here before and I'm just as nervous." Daddy looked down at Jane and said, "Yeah, but she could have saved us all of this trouble if she had just let me marry them at home."

We saved the front left pew of the church for the Lady Vols. They were all there, a dozen of them in their most respectable dresses. "Amazing Grace" played, and then the wedding march began. Our players rose — and kept rising, and rising, until they unfolded to their full height. They looked like tall, draped curtains.

Here's the problem with inviting a basketball team to your wedding and giving them the front pew.

Nobody behind them could see.

I was finally becoming a more creative, resourceful coach. I no longer thought I had to be in control of everything and everybody; in fact, if there was one thing I'd realized, it was that once the game starts, a coach can't physically control what's happening. You can't move bodies from point A to point B.

The job of coach wasn't about being a martinet. It was about preparing people to make good independent decisions. Getting them in the right spots at the right time was as much a matter of understanding them, and *talking* to them, as it was of directing their traffic.

When she first started, the age difference was so close she had to prove a point, that she was the coach and we were players. She treated everyone the same. But we were a team that loved to play the game and had big hearts, and by our senior year she was learning what she could do with kids, and what she couldn't do. I think she understood, "I've got to do this a little different." Because she had developed a relationship with us, she knew how far she could go.

— HOLLY WARLICK

Becky Clark was a nineteen-year-old premed major from Memphis, and she was partly deaf. She had significant hearing loss that was progressively worsening, but she refused to concede to it and wanted to try out for the team. I gave her a chance, because I thought it would be a good learning exercise for all of us, and she made the team in 1980.

Becky had hearing aids, but she couldn't wear them when she was playing because sweat destroyed them. In the noise of practice and games, she couldn't make out what anyone said to her. That meant, as a team, all of us had to deal with Becky's debility, make sure she saw our eyes and read lips. "You fill in the blanks for your teammates," I told them. "No matter what the problem is. If there's any miscommunication, it's your fault."

One afternoon in practice during a defensive segment Becky ran into a screen and fell to the floor. Her teammates were supposed to warn her that a screen was coming so she could switch off — but Becky hadn't heard anybody yell "switch" and slammed right into it. We had to figure out how to help her, but she also had to figure out how to help herself. I blew the whistle.

"Becky, what happened there — tell me!" I said. "You've got to get around that pick."

"I couldn't hear my teammates holler," she said.

With Becky, the best way to communicate was visually. She needed nonverbal cues, I realized. Somehow, she had to accomplish the task of seeing what everyone else was hearing. I walked over and stood in her spot and got in a defensive stance. I went through the steps of denying the ball to an opponent and stepping around a screen from her perspective, trying to show her how to use her eyes instead of ears.

She said, "Becky, let yourself see the whole court. You've got to see that pick coming. You're going to have to use your peripheral vision, become aware of movement around and behind you as well as in front of you. The key is, you've got to anticipate. You've got to anticipate the action, anticipate the movement. Okay now, let's try it again." Coach Summitt taught me a valuable lesson during that practice session, which has served me in all phases of my life. Although I'm now deaf, I can still hear her urging me on with one simple word, "Anticipate!"

— BECKY CLARK

Players like Becky were shaping me as much as I was shaping them. Each one seemed to come with some moral, insight, or lesson about teaching. Cindy Noble, Debbie Groover, Cindy Ely, Susan Clower, Shelia Collins — they all left their impression on me. Sometimes it felt like picking a series of locks: How could I spring open their potential? My coaching was becoming more reciprocal and responsive, a matter of understanding their makeup, rather than just pulling their strings.

I had to get to know a whole new group in 1980–1981, because with Jill and Holly graduating we were virtually starting over. We'd rely on seven incoming freshmen — and only five made it through my workouts to Christmas break. We dubbed the survivors the Fearless Five. They were from all over the country — with television exposure our recruiting had gone national: Mary Ostrowski was a brilliantly talented but reticent six-two center from West Virginia. Lynne Collins was an energetic six-one forward from Virginia. Tanya Haave was an intelligent swing player from Colorado. Paula Towns, whom we called P-Town, was a six-one forward from Georgia. Pat Hatmaker was our local, a five-foot-eight greyhound of a guard from Knoxville, whom we nicknamed Rattle, because she was so bony thin. Every Monday I made our players weigh in, and Hatmaker was the only one who didn't weigh enough.

If there was a player who taught me just how much control I didn't have, it was Lynne Collins. She was a big, energetic, bass-voiced blonde whom we nicknamed

Orca for her habit of throwing herself on the floor and flopping after loose balls like a beached whale. R.B. and I had driven over to scout Lynne in a high school game, and during a time-out I watched her bite the top off a water bottle, because it was too small. She just spit out the plastic and chugged. I turned to R.B. and said, "I want that kid."

But Lynne was also what I called "an outlaw." She didn't just chug water, she chugged beer. She treated my training rules as purely optional, and right away started busting curfew. From then on she was constantly in trouble.

"Why are you always looking at *me*?" she asked.

"Because you smell like a brewery," I said.

Lynne swore I had a network of snitches all over town, waiting to call in her every transgression, which I did. She used to sing the lyrics to Michael Jackson's "Somebody's Watching Me." She would chant, "Pat Summitt's waaaaatching me. I got no privac-cccccy. . . ." We played constant cat and mouse. Once, when I heard she had been out and about, I got in my car and drove out to the strip where I knew she was likely to be. She saw my gray Oldsmobile Toronado coming down an alley toward her and broke into a run — first she tried to hide behind a bus, and then she crept behind a light pole. Finally I wrangled her into the car and told her she was not only benched, she wasn't even allowed to dress for the game. That night Lynne showed up in her street clothes — and limped to the bench so everyone would think she was injured.

After a while Lynne started going farther afield, hoping to evade detection. One afternoon I strode into practice while the players were stretching, and I made a beeline right for her. She just rolled her eyes and said, "Uh-oh."

I said, "I heard you bought a six-pack of Coors at the Pilot gas station on Northshore last night."

Northshore was twenty miles from campus.

Lynne goes, "Nope."

I raised an eyebrow.

"It was actually an eight-pack of Miller Lite," she said.

I just stared at her and tried to contain my icy smile.

"I know," Lynne said, wearily. " 'Get on the line.' "

Lynne did everything dramatically. Whenever I made the team run suicides, she screamed like it was about to kill her. She would hit the end line and wail, "OH MY GOD!" After each sprint they got ten seconds to recover, and then had to go again. One afternoon Lynne's screams got louder and louder. Every time she hit the end line, I heard, "OH MY GOD!"

After about the fourth time, I got tired of hearing it. I looked at her with daggers in my eyes and I said, "Lynne Collins, if I hear that out of you one more time, we're gonna run ten more."

Everyone around Lynne muttered, "Lynne, shut *up.*"

They ran again. This time when Lynne approached the line, everybody tensed. Her foot hit the baseline. She took a deep, gasping breath and opened her mouth, and this is what I heard: "JE-SUS CHRIST!"

Everybody just stopped dead. The gym fell totally silent and they all looked at me to see what I would do. I had to turn away because I started giggling, and next to me Nancy Darsch was giggling too, and pretty soon we were laughing so hard we had to bend over.

I was figuring out more subtle approaches to discipline. I was continually racked with worry about their well-being: How do you sleep when you feel responsible for a dozen eighteen- to twenty-year-olds with car keys, willful temperaments, raging thirsts, and surging hormones? But if I tried to police everything they did, we'd all be miserable. The answer was to borrow from Richard Head and have just a few simple rules — but make sure they feared the consequences of breaking them.

One evening I ran into two of our players, Susan Foulds and her roommate, Cindy Noble, our all-American center, at a Tennessee men's game. Lately I thought I'd smelled nicotine on them. I strolled over and took a seat next to them.

"I had a funny dream last night," I said conversationally. "I dreamed I caught you two smoking."

They blanched. There was a long, tense pause. Then Cindy spoke.

"What did you dream you did to us?"

I said coolly, "I dreamed I made you run." Then I got up and sauntered away.

But the most effective way to get their attention was to embarrass them. They liked to look good — cared about appearances. When we went on a road trip to Colorado, they spent most of their time sunbathing, oiled up and lounging outside on the hotel patio, all day. We lost by 20. I was furious — but instead of making them run sprints when we got home, I made them run right then and there, in front of the opposing fans as soon as the game was over. They were mortified. They looked good doing it though. Bronzed up.

Another time we lost at Stephen F. Austin. Horrible. She made us go into their weight room and lift weights. We had our uniforms on, and our sweats. I weighed 118 pounds and couldn't lift a bar, much less the weights. Their fans and staff were watching us. Like, "Look, there are the Lady Vols."

— PAT HATMAKER

But the young women on that team were made of something, as was anyone who survived with me. I discovered how much steel they had in them the night I drove them to a cookout thrown by some boosters, and our van blew out a tire. I pulled the shuddering van over to the shoulder of the interstate and got out and started rummaging in the back for a jack. I couldn't find one. There was no jack.

I stuck my head inside the side door and said, "All right, ladies. Everybody out of the van." They climbed out and stood around.

"Half of you on this side, and half on the

other," I said. "On the count of three, you're gonna lift, and I'll change the tire."

They stared at me incredulously. "You want us to lift a *van*?" Hatmaker asked.

"Let's go," I ordered.

They shuffled into place, doubtfully. Half of them got on one side, and half on the other. I counted to three — and they lifted that van up. I don't how they didn't blow their backs out, but they did it. Some took more weight than others — skinny Pat Hatmaker was shaking like a Chihuahua after a haircut.

I said, "Okay, hold it. Hold it."

They stood there trembling with effort until finally I said, "Okay, drop 'er down."

They were proud of it. When we got to the cookout, they said, "Sorry we're late. We got a flat and had to lift the van."

The better I got to know our players, the more I was able to search out their competitive personalities, find their insecurities, and shore them up. "Mo" Ostrowski was a magnificent, willowy pure player with tremendous reach and finesse. But she was strangely passive on the court. She lacked that drive-it-up-the-floor personality, a gimme-the-ball-and-get-out-of-my-way attitude that great scorers usually have. Some players want the ball in crucial situations, but others are more anxious; they think, *What if I don't make it? What if I miss?* Mary would hesitate. In a game against Long Beach State, we had a chance to win with a few seconds left and Mo holding the ball. She had an open shot right in front of her. But instead of shooting it, she saw Lynne Collins under the basket, and passed it — just as Lynne turned to rebound. The ball hit Lynne in the back, and we never got a shot off.

Taking a game over just didn't come naturally to her, I realized. Watching her early in her career was like looking at a skyscraper in which the elevator didn't yet go all the way to the top. It was my job to try to get the elevator all the way up. I tried begging her to shoot, and threatening her. Finally I just required it. I made a rule: she had to get off at least ten shots a game or she had to run. It worked: she ended up leading us in scoring her sophomore and senior years and made all-American.

Hatmaker had a similar shyness, though I didn't realize it at first. She was a wonderful player to watch, catlike and agile, so active that I didn't realize how much confidence she still lacked as a freshman. But I began to notice that she didn't like much physical contact. Pat was afraid of taking a charge:

when another player came at her, instead of setting her feet she would shuffle and cringe. I took care of that one day in practice: I made Pat take a charge from every player on our team, until she learned that a little bump wasn't going to break her. Physical nerve was never again an issue with Pat. In fact, she went on to become a police officer, and then a security specialist at the Oak Ridge nuclear facility. Hatmaker keeps us all safe.

But as a freshman Pat had some lingering insecurity, which I didn't realize until we were in the Final Four with a game on the line. The Fearless Five finished their freshman year by making it all the way to the national semifinals in Eugene, Oregon, where we once again met Old Dominion. The game came down to the last eleven seconds, and we had a one-point lead. I called a time-out and set up a play: I wanted to get the ball in Hatmaker's hands because she was our quickest, best ball handler and best free throw shooter.

We came out of our huddle — and I saw the players have a second huddle. Not a good sign. Then Mo Ostrowski picked up the ball and slapped it, to start the play. Hatmaker took off — and ran *away* from the play. Never looked back. Instead, our junior guard Susan Clower stepped up and received the ball and was immediately fouled. Now, Susan didn't go to the free throw line much in pressure situations.

Inside, I was livid. But everything I'd learned about communicating with players told me that it was vital to stay positive, because Susan immediately looked over to me for reassurance. How do you look back at someone who is clearly nervous, who you know isn't real comfortable in this situation? I just remember giving her the thumbs-up and telling her she was ready. And she was: Susan was playing in her third straight Final Four. She hit the first shot, looked right back over at me again. I gave her another high sign. She made the second one, and we won, 68–65.

It was a great moment for Susan and our whole team. But I couldn't celebrate, for thinking about what had just happened. On the way to the locker room, Mo Ostrowski caught up with me. "I've got to tell you something," she said. "After our huddle, we had another huddle."

I said, "I noticed."

"Hatmaker told us she did not want the ball," Mary said.

When I got to the locker room, Pat was sitting right in the front row. She made immediate eye contact with me, which was important because it meant she wanted to confront what had happened. It was a brave reaction and I respected her for it. But it was also my responsibility to call her out. "I can't believe you wouldn't want the ball, and I can't believe we put you in this situation," I said, "and you let the whole team down." But I didn't want to get so caught up in how upset I was with Pat that we failed to prepare for tomorrow — we had a championship game to play against Louisiana Tech. I started to pump her back up. "You'll be okay," I said. "You're going to learn from this. Now, let's move on."

But I was the person who learned the most that day. I'd not done a good job of understanding the players I was working with and how they responded to pressures. My most important call of the game was designed to get the ball to Hatmaker, and Hatmaker didn't want the ball. Not once had I sat with her and said, "How would you feel if we're in this situation?" I should have known. Should have talked to her more — or better yet, listened to her.

That I still had a lot to learn showed in the championship game: Louisiana Tech killed us, 79–59. We were too young; we fell behind by 11 at halftime and I got outcoached by a couple of veterans on the Louisiana Tech sideline named Sonja Hogg and Leon Barmore, Sonja's assistant. It was the first time we ever allowed a TV camera in our locker room, and NBC caught me live trying to encourage my players, which earned us the consolation of sympathy mail.

People started saying we were "always the bridesmaid, never the bride." We just couldn't seem to win — we always came up a little short — and the following year we were disappointed yet again. As seniors, the Fearless Five carried us to the brink of another national championship, this one at Pauley Pavilion in Los Angeles. Mild "Mo" Ostrowski finally rose to her full height and set an NCAA record in the semifinals with 35 points and 17 rebounds against Cheney State. In the title game, we met a team from Southern California that was one of the greatest ever assembled, starring an array of Hall of Famers and Olympians in Cheryl Miller, Cynthia Cooper, Pam and Paula McGee, and JaMaiia Bond.

It was a huge opportunity: I'd been named head coach of our '84 Olympic team, which meant a crack at a rare double victory, a championship and a gold medal in the space of a few months. And it almost happened. We led Southern Cal for thirty-three minutes. It was right there; we could almost feel the trophy in our hands. But then our kids wore down. We made a couple of tired turnovers, and the Trojans surged over the last five minutes, to a 72–61 victory.

I'll say this for us: we were good losers. It was our fifth trip to the Final Four in a seven-year stretch, and we'd lost every time. I racked my brain trying to figure out what the difference was between us and the teams that won. "What do we need to do?" I asked Nancy. "Is it the players? Is it me?"

I took to my bed, sick, and didn't get up for two days. I shuffled around in my pajamas. I couldn't eat; I couldn't sleep. I blamed myself. It was me: I was the one responsible. *You let it get away. You should have done something different.* I was simply still learning against older and more experienced coaches. I stared at the tape trying to analyze my weakness: If I had gone to a zone, would it have changed the momentum? Why didn't I switch defenses? Should I have conditioned us differently, so we had fresher legs? I felt like I cost us, whether because I was stubborn, or limited, not able to see the entire floor. I gritted my teeth and said, "Someday, we're going to win a championship."

Commitment is all about risk: the payoff

is either heartbreak or exhilaration. But it's also about tedium, the willingness to persevere through problems without quitting and, more important, without demoralization. It's a kind of faith. In retrospect, those seasons weren't failures: the only thing we failed to do was win one more game. As hard as I took our losses, there was dignity in them. We were willing to fail. How we behaved in those moments was, of course, as self-defining as winning could ever be, and that was a lesson that translated off the court. Both in marriage and in work, I'd discovered my own heart, and its capacity for devoting sustained, focused attention to something other than myself. In time I would go from feeling like we would never win, to feeling like you couldn't ever count us out again.

Sometimes I wish God hadn't given me so many issues.

What kind of issues?

Personal issues.

Can you tell me about them?

I guess they made me who I am. I guess they made me better. One thing I've learned.

What?

How powerful God is.

— April 14, 2012, Knoxville, Tennessee, eleven months after diagnosis

6
PROFESSIONAL WOMAN

After years of defending my right to an unconventional job, all I wanted was the most conventional female role, to be a mother. But for the first time in my life, I found something I couldn't will myself to do. I could change a tractor tire, chop tobacco, and get a team to the Final Four, but I couldn't do the most fundamental thing in the world: bear a child.

R.B. and I had settled into married life smoothly, with the exception of a couple of minor adjustments. At heart I was a traditionalist when it came to family, and I liked to cook dinner at home every night. One evening I was stirring something on the stovetop when R.B. wandered in and began lecturing me because I used the big gas ring instead of the small one. "Now listen," I said, "if you want this marriage to last, when I'm cooking you need to just get out of the way."

We both had grown up in homes crowded with children — R.B. was the oldest of four — and we talked for hours about whether to have four children or five. I hoped for at least one daughter, so I could raise a strong woman. I was sure I could juggle motherhood with coaching, though the job had become more and more demanding — and deeply preoccupying. One night, I walked in the house without even noticing a new car in the driveway. R.B. said, "What do you think?"

"About what?" I said.

"Did you park in the garage?"

"Yes."

"What did you see?"

There was a huge new gleaming SUV there, and I was so lost in thought that I had pulled up right alongside it and never registered it.

I had taken my ability to have a baby for granted. I don't remember the exact dates or circumstances anymore — Alzheimer's treats painful and joyful recollections equally. I just remember how thrilled I was each time I learned I was pregnant, and then the abrupt, empty despondency when I no longer was. Between 1982 and 1989, I suffered four miscarriages.

I barely had time to feel like an expectant

mother the first time it happened, early in my first trimester. The doctor explained that it wasn't uncommon; almost a quarter of pregnancies end in miscarriage, and the vast majority of women go on to healthy pregnancies. I wiped the tears off my face. "We'll just try again," I told R.B., and to improve our chances I made myself as healthy as possible and quit drinking alcohol at dinner in favor of iced tea.

But I wasn't in the vast majority. I lost another baby. And then another, this time not as early. I was pregnant long enough to feel that there were two of us in my body, and to be physically knocked down by the grief when I felt alone again.

"Why is this happening to me?" I asked my doctors. They had no easy answer: any number of possible factors could cause recurrent miscarriage, and sometimes an underlying cause was never found. I underwent a laparoscopy test, fairly new at the time. When I woke up, the doctor told me, "Everything looks fine."

R.B. came in beaming, hugged me, and took hold of my hand. I caught him off guard by bursting into tears. "What's wrong?" he said.

"I was so worried that we couldn't have children," I said, "and I didn't want to disappoint you."

I was concerned that stress could be the cause: pressure in coaching was ever present, almost a state of being. But the doctors told me there was no evidence linking recurrent miscarriage and work stress; it wasn't the job's fault. Nevertheless, we took a brief hiatus from trying to have a child in the summer of 1984, because I was under especially intense strain: I had gone straight from the Final Four to preparing for the Olympics in Los Angeles, where the USA team was heavily favored. If we didn't deliver a gold medal in women's basketball, it would be because I screwed it up. "I've got to do this," I told R.B. I'd never live it down if we lost.

The Olympics were exhilarating and distracting, and a solace for the personal losses of those years. For forgetting all your troubles there is nothing like watching human beings literally seem to fly. The '84 Olympics had a lot of those, and the basketball tournament featured two in particular for the United States in Cheryl Miller and Michael Jordan. Being around those gliding, magical artists and meeting and working with other elites once again took me to a whole new level as a professional.

My male counterpart was Bobby Knight,

the Indiana University coach known for his disciplined teams, his incandescent temper, and his penchant for saying the outrageous. I learned a lot from Bobby, with whom I became great friends, once I got past an early encounter. We met for the first time at a huge press event in Indianapolis to introduce us as the USA head coaches. I was walking ahead of Bobby down a hallway, when he said, "You know, you got a great ass."

I laughed. Then, with a smile still on my face, I said, "Don't ever say anything like that to me again." Bobby just grinned back largely — he had a wonderful smile — and shrugged it off. So did I. Underneath it all I knew he respected me, and he was just being a provocateur. A few years later when his son Patrick wanted to be a coach, Bobby sent him to Knoxville to observe our practices for a couple of days, telling him there was no one better to learn from.

> They did go on and become friends in a big way. I probably wouldn't have handled it. But she laughed at it.
>
> — Nancy Darsch

Bobby and I bonded over the pressure and honor we felt as Olympic coaches. It was

274

compounded for me by the fact that I was young for the job, only thirty-two, still relatively unproven, and I was also the only female coach in the entire Olympic tournament. Although it was a great compliment, it came with an unwritten statement: "You better win." It was widely acknowledged that the United States had the most dominant player in the world in Cheryl Miller, and anything other than a victory would be viewed as an underachievement. Not a day went by that I didn't think about the fact that I'd never won a collegiate championship, yet I was expected to deliver a gold medal.

The stress was relentless, and it aged me. You know how a president grays throughout his term? That was how I aged in the summer of '84. It made me more demanding than ever, especially on the two Tennesseans who were on our squad, Lea Henry and Cindy Noble, who became my targets and outlets when I needed to vent. Fortunately I had a great complement in the late great Kay Yow, whose style was the exact opposite of mine. Kay was the head coach at North Carolina State, where for thirty-four years she turned out players of distinction and won over 700 games despite hardly ever raising her voice, which was as soft as flannel.

Kay's gentleness was not only good for the players; it was good for me. Where I made demands, she questioned and suggested. I became a better coach just by listening to her, and she gave me one of the great lessons of my career in the week before the Opening Ceremonies. We were walking back to our condo from practice, after I'd been particularly hard on Lea and Cindy.

Kay very calmly and sweetly said, "You know, Pat, how much better do you think Lea Henry and Cindy Noble are going to *get* at this point?"

She was saying ease up — it's enough. I had reached the point of diminishing returns. "I think they are both trying really hard to please you, but how much more can they possibly do?" she said. "I just wonder if you've really thought about that."

I said, suddenly self-conscious, "Kay, that's a good point."

That squad didn't need much pushing from me. They were a women's Dream Team: in addition to Miller, we had the towering Anne Donovan from Old Dominion; a fire-eyed little guard from Louisiana Tech named Kim Mulkey; the great versatile future Hall of Famer Teresa Edwards; our captain, Lynette Woodard, of Kansas; and Pam McGee of USC. There were a lot of epic performances at the Los Angeles Games from athletes like Carl Lewis and Mary Lou Retton. But one of them came from us: we swept the competition, going 6-0, winning every game by almost 33 points. After we beat South Korea by a score of 89–55 in the gold medal game, making it a talent show in front of a packed home crowd in the Forum, the squad shocked me by lifting me up and carrying me to center court. In the photos you can see my white high heels.

> They picked her up and threw her in the air. It was a wonderful moment — it's better than getting Gatorade thrown on you. And it showed the respect and love they had for her.
>
> — NANCY DARSCH

Our performance was so sensational that it created rumors that I might retire. The talk was that now I had won a gold medal, I would seize the chance to go out on top. Bobby Knight told me, "After this you need to go back home and have kids." He couldn't know what a sensitive topic it was, or that my father shared his opinion. My father insisted it would never get better than this: I'd finished second in the NCAAs and won a gold medal in the same year, and how could I ever top that? It was time to do something else. "You need to retire and start your family," he said.

In retrospect, I think both he and my mother worried about what the stress of the job was doing to me, and whether it contributed to my miscarriages. I had gotten thin during the Olympics, and there were circles under my eyes. My father also understood that part of what drove me professionally was the inability to ever please him enough to get a compliment from him. Telling me to retire was his way of saying, "You've done well. You can stop striving for my approval now." But, of course, Daddy couldn't say what he really meant.

He could never really say or admit, "I was flat-out wrong." But he had his way of conceding. He couldn't say, "Trish, I am so pleased with you, and I love you so much, and you don't have to do any more. I think you ought to hang it up and enjoy the fruits of these labors." He couldn't say that. He just said, "You ought to retire." Period.

— R.B. SUMMITT

"Dad, I can have a family and still coach," I said.

I knew what I wanted professionally, and understood what it would take to get there, but I was trying too hard to make it happen. Which was the way I did everything. Even snow-ski.

The first time I tried to ski I was in Gatlinburg, Tennessee, one winter with my sister-in-law. She advised me to start on the beginners' slope, but do I look like someone who goes to the bunny hill? Instead I took the ski lift all the way to the top, and during the ride I watched the skiers beneath me for a quick how-to lesson. I got so caught up in studying them that I didn't get off the lift — just sat in the chair as it turned the corner and headed back down the slope.

Now, I certainly wasn't going to ride the lift all the way back down the mountain and have people think I didn't have the sense to get off. So I decided to jump. I was about twelve feet up when I dropped out of the chair. I landed face-first in the snow, knocking the wind out of me. I lay there for a moment and thought, *Maybe nobody saw me.* Then a voice came over the public address system.

"ARE YOU HURT?" the voice said. "DO

YOU NEED ASSISTANCE?"

I didn't answer. I thought, *Well, at least they don't know who I am.*

But then the voice spoke again. It boomed, "COACH SUMMITT? ARE YOU OKAY? DO YOU NEED HELP?"

I just waved.

It wasn't in my nature to ask for help with anything. For years I'd managed the Tennessee program almost single-handedly, and when I did delegate, it was only to my closest associate, Nancy Darsch. But in 1985 I had no choice but to seek help, because Nancy left us; after seven years as my right hand, and also my eyes, a brilliant scout and tactician who helped us to five Final Fours in seven years, she took the head coaching job at Ohio State.

Fortunately, thanks to a new NCAA rule expanding coaching staffs, I was allowed to replace Nancy with not one but two assistants. I also had help in our athletic director, Joan Cronan, a velvet-gloved, hairsprayed force who had arrived in 1983 and was turning us into the most prominent women's athletic program in the country. Joan had the air of a gracious Louisiana hostess, unless you messed up; then you found yourself quietly disinvited from the party. She was a superb fund-raiser who slowly but surely built our budget, and she told me to go after the best assistants money could buy.

I started out looking for a couple of good hires, but what I got instead were Mickie DeMoss and Holly Warlick, who over the next twenty-eight years would be my mainstays, coconspirators, partners in mischief, emotional counselors, equalizers, truth tellers, comforters, and favorite dinner companions. We were a combination of floor show and secret society.

I'd known Mickie Faye DeMoss for some time. She was a comical, fierce little person who had built a reputation as the best recruiter in the business at Auburn University, as well as a great bench coach. She was a renowned storyteller who liked to spin tales of growing up in Tallulah, Louisiana, where her mother, Wilma, owned a combination bar and grocery store called the Delta Lounge. She got her frankness and wit from Wilma, a five-foot firecracker whom I came to adore. Wilma was a whiskey-sipping, sharp social observer with a way of jabbing the pretense out of people, especially when she was into her beloved Crown Royal blend. She had her own vocabulary and a set of sayings that we repeated constantly.

"If you'll just keep your mouth shut, nobody will know you're a fool," she'd say.

When somebody talked too much, she'd say, "Sounds like a duck with a whistle up its butt."

When she was putting on her makeup, she'd sigh and say, "You can't ruin ruin."

If she decided someone didn't know what they were talking about, she said, "They don't know sheep shit from cotton seed."

But when Wilma got really, really angry, she'd say, "Makes my butt want a dip of snuff."

Mickie and Wilma were devoted to each other, though it wasn't the most conventional mother-daughter relationship. Mickie was badly pigeon-toed as a little girl and had to wear leg braces, and Wilma was afraid that Mickie was too sensitive about it. Mickie claims that Wilma's way of toughening her up was to set her on the bar of the Delta Lounge and make her dance the jitterbug in her braces, while singing, "Goin' to Kansas City!" until everybody applauded. "Buddy, I danced until sparks flew," Mickie says. The result of this unusual exercise in child rearing was one of the feistier people I'd ever met.

When Mickie came to Tennessee for the job interview, I asked, "Do you think you can bring in the players to get us over the hump, to take us to the next level so we can win a national championship?" Her answer was pure Mickie.

"That's not the question," she said, bridling. "I'll get you the players. Do you think you have what it takes as a head coach to win it?"

I just glared at her. "Oh, I have what it takes."

I thought, "Did I really just say that?" But that was the level of confidence I had in my ability, and that's the level of confidence she had in her ability to win a championship. So you put those two together, we had a winning combo.
— MICKIE DeMOSS

Holly Warlick had grown up into an engaging, endlessly good-natured adult, though with the same competitive edge she'd had as a player. Hiring her was a no-brainer. After she left Tennessee, she'd gotten her master's degree at Virginia Tech and migrated to Nebraska as an assistant coach. I called her and said I wanted to hire a former player, someone who could teach our philosophy, but also "offer personal testimony that it was possible to live through playing for me." I asked if she would be interested.

She said, "I can be there in fifteen hours, unless you need me in eight."

The first week Holly was on the job, I realized that life at work was never going to be the same. She and Mickie shared an office next to mine, and one day I walked into it to see that Holly had found a picture of me, in a little green skirt and little green sweater, and blown it up and mounted it on the wall. She had also signed it: "To Holly and Mickie, keep up the great work! Love, Pat." I just about died laughing and didn't stop for the next two decades.

They were capable of outrageous stunts and were always doing things to keep us loose. That first season together we took a road trip to Los Angeles, where Mickie managed to talk her way onto the game show *The Price Is Right* by telling the screeners that she was a professional mud wrestler. "Come on down!" the host shouted. Mickie proceeded to win the Grand Showcase, with the help of one of our players, Jennifer Tuggle, who was a math major. She got a trip to New Zealand, motor scooters, a bedroom and living room set, a grandfather clock, stereo equipment, a washer-dryer, and other fabulous prizes too numerous to mention.

Together, Mickie, Holly, and I had that

quality known as good chemistry. For some reason, we struck the right balance of laughter and serious purpose — once they got used to my hard-driving pace.

Among Holly's first assignments was a road trip with me to Birmingham for a Southeastern Conference meeting. I had a new car, a beautiful turbocharged Datsun 280z, champagne colored with a glass T-top. Holly strapped herself into the passenger seat and I hit the gas. The velocity slammed her back in her seat.

> I looked over at the speedometer going through Chattanooga and the needle was totally buried. I didn't say a word because I was still in the player-coach relationship. But I'm thinking, Holy ——, we're gonna get killed. I held the newspaper up in front of my face like I was reading, 'cause I thought, We're gonna get killed, and I don't want to see my death.
>
> — HOLLY WARLICK

When we got to the outskirts of Birmingham, I pulled over and handed her the keys and said, "You drive, I have to put on my makeup." Holly got behind the wheel.

"Now be careful," I said.

Holly answered, "At least you'll see the

needle."

Mickie and Holly eventually convinced me to slow down and realize that sometimes less was more. But back then I was inclined to think more was more, and the 1985–1986 Lady Vols felt my excesses. We were a young team, with eight players who were either freshmen or sophomores, and I resorted to some radical means to teach them good habits and high standards.

That season we lost ten games, including a bitter upset to our instate rival Vanderbilt. We had never lost to Vandy before, and I didn't take it well, and I didn't intend for anyone else to take it well either. As we trooped back onto the team bus, R.B. said, "Where are we eating?"

"Eat? We're not eating," I said. "We might *choke* on it."

I think she hated losing more than she liked winning. Losing was like death. I mean it was miserable. She instilled a great fear of losing, and it was a real motivator.

— SHELLEY SEXTON COLLIER

We got back to campus at about two A.M., and the kids filed off the bus ready to trudge back to their dorms. But I said, "Where do

286

you think you're going?" They froze, afraid to answer. I said, "Everybody in my office. We're going over this game."

The whole team, including Mickie and Holly, jammed into my little office in Stokely. The players sat on the floor with their knees up to their chests. I passed out paper and pencils and loaded the game film into a video player. I told them to watch themselves, and to make a note every time they didn't run the floor hard.

I was petrified, and I didn't even play that night. I was writing down things like "My shoe was untied." Anything that might make her happy.
— KATHY SPINKS GRIZZELL

When the tape ended, it was close to four A.M. I said, "You have exactly two minutes to get to the locker room and put your gear on. I'll see you on the court."

When they went into the locker room, they found a pile of fuming, sweaty uniforms in the middle of the floor. They could just put those back on, I said. "I'm not making the managers do extra laundry," I said. "Why should they pay for your mistakes?"

I told them to get out their lists and made them run a thirty-second suicide for every instance in which they hadn't sprinted the floor — and some of their lists were fifteen items long. They ran until they couldn't feel their legs. It was about six A.M. when we finally finished. "Y'all go get some breakfast, and get your bitching out of your system," I said. "And you better not miss your 7:50 classes."

I made the newspapers for that one; someone saw all the lights on in the gym at 4:30 A.M. After the story ran, the university president, Dr. Joe Johnson, called me and suggested that perhaps wind sprints at 4:30 A.M. didn't enhance student life. I had to agree.

But I didn't punish our players just to make myself feel better; those workouts had a purpose. I was trying to teach them a lesson about commitment. I measured our performance by two things: effort and execution. I was willing to coach execution for as long, and as forgivingly, as our players needed me to. I was a taskmaster, but a patient one, when it came to execution. But I wasn't patient or forgiving about effort. Lack of effort was tantamount to a lack of respect for our teammates and coaching staff and for me. With a lack of effort, one lackadaisical player compromised the efforts of all of us.

I think in Pat's mind, the more I got to know her, there wasn't anything she couldn't do, whether it was change a tractor tire or run an Olympic trial. Pat was a doer. It was all about action, all about let's get to work. She wasn't a planner and a thinker and let's analyze this. It was about action. "DeMoss, you get over here and put that there." And maybe it was wrong, but we'd just redo it. She didn't mind redoing it. She'd do it sixteen times if she had to. She coached every day like it was the national championship game. Every practice was coached like that. It was never a letup. I can't ever remember a day where she was tired, ever.

— MICKIE DEMOSS

Most college-age women didn't know what kind of effort they were capable of. Didn't have a clue. But I did. There is an old saying: a champion is someone who is willing to be uncomfortable. My message to that team at 4:30 A.M. was: "This is *what it takes.* I've shown you what it requires, what real effort looks like. Now you know, and if you turn away from it, take a shortcut, you'll be settling for less. And if you do it once, you'll do it for the rest of your life."

Why did it work? How could I harangue

them, and drive them at 4:30 in the morning, and get results? Why did they accept it, instead of quit or revolt? The answer was that I had become sure of and secure in my relationships with our players. My demandingness was based in a fundamental sense that every kid had potential greatness in her — and they understood that, because I made it clear to them. I'd learned the single most important principle of teaching: they don't care how much you know, unless they know how much you care.

A player named Bridgette Gordon had as much to do with bringing me to that realization as anyone. Bridgette was a six-foot forward from DeLand, Florida, whom everybody called "Pat's little girl." More than a hundred schools had pursued her, but she chose us after her mother, Marjorie, a nurse's assistant who was trying to raise eight kids alone after a divorce, made me promise to treat Bridgette like my own daughter. We were sitting on Marjorie's front porch when she said, "Bridgette's so young and she's never been anywhere, Pat. Please take care of her."

It was a relationship I never expected to have in coaching: surrogate mother. I was taken aback. But something made me accept it: sitting on the porch that day, I promised Marjorie that I would treat Bridgette like my own daughter. The fact was, I had my share of motherly feelings and needed someplace to put them, and, well, here were all these kids right in front of me. I already felt deeply committed to them, and surrogate parenthood was just a small last emotional step. And Bridgette was adorable, with a crooked perpetual smile, and brown eyes so animated they almost shot sparks.

But I was an inexperienced mother figure, and during Bridgette's freshman year, I made some mistakes with her — the kind any new parent makes when trying to strike a balance between nurture and discipline, watchfulness and hovering, pride and demand. To complicate matters, I was jumping right in with a teenager, and Bridgette was a typical one, moody, smart-mouthed, with a habit of rolling her eyes and mumbling under her breath when she was spoken to. Which drove me crazy.

Pat could ride you for five straight hours, and then with a snap, at three o'clock, right after practice, she'd invite me into her office and want to know how my day was. She'd ask how my mother was doing. I'd think, "You just rode me for five hours and you want to know how me and my mama's doing? I'm doing fine — and I don't want to talk to you."

— BRIDGETTE GORDON

When I scheduled a three-mile training run, and it rained, Bridgette assumed I'd cancel it. "Get your rain suits on, that's what I bought 'em for," I said. Bridgette sighed, and murmured under her breath. When it snowed, she cut class, for which I made her do a five A.M. workout. I got on her for everything from her body language to dress; she had a taste for rattling gold jewelry and was always styling her high wedge of hair in the latest do.

She said, "Respect is not demanded, it's earned. So if you want to be respected, this is how you carry yourself. That Lady Vols across your chest is not about Bridgette Gordon, it's about this program and the people before you, and the people before them, and you're going to carry yourself like a lady, and act like a lady, on and off this court. You're going to dress appropriately, carry yourself appropriately." Forget about basketball, she taught me how to be a woman, demanded I act like a woman.

— BRIDGETTE GORDON

But Bridgette almost left the program at Christmas that season because of one of my parental overreactions. We'd gone to Hawaii for a tournament, and early one morning I got word that Bridgette's first semester report card had come in, and it wasn't good. In fact, it said her grade point average was 0.0. I learned later that her first-quarter grades had been withheld because she had some unpaid library fines, but I didn't know that yet — I just thought Bridgette had cut so many classes she had no grades. I flew off the handle. I found Mickie and Holly on Waikiki Beach and told them, "I just found out Bridgette's grades. She's got a goose egg. We've got to go talk to her."

Mickie pointed to the surf. I saw Bridgette, in a yellow bathing suit and swim cap, hanging ten on a surfboard and heading into shore. I waved her over.

"Bridgette Gordon, I knew you'd been acting funny!"

"Ma'am?"

"Did I tell you that you could speak?"

"No, ma'am."

"Your GPA is 0.0."

"Excuse me? But . . ."

"Did I tell you to speak?"

"No, ma'am."

"I've had just about enough of you. I'm tired of worrying myself to death over you. I ought to send you back to Florida on a raft with a slow leak."

I started crying and I said, "A raft from Hawaii? What kind of person are you?"
— BRIDGETTE GORDON

I stormed off, leaving Mickie and Holly to talk to Bridgette more calmly and try to figure out what had happened. The crisis was resolved when we got word that Bridgette was in good academic standing but owed money to the library. By then Bridgette was mad.

"You know what?" she told Mickie. "When I go home for Christmas, I'm not coming back. So she doesn't *have* to worry about me anymore."

But when Bridgette got home to DeLand for the holidays and told Marjorie she didn't intend to return to Tennessee, Marjorie just smiled and said, "Oh yeah, you're going back."

For all of the structure and discipline at Tennessee, I also liked to indulge Bridgette and the rest of our players, whether it was with ice cream sundaes at pregame meals, or road trips to New York and Hawaii. The reward of being a teacher is to watch the widening of young eyes when they experience something new, and one night on a road trip to Notre Dame, I got to watch Bridgette's face as she saw snow for the first time.

We came out of a restaurant into a white curtain. Bridgette was elated; she'd been hoping to see snow ever since she left Florida, and right at her feet there was a foot of it. I watched her scoop up a handful, and I said, "Do you want to go play in it?" Bridgette's eyes turned into bright pennies and she nodded.

"If you've never seen snow, then you've never done a doughnut, have you?"

She shook her head. "Come on," I said, and pulled my rental car keys out of my purse. Bridgette and a couple of other players loaded into the passenger seats, and I said, "Buckle up." The empty parking lot was carpeted in white. I said, "Hang on." I hit the accelerator — and then the brake — and spun the wheel. The car went into a 360, sliding across the snow-slick asphalt, and the kids shrieked with pleasure. In the seat next to me I heard Bridgette expel her breath, "Whoooo." Bridgette couldn't get over it. I did several 360s before I got tired of seeing Bridgette's eyes widen. Finally she said, "Okay, I think I've seen enough snow now."

At the end of that season I took Bridgette home to Henrietta with me. She was scheduled to fly out of Nashville to an all-star international tournament called the Olympic Festival, and I was going to the farm that same week, so I invited her to come meet my family and to see where I'd come from; it was my way of saying to her, "You're part of my family too." We walked around the tobacco fields and I explained to her how I'd grown up. She stared at the cows and other livestock and watched the picking of tomatoes and snap peas in the garden behind the house. She sat down with us for a large family supper and watched how my mother served and waited on everybody at the table.

"Do you ever rest, Miss Hazel?" Bridgette asked.

Mama just laughed and shook her head.

Pat was my mother away from home. And she took me home like the daughter she didn't have.

— BRIDGETTE GORDON

After that, Bridgette didn't roll her eyes and mumble at me anymore. She looked me in the eye, and even sometimes teasingly called me "Treesh," like she'd heard my family do. By the time Bridgette graduated with a degree in political science, everybody would call her "Little Pat," or "Little Trish," or "Pat Junior." Some of our players just called her "Pat's pet." But Bridgette told them, "She gets on me harder than she does any of you," and she was right. I got on Bridgette. But it was like I told all of them: the day I didn't get on them was the day they knew I didn't care.

If I had a great strength as a coach, it was that I got the most out of people. That very young team? The next year, they broke through and won Tennessee's first national championship.

In 1986–1987 it all finally came together for us: players, staff, and philosophy. It seemed like every kid on that team needed something more from me than just basketball coaching, a different kind of caring. They were a project, all of them interesting characters with their own issues. Some of them needed love — and some of them needed tough love.

There was Dawn Marsh, a showy junior guard from Alcoa, Tennessee, who drove me crazy with her reckless flamboyant passes behind her back, which sometimes flew into the third row. I accused her of trying to give balls away to the crowd as souvenirs. She made me so mad once I chased her down a hallway, ran her up against a wall, put a hand on either side of her head, and leaned in and said, "You been reading too many of your press clippings and they're *not* accurate." Melissa McCray was the perfect balance to Dawn: a great guard who was so churchy and responsible that our players called her "Emma," claiming she reminded them of their grandmother, and Emma was the most grandmotherly name they could think of. Melissa was the kind of leader who got her teammates up on Sunday morning after they had been out at the clubs and made them go to religious services.

Sheila Frost was a six-four sophomore forward from Pulaski, Tennessee, who was such a gentle young woman trapped in a big body that her nickname was "Pee-Wee," a tag that I loathed and forbade anyone to use.

"She is not a Pee-Wee," I announced. "She is a GIANT. We do not have any weak individuals on this team."

Carla McGhee was a six-foot-three freshman from Peoria, Illinois, with an attitude, who for much of that season wasn't even sure she wanted to stay at Tennessee. She was tough, raw, and cocky, but she only played hard in spurts. She resented the regimented aspects of the program, and our skirmish started on the very first day of fall workouts, when I made the team line up for a three-mile training run.

Carla said, "I told you black people don't do distance. I can run a fifty or a hundred or a two hundred, but I'm not going to run three miles."

I said, "I told you I don't see color. Start running."

Carla fought me throughout that year, and I kicked her out of practice on more than one occasion for loafing, or for resisting me. She'd complain that she hadn't intended to join the army. I could feel her lack of commitment, and one day I chased her down outside of Stokely and demanded to know what her issue was.

She said, "You need to just go on, Pat, before I say something we'll both regret."

"Say it," I said. "You *say* it."

"I think I need to transfer," she said. "I think I need to play for a black coach. I want to go play for Vivian Stringer."

I told her I could arrange that — Iowa's Vivian Stringer was a good friend of mine.

Then we both calmed down, and we sat on some steps and really talked. I told her to think about it and if she was serious, I'd help her transfer anyplace in the country. We reached an uneasy truce. I could afford to be calm, because I knew Carla's mother wasn't going to let her go anywhere.

No one was more needy than Kathy Spinks, financially. She was a six-foot-two broad-shouldered young woman with a tumble of auburn hair, and she came from a little coal-mining town, Belfry, Kentucky, so far up in the hills that the roads didn't have guardrails. Her home was not unlike the one I'd been born in. I can remember the winding mountain road, and the coal trucks that rumbled by, and then the little cabin with no phone or running water. You could see that even the basics, food and clothing, were hard to come by for that family.

Here I came in my good suit and high heels, stepping across their wooden porch. Several schools were recruiting Kathy, including Kentucky, and it was a confusing process for them. But her father solved it by telling her, "You're going to play for that Olympic coach."

I think I'm the only person that ever played

for Tennessee that's been grand marshal of a King Coal Parade.

— KATHY SPINKS GRIZZELL

When Kathy checked into her freshman dorm, it was the first time in her life she'd had a telephone and an indoor shower. Yet when her mother dropped her off, Kathy was wearing a suit exactly like the one I'd worn to her home on my visit. Her mother had studied it and then sewn a replica of it for her daughter. That's how proud those people were.

I kept Kathy's background a secret from our players; I knew what it was to feel backward and exposed. I could see her studying others, wanting to fit in but not being sure of how to do it or what to say. When we went to restaurants, she always ordered the same thing, "a cheeseburger and fries." It hit me that she didn't know most of the items on the menu and didn't want to seem uncouth. I began to claim the seat next to her and would quietly order for her, so she had some variety and learned different cuisines.

One thing Kathy couldn't hide was the fact that she'd never seen a black person before she came to Tennessee. She stared at her roommate, Cheryl Littlejohn, a center

301

from Gastonia, North Carolina, and said, "So, the inside of your hands are pink?"

Kathy had moments when it was too overwhelming for her and she was tempted to run back to Belfry in tears. At one point during the '87 season, she fell behind academically. "Pat, I'm gonna fail," she said. "No, you're not," I said. "You can do this. I'm not ignorant as to how you grew up. I know exactly. You're a lot like me. You can overcome anything." Everybody in the athletic department was pulling for her, but no one pulled harder than Kathy herself. She not only passed — she eventually made the dean's list.

> She threw the gauntlet down. She said, "I overcame it, now what are *you* going to do?" I think the phrase she used was, "Are you going to be a pantywaist about it?"
> — KATHY SPINKS GRIZZELL

A championship season, as it turned out, wasn't a matter of magical transformation, of something that had been hard suddenly becoming easy. It was a season with as many problems as we'd ever had. There wasn't a single all-American on our roster, and we struggled to climb the rankings all year. But we had *something*. A quality. We had people like Kathy Spinks.

Kathy was one of our so-called corn-fed chicks, a mocking name opponents eventually gave our beefy, muscular blue-collar frontcourt, a group that included Carla McGhee, Cheryl Littlejohn, Karla Horton, and Jennifer Tuggle. The corn-fed chicks battled and banged through the toughest schedule in the country; we played twenty teams ranked in the top 20 and lost to a half dozen of them. But we made our opponents feel it. Carla McGhee even wore elbow pads that made her biceps pop.

Just after Christmas we met the Texas Longhorns, the defending national champions, with whom there was no love lost; just a couple of weeks earlier we had wrested the number one ranking from them. When Karla Horton turned to sprint down the court, she accidentally ran into a Longhorn, and the player went down in a heap because Karla was so hard packed with muscle. During the injury time-out, Texas coach Jody Conradt, who was normally a friend of mine, walked down to our bench and began poking me angrily in the chest. "If you'd teach your kids how to play proper defense, you might win a national championship someday!" she said. I just stood there and kept my mouth shut out of respect for Jody, but our bench went nuts. Holly was furious and jumped up, saying, "Don't take that off her, Summitt!" We lost, but from that day on we called Texas "the wrong shade of orange" and vowed to get revenge at the Final Four, which was to be held in Austin that year.

To go with the corn-fed chicks, we had great leadership in the backcourt. Mickie kept her promise and brought in the best freshman in the country, a spectacular guard from Flint, Michigan, named Tonya Edwards, who was so tough she reminded me of a bramble patch. Then there was our angel-faced point guard Shelley Sexton, a senior from nearby Lake City. Shelley was a charismatic player, but she had a drawback: she was sweet. It was the point guard's job to be the floor general, to issue orders and to hold her teammates accountable. But Shelley was soft-spoken and gentle, and she hated to criticize. She'd say, "It's okay, it's okay." I'd shout back at her, no, it was *not* okay.

"You're too *nice,*" I told her in front of the team. "Nice girls finish last."

To teach Shelley to be more forceful, I resorted to a method you wouldn't find in any instructional. I made her plan and run a practice. She had to design the workout, set up the drills, push her teammates through them, and decide when something had been done well enough. I never said a word.

> For a good hour and a half she just stood there and watched. I was drained. Not only do you have to talk, you are in the drill. I just remember being mentally exhausted after that practice. But what a great way to develop leadership and ownership.
> — SHELLEY SEXTON COLLIER

By the time we got to the Final Four in Austin, I had a different attitude and feeling than I'd ever had about a team before. I felt at peace. Nobody expected much out of us — we were the lowest-ranked team there — but I was relaxed and completely confident in our kids, who had paid the price. I no longer felt it was up to me to make it happen; they had a certainty about them. When we checked into our Embassy Suites hotel in Austin, Karla Horton and Shelley Sexton came to my room. They looked me in the eye and said, "Pat, we came here to win a championship. We're going to cut down nets."

In the semifinals we stunned Long Beach State, the highest-scoring team in the na-

305

tion, 74–64. That set up a championship game with our old nemesis Louisiana Tech, which had upset Texas in the other semifinal to spare us the chore of playing the wrong orange on their home court. We had every reason to fear Louisiana Tech: they had beaten us early in the season by a dozen points, and my lifetime record against them was 1-11.

But here's how confident we were: at our practice on the morning of the game, we didn't touch a basketball. Instead I had the team lie on the floor of the Erwin Center, with their heads in the jump circle, and close their eyes. Then Mickie, Holly, and I talked them through the scouting report. It was almost hypnotic; the only lights in the arena were the center lights, shining on the circle. Even the CBS technicians froze, stopped what they were doing, and a hush fell.

In a calm, steady, self-assured voice I said, "Here's what's gonna happen." We went through our offense, asked the players to see it, to think about how it was designed. Envision how they would get around a screen. See how the game would ebb and flow, we said. See yourselves as national champions.

After that, there was a silence in my head

all day. By tip-off I was only anxious about one thing: I wanted women's basketball to look good for the CBS national television audience, so the game could grow. I chose my best suit, a blue-and-black-striped number with big square shoulder pads and the long midcalf hemline of the 1980s, and I curled my hair.

It was a rout. We held Tech to their lowest score ever, 67–44. Had them from the get-go. The corn-fed chicks set big, wide, immovable screens for Bridgette, who curled around them into the lane and hit beautiful little jumpers. Our players knew everything Tech wanted to do before they did it — wherever they went, the Lady Vols were already there waiting.

We were practically standing in their spots calling their plays out.
                    — SHELLEY SEXTON COLLIER

The second half was a matter of running the clock out. The last seven minutes seemed to take forever — each minute felt like an hour. I'd glance at the board, and only ten seconds had ticked off. After what seemed like another hour I'd peek again, and only forty-five seconds had gone by. Finally, the last few seconds wound down.

The horn sounded, and it was like my ears popped. Shelley Sexton threw the ball in the air and screamed with joy. There was a distant, jubilant bloc of sound from the Lady Vols cheering section behind us — I stood on tiptoe and peered upward and spotted my family and held up my arm. Then the biggest corn-fed chick of all, Karla Horton, ran over, picked me up, and threw me over her shoulder like I was a two-by-four.

It felt every bit as good as I imagined — every bit. I felt flooded with a sense of completion, and gratitude. I hugged every single Lady Vol and thanked them individually for making it happen. I said, "This team has played as hard and as smart as I could ask any team to play."

Shelley Sexton was the one who summed it up best. "Sometimes you have to go through hard times to get where you want to go," she said.

We were due — long due. But the funny thing was, once it finally happened, we barely knew how to celebrate. We got some shirts that said DON'T MESS WITH TEXAS, and crossed out the Texas and replaced it with Tennessee, and put them on. Mickie, Holly, Joan, and I jumped in a cab and went to Austin's famed Sixth Street, but most of the places were closed because it was a Sunday. We ducked into a convenience store and bought some cigars, because we felt like that was what winners were supposed to do.

Didn't even know how to light 'em. We just weren't prepared for a celebration. That changed.

— MICKIE DEMOSS

The next morning we piled on a plane for home. Shelley was carrying the national championship trophy, and as she took her seat she yelled down the aisle.

"Hey, Pat!"

"What?"

"Nice girls don't always finish last."

I started laughing. Shelley took her seat, and buckled in, and turned to Cheryl Little-john. "Nice girls don't finish last," she said again.

We came home to thousands of people. The airport was packed and the streets were lined with fans holding up balloons. Cars honked at us, and a fire and police escort led us through the streets. A fire truck even spritzed us with water plumes. It was the best part of winning, to find out how much people cared. Every business in town had a Lady Vols sign in the window; everybody seemed to feel a piece of ownership, from the dry cleaner to the drugstore.

The fans were all waving something in their hands. I looked closer.

They were ears of corn.

The truth? Winning is impermanent. It's as vanishing as the champagne in the empty bottle. After the din and the celebration, what lingers is not the cold metal trophy but the feeling of warm exultation you shared with one another. While you are still looking back over your shoulder, a season ends and a new one begins. The leaves turn over, and so do the kids.

We went to four consecutive NCAA Final Fours from 1986 to 1989, and won two of them, and I can't separate them in my memory anymore without prompting or pictures. But what I do remember is the intensity of certain events:

• In December of 1987, finally playing in front of the roaring, sold-out crowd I'd always envisioned, when Texas came to Knoxville for a number one versus number two rematch in our new Thompson-Boling Arena. The game traffic was so heavy I had to park my car on the shoulder of the road and I half jogged in my high heels, picking my way across a railroad track, to make tip-off. I'd just as soon have missed the game: Texas humiliated us, 97–78, and I was so angry I had the score painted on the wall of our pretty new locker room — in orange numerals three feet high — and for the rest of the season every drill we did had to be done in ninety-seven seconds.

• Making that squad run four-hundred-yard dashes to get them in shape, telling them that we had two kind of players, "tunas" and "rabbits," and declaring, "I'm not having any fat girls on this team."

• Wearing a bright orange outfit with white shoes on the sideline against Stanford, and walking off the court to hear a fan shout, "Hey, Coach Summitt! My boyfriend dresses better than you!"

• On April 1, 1988, at the Final Four in Tacoma, placing a prank call to Mickie and Holly's room at 7:30 A.M. on the morning of our semifinal rematch with Louisiana Tech, telling them that four of our starters had been hospitalized with food poisoning, and bringing Holly to tears before I said, "April Fool's."

• Losing to Louisiana Tech that night, 68–59, and listening to senior Kathy Spinks sob so hard in the locker room that I said, "Handle it, Kathy." Then adding, "Tennessee has been good for you, and you've been good to Tennessee." Telling the whole team, "You've experienced more highs than 90 percent of the population, just remember that, and learn from the lows. There would be no highs without the lows."

In the spring of 1989, on our way to our second national championship in three years, I was so superstitious that I went a month without shaving my legs. We had a dominant team with a 35-2 record, but the deeper we went into the NCAA tournament, the more convinced we became that if we changed a thing, the spell might break. With every game, our superstitions increased and gathered force.

We had to eat only Bluebell ice cream. We had to keep every heads-up penny we found — and God forbid you should come across one showing tails. *Don't touch it, don't even look at it,* we cautioned one another. We had to wear the same makeup and do our hair the same for every game.

Mickie would ask Holly, "Do you have the same eye shadow on?"

"Yep."

"Good."

When I made the mistake of telling them that I hadn't shaved my legs, from then on Mickie and Holly forbade me to touch a razor. Mickie asked every morning, "Pat, are your legs unshaved?"

"Yep."

"Good."

But on the day that we met Auburn for the national championship, I couldn't stand it anymore. My outfit required that I wear white hose, and there was no way I was appearing on national television with the legs of a German shepherd showing through my stockings. Anyway, by then we had beaten every opponent in the tournament by an average of 22 points, and I was convinced our team was strong enough to withstand a little superstition.

When Mickie and Holly walked into the pregame locker room, I broke the news to them.

"Y'all, before you even ask me, I shaved my legs this morning."

"You did *what?*" Mickie screamed.

Holly buried her head in her hands. It was the worst news she'd had in weeks.

"I had to," I said. "I'm wearing white hose."

Mickie was furious. "You sacrificed the betterment of our team for your *appearance?*" she said. "Why would you do that?"

"DeMoss, you need to relax and get out of this locker room and go calm down.

We're gonna win this ball game."

"How do you know we're gonna win it? HOW DO YOU KNOW?"

"Because I know."

I remember thinking, Now that's confidence right there.

— MICKIE DEMOSS

I was confident, and I was right. The Lady Vols beat Auburn by the score of 76–60, behind a 27-point performance from my little girl, Bridgette Gordon. There was a moment of doubt in the second half, when Auburn, led by a tenacious dervish of a guard named Ruthie Bolton, cut our lead to just three points, 50–47. Bridgette had gone suddenly passive and quiet on the floor, and I called a time-out.

Bridgette sat in the huddle with a hand over her mouth. I got within about three inches of her nose, and I said, "You've got about twenty more minutes left in your college career; why are you saving your energy?"

Bridgette just looked at me and mumbled something through her hand.

"Bridgette Gordon, quit being a baby! Get your HAND off your mouth and listen to me," I said. "I can't believe Ruthie Bolton wants this game more than you, because right now, she sure is outplaying you. Don't you hide on us!"

Bridgette just nodded and didn't say anything. It was a repeat of a conversation we'd had almost weekly for four years. "You've got to be the hero or the goat when the game is on the line," I'd told her. "In the eyes of the spectator when the game is over, you're going to be one or the other. But if you stick your neck out, I'll never criticize you for winding up the goat. Just don't let the fear of failure get in your way."

Bridgette went back onto the floor and wrote her name all over the championship trophy. She knocked down three straight jumpers — a series of power dribbles, jump-stops, and little pops into the net. She nailed six points in a row to send us on a 13–4 run to open the game up again.

> I looked at her like, "Is *this* what you mean?"
>
> — BRIDGETTE GORDON

But after it was over, I discovered the reason Bridgette had gone quiet and kept her hand over her mouth. She'd taken an elbow to the face, and one of her teeth was almost completely knocked out. The inside of her mouth was filled with blood, and her tooth was just barely hanging on.

> I wasn't thinking about a title. I was thinking about how I was going to look toothless.
>
> — BRIDGETTE GORDON

I was struck once again by how little control I really had — I would never score a basket for Tennessee. When I found out that Bridgette needed to have her mouth treated by a doctor, I felt so guilty I almost cried. I told the press, "I can't say enough about what she means to this team. To this program. And to me."

This time we knew how to have a victory party. The kids were big into dancing, and all season long they had begged me to show them my moves. I said, "I don't dance." But when it got to tournament time, Bridgette and I made a wager. She said, "If we win, will you dance?" I replied, "If you win a championship, I'll dance on a table." Well, as soon as the buzzer sounded, Bridgette went on CBS for the postgame interview and told a national television audience, "What you really need to tune in to is Pat dancing on a table tonight."

All the kids could talk about in the locker room was how much fun it was going to be to watch me make a fool of myself. Joan Cronan had arranged a victory party for us at the home of a Tennessee booster who had a home on Puget Sound, and the kids were almost giddy as they loaded onto the team bus. As soon as we walked in the door, everybody stopped dead and stared into the living room.

> I saw it was a glass coffee table, and I nearly croaked. But as always, Pat rose to the occasion.
>
> — JOAN CRONAN

Somebody started up '60s Motown on a stereo. The kids gathered around the table, clapping and chanting while I tested the glass. When I kicked off my shoes and hitched up my slacks and stepped on the table, they erupted into squeals. Bridgette hopped up on one side of me, and Carla McGhee on the other, and I showed them my moves on that slick glass.

> She went to dancing like a country girl, and we all fell out. A big old country girl.
>
> — BRIDGETTE GORDON

It was not the most elegant display, and I don't know how we didn't break the table, but that dance was the highlight of those years. Not for the reason you might expect, either. It was the highlight because Carla McGhee was well enough to dance with me.

It had been a long three years for Carla and me, since her threat to transfer. Back in the fall of '87, when we were all still feeling the after-glow from our first national championship victory, Carla had a terrible car accident. On the day before we were to start practicing for the '88 season, she and a friend were driving through Knoxville when another car plowed into them. The force of the crash threw her through the windshield. The rescue crew had to cut the top of the car away to get to her, and when they pulled her out, they couldn't believe how badly she was broken up.

She was in a coma when I reached her hospital bedside, and her face and body were so shattered and swollen I didn't recognize her. She had broken all but two bones in her face and several more in her body. Her right arm, her hip, her jaw, and her voice box were badly damaged.

Spectators, people on the outside, always supposed that the worst thing that could happen to me as a coach was to lose in a big game. Wrong. The worst thing that could happen was to stand by helplessly and see a player hurt. It was an ever-present dread and the worst, most helpless aspect of the job. Parents sent their children to me in pristine condition, unmarked, and perfectly healthy. Every injury they sustained in my care, every little nick and scar, was a personal reproach. So imagine the feeling of looking down at young Carla McGhee and trying to summon the words to tell her mother, Joyce, and her foster mother, Clare, "I'm so sorry, your daughter is in a coma and they'll have to try to put her beautiful face back together as best they can."

Carla stayed in a coma for three days. I'd have given anything for the slightest sign of her swagger, anything for a smart-aleck word. When she finally woke up, I said, "I don't care if you ever pick up a ball again, but you've got to fight. You've got to recover. Promise me you won't let this ruin your life."

Carla couldn't reply — her vocal cords were too damaged to speak. She had to communicate by writing on a scratch pad, or by ringing a bell. She was in the hospital for two months while she underwent a series of reconstructive surgeries and skin grafts. She finally left at Thanksgiving, on crutches.

Even after Carla began to heal physically, she went through a difficult time emotionally. She still felt torn up inside and had dark, depressing thoughts about death. It took a year of rehab before she was able to run well enough to rejoin the team, and even then she was still uncertain and afraid of contact. "I feel like something in me might break," she said.

Carla worked, and worked, and by the start of the 1989 season she was a starter for us again, even though sprints still hurt her hip. It was a delicate coaching job, to be sensitive to her pain and fear, yet try to push her through it. "The body is amazing," I said. "So let it *be* amazing." But it was Carla who was amazing. When she stood on a coffee table with me, she still wasn't even completely 100 percent.

It would take a few years — but eventually she became whole again. She went on to get her diploma in sports management and was named to the 1996 Olympic team that won a gold medal in Atlanta under my friend Stanford head coach Tara VanDerveer, who said she took Carla for her sheer toughness. After the Olympics, Carla was a founding player in the WNBA and competed for several seasons before retiring in 2003. She's now the director of basketball operations at the University of Nevada–Reno.

Winning helps define loss, and the loss

helps define winning. You can't have one without the other, and if you did, you wouldn't know how to feel about it. Carla's accident — the fear of losing her, but then regaining her — put winning and losing in their proper context.

So did a more personal loss in 1989. Just a few months after our championship, I suffered my fourth miscarriage. This one wasn't early. It was far enough along that I had let myself hope that it would be a healthy pregnancy. It wasn't. I carried the baby for almost twelve weeks, and when I lost it, the miscarriage was incomplete and I had to go into the hospital for a procedure. Tears trickled down my face on the day that I told Mickie I would be absent from work, and why.

> She was very emotional about it. She was crying and said, "I have to have a D and C." I said, "What exactly is that?" And then she explained, and I understood why she was so emotional about it.
> — MICKIE DEMOSS

I thought I knew pain and how to handle it. I'd dislocated my jaw, blown my knee, and had a nail driven through my foot. I'd broken bones and torn muscles. But nothing prepared me for the tear in my soul that was my fourth miscarriage. Who would that lost baby have been? Athletic and stubborn chinned, no doubt. Blue eyed? Maybe. I grieved over characteristics of a child I'd never hold or see.

Over the next few months, R.B. and I discussed all kinds of options and treatments with my doctors. I was almost thirty-eight years old and a sense of desperation was creeping in. The cure for inner pain is time. But what's the cure for running out of time? The temporary answer was to keep hoping, and to pour my feelings into other people's children. I reminded myself that at least I had a dozen daughters.

My sister, Linda, was six years younger than me, but she already had two little girls, named Lindsey and Casey. When they came to visit, I would hold them and brush their hair. Casey was particular about hers and would whisper to Linda, "Mama, please don't let her do my hair!"

Linda knew what I was feeling and would say, "She doesn't have a little girl. Let her fix your bangs."

I wasn't at my best over the next few months after the miscarriage. The 1990 season was disappointing — as was often the case coming off a national championship. We were as talented as any team in the country, but we were uneven, and complacent. We should have had a powerful incentive: the NCAA Final Four was to be held in Knoxville, which meant we had a chance to win a championship on our home floor. But we seemed to think it would be handed to us, and I had a hard time motivating that group.

In December we went out west and lost to Stanford by 14 points. I was mad all the way home and decided our players had become overly entitled and weren't playing Tennessee's brand of ball. When we got home, I evicted them from our locker room. We had a new palatial, state-of-the-art clubhouse thanks to Joan Cronan, and I decided they didn't deserve it. Told them they hadn't earned such luxurious digs. I moved them to a visitors' locker room with nothing in it but a few folding chairs and blank walls.

They stayed there for a month. Every day Mickie or Holly would say, "Have they earned their way back in yet?" And I'd say, "Nope. They haven't shown me they can sustain it." Word got around, and *USA Today* did a story about how I'd thrown them out of their own locker room because they hadn't "paid the rent." Finally, in February,

I let them back in.

But I never made enough of an impression to cure their inconsistency, and everything I worried about came true. We went to the NCAA regionals in Norfolk, Virginia, expecting a walkover into the Final Four. Signs in the arena said THE ONLY WAY TO KNOXVILLE IS THROUGH TENNESSEE. Our marketing department had thousands of T-shirts printed up that said TENNESSEE AND THE FINAL THREE.

But in the regional final we met Virginia, led by a thorny guard out of Philly named Dawn Staley, who didn't seem to know she was supposed to let us waltz to the Final Four. Nothing would fall for us — we missed routine free throws, blew layups. We lost in overtime, 79–75, and at the end of the game, I knelt on the court, elbow on my knee and with my chin in my hand, woebegone, flicking my eyes up at that ugly scoreboard.

The Final Four would be in Knoxville — and the Lady Vols wouldn't be in it. It was the all-time low, the worst loss ever. I felt a sense of utter failure, and guilt that we'd let everybody in Knoxville down. When I walked into the locker room, I could see the kids visibly dreaded what I might say to them. At first I couldn't even speak, and when I finally found some words, they were uncharacteristically subdued. We would go back to Knoxville and act as gracious hostesses, I informed them, for the teams who had earned their way there.

> Pat was just sick, you heard it in her voice. But we were wondering why she wasn't yelling and getting overly excited.
> — DAEDRA CHARLES

Afterward I climbed into a van with our staff and Joan Cronan for the ride to the airport. Joan said, "I guess we'll just have to eat all those thousands of T-shirts back in Knoxville."

I said, "Oh no. That will be our practice gear next year, I promise."

Then I broke down and started crying — and couldn't stop. I cried all the way to the plane, and for much of the rest of the night. I cried to the point that it was completely out of proportion.

When we got back to Knoxville, I dropped a box of those T-shirts in our locker room with a thunk and told the team they would be wearing them for the foreseeable future. I also told them they would be working at the Final Four: among their duties was to serve as humiliated tour guides of our beautiful locker room, the one they had been kicked out of.

We all sat there in the bleachers of Thompson-Boling Arena and watched Stanford win the national championship on our home floor. It was a relief when it was over, and we could put it behind us.

We got over the loss and by the time spring workouts began, I had more reason than usual to focus on the future rather than dwell on past failures. One afternoon, a bright, laser-eyed sophomore named Debbie Hawhee came dribbling over to the sideline where I was standing.

"I dreamed you had a baby," she said.

Mickie was next to me, and her eyes widened into saucers. I said, shocked, and a little testily, "What'd you dream that for?"

"I don't know," she said. "But they took you away in an ambulance and you came back with a baby."

Not long afterward, I convened a team meeting to address some issues. First of all, I offered a transfer to anyone who wanted to leave. We were going to work harder than ever, I declared, because I didn't intend to live through another season of such uneven effort, and anyone who wasn't committed needed to move on. "If you don't want to be here, I'll help you go anywhere you want," I said.

Second, I had a personal announcement to make.

People on the staff had noticed that I was only drinking iced tea at dinner. When they asked if I was sick, I lied and said yes. But weeks went by and I kept telling the same fib, and it turned into the longest ailment in history. I kept the secret long past the first trimester, because I wanted to be sure. But after what Deb Hawhee said, I had realized there would be no fooling people for much longer.

"I'm five months pregnant," I told the team. "The baby is due in September."

After all the high-pitched whooping died down, and the kids finished trying to break my back with muscle-bound hugs, Mickie said excitedly, "And Debbie Hawhee knew! She's psychic!"

What's bothering you?

Did you read that paragraph in Sports Illustrated?

The one about life expectancy for people with Alzheimer's?

Yes.

I read it.

What did you think?

Look, I think it's a guess, and a bad one. It's an average.

[Crying]

What upsets you the most?

I want to see my son grow up.

— December 13, 2011, Piscataway, New Jersey, on the road with the Lady Vols, seven months after diagnosis

7
WORKING MOTHER

I was the most healthful, shake-drinking, yoga-stretching expectant mother you ever saw. You didn't hear me complaining about swollen ankles; I power walked five miles every morning and was so fit that at seven months I barely looked pregnant. But finally, the bump began to grow. It looked like a flotation device.

R.B. and I talked about names, and of course, Mickie and Holly jumped in with their opinions. I made the mistake of suggesting "Brandy" for a little girl because I thought it sounded pretty, which R.B. liked, but it drove Mickie and Holly crazy. They refused to let me subject the baby to such a sugary little identity. They were simply not having it.

"What's wrong with Brandy?" I said. "It's a sweet name."

"No!" Mickie said. "Not unless her middle name is Alexander."

Eventually we learned we had a boy on the way and settled on Ross Tyler. Even in the womb he was a mild-mannered, easy baby. He caused no nausea or moodiness, none of the usual complaints. I had just a couple of very small, quirky symptoms: all of a sudden I couldn't bear the smell of whiskey, and even more odd was my reaction to a particular brand of toothpaste. We attended a class for expectant parents, and the teacher asked us to name our various ailments. When other mothers discussed their morning sickness, I raised my hand and said, "For some reason Crest toothpaste absolutely turns my stomach." The teacher just stared back at me, blankly. "I've never heard that one before in my life," she said.

I took to pregnancy like an athlete, determined to be in peak condition for my labor. I was well into my third trimester when I led our team on a strenuous hike to the top of Mount LeConte — it was the third-highest peak in the Smoky Mountains at 6,593 feet, and you should have heard the Lady Vols huffing to keep up, trying to avoid the humiliation of being outclimbed by the pregnant lady.

I power walked right up until the day I delivered, and on those walks I would have conversations with Tyler. I had an idea that

I could get a head start on bonding with him and made it a point to speak aloud to him every morning, and again at night, imagining that he would get to know the sound of my voice. I would tell him about my day or my hopes for him. "I can't wait until you get here," I'd say. "I think you're probably going to be a little redheaded boy. There's a lot of redheads in the Head family. Redheaded boys with a temper."

The last conversation I had with him while he was still inside me was on the morning of September 20, 1990. I was two weeks from my due date, and I'd had a bad night, couldn't sleep, and was up and down with a backache and a constant need to go to the bathroom. Which should have told me something. I was scheduled to fly to Pennsylvania for the day with Mickie to see our most important recruit, an electric, bouncing guard named Michelle Marciniak, who was the top high school player in the country. R.B. was adamantly opposed to the trip. "Boys tend to come early," he warned. We bickered about it, until I called my obstetrician, Dr. Leonard Brabson, who, though he wasn't overly thrilled at the idea, didn't forbid it either. I told R.B. I was going ahead with the trip.

But that morning as I walked, I wondered

if R.B. was right. I only made it two and a half miles before my back started aching. I said to my stomach, "Buddy, it's hot for a walk today," and I turned back to our new home, a pretty wood-and-stone place on the banks of the Little River, a Fort Loudoun Lake tributary, only five miles from campus to make the commute with the baby easier. I went out on the back porch, and I sat down in the sun and drank a tall glass of water while I looked at the river. "You know, Tyler, I don't know about this trip today," I said. "I'm not real sure we need to go."

But then I did my usual deal: I told myself I could handle it. Michelle was taking visits from every big-name coach in the country, and we couldn't afford not to go, I rationalized. Also, I had booked a charter flight on the university's plane, at the suggestion of Joan Cronan, who didn't want me flying commercial, and I was reluctant to cancel.

"I'm going to be all right," I said. "Mom will be all right, so let's get dressed."

I always think I have time to do one more thing.

Mickie and I went to the airport and boarded the charter flight to Macungie, Pennsylvania. But I was very uncomfortable on the plane, constantly shifting in my seat to ease my back. Then, just as we landed —

I felt — something. I looked at Mickie. She said, "What's wrong with you?"

"Mickie, I think maybe my water just broke."

"What does that mean?"

"That means I'm getting ready to have Tyler."

Her eyes widened. "We're going home," she said.

I said, "No, wait. Let me call the doctor."

We got off the plane, and I found a restroom and some paper towels. Then I called Dr. Brabson on a pay phone, and described what had happened, and asked if I needed to turn right around. He said that I was probably still several hours from delivering, and women having their first babies tended to labor longer. "Do you want to stay and make the visit?" he asked.

"Well, I don't want to overreact," I said. "I chartered the plane and flew up here, so I guess I do."

I had heard a million stories of women who rushed to the hospital thinking they were having their baby, only to be sent home again. *Embarrassing,* I told myself. *Don't be one of those.* Plus it was a crucial business trip — I wanted to see Michelle Marciniak in orange. "I'm okay," I said. Brabson told me that since it was only a two-hour flight back to Knoxville I was probably fine, but I would want to keep it short.

I hung up the phone and said to Mickie, "He says I can make the visit."

Mickie said, "Are you *kidding* me?"

She was a nervous wreck as we got in our rental car and drove to the Marciniak residence. When we got there, Michelle was still at school, but her mother, Betsy, opened the door. She gave me a hug and said, "How are you doing, Pat?"

"Well, I'm in labor," I said.

Betsy said, "What are you doing in my house?"

I explained that my doctor said it would be several hours before the baby came, and I wanted to make the effort to talk to Michelle. "Just don't tell her," I said. "I don't want her to be distracted." Betsy looked at me skeptically, but I promised her I was fine.

Just then Michelle walked in, radiating star quality. She was tall for a guard, almost six feet, with a kind of gleam to her, an open-faced girl with a shelf of white-blond bangs that hung over saucerlike blue eyes. The entire family gathered in the living room, and Mickie laid a large embossed book on the coffee table, and we began our song and dance about the virtues of the

University of Tennessee, showing her pictures of the dorms and other facilities. But any hope I had for a calm, undistracted visit disappeared. Everyone in the room was tense, including the family dog.

> So I walk in, and something seems a little bit strange, everyone's on edge. I didn't have a clue, but I knew that things weren't right. People were not relaxed. My dad's sitting on the edge of the sofa jingling his change in his pocket, and my dog Frosty is running around like crazy.
>
> — MICHELLE MARCINIAK

It was the most rushed, hurried presentation ever. Mickie flipped the pages and talked so fast that she sounded like she was motorized. She said, "This is the dorm this is where you'll sleep this is the cafeteria this is where you'll eat this is the weight room this is where you'll train . . ."

All of sudden, I felt a spasm. I made a small sound, stood up and excused myself, and went to the bathroom. My back was killing me — I suspected I was having contractions, but I never envisioned feeling them in my back. After a bit it eased, and I went back in the living room and sat down again. Mickie was still flipping through pictures, saying, "This is the student center this is the academic support center where you'll study this is the administration building . . ."

I felt another contraction. I suppressed a moan, stood up and excused myself again, and went into the other room to call Dr. Brabson. I explained the situation, and he said, "Why don't you just come on home."

Pat is getting up and going to the bathroom, and coming back in. Gets up, uses the phone, and comes back in. Gets up, uses the bathroom, comes back in. Gets up, uses the phone. And I'm like, Okay, seriously, what is going on?
— MICHELLE MARCINIAK

I walked back in the living room, and I said, "Michelle, I'm afraid we have to cut this visit short. The baby is on its way." All of a sudden it clicked with her why her dad was pacing and fiddling with the change in his pocket. I turned to Mickie. "We've got to go. Now," I said.

Michelle stared at me with big alarmed seventeen-year-old eyes that said, *Are you about to have a baby on my couch?* Everyone immediately went into motion. Mickie babbled that she wasn't sure she could find

337

her way back to the airport, so Michelle and her brother Steve offered to lead us there in their car. We went speeding through town at eighty miles per hour — and at one point took a shortcut the wrong way down a one-way street. As we wove through traffic, I went into another contraction and tilted the passenger seat all the way back and started groaning again.

I look back in the rearview mirror, and I see Pat's feet on the dashboard. Her head is back and you can tell she's in a lot of pain. And we're flying. We go through stoplights, Do Not Enters, stop signs, just to get to the private airport.
— MICHELLE MARCINIAK

We finally got to the area where the private planes were parked, and we pulled onto the tarmac. Michelle and Steve stopped at the gate and watched us with their fingers up on a chain-link fence. Here's what they witnessed: I walked up the steps and boarded UT's King Air 200, while Mickie hurriedly ran up the steps of another plane. Michelle turned to Steve and said, "Did you see what I just saw?" Mickie got on the wrong plane. I was the one in labor, but she was the one who was totally flustered. A pilot said to Mickie, "Can I help you?," and she realized her mistake and ran back down the gangway and found her way to our plane.

I settled in my seat and thought about R.B. I had called him just before we left the terminal. I said, "Well, my water broke, and I'm on my way back."

"Oh boy," he said. "Okay."

I knew the thing to do was to be calm. I remember looking at my officemate and grinning, and saying, "Well, are you still in Pennsylvania?" I think she said, "Yes, Mickie tried to get us killed going back to the airport," and we laughed, and I said, "Well, what do you need me to do?"
— R.B. SUMMITT

R.B. said, "Do you think you need an ambulance?"

"That might not be a bad idea," I said.

I explained to our pilots, Dave Curry and Steve Rogers, that I was in labor, and I asked if they had any wine on board; I had read in one of my pregnancy books that a glass of red wine could slow contractions.

"No," Dave said, "but there is a bottle of bourbon on board."

"Well, give me that," I said.

He brought me a plastic cup full of it, but I took one whiff and turned my head away. I couldn't possibly drink it. "Here," I said, and handed it to Mickie.

She belted a big swallow. Tossed it right down.

The pilots asked for an emergency takeoff and got clearance. As the wheels went up I fished around in my briefcase and handed Mickie an emergency pamphlet I carried on how to deliver a baby. She accepted it, with a look of stark terror, and began reading — and downed another belt of bourbon.

We were airborne when the contractions began again, and this time the spasms were so bad I couldn't sit in my seat. I got down on my hands and knees in the narrow aisle, moaning. Mickie rubbed my back, but my moaning got louder and turned into a wail. Mickie jabbered at me nervously about Ruthie Bolton, the great Auburn player who came from a family of twenty-one children.

"It's okay, Pat; just think about Ruthie Bolton's mother. She had twenty-one children. If she had twenty-one, you can have one."

I said, "Mickie, you have to calm down."

Then a contraction struck and I wailed again, and the noise made its way to the cockpit, where our pilots were growing nervous. They radioed ahead and asked for an emergency landing at the closest airport, which was Roanoke, Virginia. Steve came to the back of the plane, where I was still on all fours.

Steve whispered to Mickie that they wanted to land the plane and get me to a hospital. After he returned to the cockpit, Mickie said, "Pat, they want to put us down in Virginia and get you an ambulance."

Now, I had no intention of giving birth to my baby in Virginia. Virginia was the school that had knocked us out of the NCAA tournament, and caused me so much pain. As far as I was concerned at that moment, it was a hateful state with absolutely nothing to recommend it. My baby wasn't going to be born anywhere but Tennessee. My home was in Tennessee, and my husband was in Tennessee. R.B. was going to be present at the birth of our son — it had taken us ten years to bring Tyler into the world, and I didn't want him to miss it. He hadn't wanted me to make the trip in the first place, and I owed it to him to get home if I possibly could. I did not want to face him if our son was born in Virginia.

Between breaths and clenched teeth, I said, "Mickie, you go tell them that if they land this plane in Virginia, they're going to have a *madwoman* on their hands."

Our pilot Steve had actually helped deliver two of his children with a midwife, but that was in a bathtub, not in an airplane flying in turbulence. He decided he didn't want to try it, and he hit the throttle, hard. I found out later we burned nine hundred gallons of fuel in an hour, flew so fast that the plane would have black exhaust streaks along the sides when we landed.

R.B. was waiting for me on the ground with an ambulance, and I thought he was going to climb over the seat and drive it himself. We got to St. Mary's Hospital at about 7:30 P.M., and by then it had gone out over radio scanners that the UT plane had requested an ambulance for Coach Summitt, so it was all over Knoxville that I was in labor. We checked in under the name Patricia Smith for privacy, which led to a scene when Holly came to the hospital and tried to find us. Mickie had called and left a message on her answering machine to tell her what was happening.

Mickie's voice said, so nice and calm and steady, "Holly, uhhhhhh, Pat has gone into labor." She was so calm I knew something was wrong. I was running around like I was the daddy.

— HOLLY WARLICK

When Holly arrived at the hospital, an administrator wouldn't tell her what room I was in. Holly said, "Well, I *will* find her," and she charged up the stairs and ran around the maternity ward, yelling, "Pat? PAT? Where's Pat Summitt?" We heard her voice out in the hall, and R.B. went and got her. She walked into my room carrying a bottle of champagne in a brown paper bag.

Dr. Brabson arrived to examine me and explained that Tyler was in the "posterior" position, meaning that he was turned in the womb toward my stomach, which was why I felt the contractions in my back. He didn't want to do a Cesarean, because he felt that with some patience he could turn Tyler around, but it would be a while before I gave birth, and I'd be in some distress. I said, "I've got to have an epidural." I was over being brave. An attendant came in to give it to me and said, "This is going to hurt."

I replied, "Just hurry up and do it. Because after this, nothing is ever going to hurt again."

Tyler didn't appear for four more impatient hours. I watched some TV and visited with the nurses who all came in to chat. In the meanwhile, Dr. Brabson kept going out and delivering other babies. He'd come back to my room and say, "Another boy!" Finally I said, "Don't you leave this room again."

When it was time to deliver, a nurse asked R.B. and me if we wanted any other family in there with us. We hadn't planned on it, but we looked at Mickie and Holly and said, "Stay." At that moment, they felt as close as sisters.

I thought I was a tough coach until I met my delivery room nurse. She talked to me like I talked to our players. "We're gonna have this baby *now,*" she ordered me. When I cried out, she said, "Come on, aren't you tougher than that?" Mickie and Holly burst out laughing; they said the nurse sounded just like I did in practice.

My son was born at 12:18 A.M. on September 21, 1990. R.B. was right by me, and we locked hands while I pushed. He was saying, "You're doing great, you're doing great." Mickie couldn't bear to watch; her nerves were too shot from the plane ride, so she turned away to the window. But Holly stood right next to Dr. Brabson and saw every second of Tyler's delivery, and she would say later that it was a greater moment in her life than any championship we ever won.

First his head emerged, and then his little arm popped out. Then the doctor lifted him and laid him in my arms.

He was born and before the nurse even started cleaning him up, Pat said, "Hey, Tyler." His head turned right around, and they made eye contact. It was obvious that he knew that voice. And there was a bond right there that words can't describe, for all of us.

— R.B. SUMMITT

When Tyler's little face and eyes rolled toward me, I knew that he had heard every word I'd said to him for the last nine months. After the nurse cleaned him up, Mickie and Holly huddled around me to peer at him. That's when Mickie said, "He's got kind of a cone head." I started giggling, because in fact his head was pointy. Holly said, "Mickie, you need to shut up!"

I was exhausted, but before I fell asleep I made four calls. I dialed my mother, and then my mother-in-law, and my sister, and I told them about Tyler's arrival, and how much I loved them all. Then I dialed one more number. It answered on the first ring.

> I was up. I was waiting to hear from them, a nervous wreck. Pat called me right after she had Tyler. It was around one A.M. and she was exhausted, but she said, "Michelle, I wanted to let you know I have a little baby boy, Ross Tyler Summitt."
> — MICHELLE MARCINIAK

Our players were conditioning on the track at six the next morning when they heard Tyler had arrived. After they finished their four-hundred-meter sprints, they all trooped over to the hospital and sat around on my bed. I remember a forward named Lisa Harrison sitting at the foot of it, holding Tyler in her arms. It was obvious that he was going to be our own gender diversification program when he pulled his first trick by wetting all over Joan Cronan. I was changing him when Joan leaned over to take a closer look, and he just let it go like a fire hose over the front of her nice red dress.

We all burst out laughing, including Joan, who said, "I'm not used to being around boys."

The kids hoped that Tyler would sweeten me up and keep me at home for a while. But I was right back to work a little more than a week after Tyler was born; I just carried him with me to the gym in his portable car seat. I didn't have a choice: it was September, our players were back on campus, and the 1990–1991 season was just a couple of months away. I was lucky that my job wasn't a nine-to-five affair; my hours were flexible, and I could sleep in every morning while our players were in class and take my infant son to the office with me. I felt great; I was full of love and excitement, and the fatigue of middle-of-the-night feedings was nothing a catnap couldn't cure. Ty attended his first Lady Vols practice when he was eight days old, sitting on the sidelines out of the way.

I loved everything about being a mother; there were no hard parts for me. I'd had so many miscarriages, lost so many children, that anything to do with an infant seemed wonderful to me. I took Ty everywhere; he was always in my arms, and no new mother ever had more help than I did. I had a wonderful nanny, Vanessa Best Hodges, but our whole team and staff also cared for Tyler; he had a dozen older sisters and stand-in babysitters. Mickie and Holly carried him around constantly and teasingly called him their "sack of taters." Then there was my devoted longtime secretary, Katie Wynn; our first-rate medical trainer, Jenny Moshak; and an expert media director, Debby Jennings, all of whom felt more like family than staff and were always there to help haul his diaper bag and stroller or be in charge of his bottles and toys.

I don't know that I consciously set out to create a "family model" of success at Tennessee, but that's what we grew into once I became a mother. Partly it was by necessity. I relied on others for so much help with Tyler on the job — to sterilize his bottles, feed him, change him, tend to him, and play with him — that it didn't make sense to treat my staff like employees, or our players like mere students. We were all collaborators in this ambitious ongoing project that was Tennessee basketball, and then here came Ty, who was this fascinating addition and new facet to the experiment.

When Tyler came along, he had a tremendous impact. Family had always been important to her, but Tyler took that to a whole new level. Ty was so good for her with the players, because behind all that demandingness was an unconditional love, and that's a difficult balance, but she struck it.

— BILLIE MOORE

He was an ideal baby boy, so blond he was towheaded, with large, swimming blue eyes, and a placid temperament, and everyone doted on him. The players loved to see him arrive with our nanny at practice, because that meant I might go a little easier on them and cut practice short. As soon as we finished, I'd sweep him up into my arms.

Ty was around so much that when he was just six months old, he learned to imitate me while I was coaching. He was in his high chair one day, gazing back at R.B. and me with those solemn blue eyes, when suddenly he raised his arm up and pointed like I did when I called out a play. We just died laughing.

We loved it when Ty would show up because we knew practice was about to be over. I just remember this fierce competitor, someone who didn't allow you to cut corners and who gave us the discipline to win, but then you saw this gentle side of her when Ty would come around; she would just melt. I remember she would reach out and scoop him up and he would have the biggest smile, and it really touched us. Even as tough as she was on us, we knew there was this other side of her. And I remember her sharing Ty with us. We would fly commercial and we would pass Ty around. Maybe I would have him, or someone else would. She allowed us to be a part of his early development.

— Nikki Caldwell

I brought Tyler to every game; he was attached to my hip in the locker room, where I would feed him and hold him until right before tip-off. I even carried him on my shoulder while I was giving our team their pre-game talk. Then right before game time, I'd hand him off to Vanessa or R.B. We put cotton in his ears to block out the crowd noise, and he would lie in R.B.'s arms up in the stands and, believe it or not, usually fall asleep.

Ty's sleeping, in fact, became another one of our superstitions: R.B. swore that if we were in a tight game and Ty dozed off, we always won. He'd look down and see Ty's eyes shut, and sit back relieved, sure that we were going to be okay. It got so everybody took it as a good sign. We'd be in a tough spot, and Joan would look over at R.B. and ask, "Is Tyler asleep?"

I could hardly get our players to put him down. They handled him constantly, especially our senior leader Daedra Charles, who acted like Ty was partly *her* son. Daedra was always leaving lipstick marks on his forehead, until it became yet another superstition: Daedra had to kiss Tyler before the tip-off of every game for good luck.

I was lucky to have Daedra Charles on our team at the same time I was trying to adjust to coaching with a new baby. She was such a strong, mature leader of our team that I could actually delegate responsibility for team discipline to her — she became my partner-enforcer on the floor, and you didn't want to mess with Daedra. She was a muscled six-three center from Detroit, Michigan, whom we called "Train," which was short for "Night Train," because she was so forceful around the basket. Take a basketball out of her hands and she emanated sweetness, with deep brown almond eyes and a triangular face with high cheekbones that framed a brilliant smile. But on and off the court she meant serious business.

She hadn't started out that way. Daedra's ACT test score coming out of high school didn't meet the minimum NCAA eligibility requirement, which meant she had to sit out her freshman year while she got squared away and more serious academically. When other schools gave up on recruiting her, I said to her, "We want you regardless. It doesn't matter to me if you had trouble on your test scores; I'm recruiting you because I want to help you be a better person and *also* a basketball player." That was just the foot we started off on, and Daedra felt an extra measure of loyalty because of it.

That spoke to me. It wasn't all about "I want you to play ball." It was, "I care about you as a person and an individual and want you to have both, to be successful at both." And they never gave up on me.

— DAEDRA CHARLES

Daedra also had to get her fitness up to our level before she could play. In the summer before she came to school, I called once a week and reminded her that when she got to Tennessee she'd have to pass a conditioning test, a three-mile cross-country run through some woods near campus. "Are you running your three miles every day?" I'd ask. "Yes, ma'am, I am," she'd say.

Well, she got to Knoxville and the day of the three-mile run came. Our team took off running, but Daedra only made it one mile before she dropped to the side of the path and stopped, panting. I pulled up next to her, and I said, "Now, Train, you *told* me you'd been working out and running three miles a day!"

"Yes, ma'am, I have been," she said.

"Tell me what you were doing."

"Well, I ran a mile and a half in the morning. And a mile and a half at night."

I glared at her — I couldn't believe it. I ordered her back to the starting line, and told her I'd deal with her later, and then ran to catch up with the rest of the team.

For the next several weeks I made Daedra get up early in the morning and run three miles. She protested that the trees gave her asthma. "Is that a willow?" she asked one morning. When I said yes, she started gasping and she said, "I'm allergic."

"I will get it cut right down," I said sarcastically.

It was child abuse. I should have called Child Protective Services.
— DAEDRA CHARLES

But Daedra grew into our most conscientious leader, and by her senior season in 1990–1991 she was running the team. I hardly had to say a word, because by the time I saw a problem, Daedra had already solved it. I'd bring it up, and she'd say, "We took care of it." Or she would come into my office and say, "I need to tell you about a team issue in confidence, and this is what I think you should do about it." I found myself following her advice.

It was like having an oldest child you could depend on to babysit all the others. The result was a season in which I could just teach and didn't have to worry about motivating the Lady Vols. There was a big difference: motivating is a lot harder than teaching, because you have to give more of yourself, constantly rack your brain to think about how to start somebody's engine, what to say or do that might get them going. On almost every team there were a couple of players who drove me crazy because they weren't motivated; we'd have ten kids busting it in practice, and one or two trying to cut corners. But everybody followed Daedra's lead: they saw how hard our senior star busted it and didn't dare go less than all out, for fear of what she might say.

Coaching and parenting had more than a little in common, I realized. The point of both was the same: to nurture young people to maturity. The previous spring after our painful experience watching Stanford win a championship on our home court, I'd told Daedra and the rest of our players they had to take more responsibility for themselves, and for what happened on the court. I couldn't drive them to a championship with a whip and a chair, like a lion tamer. It was too draining. They had to meet me halfway.

"I can't score for you, or get a rebound for you, I can only give you the information to be successful," I said.

Teaching and pupildom were a mutual exercise, I told them. "I will help you if you work with me. But you have to buy into what I'm teaching. I'll give you all the tools to put you in the position to win. But then *you* have to walk through that door. I'll get you to that point — then *you* have to take those final steps."

It wasn't just about working hard on the court, either. Everything within our system was increasingly designed to teach players to make good independent judgments. I was beginning to change the way we practiced; to encourage players to think for themselves I created game situations that forced them to make their own decisions. I'd put two minutes on the clock and a certain score on the board, and then tell them, "Have at it." I'd just stand there with my arms folded. After the segment, we'd talk about their responses, why they made their decisions, so they understood good ones and bad ones. The formal term for it in education is "situational learning." I couldn't stop a game, the way I did a practice, to correct them. I couldn't say, "Wait a minute, you didn't use your screen, and you didn't set your teammate up." All I could do was try to give them the knowledge and confidence to correct themselves, and perform when it counted in a big game situation.

Instead of *giving* them a playbook, I made them draw up all our schemes in their own notebooks. Rather than *giving* them a handout of team policies, I made them write them out. Writing things down would give them better recall and help them etch schemes in their minds, internalizing our offenses and defenses and out-of-bounds plays.

I also made our team rules fewer and simpler. I'd learned that if you have one hundred rules, then you have to police them, and kids are going to break them, and that just creates problems. Better to have a few rules, but strictly enforce them. I treated them as adults, until they gave me a reason not to, and usually they didn't. As long as they abided by the rules, I was pretty flexible. But if they didn't, I could be as tough as any person they'd ever met. But I also prided myself on being fair, firm, and consistent.

We acquired such a reputation for being highly disciplined in everything we did that kids from other schools called us the Cookie Factory. They said we turned out "cookie-cutter" players, teased us that our program was too regimented. But it was my observation that young people wanted discipline, even craved it, because they wanted to succeed. They wanted an environment of healthy structure, one in which they felt I cared about them and cared that they did things the right way. Deep down they understood there was a relationship between discipline and success, and they wanted me to show it to them.

Our rules and policies were just another expression of caring. There is an old saying, "Rules without relationship result in rebellion." The thing I tried to emphasize first and foremost was that we were all family — and you take care of and protect your family. We literally lived together: we traveled together, ate together, practiced together, did community service projects together, had classes and even summer school and camps together. Add it all up, and we spent around three hundred days a year together.

Pat would say, "You win with the person next to you. This is your family and you need to protect the family. You live in a fishbowl and there is an image you must uphold; you are an extension not only of your own family, but the UT family, and everything you do has consequences for everybody."

— NIKKI CALDWELL

A pickpocket got a load of our protectiveness on a road trip to Chicago. We checked into the Marriott on Michigan Avenue and then set out for a walk to do some shopping. Debbie Hawhee was just a youngster from Greeneville, Tennessee, and she had not spent much time in cities. As she stood at a street corner she was so busy staring around that she was oblivious to the fact that a man next to her was surreptitiously digging through her bag. All of a sudden the thief was surrounded by towering Lady Vol Amazons. Our trainer, Jenny Moshak, saw it first and shoved him away, and then Carla McGhee took over. After they ran the thief off, Carla scolded Debbie. "If you're gonna be in the city, you got to guard your stuff," she said.

Each policy told our kids what we really cared about: the Lady Vols had a 100 percent graduation rate; every kid who played for four years got her degree, and that didn't happen without rules and policies. Our reputation on campus was for caring about their academics first, without compromise. "Class is not an optional situation," I said. Lady Vols were required to sit in the first three rows of every lecture so their professors knew they were there, and no cuts or unexcused absences were permitted. If you cut a class, you didn't play in the next game. Period.

We cared about commitment. Every season I told them the exact dollar value of their scholarships and explained that we expected them to fulfill their end of that deal. "It's not going to be any bed of roses," I said. "You'll work for every dime. There is nothing free about it." That meant committing to our conditioning regimens. "Your head, your heart, and both feet better be in this program," I'd say. On Monday, Wednesday, and Friday they had weights at 5:30 A.M. On Tuesday, Thursday, and Saturday they sprinted on the track. Classes started at 8:00 A.M., and as soon as they were over, players were expected to be taped, stretched, and ready for practice, which usually lasted three hours. After practice they showered, ate, and went to mandatory study hall every evening until 8:00 P.M. (I'd learned from experience that the best way to keep players out of trouble was to make sure they were too worn out to get into much.)

The penalties for breaking any of our team policies were clear-cut; there were no mysteries about how I'd react. They were matter-of-fact and designed to show players how interconnected they all were to each other's success. Let's say somebody didn't get her study hall hours in. I made the whole team get up and run at six the next morning, and from then on they would police each other. Nobody wanted to chance it again. I usually had to penalize them only one time as freshmen.

We cared about their reputations and appearance. We didn't have a dress code, but we didn't allow hats or tattoos, or jeans when we traveled, because the players were representatives of a university. We cared about being respectful. No one was allowed to get a technical foul except the head coach. We didn't use foul language — I didn't even swear much in private, because I wasn't allowed to growing up, and I just never thought it was real tasteful. (Though occasionally the team would drive me to say, "What the hell do y'all think you're doing?") We made eye contact when we were spoken to, and we were polite whether we were dealing with a high-dollar donor, or a waitress, or a housekeeper. When we stayed in hotels, I insisted they keep their rooms in decent shape.

> Pat used to say when we left the hotel, Go back in and cut the lights off. You don't leave a place with the lights on and the TV on. We always had to go back and double-check. It was a little thing about respecting others.
> — REGINA CLARK

All this added up to a tremendous sense of pride within our program. We all cared equally about the Lady Vols logo, because we felt that over the years it had begun to acquire more than just the imprint of excellence from championships. It had begun to suggest a kind of character. Discipline on and off the court, adherence to deadlines, no tolerance for excuses — all these things were lessons in self-presentation, and the grounds for self-respect.

Daedra took our rules to heart as much as any player. Here's how accountable she was: she turned in a recruit for a morals violation. The young lady in question was a high school player visiting Tennessee, and Daedra was her hostess in the dorm. She woke up in the night and found that the young woman wasn't in her bed and assumed she'd gone to the restroom. But in the morning when Daedra asked, "Where'd you go last night?," the recruit replied that she had been with a football player she had met earlier in the day.

"All *night*?" Daedra said, shocked.

"Yeah, and it was fun, too," the recruit said.

Daedra decided she had to tell me. Only, she couldn't bring herself to use the word *sex* to her head coach; it made her too self-conscious. I think the more halting, dodging term she used was "chickabowwow," which years later still made Mickie, Holly, and me gasp with laughter. We sent the recruit on her way, after a sharp lecture.

Involvement in the private lives of players was a delicate issue that didn't exactly fall under my job description, but it required constant consideration. It was a complicated subject: I didn't want to be too invasive, yet I also felt responsible for them and knew their families were relying on me to protect them. Also, private lives could intrude on our team; on more than one occasion we'd had situations of jealousy. I tried to approach it like a parent: give them the information with which to make good decisions. We had campus experts talk to them about safe sex, but I added my own opinion on certain matters, learned from experience, such as the entitlement of football players.

Social lives, I told Daedra, better be conducted in an adult, discreet, responsible way. I didn't want to interfere with their lives, and I wouldn't show up unannounced on their doorsteps, any more than I wanted them interfering in mine or showing up at my doorstep unannounced. But I did say, "Don't let me find out about your business. If it reaches me, then that means you haven't kept it private. If I find out about your business, then I will be *in* your business."

It was Daedra who helped me deal with the team when I learned some players had been sneaking their boyfriends into their rooms after game-night curfew. Early on the morning of a road trip, I saw the boyfriend of one of our players drop her off at the team bus. She was a great player for us, whom I was personally fond of, one of those who had sat on my hospital bed the morning Tyler was born. But breaking curfew was a team violation. When we got to the airport, I told the team, "Circle up." We started every practice with a circle and that was a time to lay issues out in the open. "Circle up" meant we had something to discuss.

They gathered around and I said, "Raise your hand if you've had any males in your dorm room or apartment after curfew." Daedra raised hers, but nobody else did. Now here was a second discipline issue: I knew they were lying. So I said, "We will finish this on the plane. And you better not lie to me. You think about this; I want to know the truth."

I boarded the plane, and Daedra took over. "Y'all better tell the truth, because you know that she knows."

Debbie Hawhee said, "It's none of her business."

Daedra said, "Yes, it is her business, because apparently people are putting our business on the street."

Lisa Harrison said, "I know for a fact that people have their boyfriends over."

Daedra rounded on her. "You don't throw people under the bus. Don't you ever do your sisters like that again. Now listen to me. We got to circle up, and everybody's got to tell Pat their business."

That's how Daedra ran our team. On another occasion I had to talk to her because I'd gotten calls that some of our team were out at a bar called Ivys. They were only drinking Coca-Cola, Daedra swore, and I accepted that. But I told her it didn't matter; what mattered was the perception that they were sitting around in Knoxville bars. "Listen, I get calls all the time," I said. "Everybody knows y'all. And you don't know who I know. So you better do the right thing."

Daedra called the team together. "Don't even get caught with a cup in your hand," she said.

> Oh, heck, she had informants. Everybody knew us. I'd say, "How'd my mama know that?" I called her Mama because she acted like my mama, and they shared the same birthday.
> — DAEDRA CHARLES

Just like in a family, I didn't want our players running to me with every little squabble. Conflict resolution was a big part of what we taught in our huddles: if there was an issue, I wanted them to "circle up" and talk to each other about it face-to-face. I taught them how to run their own meetings without coaches, how to have a discussion and confront their issues in a constructive way, rather than backbiting. "Y'all need to figure this out for yourselves," I'd say.

Realistically, not every player was going to feel like a sister. They had their dislikes, rivalries, jealousies, and squabbles over playing time. Some players were very close, and others just didn't seem to speak the same language, and there was no rhyme or reason to it: Debbie Hawhee and Regina Clark were the closest of friends, even though Debbie was a Tennessean and Regina was from Saginaw, Michigan, whereas Debbie and Daedra didn't see eye to eye at all; Debbie resented Daedra's take-charge manner. But they had to learn to say, "Don't talk to me in that tone." I encouraged them to work it out among themselves, and by the time Daedra was a senior, Debbie could say to her, "I don't really like you that much, but I respect you." Daedra said, "Well, thank you."

I constantly tried to find new ways to get the family message across. I began to write our players notes, because I knew that getting mail from home was important to kids at college. It occurred to me that when I had recruited them, I sent them warm notes and encouraging letters all the time — written words from me had attracted them to Tennessee in the first place. But once they got to campus they no longer heard from me in that way. I didn't want them to suddenly stop getting mail from me, I decided. So I began to jot down thoughts and encouragements and stick them in their lockers. It was a personal touch that I wanted them to have. I could say the same thing twenty-five times, but when it was written down, just reading it once in permanent ink could make all the difference.

> Certain letters were uplifting, and when I got sad, I would go read those letters and it would help me. They were handwritten. Not typed, and they were personal.
> — DAEDRA CHARLES

I fed them. I had them over to the house as often as NCAA rules would allow, and I home-cooked for them. I'd ask them what their favorite foods were, and whatever they asked for, they got. Which meant there were some nights when pigs' knuckles and collard greens were on the table. Also fried okra, steaks, fried shrimp, red velvet cake. I got my own mother to come visit and help me cook for them.

I loved to take our players traveling. As the program grew, we began to make summer trips overseas for tournaments — one summer we went to Brazil, and we spent a Christmas break playing a tournament in London — and for many of them, it was their first trip out of the country. They'd never had passports, or certain shots, or sat in restaurants with rows of silverware. Teaching manners was part of parenting, and before we left, I had an etiquette expert come to our locker room and give them a lesson in tableware, how to tell a dessert fork from the main course utensils. I also gave them a lesson in foreign currency exchanges. When we went out to dinner, I urged them to try new dishes. Regina Clark, from Saginaw, had never tasted lobster before. "Try it," I urged her. "Try something new. Don't always order the same thing."

Some of our players had never been much of anywhere, just as I hadn't at their age, and travel was disconcerting to them, and they needed reassuring. Marlene Jeter, a redshirt freshman on the 1991 squad, had never stayed in a hotel with turn-down service. When we went to the Final Four in New Orleans at the end of that season, Marlene, who was from Union, South Carolina, came to my room to report that she'd been "robbed" in her Fairmont Hotel room. I said, "What's missing?" She said, "Nothing, but someone's been in my room." The bedcover was turned down, and there were chocolates on her pillow.

Maybe because of Tyler, I began to hear the sound of my own voice when I talked to our players. A common complaint from them was: "Pat is never satisfied with me; she makes me feel like I can't do anything right." Over the years I'd tried to change that. I complimented them, but for some reason they didn't register it, whereas they tended to hang on to the critical things I said. Even more important, when they didn't hear my voice at all, they assumed I must be unhappy with them. Which taught me a fundamental lesson: in the absence of feedback, people will fill in the blanks with a negative. They will assume you don't care about them or don't like them.

I told them "great job" more than they gave me credit for. But I wasn't going to be their cheerleader, either, and say rah-rah every time they sprinted down the floor, because they were *supposed* to sprint. Let's say Jody Adams made six passes, set four screens, or made five cuts. I couldn't possibly compliment her for doing all those things. It would just clog the gym with chatter. With too much praise you lose your effectiveness — just as too much criticism loses effectiveness. Eventually they tune you out.

With R.B.'s help, I devised an exercise in communication. Sitting at the dinner table one night R.B. said: "Look, let's come up with a system in which they have to verbalize both negatives and positives, because they tend only to hear negatives. Is there a way that you can bring some emphasis to the positives so that they are more aware of it?"

I decided to make our players say "two points" out loud whenever I gave them a compliment, whereas if I gave them a criticism, they had to say "rebound," meaning shake it off, take the lesson, and then move on. It sounds like a silly thing, but it was surprising how much better it made everybody feel, and we all started injecting it into our everyday conversation. A player would drop by the office and I'd say, "That's a cute outfit," and she'd say, "Two points."

That's not to say I became mild mannered. I was still a teacher who employed high-volume and, occasionally, withering sarcasm if the case demanded it. Which it did one day in practice when ESPN was filming us. Debbie Hawhee was a brilliant student who carried a 3.95 grade point average in literature. She would read the Greeks all day and then come to practice and sprint all out for three hours. Somehow, despite the workload, she would graduate a semester early, and she eventually went on to become a highly regarded literature professor at

Penn State. But on this day, she was having trouble grasping the principles of a full-court press. I stopped practice.

"Hawhee!" I hollered. "What's your GPA?"

Debbie just stood there, unwilling to say it aloud. "Unnnnnh," she said.

"It's a 3.95," I said. "And you can't figure out where to go?"

She was mortified.

Our program was no paradise, and my methods weren't faultless. I don't want to give the impression that every kid I touched magically became an all-American with a degree. Tennessee wasn't for everyone, and everyone wasn't for Tennessee. There were some players who didn't consider me family, whom I either failed to reach or I mishandled. In thirty-eight years, a total of thirty-four players either left the team or transferred. Their reasons were various: three of them were medical casualties, their careers cut short by injury; five were walk-ons who subsequently walked off; two left to play other sports; one left to get married; and four had overwhelming cases of homesickness. But the rest transferred because they either wanted more playing time or found me too demanding, or weren't a good fit.

I stayed with every one of them for as long as I thought there was some hope that they would get it. Even now, I prefer to think I didn't give up on them — they gave up on themselves, came to me and said, "I can't do this," or "I don't want to do this."

To be frank, some of those who stayed all four years weren't that enchanted with me either. Fortunately, they were gifted and resilient, and the stresses of the program usually developed them — in the end. But some didn't always get the caring part, only the yelling. Some felt used. Some didn't like a white lady with a southern accent barking at them. Each night at home, I would hold Tyler and chew my lip over whether I was being too harsh.

I was especially intense with the 1991 team because I was determined to make up for the dreadful loss to Virginia the previous year. It was an exhausting season, between learning to be a mother and trying to bring along a team that was half veterans and half freshmen. I juggled eleven different lineups, trying to find the right combination around Daedra, our anchor. "The first five in the game might not be the last five," I warned them. It wasn't the greatest Lady Vols team we ever put on the floor; we had some significant deficits and flaws, and nothing came particularly easy to us. We spent much of the season doing what I called "power drills": a dozen kids would get into a defensive crouch, and I'd tell them to imagine the power in their backsides as they'd slide around the perimeter of the court, chanting, "Power power power power."

But led by Daedra, they gradually grew into one of the most powerful, physical, and tenacious groups I ever had. Our point guard was a tiny five-foot-four Tennessean named Jody Adams, who looked so small on the floor it was like watching a hobbit with braids. Our two-guard was a gifted slasher-scorer from Canton, Michigan, named Dena Head, who seemed eternally and deceptively sleepy. Off the bench, Nikki Caldwell was a long-limbed freshman from nearby Oak Ridge, Tennessee, with a bass voice and such concentrated intensity she reminded me of myself.

Peggy Evans was a wonderfully attacking six-foot freshman forward from Detroit who clearly chafed to be a great player but needed some discipline and consistency in her game. Peggy was also one of those who didn't like being snapped at by me. Most of the time she wore a smile on her face, but when I told her to run, she got visibly resentful — quite possibly because on one occasion, I told her to run the stadium stairs and forgot about her. I looked up, much, much later in practice, and she was in tears because her legs were aching so.

As the '91 NCAA tournament approached I ratcheted up my intensity, and one day in practice I pushed Peggy too hard, and she had had it with me. It was right before the NCAA tournament, when I was always at my most demanding, and I'd decided I didn't like her pace running the floor. I started tearing into her — but that only made her slower.

"We're going with or without you," I threatened. "I'll leave your butt behind if I have to."

Daedra came running across the floor. "Pat, let me handle this," she said.

I stopped. Maybe Daedra's kinder voice was what Peggy needed. "Okay, Dae," I said. "But you better straighten it out." Daedra did — she talked quietly to Peggy for a minute, and Peggy settled down and became a huge factor for us in the postseason.

Once I had a strong enough connection with a player, as I did with Daedra, I could be as blunt and confrontational as I needed to be without worrying about our relationship. When I had a sense that Daedra needed her buttons pressed, I did it. That was the case with us when we got to the 1991 Final Four in New Orleans.

It was such a closely competitive tournament that there was no time for sweet little exercises like "rebound" and "two points," because our backs were to the wall in every single game. It seemed like I shouted us through the tournament, and by the time we got to New Orleans, my voice was thoroughly shredded; I was so hoarse I had trouble making myself heard in the huddle.

In the semifinals, we trailed Stanford 28–21 at halftime, and Daedra wasn't playing well. She was fumbling the ball and missing easy shots under the basket, and I could tell it was because she was feeling pressure that it could be her last game. She needed to fight through it — and sometimes anger could help a player like Daedra punch through to the other side, into a great performance.

I happened to know that she had just been named Tennessee's first winner of the Wade Trophy, named for Margaret Wade, which went to the best women's college basketball player in the nation, but it hadn't been made public yet. During the halftime break, I gave our team some basic instructions, and then I said, "Everybody out of the locker room except for Train."

After the room cleared out, I got in Daedra's face and told her about the award. "You're only the best player in the country," I said, seething. "You've been named winner of the Wade Trophy, the most prestigious prize in basketball — and you're playing like you just learned the game. Everybody in the country is going to say, 'Why did *she* win it?' Is this the best game that the nation's best player can play tonight?"

> I'm, like, Are we watching the same game? But she needed me to do more. She knew she could ride me and I would rise if I got that extra push. She jumped me, and those big blue eyes were piercing through me. I said, "I got you, Pat."
> — DAEDRA CHARLES

Daedra went back out on the floor and said to Jody and Nikki, "Y'all get me the ball. Let's go to work." That's exactly what they did. Daedra kept her hand up for the ball the entire second half. They'd lob it in to her, and she'd catch it and spin and kiss it off the glass. Daedra ended up with 18 points, and we won, 68–60.

That set up a national championship game that would endure as one of the most emotional and hard fought of my thirty-eight years. Our opponent would be, of all schools, Virginia. The dreaded, hated team that had broken our hearts a year earlier, the flagship school of the state in which I refused to let my son be born because the memory of that loss was so painful. The morning of the game, I dressed six-month-old Tyler in his little jumper and pulled a T-shirt over his head that we'd had made specially for the occasion.

It had an encircled Virginia Cavaliers logo on it, with a red line drawn through it.

Then I put him in a pair of tiny sneakers. No baby shoes for my boy. He was a baller right from the start.

My own fashion statement was a snow-white suit with gigantic shoulder pads. On both sidelines, the coaches looked like Cinderellas. Virginia coach Debbie Ryan had on a floral dress with puffed sleeves, and Mickie and Holly wore long pastel purple and violet dresses with hemlines to midcalf. It was the Laura Ashley era. We all looked like we were wrapped in designer curtains.

But I wasn't so crazy about the fashion statements of our senior Daedra Charles and rookie Nikki Caldwell, who proudly showed up with their jersey numerals shaved in the backs of their heads. My mouth fell open. I blamed Daedra. One of our team sayings was "To have a great leader you must have eager followers." In this case, Daedra was the great leader and Nikki was the eager follower. They had gone to the hairdresser together to have their necks shaved — they both wore short wedge haircuts. Daedra told the hairdresser she wanted something special. "I want number 32 in my hair." Nikki promptly imitated her.

> Years later I said, "Isn't that better than getting tatted? My hair can grow back and a tat is for life."
>
> — Nikki Caldwell

Mickie tried to be the buffer. She said, "Now, Pat, don't say a word. This is the Final Four." But I wasn't having it. I couldn't wait to get into them. I went to them and put my hands on both their shoulders and leaned in — close. "You'd better show up and play," I said. "This is not an individual game, and you don't draw attention to yourself that way. You better *hope* we win."

I told the whole team the same thing. There was no inspiring, Knute Rockne win-one-for-the-Gipper speech from me that day. The truth was, I knew that we weren't as talented as Virginia — they were bigger, taller, and more skilled, and I feared we had no one who could match Dawn Staley's weaving, acrobatic genius. All we had were warriors with a taste for grinding. I made the calculated decision to appeal to their combativeness. I said, "We better not lose this game, because I can't take another year of losing to Virginia. Can you? I *refuse* to lose. We are *not* losing to Dawn Staley again. If we do — y'all don't want to go home with me. I will be a madwoman."

Then I turned to Daedra. "If we don't win, it's going to be *your* fault, because *you* didn't come ready to play." Daedra just nodded. "Okay, I got you."

But at first, it looked like we had no business being in the championship game. We trailed Virginia by 10 points in the first half — Daedra couldn't make a shot and neither could anyone else. The only thing that kept us in was sleepy-eyed Dena Head, who went on a tear; we came up with a little isolation play for her and she worked it to perfection. Virginia was so preoccupied with collapsing on Daedra that Dena just kept slashing to the basket and either getting a layup or a foul. Slowly, we crawled back in it, and we led 27–26 by halftime.

But by then, Daedra had picked up three

fouls. We were as superstitious as ever, and Daedra decided that she had tempted fate because during pregame warm-ups, she hadn't been able to find Tyler and kiss his forehead. Daedra looked up in the stands and yelled to R.B. He handed Tyler down through the crowd — I looked up and saw our baby being passed around by strangers over the railing to Daedra. She put her lipstick imprint on his forehead. Our nanny, Vanessa, ran down out of the stands to fetch him and carry him back to R.B.

I still don't know how we did it. We were down 5 points with 1:21 to go. It was a matter of every player making a small difference with a hustle play — Lisa Harrison rose in the air and snatched a rebound — she would have 25 in two games in that Final Four. Caldwell raced the length of the court like a woman possessed to block a Virginia fast break. And a staffer offered a great suggestion. During a crucial time-out down the stretch, our graduate assistant Angela Lawson, a former guard for Louisiana Tech's 1988 national championship team, told me she had a play that she guaranteed would get us two points. "How do you know?" I said. She answered, "Well, we ran it to beat Tennessee." I gave her my seat in the huddle, and she drew it up.

It worked: Dena Head sprang free and hit a little leaner. We were still down by 2 points, but then Dena drew a foul with three seconds left. She went to the line for two free throws that could send it to overtime. Virginia called a time-out to try to ice her.

A time-out lasts sixty seconds, and in that brief, hectic segment you have to send a message that your players will believe in and trust. I'd learned that *the first thing you say, and the last thing you say, will stick.* Everything else goes in one ear and out the other. It was critical that the message they heard from me was positive — I had to instill confidence. "When Dena makes these free throws," I began, and gave our players some defensive instructions. Then, right before the huddle broke, I repeated it. "When Dena makes the free throws . . ."

Up in the stands, Joan Cronan turned to R.B. "Is Ty asleep?" she asked.

"Yes." R.B. beamed.

Tyler knew before anybody we were going to win that game. Dena sank both free throws. We still had to survive a pell-mell Dawn Staley drive to the basket that nearly went in, but it ticked off the rim, and regulation ended with the score 60–60. I said, "Yes! Yes!" Overtime was no waltz. The game was so physical that four players fouled out — including Daedra and Peggy. But Dena, who would wind up with 28 points, staked us to a 70–64 lead with another pair of free throws, and just before she hit them, she looked over at Daedra on the bench. "This is for you, Train," she said. It still wasn't quite over — the indomitable Staley banked in a three-pointer with four seconds left to cut it to 70–67. But Jody Adams raced her dribble up the court, and the clock mercifully expired.

Suddenly a ring of Lady Vols surrounded me; Mickie and Holly grabbed me in a group hug. As soon as they released me, Caldwell was hanging on one shoulder, and Daedra was on the other. Then someone handed Tyler down through the crowd again, and he was in my arms. It was Tennessee's third national championship in five years — but for me, it felt like a first. I'd never won one that felt so complete.

There was a huge amount of trust that transpired in that last segment and then overtime. There was no look in Pat's eye that showed any type of defeat. There was just a huge bond between us, because the foundation had been laid.

— NIKKI CALDWELL

I forgot all about the shaved hair. That night, we told the kids we would do whatever they wanted to celebrate, and they announced they wanted to see Bourbon Street. We took them out, and fed them crawfish, and then we wandered through the French Quarter listening to the tinny music and sticking our heads into the various dives. Which allowed Deb Hawhee to get off one of the great one-liners in program history.

One of the joints our players peered into was a burlesque club. They giggled and carried on at the sight of the dancers, until Joan Cronan scolded them, saying, "That's somebody's daughter." We crossed the street and continued our wanderings, until we came to another club. This one starred a burlesque queen named Lily St. Clair — who was showing her age. The kids peeked through the open door at Lily, and Deb couldn't resist.

"That's somebody's mother," she said.

The Head Family was too big for one little sofa. From left: Charles, Tommy, Kenneth, Pat, baby Linda, and my mother and father, Hazel and Richard.

Photo courtesy of Head Family.

Richard Head holds the newest addition to his log cabin family, baby Patricia Sue, his fourth child and first daughter.

Courtesy of the Head Family.

The skinny girl they called Bone, standing in front of the hay barn where we played ball.

Photo courtesy of Head Family.

A hayloft on the family spread.
Photo by Sally Jenkins.

The house my father moved us to across the county line so I could play basketball. From the roof you could see the drag races.
Photo by Sally Jenkins.

Trisha Sue Head in action at the University of Tennessee, Martin, with her hand-sewn numerals. The court was the one place I felt confident.

Photo by William Ewart.

The co-captain of the 1976 U.S. Olympic team shows off her silver medal shooting form. My coach and mentor Billie Moore is in the background in a white team jacket.

© Rich Clarkson/Rich Clarkson & Associates.

My coaching style on the sideline was very animated, as was my early taste in plaids.

© **Knoxville News Sentinel.**

Carried around the court by the USA team after winning the Olympic gold medal in 1984.

Photo by Debby Jennings.

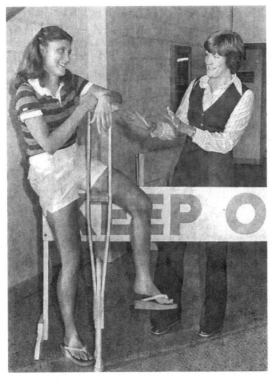

Teasing with Lisa McGill, who was still on crutches after her serious accident. A coach's worst nightmare wasn't losing, it was injury.

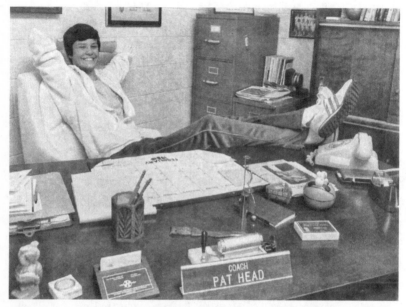

Jill Rankin was the first player who made fun of me — to my face. She takes liberties in my cubbyhole office, circa 1978.

*Mom loves her work. Writing pre-
game instructions with one hand,
burping Tyler with the other.*

Photo by R.B. Summitt.

Celebrating our first national championship under the scoreboard in 1987. It took seven Final Four losses to learn how to win one.

© **Knoxville News Sentinel.**

My son, Tyler Summitt, the love of my life, aged one. He attended his first practice eight days after he was born, and took his first Lady Vols road trip at two weeks old.

Photo by William Ewart.

Newborn Tyler attends practice, watched over by Daedra Charles, while Dena Head examines his perfect feet.

© Knoxville News Sentinel.

I made a family dinner for R.B. and Tyler every night. It was a priority no matter what the score or the season.

Photo courtesy of Pat Summitt.

The Summitt family in our happiest days.

Photo courtesy of Pat Summitt

Tyler was always a part of our bench. Notice the whistle around his neck.

Photo courtesy of Pat Summitt.

I was forty-three before I got my first hug from my father.
© Patrick Murphy-Racey.

With my parents, Richard and Hazel, at an NCAA Final Four party in the 1990s.
Photo courtesy of Jane Brown Clark.

With my mother on the night in 2005 when we broke the all-time record for NCAA Division I victories with 880. Tennessee honored me by naming the court The Summitt.

© **Knoxville News Sentinel.**

My parents in the stands at the 1998 NCAA Final Four. "That's about the best job you ever done," my father said.

Basketball took the Tennessee Lady Vols places we could never have imagined. Visting Westminster Cathedral, London, during a summer tournament swing overseas.

Photo by Debby Jennings.

I literally dressed down Michelle Marciniak in the NCAA Sweet 16, March 24, 1994. She kept the picture on her dashboard for a year.

Photo by Tom Ewart.

What it's all about: Kellie Jolly and Chamique Holds-claw receive their degrees, 1999.

Holly Warlick and I have known each other so long we think exactly alike. She was the logical successor at Tennessee.

Coaching Glory Johnson with one hand tied behind my back — after fighting off a raccoon. It was a tough period: I lost my father and my marriage, and began having serious health problems.

My great friend Mickie DeMoss always told me what I needed to hear, not what I wanted to hear.

© **Knoxville News Sentinel.**

Confrontation equals honesty equals performance. Calling o
our players in the locker room during the 2012 season.
© Patrick Murphy-Racey.

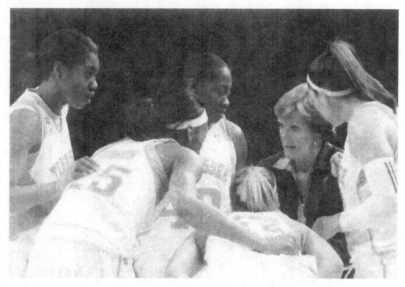

The huddle: you have sixty seconds to communicate, ar
they will only remember the first thing you say, and the la
Coaching my last team, 2012 season.
© Knoxville News Sentinel.

Tyler Summitt, twenty-one, new assistant coach at Marquette University and all-around phenom, works the bench while his mother watches over his shoulder during the 2012-2013 season.

© Patrick Murphy-Racey

Tyler visiting his mother at home in the fall of 2012.
© *Lookalike Productions.*

I want to ask you a tough question.

Okay.

If you could trade your championships for your health back, would you?

Uhhhh. That's not even realistic.

I know. But I'd like to hear how you feel.

[Pause]

I would give back every one of my trophies to still be coaching.

That says it's the teaching you really love, more than the winning.

That's right.

It also says that retirement is a deep wound.

Yes. It is.

— June 23, 2012, at night driving from Henrietta back to Knoxville with the tape recorder off, thirteen months after diagnosis

8
CHAMPION, PART I

The price of love is entanglement. My son became an inseparable part of our team and locker room, with no boundary between family and work anymore, and that led to emotional complications. For one thing, it divided Tyler's loyalties. He got crushes on our players, and when I'd yell at them, he would form a deep creased frown between his eyes and give me the cold shoulder. "I'm sleeping in the garage with Micey," he'd announce. Micey was the cat.

For some reason, Tyler was drawn to the young women I had the most complicated relationships with, players on whom I practiced the toughest love. The first great obsession of his life was Vonda Ward, and it was a May-December romance; he was three and she was twenty. I couldn't believe it, because it's fair to say that I never had a more complex relationship with a player than the one I had with Vonda Ward of

Northfield, Ohio. I loved Vonda and found her enormously interesting — she was an unusual, even extraordinary young woman who moved to a different drummer — but she frustrated me as a ballplayer. She was built like a superhero, a lithe six foot six with muscles everywhere, crowned with a blaze of yellow-gold hair that Tyler found enthralling. But Vonda had just one drawback: she was as hardheaded as a young Pat Summitt.

Vonda wanted to be a finesse player; I wanted her to be a physical, dominating force in the paint. Vonda wasn't having it; she was going to play the game her way. I'd tell her to do something, and she would stand there and stare back at me intractably, hands on her hips and rolling her eyes, until I came unglued. It was all-out war. I tried threatening, benching, withering sarcasm.

"I've never seen a post player before who is six six and wants to play as if she's five six," I said, exasperated.

Courage wasn't the issue with Vonda, far from it. She had a fascination with firefighters, and in her free time she trained as a volunteer with the Knoxville fire department. When I found out, I was tremendously proud — but it got under my skin, irritated me, too.

"You'll run into a burning building, but you won't deny the high post!" I hollered.

One day Vonda so frustrated me in practice that I grabbed a ball and drop-kicked it into the stands. Sank my toe into it as hard as I could and watched it soar into the upper loges. Then I kicked her out of the gym. "Just get out," I said. "Go." But the frustration was mutual. Vonda walked into the locker room — and punched a wall, literally put her fist in it. She was aiming for drywall, but she missed and instead hit concrete and gave herself a boxer's fracture. That's who Vonda was; a few years later she would become a heavyweight prizefighter and win a women's world title.

Knocking heads with stubborn young players was often a necessary part of their evolution. Sometimes it was the only way to convince self-concerned eighteen- to twenty-one-year-olds to set aside their insecurities, cares, motives, and agendas and buy into something as self-sacrificing as the Tennessee program. Usually, I could set my watch by their development. As freshmen and sophomores they were resistant and defensive, unable to bear criticism. Then they'd grow up, and by their junior and senior years they understood we were in it together, and they even got to like the sound of my voice.

But no two players were alike. Some were average adolescents with the usual sensitive feelings; others had truly serious deficits. I was learning that they each had different pressure points — and that was the interesting part of the job. I picked up a saying from the legendary UCLA coach John Wooden: "I don't treat them all the same, but I treat them all fairly." I asked all our players to achieve the same standard, but I couldn't ask all of them in the same way. Some took longer than others, and I'd think, *How long do I have to wait before she gets it?*

Having Tyler around was good for me, because he smoothed my hard edges and was a reminder to be patient, that each young woman was unique and their development happened at different speeds. Practice would end, and Tyler would sprint over to Vonda because he just had to be with her, and I'd grin at the sight of six-foot-six Vonda picking him up. But by then, Vonda was often in no mood to smile back.

"I don't know why they can't separate," I'd say to Mickie and Holly.

"Pat, first of all, they're kids," Mickie would say. "And two, they're getting yelled at. When you're the yeller, you can let go of it a little easier."

"I don't know why they fight me."

Raising a son in the midst of a women's basketball team meant an unconventional childhood, but I tried to give Tyler some choice in that. As soon as he was old enough to understand, I said, "You can come with us, or you can stay at home with the nanny and play. It's up to you. But if you come along, you have to behave. You have to promise to be good."

He wanted to come along, and he was good. He rode in the back of the bus, a tiny figure sandwiched between our players. He sat on the end of the bench during games, looking like a miniature assistant coach in khakis, blazer, and a clip-on tie.

I gave him odd jobs to do; he was just four when I handed him my briefcase and he started lugging it for me. When he got a little bigger I put him in charge of the little orange stool that I sat on in our huddles. During time-outs, he would run over and set it up for me, then scamper out of the way. He'd watch Mom give her speech in the huddle, then dart in and carry it back to its place at the end of the bench. As he got older he decided his role was to take care of me; he made sure I had bottled water and cough drops on the bench to soothe my throat, which got so raw from yelling, and rubbed my shoulders when he thought I was stressed.

It wasn't the most orthodox parenting style; I couldn't name another head coach who sat his or her child on the bench during games and wove him into the team to such a degree. But I thought it was crucial for Tyler to feel involved in my work, so that basketball was never something that took his mother away from him. Even in the most intense games, I would wander down the bench to speak to him, just to give him a moment of attention. To let him know that he always came first, that he was important to me regardless of the score. "What do you think, Tyman?" I'd say.

> I would say something, and I don't even know if it was right, but she'd nod and go, "Huh. Okay." And she'd walk back.
>
> — TYLER SUMMITT

Hopefully, Tyler never questioned whether he was my main priority. In 1991, my friend Kim Mulkey called me. She was a young, newly pregnant head coach at Baylor, and she was worried about her ability to be a coach and a mother at the same time. I reassured her. "You will never neglect your children," I said. "You will neglect your job

392

for your children." I believe we've both gotten it right.

I enrolled Ty in a primary school just off campus, no more than a thousand yards from Thompson-Boling Arena, so I could take him to school and pick him up every afternoon myself. He came to practice with me and would romp around with our student managers on the sideline or climb the bleachers exploring the TV booth. After practice we'd go home and I'd cook — we ate as a family every single night, no matter how late the hour or how tired I was, and R.B. and I did our best not to talk basketball at the table. After the dishes, I'd pop a tape in the video player, and if it wasn't too late, Tyler would sit on the couch with me. Every now and then he'd look at me and say, "Mama, can we watch something on TV other than basketball?" I'd give him his choice and we'd watch for a while, and then I'd put him to bed and go back to work.

I'd go to sleep listening to her scream at the TV, watching film of practice.
— TYLER SUMMITT

Somehow, he naturally understood to be quiet when I was talking to the players; he'd just stand in the shadows and watch. He was so ever present and accepted by our players, in fact, that I had to teach him a lesson about discretion. While I sat up front on our buses and planes with the coaches, he would travel in the back with the players, doing his little-boy homework while they read their textbooks. He listened to their chatter and, inevitably, he also heard their bitching sessions. Once, when he was about five, he came to me and repeated something they'd said.

"They told you that?" I said.

"Yes."

"You don't need to tell me that."

"Why not?" he said.

Tyler thought he was helping by passing on information. But it made me uneasy to think of my five-year-old as a spy.

"What you talk about with them stays between you and them," I said. "And when I tell you something, it stays between us. Period."

There were worse educations for a little boy than to hang around a women's basketball team, I figured, although when he began learning the words to So So Def All-Stars and dancing hip-hop in the back of the bus, I wondered. One result of being around a bunch of smart-aleck collegians who treated him like an adult was that sometimes I feared he was growing up a little too fast. He was just five when he started eyeing the presents under the Christmas tree, and then gazing at the chimney skeptically.

"Mama, are you Santa Claus?" he asked.

I stared down at him, with my hands on my hips. He came up to my kneecap.

"Do I *look* like Santa Claus?" I demanded.

It was obviously going to be a peculiar upbringing, and I was curious to see how he would turn out. As soon as Tyler was old enough to discuss it, I asked him what he wanted to be when he grew up.

"A tree cutter," he announced.

"Why a tree cutter?" I asked him.

It took a while to get to the bottom of it, but it turned out that he hero-worshipped one of our student managers who majored in forestry. It was a passing interest. A few months later, I asked him the same question again, hoping that this time his answer would be astronaut, or president of the United States. But it wasn't.

He said, "I want to be a manager."

"You mean like a basketball manager?" I said.

"Yes."

"Son, there'll come a time when you need to make some money. If I were you, I'd probably stay away from that particular career."

I advised Tyler that he could be anything he wanted, but I hoped he avoided the same line of work as his mother. I wanted him to be his own man — "Be anything but a coach," I said. But I'm not quite sure what I expected, given how enmeshed he was with our team.

The fact is I raised my own son almost as if he was another player. Tyler saw very early the repercussions when our team didn't do something right or misbehaved, and it gave him a healthy respect for my authority. I don't recall him ever throwing tantrums, or even crying very much. He was a limpid-eyed, sweet-mannered child who, at worst, got a little antic and red cheeked when he was excited, but he never wailed with tears. A good deal of the credit for that goes to a young woman named LaTina Dunn Haynes, who became his nanny when he was just three and remains a part of the family to this day; Tyler was the ring bearer at her wedding.

My philosophy when it came to rules with Tyler was the same as it was for our team: I only had a few, and I was strict about them. He was to say "yes" instead of "yeah," look people in the eye, and give a firm handshake. I talked to him like a grown-up; I knew kids who were still talking baby talk as teenagers, and it made me cringe. "If you act like an adult, I'll treat you like an adult," I said. He cleaned his own room and cleared his plate from the table as soon as he was able, and schoolwork came first, which wasn't a problem because he was smarter than his mother. I recall just one poor mark ever — on his first-grade report card. "You're better than this," I said sharply, and handed it back to him. From then on it would be mostly straight A's.

> Our family was run the way her team was run. So you do something wrong, there is a consequence. Just like with her players. It was "Hey, you do the right thing the right way, and I won't yell at you." How she ran her team, that's how it was at home.
> — TYLER SUMMITT

Like my father, I figured out quickly that you could influence a child with just a look or a tone and save yourself a lot of trouble. Tyler went through a phase when he was attracted to shiny things, and he was always lifting car keys off people's desks to play with them, and then losing them. Mickie and Holly and I constantly had to hunt for them. I caught him at it one day and leaned down to give him a lecture, with my infamous glare.

He said, "Mama, will you just do one thing before you yell at me?"

"What?" I said.

"Please put your sunglasses on."

The worst trouble he ever got in was when he went down to our dock to go fishing alone, which he was not supposed to do. I searched for him in a panic for fifteen minutes before I spotted him down by the river, which made me panic even more, because he could have drowned. "ROSS TYLER SUMMITT!" I hollered. I sent his father down to give him a lick for every step back up to the house. There were forty-four of them. He would take a step, and *whoosh*. He'd take another step, and *whoosh*. R.B. barely touched him, but it killed his pride.

Disappointing her was worse than any whipping.

— TYLER SUMMITT

There was one way I didn't imitate my father as a parent: I told Tyler I loved him every single day and kissed him every chance I got. He always knew from my voice and touch that he was the most precious thing in the world to me. My father had never yet hugged me or told me he loved me, or given me a direct sign of affection. I was old enough and secure enough in myself to not fear him anymore, but with age came something else: incomprehension. How could a father be so undemonstrative, and what had it done to me?

R.B. and I took Tyler to Henrietta for every holiday, and as I watched Tyler with my father, I saw that the grandkids got a softer side of Richard Head. Tyler crawled in Daddy's lap, and they would talk about his hunting beagles. My little nieces would throw their arms around him, saying, "Granddaddy, give me a kiss."

He'd say, "Awwww, girl."

My parents were aging, and the years of farmwork accelerated the process. My father had had two knee replacements and a mini-stroke that left him slightly dimmed. For some reason it also made him more talkative — he even teased with Tyler. During a family visit once we were all sitting at the supper table eating in silence, when all of a sudden Daddy looked at Tyler, and said, "Tyler, would you rather have a hundred-dollar bill, or a cow?"

Tyler looked at me. I said, "I'm not saying anything. You need to figure it out for yourself." R.B. knew not to say anything either, because he had learned from long experience that when Richard Head spoke, you shut up. I watched Tyler try to puzzle it out. The expression on his angelic face said *I don't need any milk because I got some right in front of me; Granny just filled my glass.*

Ty said hesitantly, "The money?"

Daddy's shoulders shook with laughter, and everybody smiled. I leaned over and told Ty, "A cow is worth about eight hundred dollars." That was Daddy's idea of a joke.

Tyler sensed the distance between his grandfather and me, but he didn't know what it was. I explained to him that Mister Richard had been a lot different when I was growing up, and I told him some stories about the lickings we got.

One day Mom asked me to go find the sugar in the pantry. I went in there and I did a halfhearted look, and I came back and said, "Mom, can you help me?" And she told me a story about how Granddaddy would take her out in the field and say, "I need this done." And if you couldn't do it, you'd probably get a whipping. And if you didn't do it on time, you'd get a whipping. And if you didn't do it right, you'd get a whipping. I went back and found the sugar. And from there on out I was sweating bullets when she would ask me to do something.

— TYLER SUMMITT

I never wanted my own son to fear me or wonder about my affection for him. I *had* to get it right with Tyler — because I wasn't going to get any second chances to raise a child. He would be my one and only.

R.B. and I were finally forced to accept that we would have no more children. We had continued to hope and to try after Tyler, but I suffered two more miscarriages. Finally, the grief not only put me to bed, it caused a marital crisis. I would lose a baby and feel like R.B. almost blamed me for not doing something right. We argued about whether to adopt; I was in favor but he wasn't and wanted to keep trying for a biological child. Finally, I told R.B. I just couldn't bear another failure. "I can't do this anymore," I said.

The miscarriages really knocked her down. And we had some arguments about that, I will just tell you. I felt like she didn't go to the next level. She felt like she knew in

401

her heart it wouldn't have mattered.

— R.B. SUMMITT

But finally we reached a peace. We agreed to be grateful we were blessed with Tyler, our healthy, easy-as-a-breeze boy who gave us so much pleasure. With that acceptance, for the next few years I experienced total contentment, the most completely happy, balanced period of my life.

Motherhood with Tyler so softened and gratified me that people began to remark on it. Trish Roberts was one of them. She came back to visit and after watching me in practice one day, she said wonderingly to Holly, "Pat's mellowed."

"Oh, Lord, don't tell her that," Holly said. "She'll tear the doors off."

Bridgette Gordon noticed it too. She had been playing overseas in Como, Italy, after graduating, but she came back to Knoxville in the summers to work at our annual basketball camps. She was sitting in our locker room during a break in the summer of '94 when one of our new freshmen, Abby Conklin, came in. Abby said, "Pat, I didn't have time to get my workout in today."

"That's okay," I said.

Bridgette's head almost spun in a full circle. "Excuse me?" she said. "It's *okay?*"

"She can make it up later," I said.

I said, "Wow." That's when I knew Tyler had softened her up for real.
— Bridgette Gordon

There were still times when players mistook my tough love for all toughness, and no love. The problem with running a team like a family is that it raises the emotional pitch: the investment is deeper, but you can also be disappointed and hurt by each other. One thing that all families do is fight, and they don't always fight fair.

I didn't always fight fair with Michelle Marciniak, I'll admit. All coaches are emotional manipulators at heart, and I was the very best of them. I'd become an excellent actress, learned to use all shades of my voice and eyes to get the reactions we needed from players. I could be warm or withholding depending on what served the team, and usually what looked like temper on my part was calculated.

Pat was so in tune with the players, with when to push and when to let up, when to put an arm around someone. She would seem so competitive and high-strung and demanding — and the whole time she knew exactly what she was doing. She was very much in control. She had this innate clock or measuring stick and knew how far she could go with them.

— MICKIE DeMOSS

I punched every button with Michelle, who was Tyler's second great love. Believe it or not, after the recruiting visit that ended with Tyler's birth, Michelle didn't come to Tennessee. She thought Notre Dame offered her a less crowded stage, and it was a mistake; she was instantly unhappy and began dropping me notes. "Hey, Pat, I'm following you guys," she'd write. She eventually transferred and had to sit out a year under NCAA rules, so she didn't see the court for us until the 1993–1994 season. But when she did, it was the start of a highly charged years-long clash.

I loved Michelle, but she was a headlong, reckless player who needed curbing, which created constant tension between us. In some ways we were a profound mismatch. I was all about structure, fundamentals, and discipline. Michelle was all about freelancing and risk taking. She played on pure impulse, and the press nicknamed her "Spinderella" for her showy whirls to the basket, which the crowds loved. But sometimes her gambles were scatterbrained and costly. I tried to explain, calmly at first, that it was a form of self-absorption.

"Michelle, when you go down and you do a 360 spin move and hit the woman in the third row eating popcorn with the ball, when you do that, you're not thinking about what's best for the team. You're doing what Michelle wants to do."

But Michelle was going to do it her way. She didn't talk back or show an attitude — she'd just go right back out and do the exact opposite of what I told her.

"Don't spin ever again, Michelle."

The first time an opportunity presented itself, she'd spin.

"Didn't I tell you not to spin?"

A few more minutes would go by, and I'd halt practice, and this time my voice would rise.

"Michelle! You're trying to thread a needle, throw a one-handed pass through an entire lane. It got picked off AGAIN."

Mickie and Holly thought I kept her on too short a leash and wanted me to give her more line. We argued about it, heatedly. Ego and stubbornness were part of the standard equipment for great players, Mickie insisted. "You're yanking Marciniak too soon, not letting her get into her game," she said. "Let her play through her mistakes a bit more." But I hesitated to prematurely embolden a player who was so erratic. "I know what I'm doing," I said.

> Now that I look back on it, I see where Pat was coming from. Michelle basically wasn't tamed yet. That was back when I still had the energy and the stupidity to argue. But Pat was up for a good argument. She liked the challenge of it. And I think that's what kept us all from getting too comfortable.
>
> — MICKIE DeMOSS

I felt like I always had to hold my breath with Michelle. A classic instance of her double-edged play came in our season-ending loss to Louisiana Tech in the 1994 NCAA Sweet 16. We were a 30-1 team that year, our best record in program history — but it made us wildly overconfident, and Louisiana Tech handed us a stunning upset, 71–68. Michelle came off the bench to score 14 points, but she also did something that was wholly . . . Michelle. She went down and rippled the net with a long-distance three-pointer and then showboated with her hand dangling in the air and didn't get set on defense. Tech came right down and hit a three in her face.

I was livid. I leveled her with a death ray glare and beckoned her over. As she came jogging to the bench, I shot out my arm, grabbed ahold of her jersey, and twisted it, pulling her closer. I stuck a finger in her chest and said, "Here you are, you come in and you did something really good, you hit a three. But then you gave *up* what you worked so hard for. Don't you *ever* do that again — if you do, you'll be sitting next to me. We're not here to trade baskets." A photographer from the Associated Press snapped a picture of the moment, and it ran all over the country. I wasn't proud of the photo — it looked like the Wicked Witch talking to Spinderella — and I called Michelle's mother and father the next day and assured them I wasn't in the habit of jerking their daughter around.

But Michelle liked it. She cut it out of the paper and pasted it to the dashboard of her car to remind herself of what not to do. "That's the way Pat wants me to think," she told herself.

The loss to Louisiana Tech made me sick. When we got back to Knoxville, I went to bed and didn't get up for a couple of days — not even when we had a flash flood. Torrential rains caused the Little River to rise dangerously in front of the house; it covered our dock, and then the gazebo, and began creeping up the hillside toward the porch. R.B. said, "Pat, you've got to get up, the water is rising over the dock."

I just raised my head about an inch from the pillow and said irritably, "Well, what exactly do you want *me* to do about it?"

Fortunately the river fell again, while I lay there immobile as a sandbag. What finally got me up was Michelle. Despite our skirmishes, she impressed me and gave me hope — she was a fearless, unquenchable competitor who never buckled under pressure, and when it came to effort, I wished I had twelve of her. I couldn't fault her desire to be great. I decided to bow to Mickie and Holly and hand Michelle the job of starting point guard for the following season. The morning after the flood, I called her and told her to come out to my house for a meeting. When Michelle arrived, I was on the sofa watching tape — I hadn't slept.

She had her glasses on, and that's a scary moment, because you know she was up watching film all night. You just don't want her to have glasses on. You want Pat to have her contacts in, because if she has

her contacts in, she had a little bit of sleep and she's not as cranky.
— MICHELLE MARCINIAK

I said, "I'm thinking about making you my point guard."

"Okay."

"I don't know if you can handle it."

"What would make you say that?"

"It's a lot different coming off the bench than it is starting. There is a lot more pressure on a starter."

"I disagree. I don't like coming off the bench."

"Okay," I said, "but I've been coaching this game as long as you've been alive. And I'm telling you it's not going to be easy, Michelle, and you need to trust me on that. I'm going to be a lot harder on you as a starter. But if I go with you, I'm going with you."

What Michelle didn't yet know was that there is a vast difference between playing and leading. The point guard position in basketball is one of the great tutorials on leadership, and it ought to be taught in classrooms. Anyone can perfect a dribble with muscle memory; very few people are able to organize and direct followers, which is a far more subtle and multifaceted skill.

409

Leadership is really a form of temporary authority that others grant you, and they only follow you if they find you consistently credible. It's all about perception — and if teammates find you the least bit inconsistent, moody, unpredictable, indecisive, or emotionally unreliable, then they balk and the whole team is destabilized.

Most young people are all the things I just listed, and Michelle was no different. If there is a single ingredient in leadership, it's emotional maturity.

Over the next two seasons, I intentionally did everything I could to break Michelle down. Why? Because until she completely surrendered herself and her ego, she wasn't going to become the reliable leader we needed. A willingness to do whatever it is that needs to be done regardless of self-interest is the hallmark of a mature leader. With Michelle there was a lingering note of "what about me?"

Marciniak always played hard, and five hundred miles an hour, but she'd make decisions and you'd be like, "What? Why did you do that?" You could see Pat's frustration with Michelle. She wouldn't question her drive and work ethic, but she would question her decision making in the moment.

— ABBY CONKLIN

Michelle's highly emotional style made her prone to unpredictability, and in the '95 season we couldn't afford for her to be even a little off, because early on we lost our most reliable senior guard, Tiffany Woosley, to a blown knee. We had a great senior class and I badly wanted to see them get a championship: Woosley, Vonda Ward, Nikki McCray, and Dana Johnson had built an 88-8 record in three seasons and been ranked number one in the country for most of that time. The only thing they had failed to do was reach the Final Four, which just shows that your most powerful teams don't always finish first. With Tiffany out, the seniors would be relying in large part on Michelle.

One afternoon Michelle had an absolute dog day in practice. We were running a sideline drill, and she crashed into the ball racks, and balls scattered everywhere. Well, that just irritated me to no end.

"If you're THINKING, if you're HERE, Michelle, you don't run over a ball rack," I boomed.

In the next drill, she threw the ball away at least five times on wacky, errant passes.

"Would you do that in a game?" I thundered. "You're *careless*. Everybody on the line. Let's run for Michelle's carelessness!"

Next came shooting drills. By now I'm pacing around her like a lion, and I can see that she's watching for my wrath out of the corner of her eye.

> You know where she is. You can feel that icy stare as she comes across half-court. So I take a shot — and it hits the side of the backboard.
>
> — *Michelle Marciniak*

I stopped practice.

"What was *that*?" I demanded. "What are you doing? If this is the national championship game, you would hit the side of the *backboard*? The game is on the line. We're competing for a championship. And that's what you would do? Is that right?"

Silence.

"Answer me."

She started sniffing and her chin trembled. She looked at Mickie, who shook her head faintly, as if to warn her, "Whatever you do, don't cry."

But it was too late. Michelle was bawling, tears streaming out of her eyes.

"You're crying? You're *crying*? Are you kidding? What are you crying about? You're supposed to be tough, our leader. Our point guard. And you're crying. Why? Because I'm hard on you? Well, guess what. Get used to it. You should be by now."

There were plenty of nights in the locker room when I wanted to cry, plenty of games when I was frustrated or nervous. You couldn't let people see that, I told her; if everybody on the team viewed me as a basket case, how would that make them feel? She had to project poise, control, and confidence, no matter what she felt inside. "You can't afford to do that in the presence of your team," I said later, more calmly. "That's just part of being a manager or leader."

Michelle had always worried solely about herself on the court but now she was trying to play while running an entire team, and sprinting the floor while shouting directions at the same time is harder than it looks. She had to direct the traffic, make sure everyone knew what offense we were in, manage them when they were in the wrong spots, pick them up when they were down, refocus them, encourage them.

But Michelle would go dead silent and sink into herself. She just wanted to let her spinning do the talking. I'd holler at her, and she would gaze back at me hopelessly, as if she could never get it right. Sometimes I'd kick her out of practice. "Just get out," I said. "Just go. Obviously you aren't paying attention, you don't understand what I want and how I want it, so get out. Just leave."

Michelle never knew what to do when I kicked her out of practice. Get showered? Or sit in her locker and tremble? Go back in and watch the rest of the workout from the sideline? No, the thing to do was to hang around and look remorseful, tell your teammates good job, and then cautiously approach me to ask for forgiveness.

It was like, "You're not getting a compliment from me until it's done well and it's done how I want it done." You go out and have a great practice, and her mentality is "Well, you should." Her whole motto is That's why I recruited you, because you should be the best. You have a great practice, now you should have another great practice. So the bar was set. Then that's the new standard. She's going to say, "You can't go back here anymore." So you just keep improving your situation. You always wanted to please her, and it was never good enough. You weren't going to get the compliment. What you would

414

get was a caring spirit. A few hours after practice we'd go over and eat at her home; all of a sudden Pat the mother would come out, and she would just love on us. Well, she would trick you. 'Cause you would watch this woman and this child and your heart melts and gets soft and you feel good about this relationship, like she *is* a person, she's not just this ranting raving coach trying to push your buttons.

— MICHELLE MARCINIAK

But Michelle responded and grew, and in the spring of '95 she led us back to the NCAA Final Four for the first time in three years. We went to Minneapolis — Tyler called it Minny Apples — believing it was our trophy to lose. We had an ideal mix of size and speed, and great veteran play. In addition to Michelle and Vonda, we had Dana Johnson, a bruising center out of Baltimore; Nikki McCray, a lovely, quick-footed forward from Collierville, Tennessee, who played with such urgency that she would go on to win an Olympic gold medal and star in the pros; and a junior sharp-shooter guard named Latina Davis, from Winchester, Tennessee, with a blindingly fast first step.

Our team motto that year was "One Team

with One Goal." But we had One Problem: the University of Connecticut. They were a skyrocketing, unbeaten team led by a willowy, elegant six-foot-four center named Rebecca Lobo with a smile as wide as a doorway and coached by a guy who was the first opponent I'd met who could match me for stormy intensity, Geno Auriemma. This was the inaugural year of a rivalry that, despite our quarrels over the coming years, we both agreed was an absolute masterpiece.

In order for a sport to build in the popular imagination it needs a rivalry, a gripping narrative of warring opposites. Tennessee-UConn was that for women's basketball. We were a fascinating study in primary colors: Tennessee was southern, stately, established; UConn was a come-lately easterner with hard elbows. We were slashers who preyed on teams off the dribble; they were highly orchestrated passers who picked you apart in the air. We played from the inside out; they played from the outside in. We wore bright neon orange; they wore drab blue.

There was tremendous personal contrast as well. I tried to be correct and decorous in public; Geno was a smart-ass who would take negative attention over no attention at all. You could put a microphone on me for an hour and never hear anything worse than "dadgummit"; he was notoriously foul-mouthed. I was intensely competitive but left it on the court; he was combative and carried grudges off the court. Then of course there was the most fundamental difference of all: gender. He complained about being a man working in a women's sport. To which I was always tempted to reply, "Try being a woman in a man's world."

These largely superficial, situational, and somewhat exaggerated differences would define our relationship sharply over the years. But we also had more characteristics in common than people would suppose, and we liked each other. We both loved to laugh. We both enjoyed expensive bottles of red wine. We both lived the game as if it was in us on a cellular level. We both taught it with an unrelenting energy and attention to detail. We both loved our players with a loyal, familial devotion that gave us, and them, equal amounts of pleasure and agony. And we were both kinder people than we appeared to outsiders.

We could both get enraged at officials. The first time we ever met face-to-face was on the court at Stokely Arena in the mid-1980s. Geno was then an assistant at the dread Virginia under my friend Debbie Ryan. It was halftime and I headed straight for a referee to complain about the lousy calls. Just as I got there, here came this irate Italian with a dark widow's peak and a wide-open mouth, swearing at the top of his lungs, until the official gave him a technical. I just stood there, amused. "I agree a hundred percent," I said.

> Strange as it might sound, I had a little chip on my shoulder. We're playing at UT and you know it's not going to be easy, and I thought the officials were not giving us the respect we deserved. I remember as soon as the horn sounded for the half, I ran over, and was going to give this ref a piece of my mind. And there she is. I'm thinking, "What is she doing out here?" And I realized, she's pissed too. We got there at the same time and, stupid me, I opened my mouth first. The ref hits me with a technical. She just walks away, like, "Well, I got my trip accomplished." Now I got to walk into our locker room and say, "By the way, they got two more points."
>
> — GENO AURIEMMA

Another thing Geno and I had in common was that we agreed women's basketball needed to be on television more in order to grow. In the summer of '94, I got a call from him asking if we would play UConn in a made-for-TV game on ESPN on Martin Luther King Day. It wasn't the most advantageous matchup for us; UConn was clearly an ascendant and dangerous top 5 team. What's more, the game would be at Connecticut, which meant it could easily be a loss for us.

> Everybody worth a damn said no, because it was going to be at our place. ESPN asked me, "Do you think she would play?" So I called her and she said, "Yeah." And I said, "I told you she would play. She's not like the rest of these people."
> — GENO AURIEMMA

I couldn't say no. I'd always felt a tremendous responsibility to give back to the game; I could never repay what it had given me and meant to me. It had changed my life, and I always wanted to promote it so it could change other women's lives, too. So I said yes. And we lost. We went to Gampel Pavilion on MLK Day as the number one ranked team in the country. The Huskies were ranked number two, and the press was three deep. The Huskies were the hungrier team that day and whipped us 77–66.

But in Minneapolis we had a chance for revenge in the game that mattered more: the national championship. We were the best two teams in the country by a mile, and knew it, and so did a sellout crowd of more than eighteen thousand that packed the Target Center. For forty minutes the kids warred, and they produced an instant classic that is still replayed on ESPN. Vonda Ward and Dana Johnson dueled with Lobo and Kara Wolters, while on the perimeter Marciniak sparred with an inexhaustible, scrapping UConn guard named Jennifer Rizzotti.

> We were getting ready to play them and all the geniuses were saying, "You can't run your offense against them, how you gonna run your offense?" I said, "Bull, the same way. We will run our offense against them." Uh-uh, they won't let you. The first three times up the floor we can't make a pass. And I'm like, holy Christ, they must be right.
>
> — GENO AURIEMMA

Michelle fought like a lion — but she was all over the map. Early in the game she came down and spun on Rizzotti, did her patented

Spinderella whirl, and got an open bucket. It was a great play — and the worst thing that could have happened, because now she was overexcited and started jacking up bad shots. I called her over and tore into her. Which was a mistake on my part. I was tired of not getting through to her, and instead of being calm, I matched her emotion. "You need to sit down and think about this!" I snapped. "Just watch, and get your head in the game."

I didn't leave her there for long. When a player makes a mistake, you always want to put them back in quickly — you don't just berate them and sit them down with no chance for redemption.

We took a 38–32 halftime lead, but we could never draw away. At the two-minute mark it was all tied up. But when it came down to it, we just couldn't stop UConn when we needed to most. We were in and out of schemes, trying to stymie them, but they just had too many options: if Wolters (10 points) didn't get a shot, here came Lobo (17 points); if Lobo didn't get a shot, here came Rizzotti (15 points).

We still had our eye on the trophy. We were Tennessee, after all. We had everything planned: the victory T-shirts and hats were ready to be printed, the champagne was on ice, and the catering tables were ready for a huge celebration. But UConn surged — and suddenly nothing good happened for us. Nikki McCray missed a layup. Michelle got stripped of the ball. Then she blew a free throw. And with 1:51 to go, Jen Rizzotti dashed the ball up the court and confronted Michelle — who went for the steal. The gambler took over, at the wrong time. Rizzotti went right by her and scored, giving UConn the lead, and we never got it back. Final score, 70–64.

It was a different feeling from any I'd ever had after a loss. The margin between losing and winning had been almost imperceptible. We had fought our hearts out, and we hadn't given it away, the other team had simply *taken* it from us. It came down to a handful of great plays. Unfortunately, the other kids made them.

Here's the thing that would distinguish the UConn rivalry for me: it made everybody better. The two teams had pushed each other so hard that the quality of basketball just kept rising. The first thing I did when I got back to Knoxville was call a team meeting and warn them that we'd see UConn again, and we would have to raise our game. There were a lot of rivals we felt a distinct physical edge over, against whom we were bigger, stronger, and fitter, but this wasn't one of them. UConn was our equal — and wasn't going away.

One thing a painful loss is good for is getting the attention of the last holdouts on your team, the kids who still haven't quite given you everything they have. I sensed that Michelle Marciniak was withholding — she was still a little too interested in doing it her way instead of mine. I also sensed that she was congratulating herself for making it to an NCAA final. I decided to expose Michelle in front of the whole team. She had gone just 3 for 11 against UConn, while Rizzotti had gone 6 for 8.

"You didn't show up," I said. "If you had shown up, we'd have won. You just weren't as focused as you should have been. You had the opportunity of a lifetime. We lost a national championship and *you* were the point guard. *You* were the leader. You had the ball in your hand 80 percent of the time."

I turned to the rest of the team. "Is there anyone in this room who doesn't think that if Michelle had her head on straight we would have won a national championship?"

The room was stony silent; no one knew what to do. I could feel them cringing inwardly, unsure of whether or not to raise their hands. No doubt, some of them thought it was a brutal thing to say. And it was. But this was the hard part that I had warned Michelle about.

"I told you last year when you were going to become the point guard that a huge responsibility comes with it," I said. "You're going to get lots of praise and lots of accolades from the outside world. But if it doesn't work, it's going to fall on you. Just like it falls on me. You're the one responsible."

I wasn't trying to be cruel; I was being honest. The standard conventional coaching manual says you don't "embarrass" players in front of their teammates, but I disagreed. Here's why: Dishonest teams don't win the big one. They cover up their losses with rationalizations and excuses that soothe their eggshell egos, and they keep making the same mistakes. But the truly ambitious teams find relief in honesty when they've lost, because it's the diagnostic tool that leads to a solution — here's what we did wrong and let's fix it, so we don't ever have to feel this way again. Great teams explain their failure; they don't excuse it. Then they pay a visit to Charles Atlas and get stronger. When you explain a loss aloud, it's no longer a tormenting mystery. I believed in that brand of honesty my whole career, and I knew at least one other coach who believed in it too.

It's great to capture the moment right then and there, while the wound it still open and you can really get them to pay attention. I used to call players in and sit them down privately and say, "This is the deal." I find myself doing it less and less, and here's why: you know when they leave your office, they're going to lie. You could say ten things and nine of them are "You are greatest in the world at nine things, but you suck going to your left." They leave and say, "Coach says I suck." I like to say things right in front of the team about reality. I like to say, This is what you're doing and this is why it's costing us, and does anybody have any questions? Because now they have to confront. They can't go their separate ways and say, "He said . . ." No. *Everybody* heard it. And everybody on the team already knows it. They just want someone else to say it. You are just the voice of the team calling out that player — and now that player has to react. They have to either admit it, and fix it, or say everybody else is wrong. And if they do that, they further separate themselves from the team. College kids are still kids and are looking for direction. What gives you the stomach to do it is you know you're right, and you're only saying what they already know and believe.

— GENO AURIEMMA

Sometimes I had to hurt a young woman to her core. Why? Because often players don't even know they are withholding something until they are pierced. When you pierce them, that's when the last of their individual egos finally pours out. Then you can show them how to rebuild in the right way. I pierced Michelle that day, and I'd do it again before her career was over. It was by no means an easy thing or pleasant thing to do, and I went home that night and held my son, who wasn't happy with me for making his latest crush unhappy. I chewed my lip and asked myself, *Do you think you were too hard on her?*

But the trouble was, it worked. I might have felt worse about such tough love if it hadn't paid off.

For twenty years, Tennessee had set the standard of excellence in the women's game — but now someone had met it. We had to learn from Connecticut the way other teams had learned from Tennessee. This wasn't a team we could outhustle, or outmuscle. We would have to outwit and outexecute them.

After losing to UConn twice in 1995, I knew that it wasn't just our players who had to get better; the coaches had to get better too. I wanted to get a grip on UConn's offense, called the Triple Post. They had beaten us twice with it and I was determined to study it, whether we ever used it or not. If you understand how to run something, then you also understand how to defend it.

Basketball to me is all about countering — attacks and counterattacks are what create tempos in a game and shifts in momentum. But you also have to counter from season to season. Mickie called us "the Counter Queens." Although we had a system with principles and core values that we didn't deviate from, strategically we adjusted dramatically over the years as the game changed. I don't know that I ever separated myself as a basketball technician, but along with Mickie and Holly as a staff, we were great at staying on the cutting edge of where the game was going, and using the marvelously evolving talents of kids. "It's what you learn after you already know everything that counts," I liked to say. Our ability to keep learning and teaching new things is what separated us and made us the best program in history.

I was by no means a master tactician, but I'd become a good enough one to make a difference on the sideline, for which I had a lot of guys in the business to thank. A great small-college legend named Don Meyer gave me his best methods, as did two Tennessee men's coaches, Don DeVoe and Kevin O'Neill. DeVoe had a young assistant named Dean Lockwood, and I plundered his bookshelves for the latest instructionals or videos. I'd see a new title in his office and say, "Can I borrow this?" Or I'd duck into DeVoe's office and say, "You got a minute? How do you defend the wing when the ball gets here?" I'd stay after work to watch the men practice.

It impressed me how much of a student she was, what a learner. Here she is, someone in such command of her world, her team and her program, and I'm twenty-six years old, and yet she's looking at my stuff saying, "What can I glean from this, what can I get out of this guy that can help us?" I would see her in Stokely standing at one end of the arena, leaning against a wall, watching us for twenty or thirty or forty minutes.

— DEAN LOCKWOOD

In seeking to counter the Triple Post, I turned to the men's game for schooling once again. The greatest employers of the Triple Post were the Chicago Bulls under Phil Jackson, the eleven-time NBA title winner. In 1994, I had added a superb third assistant coach to our staff, one with a gift for analyzing videotape, named Al Brown. When I told Al that I wanted to study the Triple Post, he offered to make a call to the Bulls' assistant Tex Winter, an acquaintance of his, who had first drawn up the scheme back in the 1940s. The Bulls graciously let our entire staff come study their system for a couple of days.

Then we came home and, as we always did, began putting our own spin on things. I moved players around on the floor, so they would understand the overall patterns better. I'd bring our big players out to the perimeter and make them run the play like a guard, so they saw the play from that angle as well as their own. When one of our bigs got upset if a guard didn't make a play, I'd say, "Fine. You go play point."

Shaking things up was good for all of us.

429

Sometimes I just shook things up because I felt a creeping complacency — because the Counter Queen sensed a need for a counter — and I shook Michelle up harder than anyone in the 1996 season. She was still prone to glory seeking and costly gambles, and I turned up the heat in practice every day even more. "You thought last year was hard," I warned her. "Wait till you see this year."

"You're SELFISH," I'd holler. "This does *not* revolve around you. This is about four other players on the floor; your *teammates.* You need to put other people first."

Michelle hated it when I screamed at her — she felt I belittled her in front of the rest of the team, especially our new freshmen, a couple of whom were the most promising players we'd ever recruited. One was a shy, fragile physical genius from New York named Chamique Holdsclaw. Another was a brilliant, tough-jawed Tennessee point guard named Kellie Jolly. I would blast Michelle, and they would just stare open-mouthed, while Michelle's shoulders curled.

Michelle begged, "I can't have my teammates seeing you yell at me like that. I'm asking you, if you could please turn your back to them when you're yelling at me. Don't let them see how mad you are." But I just used her plea as another chance to challenge her: I made her feel weak for asking.

"If that's what you want, Michelle. I guess you're just not tough then."

At the time you take everything personally, and it's all a big emotion-fest. It's all about you. You're trying to make it all about you, and she's just trying to make it all about everyone else, to win. But you fight her.

— MICHELLE MARCINIAK

Mickie and Holly winced at the way I dealt with Michelle. It was their job to soften the blows and to tell me when I'd gone too far. "Now, Pat . . . ," they'd say. I cut them off. "If I didn't think she could take it, I wouldn't say it," I replied. I knew full well that what Michelle wanted more than anything in the world was a compliment from me, and she wasn't getting it until she held the trophy. It was straight out of the playbook of a tall man back in Henrietta. Mickie and Holly just said, "There's the Richard in her."

I just think Pat was raised with — everything wasn't wonderful and grand. The way she was raised, you know, you had to fight a little bit, and she hadn't had it easy all

431

her life and her dad was tough, and that was the backbone and foundation of how she coached.

— HOLLY WARLICK

The final crisis for Michelle came at Mississippi late in her senior season. The Ole Miss gym was small and dark, and Michelle hated it there, and she played terribly that night. She had about eight turnovers, missed a bunch of free throws, and ended up fouling out. "Would you get your head on?" I demanded. "What are you doing missing free throws? You're an 85 percent free throw shooter. Sit down!" We lost, 79–72.

I was at my wit's end; Michelle was our senior leader, and if she played that way in the NCAA tournament, we'd be out of it. I walked into the locker room and said, "Everyone turn around, shut up, and sit down! Except you, Marciniak. Get up." Michelle stood.

"You had no leadership tonight. Where's your head? If you weren't so selfish, if you weren't so into yourself . . . You let every single one of these people down."

When I boarded the bus for the trip home, Michelle was sitting in the second row, looking out the window with her headphones on, her eyes welling up. Now, the second row is where the coaches and staff sit, while the players congregate in the back of the bus. It was an obvious play for my attention. I sat down next to her and pulled her headphones off. "What are you doing?" I said. "You're going to listen to music after you just played like that?"

Silence.

"You should be in the back of the bus talking to your teammates, trying to figure out what you can do. Instead you're up here listening to music."

Tears.

"You're crying? You're *crying*? Why? What, you can't take it?"

I knew that Michelle was as distressed as anyone that she'd had a bad game. But we had a month left in the season, and we were at the breaking point. Michelle either did it my way, or we would lose.

If I'd learned anything in all my years of teaching, it was that when you reach an impasse with a player, you get what you demand, not what you ask for. If players see even a waver in you, they will give you what *they* want to give. Sometimes you have to make yourself their adversary. I pushed Michelle to the brink — unapologetically — and I did it out of conviction in the oldest athletic training principle in the world: when you get right to the verge, the mind and body respond by expanding. They grow. It was a stressful and manipulative dynamic, and the finest of lines, and by this point I had a permanent trench in the bottom of my lip. But I gave Michelle an ultimatum.

Just before we got off the bus I said, "You need to think about whether you want to be a part of this team anymore."

Her head swiveled toward me in disbelief. "You heard me. I don't think you can be our point guard. I thought you could for a little while, but I don't think you can do it. So why don't you get some rest and we'll talk tomorrow, and you can let me know whether or not you want to be a part of this team anymore if you aren't starting."

It was hardball. Did I mean it? Of course not — it was my turn to gamble. But Michelle didn't know that, and she was devastated. She went home and told her mother she might quit, and then she stayed up all night weeping. She called me at six the next morning. "I want to do this; I want to be your point guard, and I want to lead this team to a championship, but I can't do it with the way you're coaching me," she said. "You've broken my spirit."

"Well, that's the last thing I'd ever want to do," I said.

"You embarrass me in front of my team-mates and it makes me feel like I can't lead them the way you want me to. I need you on my side."

"Okay, Michelle, I'll handle you more gently. But I don't want you as my starter anymore. I don't think you can handle it. I feel like I gave you every opportunity and you really showed yourself in the game last night. Then after the game you inverted so much that I just don't think this is really right for you."

"Pat, I can do it. I just need you to treat me different."

"You need *me* to treat *you* different? After aaalll the players who have come through this program? Aaalll the players who have won a national championship here? We're in the last month and a half of the season and you want me to treat you different? That just tells me you're not tough."

It's funny now. But at the time it was just heart wrenching.

"Pat, I'll show you."

"Well, you're gonna *have* to show me. Because there is nothing you can say right now."

I ignored her for about a week, would barely look at her. I played a variety of people at the point in practice, gave long minutes to our freshman Kellie Jolly, and acted like I'd put anyone at the point if I had to — anyone but Michelle. It was a total zero-tolerance policy for any more resistance, or lack of focus, or circus plays.

But Michelle did what she promised: she showed me. As the tournament began, we grudgingly met halfway. She tried to do what I asked her to do, and I didn't ride her quite as hard.

In the NCAA Elite Eight, we faced our old nemesis Virginia — and with twenty minutes to go, my worst fears seemed about to be realized. It was one of those nights when there was an invisible lid on the basket, a mysterious force that repelled our shots. We trailed at halftime in one of the most ugly games I'd ever witnessed, 27–14. I told our staff, "Well, it can't get any worse." Oh, but it could. With seventeen minutes to play, we trailed by 17 points. We had to make up a point for every minute remaining, or the season would be over.

Everybody was pressing, and Michelle more than anyone. I called her over, but by this time I'd learned not to meet her emotion with my own. I used the softest voice I could summon. "Look, Michelle, you're all right, but we need you to refocus," I said. "What I need from you is for you to calm down. We need you to finish out strong."

She maintained her composure, kept her head, and stayed positive. Michelle and Latina Davis went to work and ignited us with big baskets, and I had a sudden inspiration defensively. It was time for a counter. I was still known as a stubborn man-to-man coach, but I'd learned to vary our defenses, throw changeups, because sometimes it could make the other team hesitate, or even panic. I signaled our 13 Defense. It was a zone 1-3-1 set that we had hardly used all year. It sent Virginia into precisely the hesitation-panic mode I'd hoped. When the final buzzer sounded, we'd completed a 23-point swing, to win by 6 points. The final score was 52–46, and we were going to the Final Four in Charlotte.

Where our opponent in the semifinals would be the team we'd studied all year to beat, UConn. For the last time, I decided to press Michelle's buttons. I knew by now how much she thrived on being the central figure onstage. I said to her, "Who's the bigger star, you or Jennifer Rizzotti? She's the Player of the Year and won every all-American honor there is. But who are they going to be interviewing in a corner of the arena after the game? Is it going to be her? Or is it going to be *you*?"

Then, right before the tip-off, I finally gave Michelle the compliment she craved. "You've worked hard," I told the team, "and you're prepared." I looked at Michelle. "And you've got a *great* point guard and a *great* leader in Michelle."

With five minutes before tip-off, Michelle felt like I'd shot her with adrenaline.

This woman who just beats on you all the time suddenly gives you this compliment that you're not ready for or prepared for, at the most critical time. It worked. Hook, line, and sinker. I was in a different place in that game.

— Michelle Marciniak

What came next was one of the highest-quality ball games I ever participated in. For forty straight minutes, every player on both sides was at her best; big-time shots fell through the net from all over the court, led by Michelle, who was a driving, flashing force. The lead changed hands several times, no one able to get an advantage. It was a virtual deadlock — until, with five seconds to go, we went up by three. Everyone on our bench clasped hands, and I folded my arms and tried to contain a nervous jerking of my head. Just five more seconds.

438

But UConn had the ball and one more shot.

A Huskies great named Nykesha Sales drifted to the wing and faced up to the basket. Rizzotti swung a pass up the court to Sales — and then it happened — Michelle gambled and went for the steal. She missed by just a fraction of an inch and went flying by Sales, who caught the ball. Wide open, Sales nailed the three-pointer to send the game to overtime.

I let it go. It was Michelle's only mistake, and it was an aggressive, assertive one. As the kids jogged over to the bench, I exhaled and grimaced, repressed my frustration, and focused on the fact that we had five more minutes to play. "Ladies, we're going to buckle down and get stops," I said. "They are not going to outplay you, they are not going to beat you."

By God, they believed it, and by God, they made sure it didn't happen. It was almost like she willed them. Pat gave them this extra level that they could kick up to. It was, They are *not* going to beat you right here. When Pat would lock down and really home in and convince them that they were the better team and were going to get it done, it was just an extra air, our

439

team had an extra swagger.

— MICKIE DEMOSS

When I looked at Michelle, I could see she was completely zeroed in. There was an expression on her face of absolute dogged certainty: she had come too far to walk away a loser. And she flat took over in the extra period. She hit drives, drew fouls, and calmly knocked down her free throws. She had 21 points, and as she stepped to the free throw line for the last time, she had an almost smug look on her face. The final score was 88–83, Tennessee.

> I was extremely confident, and I also had a little edge because of what happened with Pat. I was like, I'm gonna *show* you. And that's why she did it. Because she got out of it a championship.
>
> — MICHELLE MARCINIAK

Our momentum carried over to the final against Georgia. Our life-sized mascot dog, Smokey, primed us for victory by destroying a stuffed Georgia bulldog on the court just before tip-off, spilling his insides all over the floor. That got Smokey ejected from the gym, and I protested. "It's not *our* fault the dog was a cheap toy," I said. Our players treated Georgia the same way — we won our fourth national championship by tearing Georgia apart 83–65, in front of a record TV audience for a women's game. Everybody made huge contributions: our shooting guard Latina Davis was Most Valuable Player of the NCAA East Region, our freshman Chamique Holdsclaw made all-America.

And Michelle Marciniak was the MVP of the Final Four.

There were two great reconciliations in the arena that evening. As the buzzer sounded, our players exploded with joy and jumped around like they were trying to defy gravity. I fought to suppress a smile of carbonated delight as Michelle bounded over to me expectantly. She wanted the last measure of approval she'd been waiting for, and that I'd withheld for so long. I wrapped her in a hug and said, "Ohhhh, I am so proud for you."

Then I climbed into the stands to see my family. I embraced my husband and son and turned to the railing behind which my parents and brothers and sisters-in-law were waiting. As I did so, I experienced something similar to what the young woman I'd just released must have felt.

Waiting for me, with outstretched arms, was my father. I moved into them, and he hugged me. I was forty-three years old, and it was the first one I'd ever gotten from him. I felt a rumbling in his chest, and then he spoke.

"Somebody around here knows how to coach," he said.

> I really think that at base the extremely tough, silent, demanding father combined with the give-no-quarter-to-the-baby-even-if-she-is-a-girl brothers she had to survive caused Pat to never feel safe and satisfied unless all these demons had been soundly beaten. When you are trying to talk to a deaf person, you keep raising your voice until you can be heard. Pat had to really do something to get any comment, let alone praise, from her dad.
> — R.B. SUMMITT

That night we had a huge celebration in the lounge of our Charlotte hotel; I vaguely remember my young friend and onetime assistant coach Carolyn Peck (1993–1995) standing atop the bar and leading us in singing "Rocky Top."

> Wish that I was on old Rocky Top, down
>   in the Tennessee hills
> Ain't no smoggy smoke on Rocky Top

Ain't no telephone bills . . .
Once there was a girl on rocky top,
Half bear the other half cat.
Wild as a mink, sweet as soda pop,
I still dream about that.

My old friend Jane Clark went upstairs to change into jeans and as she got off the elevator she ran into my parents, whose room was next to hers. Jane thought Daddy was mixed up and said, "Your room is right here."

Daddy said, "I know that. We're going down to the bar to party."

The following morning as we all staggered around trying to pack to go home, my parents came to my hotel suite to say good-bye. My father stood in the doorway, and abruptly and awkwardly, he said the words I'd been waiting forty-three years to hear.

"Now, I love you," he said.

I was stunned. I looked at him as if to say, Richard? Richard Head?

He continued, irritably. "And I don't ever want to hear about it again."

I tried not to burst out laughing, or yell hallelujah. Of course Richard Head couldn't just say, "Trish, I love you." He had to add, "And I don't ever want to hear about it again." Strangely enough, I didn't feel any great sense of relief at that moment. When I asked myself why, the answer came to me readily: I already knew he loved me. My shock was not based on the words, but on the size of the step the big man had just taken toward me, the sudden relaxing of his barricade.

For once, my father wasn't done. He had more to say.

"I don't ever want to hear again that I don't say I love you," he said. "Or that I never hug you. Or tell you how proud I am."

Then he hugged me again.

What do you think when you look at the row of trophies?

I think about the great players that made it happen, you know.

So when you see trophies, you see people.

Sure.

How good is your memory in general? Are there things you feel you should remember that you don't about some of the championships?

Oh, yeah. That's why I have you.

So you remember with prompting?

Yes. I remember, now we talk about it.

How's it feel?

Feels good.

[Laughter]

What about the stress? How stressful do you think the job was, when the team was down, the band is playing, everybody is screaming —

See, I loved that. Loved it. Living in the moment. Trying to figure out who needs the ball. Who needs to box out. Who needs to be in the game. All that kind of stuff.

You were problem solving at a mental rate that's amazing.

Yep.

And it was fun?

Oh, yeah. It's always fun, unless you lost. And then it was hell on wheels.

— May 25, 2012, Alys Beach, Florida, one year after diagnosis

9
CHAMPION, PART II

There were moments in my career when I thought I'd mastered the craft of coaching, but this wasn't one of them. Out on our home court, Stanford was cutting our team to pieces like a knife and fork. I felt exposed on the sideline, embarrassed. A wide-open space of floor opened in front of me, and a Stanford player moved into it and fluttered the net with an easy jumper for what seemed like the hundredth time. The scoreboard blinked, and I flicked my eyelashes up at it.

I turned to my staff on the sideline and said, simply, "Help me."

Farther down the bench our injured point guard Kellie Jolly, sitting with a damaged knee, looked surprised; she'd never heard me uncertain before. Mickie and Holly offered a couple of suggestions, but we all knew the answer wasn't on a clipboard. I shrugged as if to say, "I don't know who's coaching this team." I wandered down to

Tyler's seat on the end of the bench. He just looked up at me with his six-year-old wise man's eyes and held out his hands.

"I'm doing everything I can," he said.

Our defense flapped and waved at Stanford, about as effectually as laundry on a clothesline. I called a time-out and stamped my heels, but nothing prevented the slaughter. Final score: Stanford 82, Tennessee 65. The Lady Vols left the floor dispirited, their uniforms hanging on them limply, like sails with no wind.

Each season at Tennessee was its own torturous journey, but 1996–1997 was shaping up like just plain torture. We were on our way to setting a program record for losses — and for quarreling among ourselves. The Stanford game was a new low: it was our worst home loss in a decade, and it gave us a 7-3 record, our slowest start since 1984. Afterward Chamique Holdsclaw and I walked together disconsolately to a press conference to face the questions about what was wrong with the Lady Vols.

"I can't wait till next year," Chamique whispered to me.

I said, "We'll be all right." But inwardly I was thinking the same thing. *How am I going to get through this?* I wondered. We were only ten games into the season, and our schedule stretched ahead like a dark river. We were thin and injured, and had no chemistry, and if I was honest with myself, I didn't really like where this team was headed. I liked them plenty as people, lunch companions, but as competitors they were too laid-back and low energy. Nor did I always like myself as their coach.

As I looked over our roster, I saw nothing but problems with no quick fix. Kellie Jolly had torn her anterior cruciate ligament in October playing a game of pickup, literally the day before our first fall practice. I couldn't restore Kellie's knee. We had some promising freshmen in Kyra Elzy, Niya Butts, and LaShonda Stephens, but they were floundering, and it wasn't in my power to make them older overnight. We had a staunch point guard in Laurie Milligan, but she had been thrust into the starting position hurriedly because of Kellie's injury, and I couldn't fast-forward her progress.

As soon as we got Kellie's diagnosis, I knew we were in trouble. "This is going to be a long year," I told R.B. Kellie was one of Tyler's crushes, a platinum-braided kid from Sparta, Tennessee, who had taken over from Michelle Marciniak as our floor leader, and was one of the best I'd ever seen at the position. She invariably called the right play at the right moment, and sent the ball to the right place, but more than that, Kellie had a quality that everyone on our team drew from: heart. She was our most conscientious player, the daughter of a coach and schoolteacher, who got absolutely everything out of her physical talent and brought her best every day.

"Pat never gets on you," the other Lady Vols would say, enviously.

Kellie would reply, "What the heck is she going to say to me? I can't do anything more than I'm doing. I'm maxed out."

At her first team meeting as a freshman, Kellie had showed how willing she was to do what I asked. We had a plush blue leather sectional sofa that the kids loved to sink into. I marched in and said, "First things first, sit up straight and look me in the eye." Kellie sprang up from the blue cushions and sat so ramrod straight, I thought she might salute.

> I was worried that I had been leaning back on that couch and what was this woman thinking of me, because I had obviously screwed up already.
>
> — KELLIE JOLLY

Yet Kellie was unafraid of me, and our

relationship had budded early because of it. There was no strife, no tension or resistance, just a growing bond. In the spring of '96, she came to my office and gave me a gift: a photograph. Kellie's mother, Peggy, had captured the moment that my father hugged me in the stands the night we won the championship, and Kellie framed a copy of the photograph and brought it to me, a dear gesture that touched me like no overture from a player ever had.

Our team followed Kellie's lead in everything, and her absence left a huge void. She underwent surgery to have a new ACL grafted into her knee, and as soon as the doctor pronounced her well enough, she began rehabbing for six hours a day. Her goal was to get back on the floor before the season was over, and every time the Lady Vols took the court for a big game without her, she agonized. Just before the Stanford tip-off, she had gone into the bathroom and dissolved in tears.

I felt powerless to help our team, and I wasn't dealing with it well. I juggled different lineups, looking for one that might click — I would try thirteen different combinations by the season's end. My response to problems was to work harder, push harder, to fight even harder. But there were some things grinding couldn't cure.

Nothing was working. We were a team of mistakes, mishaps, missed connections, and misunderstandings. My greatest misunderstanding was with senior Abby Conklin. It was a continual challenge to try to read kids, to peer into their hearts, or in their heads, and hoping to gain a little insight, I had turned to something called the Predictive Index, a personality assessment test that business managers used to put people in the right job. It was an advance over just going to a player's guidance counselor, which was what I had done in the old days. The PI gave me an outline of a player's emotional strengths and insecurities, and what might motivate her.

But the PI was useless with Abby. She took it three times, with three completely different results. The first time she took it, she didn't believe the profile was really hers, so she asked to take it again, and then again. Each time she would decide who she wanted to be and make different choices. That was Abby.

She was a six-foot-three forward with a beautiful, arcing three-point shot, smooth as the lank brown ponytail she wore on the back of her head like a martial arts master. But she struggled with self-doubt as a ballplayer. She came from farm country in Charlestown, Indiana, where her father, Harlo, ran a nursery and a greenhouse, and Harlo wanted to keep her in the Midwest. He told Abby he didn't think she could cut it with us, that she was a half step slow. "I just don't think she's good enough," he told me frankly.

I said, "Harlo, why don't you let me make that decision? I don't tell you how to grow flowers."

But if you hear something enough, you believe it, and Abby heard she wasn't good enough. With Michelle Marciniak, the challenge had been to curb her self-regard and high emotion, but with Abby it was the dead opposite. She lacked confidence in certain areas, and she covered it up with a demeanor that could seem almost indifferent. I didn't do the best job of understanding that, and I mishandled her at times. I was so unsure in my dealings with Abby that sometimes I gave her praise and criticism even in the same breath.

"CONKLIN! Get off the court! You act like a whipped puppy! I went to Indiana to get a competitor and instead I got you!"

I just stood in the shower for a long time debating, Can I pack my car up and be

453

back in Indiana by about nine?

— ABBY CONKLIN

"Conklin! You had 18 points in that game, nobody in the country can stop you — but you gave *up* 17. So basically you were worth one point on the floor!"

From her perspective, Abby felt like she could never please me. When she shot the ball too much, I told her maybe she was too selfish to play basketball; maybe she should play golf. That only made her quit shooting altogether. She'd pass up an open shot and give the ball to Chamique. I snapped, "I didn't recruit you for your passing skills." I would rail at her, just to try to provoke any reaction. *Fight back!* I would think.

Every day in practice Pat put you in the most adverse, tough situations that she could, verbally, physically, and mentally; she got you spinning. And you had to control yourself and get through it or you would get buried. Pat would bury you.

— ABBY CONKLIN

Abby didn't like being crowded and confronted by me, and her way of dealing with it was avoidance, or sarcasm. She was witty, in her dry, low-key way. One day the kids teasingly suggested I should get a tattoo and launched into a discussion of what emblem would be right for me. Abby said wickedly, "A heart."

We almost never talked unless it was on the practice floor, where she absorbed instruction with a detached air that I wrongly interpreted as apathy. Abby would just bolt out of the gym as soon as the workout was over, and the result was a wall of silence between us.

But by '97 Abby was a senior, and as the crisis of our season deepened, I badly needed her to be emotionally engaged, because we were desperate for a leader and a more complete player. It all came to a head in the Stanford game. Our defensive game plan was for Abby to contest any Stanford entries to a particular spot on the court. "Deny the high post," I instructed her. But Abby was worried that if she denied, Stanford would drive right past her for a layup. She lost confidence and decided, all on her own, to play containment. She dropped four feet off her player. Our plan collapsed, Stanford got wide-open shots, and we got run over.

In my mind I was trying to cause the least amount of damage. So now I'm not playing her game plan and if one person is not playing it, it all breaks down.

— ABBY CONKLIN

There was a fine line between being demanding and being negative, and after the Stanford loss, I crossed it. The next day in a team meeting, I went at Abby. I'd been up until four A.M. screaming at the game film. I started off by saying, "Let's face it, we're handcuffed because Abby Conklin won't defend or rebound." Then I pointed at her. "What was the one thing I asked you to do?" I asked Abby. She had given up the middle of the floor, and they had torn us apart in the middle, I said.

Abby retorted, "I don't agree," and started to haggle with me about what we should have done against Stanford.

I stared at her. A senior was questioning my judgment in front of the entire team — a team that was losing. A team that was young, injured, and uncertain and that I was struggling to hold together, and which Abby had just done her best to pull apart at the seams. Most days in practice Abby was low on feedback. Suddenly, on this day of all days, she decided to give me some, by defying me in front of her teammates.

I said tightly, "You're more stubborn than

you are smart. And you're gonna kill this team with it."

Abby felt terrible about it, I learned later. She had reacted defensively in the face of my criticism and blurted it out. She wanted to be part of the solution, but she didn't know how to express it. At the time, however, all I heard was the mutiny in her words.

After practice, Abby came to the coaches' locker room and tried to apologize, but by then my simmering had risen to a boil. I was drinking a cup of water, and it practically turned to steam when she came through the door.

Abby said, "Pat, I want to apologize . . ."

Before she could finish, I threw the cup at the wall. It was just a paper Gatorade cup, but I flung it so hard it showered us all like a tsunami.

Pat had water in her hand and she flung it, and I thought, "Oh my God." I thought she was swinging to hit her. I thought her head was gonna come off. As competitive as Pat was, I never thought she would put her hands on somebody, but at that moment I thought Abby might've pushed her past the brink of her consciousness. The

water just hit the wall and went everywhere.

— HOLLY WARLICK

"I don't know why you don't respect me,
Abby," I said. "But you've hurt me worse
than any player ever has."

"I'm sorry. I just want to apologize."

"I don't accept your apology. I'm not
gonna accept it. *Maybe* I'll accept it by the
end of the year. But right now you need to
get out of here."

Abby backed out of the room, leaving me
alone with Mickie and Holly, who were
toweling off.

"Pat, I thought you were going to hit her,"
Holly said.

"I wish I could," I said.

For once my anger wasn't an act. I felt
betrayed by a senior I should have been able
to depend on, and I had a hard time getting
over it. Over the next few days I became the
one who was more stubborn than smart. I
took Abby out of the starting lineup for the
next game against Texas Tech, and she was
so anxious to get back in my good graces
that she answered with a career-high 26
points off the bench. "Way to respond," I
told her. But it also only made me angrier;
why didn't she do that all the time?

My hard feelings festered through a disastrous four-game road trip. We lost to Arkansas for the first time in school history. I wasn't speaking to Abby — or much of anybody — and she was starting to play more poorly than she ever had.

We went to UConn, never an easy trip, and in this instance it was like walking into the mouth of a dragon. They were the top-ranked team in the country, and we got destroyed, 72–57. We hit new season lows for points and shooting percentage.

Most of the time after a loss it was a very eerie feeling. Pat would walk in and wouldn't just immediately start blasting. She doesn't say a word, which is way worse. She just kind of looks at you. I could imitate her: She catches her breath, and then shakes her head very slowly, and looks down at you. Then she says in a very soft voice, "I'm embarrassed," or she would call us out individually, and that wasn't a low voice, it was more aggressive. You actually felt like you hurt her. That was pretty powerful for me, and most of my teammates, whether it was because you disgraced the uniform or the program or yourself. For me, I felt like my insides were ripped up. For players who were not so innately competitive, it made you question, "Why am I not feeling that way too?" And now she's got you.

— KELLIE JOLLY

We had five losses and it was only January, and the road trip still wasn't over. Our next opponent was second-ranked Old Dominion, and we flew to Norfolk, Virginia, stopping in Washington, D.C., to change planes. I sat in the airport, with Tyler asleep on my lap, drained and dispirited. Across the terminal, I spotted the North Carolina basketball team and my old friend Sylvia Rhyne Hatchell, who were also passing through on a road trip. I must have looked pitiful, because Sylvia came over and dropped a hand on my shoulder.

"How you doing, Pat?"

"Oh, I'm doing all right," I said.

"Well, just hang in there till next year," she said.

In Norfolk, we checked into the hotel, and Holly, Mickie, and I went for a drink on the waterfront. We studied our schedule, counting up the teams we thought we could beat versus the potential losses. There was hardly a game we felt sure about; a silence fell over the table. "We could be the first Tennessee team that doesn't even get into the NCAA tournament," Mickie said.

I clenched my jaw. I'd had this same argument at home with R.B. He stared at our schedule with his cautious, analytical banker's eye and announced, "We won't win twenty games."

"Oh yes we will," I said.

"I don't see how."

"Let me tell you something," I said. "We are not waiting until next year."

I refused to give up. I spent the next day soul searching with our entire team. I met with each player individually, starting with Abby. Mickie had finally intervened and, as always, told me what I needed to hear instead of what I wanted to hear. "Pat, you have to sit down and talk to Abby or we're going to lose her for the year," she said. My problems with Abby were affecting the whole team's well-being, including Mickie's.

"Either get rid of me, or do something, because I can't take it anymore," Mickie said. "Y'all have got to come to some kind of truce."

"She needs to come to me," I said.

"You're the adult," Mickie said.

"I don't know why they fight me."

"Pat, what are we fighting over? Aren't we all on the same side?"

Mickie was right, of course. I found Abby

in the hotel, and we sat and talked. I made a rare concession: for once, I told a player that I was wrong.

"I need to be the adult in this situation, and I haven't been," I said.

Abby replied, "Pat, I don't think you understand how much I do care about this team."

Abby wanted to be a stronger personality and emotional leader for the team, she said, but she just didn't know how. "I'll help you," I said. I suggested she talk to my old friend Michelle Marciniak, and I set up a phone date for the two of them. Michelle had learned how to cope with my demands, and Abby could too.

"Look, when Pat yells at you, that's actually how she shows she has confidence in you," Michelle told her. "When she ignores you, that's when you're in trouble."

The meeting with Abby was just the first of many that day. The entire team gathered in my room for a team therapy session that lasted for five hours, and it lingers in the memory of the people in the room for its gut-spilling honesty and frequency of tears. "Why did you come to Tennessee?" I asked all of them. "What did you think we were about?" Any notion I had that the team was too laid-back or they didn't care was dispelled. Every kid in the room cried. We die laughing about it at reunions now, but at the time there was nothing amusing about it, because everyone was so distraught. The line most often quoted came from our young center LaShonda Stephens, who was crying so hard she couldn't catch her breath.

"I thought this was s-s-supposed to be fun!" she said.

The next night we played with our whole hearts and delivered our feistiest performance of the year. We actually built a 10-point lead on Old Dominion deep into the second half. But we couldn't hold on: the refs called six fouls on us in the space of two minutes, and ODU staged a comeback. It was our third loss in four games.

When I walked in the locker room, Abby was kicking garbage cans across the room. Holdsclaw had her head in her arms, and young Kyra Elzy was crying so hard I could hear her hitch. Kyra was just a naive freshman, but she'd had the duty all night of trying to guard Ticha Penicheiro, a dashing all-American who was the best guard in the country. We had prepped Kyra as best we could, but Penicheiro had hung 25 points on her.

I'd never seen a team so pained by a loss — and while I felt awful, I was also relieved.

It was the emotional buy-in I'd been waiting for. "Listen up," I said. "Get your heads
up. If you give effort like this all the time, if
you fight like this, I'm telling you, I promise
you, we'll be there in March. You hadn't
fought like this every night. I *enjoyed*
coaching this team tonight." I told Kyra that
we would see Old Dominion again, in the
NCAA tournament, and she would get
another shot at Penicheiro. Next time we'd
make sure she was ready.

> Somehow Pat really picked us up. She
> praised us, and I will be honest, if she had
> been critical at that point, we'd have been
> done. We were quite immature and not
> real stable at that point. That was a huge
> moment.
>
> — KELLIE JOLLY

Kyra Elzy hated to lose as much as any
young woman I'd ever met. She was a
Kentuckian who had been coming to our
basketball camps since the age of fourteen;
the first time I ever saw her she was wearing
a Western Kentucky T-shirt. I grabbed her
by it. "Future Lady Vols don't come here
with another college's shirt on," I said. We
recruited Kyra all through high school, and
one of the reasons I wanted her in orange

was because of the way she reacted when she lost. The night her high school team dropped a heartbreaker in the state championship, she threw herself across her bed, screaming and crying, while her grandmother stood out in the hall saying, "Baby, baby, what happened? Oh, baby, you can't win 'em all." Kyra acted like she didn't want to live to see another day. I called her house that night and I said, "I know it hurts now, but we're gonna win a national championship while you're here and you'll forget all about a state championship."

But then Kyra got to Tennessee in the fall of '96 and I'd started in on her. She was a long, slim, limber kid who looked like a rare flower, and she was my second-favorite target after Abby. Kyra was a lovely, sweet person, but I badgered her to get meaner. "I would take you to lunch," I said contemptuously, "but I wouldn't take you to war." The second half of the season I transitioned to another taunt: I told her, "We're a two-guard away from winning a championship." If *only* we had someone who could play her position, I said.

Kyra would go into Mickie's or Holly's office and say she'd had it, she was going back to LaGrange, Kentucky. Mickie would calm her down. "Now, Elzy, hang in there;

as long as Pat is on you, she knows you have it in you. She's just trying to get it out of you."

She rode me like a Kentucky Derby horse.
— KYRA ELZY

All season long my father asked me why I kept playing Elzy and our other freshman, Niya Butts. They were unfinished players who were getting schooled by our opponents. But they were also quick, and long, and they were so committed to getting better that I could say to Richard, "I'm telling you, Dad, they're going to be factors for us in March."

The dramas continued; it never got easier. Kellie Jolly, after working for six hours a day, made a near-miraculous recovery from her knee surgery and rejoined us with fourteen games left on the schedule — it seemed like a luxury to have two healthy guards in the backcourt — but it was short-lived, because senior Laurie Milligan promptly suffered a season-ending injury against Alabama, dislocating her kneecap.

We lost ten games, to equal the worst season in my tenure. They got booed and heard insults from the stands, and I said a few things that toughened up their skin too.

When Louisiana Tech whipped us 98–80, I said, "I feel like I'm coaching a seventh-grade team." We fell out of the top 10 in the rankings for the first time in a decade. During the Southeastern Conference tournament, Abby went into such a terrible shooting slump that she ended up weeping in my arms in a hotel hallway.

But just before the NCAA tournament was about to begin, we had another meeting. I didn't care what our record was anymore; our team had learned from all that losing, and we were a far better team in March than we had been in January. It would be a hard road to the Final Four in Cincinnati, I told them, but we were capable of it, if we were willing to keep working on our weaknesses, right up until the end. "What do you want to do?" I asked them. This time Abby answered in just the right tone.

"We want to go to Cincinnati," she said.

But then we got our tournament draw: to get to the Final Four we'd have to go through the number one team in the country, UConn. The same UConn team that had destroyed us a couple of months earlier by a score of 72–57. The same UConn team that was undefeated and top ranked at 33-0 and had a massive force in the paint in the six-foot-eight Kara Wolters.

We had ten losses and our tallest player was six foot four. But I told our team, "I like our chances. I feel great about this matchup." Why? Because they were the same team we'd seen the last time — but I knew we were a different one, with a whole new outlook. All the pressure would be on them, while no one expected anything out of us.

We practiced like dogs for a week, and when I was tough on them, Abby was the one who kept everyone on the same page. "If there is a championship in us, that woman will get it out of us," she told everybody.

The Counter Queens had studied UConn and were prepared. We knew how UConn wanted to pass, move, and cut, and we thought we could take some things away. As far as Wolters, "We're gonna put an orange uniform on her before she ever gets to the paint," I told our centers Pashen Thompson and Tiffani Johnson. "When she gets ready to take a shower and pulls off her uniform, it's gonna be orange."

But the biggest counter would simply be how much better we were. Our glaring weaknesses were gone. Abby Conklin was a different leader: an openly caring one. She had always been one of our most selfless players, and that virtue began to shine through. Kyra Elzy and Niya Butts had become great on-the-ball defenders. Elzy had become a scoring threat, too, and nobody knew it but us. Most important, with Kellie Jolly back we were a more confident, attacking team. I told Kellie she had the green light. "You've got to be more offensive minded than you have been all year," I said.

We were the biggest underdogs in the tournament. So much so that when the Lady Vols went out to warm up for the game, we saw tournament officials giving instructions to the UConn staff about how the award presentations would go. No one bothered to clue us in, we noticed. They just ignored us. Our kids stared across the court balefully — it only made them determined to deliver the shock of the year.

I will never forget taking the floor and there was no doubt in my mind we were going to win that game. I just remember in warmups looking at the other end of the floor and seeing UConn's players and knowing we were going to beat them, because they had no idea what they were up against.
— KELLIE JOLLY

The ball went up. Second possession of the game, Kellie slashed straight through the UConn defense — and hit a layup. Next, it was Kyra's turn. She caught the ball on the perimeter, and you could almost feel the UConn defense lay off her, because they didn't think she was a shooter. Kyra launched a three — and boom, it ripped through the net.

> I don't know how Pat did it. That's part of her magic. We were broke down, disappointed, we had fallen out of the top 10 for the first time in I don't know how many years. But we were, like, "Bring it on, let's GO." We came out and punched them and I don't think they knew what hit 'em.
>
> — KYRA ELZY

Our game plan worked almost to perfection. Kyra and Niya's defense harassed the UConn guards into horrendous shooting; they made just 6 of 27 shots. By the end of the game, Kellie would score 19 points. We led 45–33 at the half and still had a 14-point lead with a minute to go. Final score: Tennessee 91, UConn 81.

It was the most unlikely game we'd ever win over the Huskies. No one had gotten within single digits of them all season, and here we came with 91 points. Geno would admit that he simply wasn't prepared for what we threw at him that day — but in a way he was partly responsible. It was a case of our greatest adversary pushing us to another level, and he would reply in the coming years by raising his own team to a higher level.

> You learn. You got to expect that when you beat someone one way, they may do something completely different the next time. And son of a bitch if Pat didn't come out in that game and do some things different.
>
> — GENO AURIEMMA

When we boarded our bus that night headed to Cincinnati for the Final Four, I said, "It's been a *long* year, but I told you if you believed in each other we would be here. Doesn't this feel good? Now don't just go to Cincinnati happy to be there. Go out and bring that trophy *home.*"

And they did. We met Old Dominion again for the championship, and this time we were ready for them. I knew it just one minute into the game; our defensive presence was so intense, the look in our eyes so bright, that I thought, *We got a repeat right here.* Kyra Elzy was Ticha Penicheiro's nightmare. Here's how much Kyra had grown: she held Penicheiro to just 10 points — and forced her into 11 turnovers. "She had those long slender arms that seemed to go on forever," Penicheiro said. Kellie Jolly broke two NCAA Final Four records, Chamique Holdsclaw was named tournament MVP, and as for Abby Conklin, she knocked down four of five shots to break the game open and was our second-leading scorer.

> When you look at where we started, and where we ended up, how she got us to that point without us killing each other and her killing us, that was remarkable.
> — KELLIE JOLLY

There had been so many days when I walked out of practice and asked our staff, "Do you think I was too hard on them today?" and they had answered, "Yes, we think you were too hard today." I know I was too hard on Abby. It's an open question whether we'd have lost fewer games if I had gone about it differently, but I didn't know any other way, except to keep working until we had turned our negatives into positives. Fortunately, a young woman who wasn't sure she was good enough to play at Tennessee turned out to be exceptional — and exceptionally tough. By the time Abby Conklin finished her career at UT, she had played in three national championship games and won two of them.

No team had ever won a national title with ten losses. The worst season we ever had turned into one of the best we ever had, because we had finally quit fighting with one another — but we never quit fighting.

Our "three-peat" of championships from 1996 to 1998 looks in the record book now like a solid block of triumph, but each one was distinct; the casts changed and we took dramatically different routes. There were moments in those years that I felt a fine professional control — but I'd be lying if I said that every motivational technique and rapid-fire decision I made was a matter of brilliant calculation. Just as often they were a result of pure feel. Here's the truth: sometimes, the game plays you.

You labor into a headwind, and then suddenly the wind shifts and it's at your back. In a way, the most absurd, hard-to-fathom aspect of the '97 championship was what followed: the almost effortless, record-breaking 39-0 undefeated season in '98 that was our finest ever.

I knew right away it would be a different kind of year when even our practices had an extra intensity. We had four new players, freshmen who burst onto the floor like atomic elements. Tamika Catchings of Duncanville, Texas, Semeka Randall of Cleveland, Ohio, Kristen "Ace" Clement of Philadelphia, Pennsylvania, and Teresa Geter of Columbia, South Carolina, were called the greatest recruiting class in history, and they lived up to it. They were so powerful and so hot burning that I worried they would flame out.

For the first and only time in my life, a team would outstrip my own ambition and vision for them. It wasn't my job to push them, I quickly discovered — it was my job to slow them down, tell them when to stop. That fall, one of our veteran players, Misty Greene, called Abby Conklin to deliver an incredulous report.

"Bud, you wouldn't believe it," she said. "She asked us if we *felt* like practicing today. She was worried we were tired."

But they were also young, and needy, and as a group they would require more mothering and less pure coaching than any team I'd ever had. When we sat down for our annual "family night" meeting, in which we circled up and shared details about our parents and upbringing, we discovered that nine of our twelve players, including all four freshmen, had been raised for much of their lives by single mothers, or grandmothers, many of whom had worked multiple jobs to send their kids to college. To this day I believe that team was driven in part by a needful urgency to repay those maternal debts.

As I studied our players and thought about how to cope with them, I looked at my own son for clues, as was becoming my habit. Watching Tyler's little mind grow made me think in new ways about the process of maturing, and how to encourage it. The idea of coaching, and parenting, wasn't to create obedient little robots moving in predetermined choreography. Discipline only took you so far. Ty had reached the age where it required constant thought to deal with him, because he'd grown into a fully conversant little master negotiator.

One afternoon in the summer after our '97 title, he had a pouting fit in the Atlanta airport during a layover. He wanted a new toy. I said, "No way." We were renovating our house that summer, and when we cleaned out his room, I was appalled at the number of toys he'd collected, to the point that I'd made him pack some of them up to take to a community center for kids who weren't as fortunate.

Tyler pouted from Concourse A to Concourse B. I was not really up for pouting, and he generally wasn't allowed to do it, but he was six, so I gave him a little leeway. But when I suggested we needed to go into a bookstore to buy a birthday gift for someone, the pout deepened and he jerked my hand.

"You're going with me," I said. "Your attitude is not good, and you need to think about someone besides yourself."

Then I said, "What little boy gets to do more than you?"

He said, "The UConn coach's kid."

I managed to contain myself and I picked up his little backpack and dumped it out. I said, "We're going to count your toys." There were twenty-five toys in there; it was like the midget car at the circus — they just kept coming out.

"Tyler, there are twenty-five toys here. Do you really think you need a new one?"

"Mama, that one's not a toy," he said, pointing.

"Okay, twenty-four. Do you really think you need another toy?"

"But I want one."

"You need to think about this, son."

Pout. Frown.

"I tell you what we'll do," I said. "If you had your own money, you could just buy a toy, right?

"Yes."

"Okay. Let's write down chores you can do that I could pay you for."

We made a list: he could make up our bed, he could feed the fish, he could feed the cats, he could wash the car. Then we talked about how much he got for each chore. Well, I created a mercenary. We got home, and he went manic with the chores and thought up new things to do for cash every day. I walked in our bedroom closet, and he had arrayed my shoes in a perfect line. "Why did you do that?" I asked.

He said, "That's one of my chores."

"How much?" I asked, faintly.

"Five dollars."

But for the most part he continued to be an easy child, coasting along in my slipstream and treating it all as a giant sleepover. There were nights on the road when he insisted on staying with Mickie or Holly. Aunt Mickie taught him how to "party" in her hotel room: she let him jump from the dresser onto the bed and sprint down the hall with nothing but his underwear on.

Our freshmen declared their need for my maternal side almost as soon as they set foot on campus. It seemed like each one of them had some raw emotional vulnerability. There was Ace Clement, one of six kids raised by her single mother, Sue. Ace had broken Wilt Chamberlain's high school scoring record back in Philadelphia, but she arrived at Tennessee with a broken heart: she had fallen hard for a pro athlete over the summer and was pining away for him. Her first question to me was "When can I go home for a weekend?" It took some time to talk her through it and persuade her to stay at Tennessee, and every day I worried that I'd wake up and find she had bolted.

> Pat wanted to know what their issues were. She didn't want to bury her head. She wanted to know, and some had more issues than others. She wanted to be needed as more than just a basketball coach. She enjoyed that, she reached out to them, and she always had the energy to do it. We had some kids that really needed structure, love, and a firm hand. And Pat was perfect for that.
>
> — MICKIE DeMoss

Semeka Randall was a powerfully built

young woman with a personality like dynamite, but she could go suddenly dark, and get a little sullen if she didn't get what she needed from me. She was emotionally hungry; she was extremely close to her mother, Bertha, who worked two jobs as a guidance counselor to support them, and had never been separated from her before. Semeka played the game with the fervor of someone who had to fight for everything; she became a great ball hawk growing up in Cleveland, where the guys she played with wouldn't pass her the ball. If she wanted it, she said, "I had to get it myself."

Bertha tried to forbid Semeka from playing pickup with the guys because it was so rough, but Semeka was always ducking out of the house to find a game. Bertha would send her to the store for milk, and Semeka would stay gone for an hour. Bertha would come marching down the street, saying, "Have you been playing ball again?" She would try to hand Semeka dolls to play with instead, but Semeka hated the dolls so much she broke them into pieces. She would tear their heads off, pull their arms off, and then their legs, and throw the pieces under her bed. That was Semeka.

"We need you to embrace your role and be an emotional leader," I said. "Do you

479

want to be that for us?"

"Yes," she said.

"Okay, then. So what do you need from me?" I asked.

"A hug," she said.

I gave it to her. When the press asked Semeka how she was adjusting to my famously vocal coaching style, Semeka answered, "If she stops yelling at me, that means she doesn't care. Evidently, she cares about me a lot."

After five championships, I felt comfortable with who I was with our players; I no longer had anything to prove or authority to establish. I didn't feel I had to strike any particular pose, and I didn't want to be withholding with this team. They didn't need it. I became more aware of which players I didn't have enough daily contact with. One afternoon I wandered over to our sophomore center LaShonda Stephens and draped an arm around her, and I literally felt her physically relax. She must have needed it, I realized.

Easily the most affectionate Lady Vol of all was Tamika Catchings. When she was a seventeen-year-old recruit, I visited her at home in Duncanville, Texas, and she said to me shyly, "You want to see my room?" I said sure. It was a tiny bedroom in the back of the apartment she shared with her mother, Wanda, who was divorced from her father, Harvey, a former NBA player. Tamika kept her room as neat as an infantryman's locker, and all over the walls were motivational slogans. She said, shyly, "You want to see my closet?" I said sure again, and she opened it and pulled out her most treasured garment. It was her uniform from a USA Junior National team.

After we left the house and got into the rental car, I said to Mickie, "It's going to kill me if we don't get that kid. It's going to kill me."

She was one of the most endearing players I'd ever met, with a face like a doll. She didn't have an ounce of artifice or emotional dishonesty. We would have only one run-in in four years. In her first practice I criticized her defensive stance and told her, "Get your hands up!" Tamika got tearful. She was usually so perfect she had never been corrected.

"Do I have to handle you with lace gloves?" I asked. "Do I have to pamper you? Or do I have to send you back to Duncanville, Texas?"

Tamika's immediate reaction was, "My mom would kill me if I got sent home." She straightened up, and after that we never had another incident.

Catch was so unspoiled that she thought every hotel room was the Ritz. Early that season we went back to my alma mater, UT-Martin, for a game, and stayed at the only hotel in town, a small Econo Lodge. It was so much bigger than her room back in Duncanville that Tamika thought it was a palace.

"I love the Econo Lodge," she said.

"Well, you just wait till we get to the Hilton," I said.

Catch was so sweetly accommodating that she even obeyed my edict about a clean locker room. Our inner dressing area had rows of handsome, highly polished wood lockers with doors on them, and every so often I would walk through there and get annoyed because the kids were so messy. They would leave their doors wide open with clothes and shoes falling out. It irked me to see the locker room we had worked so hard to get look slovenly. "How your area looks, that's a reflection on the team as a whole," I said. "What's behind closed doors, that's yours, but you never know who is walking through this locker room and you have all this stuff hanging out. Tidy it up." Of course, they would clean it up for a day or two, and then they would revert right back to sloppiness. But Tamika's area was always neat and orderly, just like her room at home.

So it was all the more surprising when I noticed that Catch was not following some of my directions on the floor. Then she blew a curfew. I knew that Catch was partly deaf: she had a condition called congenital sensorineural hearing loss. She was our quietest player; she usually communicated with a nod or shake of her head instead of speaking aloud, because she was self-conscious about her speech, which had a slight, telltale slur. But I'd been told by her high school coach that her hearing loss wasn't too significant, and she showed few signs of it.

When Catch returned to our hotel a half hour after curfew during a road trip to Stanford, however, I knew her hearing was worse than I'd realized. She admitted she hadn't heard me announce the curfew time on the team bus. She also admitted, after some gentle questions, that she couldn't hear my signals on the court in crowd noise. I decided to confront the issue, and we had her tested. It turned out Catch had "profound" hearing loss, and that she had covered up for it since she was a girl.

I asked Catch if she would consider wearing hearing aids, very small ones that were all but invisible. "I don't know if I'd be comfortable with that," she answered. Catch had hearing aids until the third grade, but other children had mercilessly teased her about how big they were, and she was so pained and embarrassed that one day she'd thrown them away in a field. She had never worn them again and instead learned to compensate to an amazing degree over the years; she read lips and smiled and laughed at jokes even when she didn't hear them. She refused to concede to the idea of "impairment" or "disability."

I replied that in my judgment she was going to be a great player who would have to appear in her share of press conferences. "You have big goals in life," I said. She was going to have to speak in public — and her hearing and speech issues were going to be more conspicuous than a hearing aid. "Tamika, we all have problems," I said. "My eyes are bad, so I wear contacts and glasses to see. My feet are bad and I have to wear orthotics. If you have a problem, why not fix it?" But the clincher may have been when I told her that I had gotten braces at the age of twenty-nine, to fix my crooked front teeth. Tamika finally agreed to try new hearing aids and also to work with our university speech therapists.

It was trial and error with the hearing aids. As with Becky Clark before her, sometimes

Tamika would sweat so much in practice or games that they would break or malfunction. We worked on her anticipation and on hand signaling. Tamika today would tell you that she actually views her hearing loss as something of an asset as an athlete, because it made her more observant and intuitive. But back then it was a struggle, and we had to stay on her to wear the hearing aids.

"Where are they?" I'd ask.

"In my locker," she'd say.

"Go get 'em," I'd say. "I'm not paying for them to sit in your locker."

The player on our '98 team who was most in need of my unconditional affection and reassurance was not a freshman. She was our centerpiece, the lead Meek, that peaking virtuoso Chamique Holdsclaw. On the court Chamique was so natural she seemed to wear the game like a second skin: she could pull up, spin, and drop a hovering finger roll all in one motion, conjuring up moves in the moment, reshaping her body in midair. But take a ball out of her hands and she was a tender, shrinking young woman.

"You look so scary!" she had blurted when I came to the Astoria Houses, a project in Queens, New York, to recruit her. Now, if anyone should have been scared it was me;

Chamique's high school coach, Vinny Cannizzaro, a former cop, had insisted on escorting me through the project with a gun inside his blazer.

Chamique's grandmother June, who had raised her, said, "Chamique, you need to apologize!" Chamique stammered something, and I just laughed and told her it was all right, she could make it up to me by coming to Tennessee.

I remember my grandmother looking at me like "I'm gonna choke you, I taught you better." But for me it was surreal. Pat Summitt was in my kitchen in the Astoria projects. I'd seen her on TV but she was in my house, and you shoulda seen the lineup out the building when she came. All the dudes were off the court. She was, like, "Are they gonna bother me?" The neighborhood wasn't the safest. But they were just lined up to see Pat Summitt.
— CHAMIQUE HOLDSCLAW

Chamique was more than the usual wounded adolescent. She'd had some horrendous episodes in her childhood; her mother, Bonita, battled alcoholism, and her father, Willie, was a diagnosed schizophrenic. June Holdsclaw was doing her best

486

to make up for it and give Chamique love and stability, but she was a tender, fragile young woman. Chamique was so sensitive that she hated it when I yelled at *other* players, much less her. The first time I turned my voice and eyes on her as a freshman, she almost went right back to New York.

I barked at her and she just stopped dead and started to walk out of the practice gym.

She said, "That's it, I quit."

On her way out of the door, she yelled, "I'm calling *Geno*! 'Cause Geno wouldn't treat me like this!"

I stood there and watched her go, nonplussed. But Mickie looked at me like a deer in the headlights.

"Pat, we got to do something, we can't afford to lose her!"

"Well, then, go get her," I said.

Mickie went running out the door. She found Chamique in the locker room muttering, "Man, I'm getting my bus ticket and going back to New York." The bus was all she could afford. Mickie said, "Look, Holdsclaw, you can't quit; you know Pat just wants the best for you. Just hang in there because at the end of the tunnel is a great reward." Chamique came back out on the court, and at the end of practice I put an arm around her and said, "Why don't you come out to the house and eat with us tonight?"

Chamique settled down, but for the next few weeks whenever she was unhappy she'd talk about that bus ticket. Of course, I knew Chamique wasn't going anywhere, because June Holdsclaw wanted her down south with us, where she'd be taken care of. She'd told Chamique flat out, "Once you go to Tennessee, you're not coming back."

It was a small thing that finally won Chamique over, completely unrelated to basketball. I thought she was underperforming in the classroom; though her grades were nothing to worry about, she was capable of more. She'd had a first-rate prep school education as a scholarship student at Christ the King in Brooklyn, which regularly sent kids on to the Ivy League. I called her in for a talk and put my hand on her shoulder.

"Just as great an athlete and player as you are, you can be just as great a student," I said. "I know what kind of work you can do. Mique, some people I can accept this from, but not you."

For some reason, that did it; that was my breakthrough with her. Chamique bore down in the classroom, and over the next two semesters her grade point average popped up to a 3.5. She never again threatened to ride a bus back to New York. All she needed to know was that I cared about her beyond basketball.

> When she told me that, it was the realest, most honest thing I ever heard. I was like wow, she really believes in me, the way she looked at me with those eyes. After that we were a match made in heaven.
> — CHAMIQUE HOLDSCLAW

The result of all this need and emotion was a team of swift, rippling electricity. The "Three Meeks," Semeka, Tamika, and Chamique, floated across the floor creating one unbelievable play after another; the ball would go flying up the court from Meek to Meek and never hit the ground. It was like watching volleyball. One of them would be our leading scorer in thirty-seven of our thirty-nine games, and it was the great pleasure of my working life to draw up plays in which all of them got to touch the ball.

> We played the game for one another.
> — CHAMIQUE HOLDSCLAW

In November we went out to Stanford for a Thanksgiving road trip, and I felt the wave of a great season building. I was sleepless, full of something. I woke up at two, four, and six A.M. Next to me in the bed, Tyler did a 360 in his sleep. I woke up once with his feet in my ribs, and again with his head in my ribs. He was a little body magnet chasing me around in his sleep. Finally I got out of bed and called up Billie Moore, who had come up for the game, and I said, "Billie, I've got to walk and talk." We went for an early morning power walk to burn off my restlessness. All my guardedness and emotional reserve were falling away with this squad and I didn't know if it was the right thing or not. I finally articulated what was brimming in me.

"This is the team I've worked my whole life for," I told Billie.

Stanford was an annual barometer game for us; if we could compete with the Cardinal, we knew we were in business. They were a consistently first-rate team, beautifully schooled by my great friend Tara VanDerveer, whom I would have happily sent my own daughter to play for, if I'd had one. Tara invariably poked holes in my team and showed me where we were weak. But that morning Tara called me and asked, "Are you excited about this game?"

"Sure I am," I said.

"I'm not," she confessed.

Tara was right to be apprehensive: it was an 18-point victory for us, 88–70. Even Billie Moore, always my toughest critic, was agape. "Holy smokes, Pat," she said. "Who's going to beat you?"

"I don't know," I said. "I don't know."

From then on, massive crowds gathered to watch us win by massive scores: we beat DePaul 125–46, Georgia 102–43, Vanderbilt 106–45.

And we beat third-ranked UConn 84–69, in Thompson-Boling Arena in front of 24,597, the largest crowd ever to witness a women's basketball game up to that point. Geno met me at half-court for the pregame handshake in such a gigantic swell of noise that I had to lean over and shout into his ear, "This is a compliment to *both* programs," and he nodded in agreement. Even the eaves were packed with people standing, until the fire marshal shut the doors and left a crowd of hundreds outside.

Kellie came in from warm-ups and said, breathlessly, "It's like a rock concert out there."

At Christmas, R.B. and I gave Tyler a go-kart, and it was his great delight to make me ride in it with him and accelerate through puddles and splash mud all over me. Our season was like that — one long roar of acceleration, a continuation of the same blowout game, each one played at the same high speed. We beat teams by an average of 30 points a night. I kept an eye on our players for fatigue; I was constantly worried they might burn out. I coddled them, and spoiled them, the way I spoiled Ty. I had them over for dinner and cooked every single item they requested. The menu: eight steaks, three kinds of chicken, fried shrimp, beans, potatoes, corn, and sweet potato pie.

As needy as they could be off the court, they were impossibly confident on it. Their locker room was full of thudding, thumping music, and when I asked what it was, Semeka told me it was their theme song, a rap entitled "No Limit Soldiers."

"I've never heard it," I said to Semeka.

"You don't want to," she said.

Ace might have required soothing talks about her love life, but on the practice court, she dove for every loose ball until she had floor burns, and she absorbed my demands with an unblinking steady resilience.

Me to Ace: "What have you learned?"

"That I'm soft."

"Prove me wrong."

"I will."

By the time of the NCAA tournament, we

were the overwhelming favorite, flatly the most deserving team in America, and I'd never desired a title so badly for a group. But we were so young I didn't know how they would react to the pressure. I was willing to go to any length to prepare them, use any manipulation to get their minds right.

"I want this for the kids," I said to Mickie and Holly. "I'll do anything to help them get it. I'll *say* anything. I'll get a technical. I'll strip."

We went to Nashville for the NCAA regionals, hosted at Vanderbilt's Memorial Gymnasium, where our Sweet 16 opponent would be Rutgers, coached by one of my best friends in the game, C. Vivian Stringer. At a pregame banquet, the Rutgers kids tried to get into the heads of our freshmen. One of them told Semeka, "I got one thing to say to you: overrated."

The next afternoon when the Lady Vols took the floor to limber up, the Rutgers kids were still at it. "It's hanging time," they said. "Get the rope." Even Vivian gave me the business when I went over to the bench to greet her. Vivian and I had a teasing relationship that went back years; we were late-night phone companions and didn't miss a chance to hit a casino together for a little blackjack, either. Memorial Gymnasium was packed to the rafters with fifteen thousand Lady Vols fans in a state of pandemonium, and as I reached out to hug Vivian, she murmured in my ear, "Fifteen thousand people. And they all have the nerve to wear orange." I pulled away giggling. The Meeks took care of any concerns I had about Rutgers, 92–60.

I knew from long experience the NCAA Elite Eight was the toughest game to win in college basketball for a favored team. It was an intermediate hurdle, but the one I dreaded most, because of the pressure to reach a Final Four. Our opponent in this one was a team every bit as fast and athletic as we were, North Carolina, coached by my old friend Sylvia Rhyne. As we watched tape of them, my tension grew. We had beaten teams all season by 30 — but margins tended to shrink in the Elite Eight, and I had a feeling we were due for a tough ball game. North Carolina was no doormat.

That night, I couldn't sleep again. I had a nightmare that I was fishing off our dock, and I got fishhooks caught in my eyes. I shuddered awake at about six A.M. and never went back to sleep. It was a premonition, I feared.

The thing you need to know about pressure is that it may be invisible, but it has physical properties. It constricts the blood flow to your smaller muscles, costing fine motor control; narrows your vision; and slows your reactions. It's real. The invisible vise of it gripped our kids against North Carolina. Suddenly their feet and hands wouldn't work, and for the first time all season they actually got outrun down the floor. Chamique went for a stretch of twenty-two minutes and only scored 2 points, because she kept fumbling the ball.

Chamique came to the bench. "The ball keeps slipping out of my hands," she said.

"Don't make excuses," I said. "Make plays."

But with 7:19 left we trailed by 61–49. We were sick, and stunned. "What can we do?" Semeka asked me desperately. "What can we do?" Holly moved to the end of the bench, hoping superstitiously that it might change our luck. Up in the stands, Tyler sat in R.B.'s lap, tremulous. "Are we going to lose?" he asked.

"It looks bad," R.B. warned him.

I called a time-out. Hoping to snap them out of it, I hurled my clipboard so hard it broke into two pieces. The shards flew in the air. "This crowd is doing everything it can to help you!" I hollered over the noise. "Now what are *you* doing? Am I coaching the wrong team? Should I be over there? You're letting them play your game! If you're going down, you're going down fighting. Whatever you need to do, do it. Claw their eyes out."

But Kellie's speech in that time-out was the more effective one. For the first and only time in her career, she raised her voice at her teammates. She slammed my footstool on the ground so hard she almost splintered the legs.

"I am NOT going home," she screamed, "so you better get out there and help me, because I can't do it alone!"

All that slamming and screaming finally broke the trance. We put on a full-court press. Suddenly the Lady Vols came alive — and turned into a swarm of sharks. There was a steady rhythm to their play: strip, steal, layup. We ran fresh players in and out, and shifted defenses, freezing the Carolina players into uncertainty. The momentum swung — hard. We scored 12 points in two minutes.

"I need some heart pills," Elzy said breathlessly on the bench. Mickie ran through ten different offenses on her clipboard, probing, looking for plays that worked. Holly grabbed me by the shoulders and looked me level in the eyes. "Get Jolly back in the game for free throws!" I nodded. We went 13 for 13 on free throws down the stretch.

And we outscored North Carolina 27–9 over those final seven minutes.

Final score: Tennessee 76, North Carolina 70.

As we came off the floor I turned to Holly, Mickie, and Al. "We're going to win the whole thing now," I said, tiredly but certainly. In the back hallway of the arena, I found my parents. My father stumped toward me with his cane and dragged me into a hug that knocked the breath out of me. He banged his cane on the floor and said, "That's about the best job you ever done. This time I admit it. I'd about give up."

That night we went to a great old Nashville café called Rotiers. "Give me your coldest beer," I said. We sat there until four A.M., reliving the game, in disbelief.

By the time we got back to Knoxville, I'd slept just five hours in two days. But instead of going to sleep, I had to go to a parent-teacher meeting at Tyler's school, and transform myself from a shouting coach to a concerned mother. Tyler's teacher had requested the meeting because he had gotten in trouble for fighting on the playground. I chatted amiably with his teacher and promised I would speak to him about it.

That night I had the talk with him. But it wasn't quite the one he expected.

"What do you do if someone pushes you?" I said.

"What?" he said.

"You push back," I said firmly.

We went to the Final Four in Kansas City and made it look like a waltz. I remember feeling tension over things that now seem small: Kellie came down with a sore throat and couldn't hit a shot in practice, and Tamika went into a shooting slump too. But we slaughtered Arkansas by almost 30 in the semifinal. On the morning of the championship game against our old foe Louisiana Tech, Tyler said, "Mama, I *love* them." I said, "I do too."

That night in the locker room I told them, "I've never been more confident of a team in my life." It was a blowout from the very outset, 93–75, touched off by Kellie, who sailed in a couple of epic three-pointers to open the game. She went on to a career-high 20, as did Catch, with 27. At halftime it was already such a rout that Tech's coach, my old friend Leon Barmore, saw us in the hallway and called out, "Hey, Pat, take it easy!"

Afterward, Leon summed up what I'd been thinking all season. "That's the greatest women's basketball team I've ever seen in all my years of coaching," he said. They were that, and more, to me: they were the only instance of perfection I would ever experience. But they were also so young and imperfect, and if I traced my delight in them back to its source, it came from that, from seeing ordinary young women, with all of their ordinary problems, do the extraordinary through sheer unchained commitment. They made me feel complete, saturated, and utterly exhausted.

When it was done, we all had the strangest reaction. I walked into the locker room, and instead of triumph, I found them in tears. They had just won the championship, and they were . . . crying.

"What's wrong?" I said, alarmed.

"We're sad it's over," they said.

As years went by, the more I thought about it, the more those seasons reminded me of something. We spent months hoping, yearning, studying, and practicing for a coveted but far-off result. We experienced deep spasmodic agonies in getting there. But when it was done and we saw the end result, it erased all the pain, and what was left was pure joy. It was exactly like childbirth. And it was my hope that all my daughters from that era, the Meeks and Kellies, the Vondas, Abbys, and Michelles, felt the same, that the pain faded and they just remembered the beauty that came out of it, like I did.

Are you all right? What is it?

I don't know. Sometimes I have these weird feelings.

What kind of feelings?

It's almost like I'm seeing things.

The doctors talked about this. You're in a safe place.

With people who love you.

I know.

What do you see?

It's hard to describe. It's like this feeling comes over me.

It's not earth-shattering.

Yes, it is.

It's okay. I'm fine.

Is it like seeing a ghost?

No. Not really.

What's it like?

It's like someone's in the house.

— May 19, 2012, Destin, Florida, one year after diagnosis

10
SINGLE MOTHER

There was a toll for all that winning: I was exhausted, played out like a loose string from the years of tension and pressure. R.B., Tyler, and I went to Jackson Hole, Wyoming, with friends for a badly needed vacation. We hiked in the mountain air, swam in lakes, and suspended training rules and enjoyed our liquid refreshments. One afternoon I went into a convenience store to buy more beer for the group. I got a case under one arm, and a case under the other, and carried them to the counter, assuming I was incognito in shorts, a tank top, a hat, and sunglasses.

The clerk said, "Hey, Coach Summitt!"

I froze, my reputation for rectitude on the line.

"I'm a student at Tennessee, working this summer at Jackson Hole. So glad to meet you."

I calmly set the beer on the counter and

looked down at it with a false innocence.

"Huh," I said. "I thought I bought milk!"

In retrospect, the expectations from the three-peat were impossible to meet. Not only were we playing at a pace that was unsustainable, I was living at one. The Tennessee Lady Vols were national icons, and people young and old gathered around our team bus four deep for autographs. *Sports Illustrated* made me the first female coach to grace the cover, and I went on *Charlie Rose* and the morning talk shows. A documentary film, *Cinderella Season: The Lady Vols Fight Back,* chronicling our '97 championship season, aired on a loop on HBO. We were so popular someone actually asked me to autograph a piece of toilet paper.

In the midst of all that, I was chairing a United Way campaign, overseeing a renovation of our house, and writing a principles-of-success book called *Reach for the Summit,* which hit the bestseller lists and made me an in-demand corporate speaker. I went on a national book-signing tour that left me with cramps in my hand. Disney called and wanted the rights to my life story; I refused. The CIA called and asked if I'd address their staff on team building; I accepted. The treadmill spun at a hundred miles an hour, and I couldn't get off. R.B., Tyler, and I were living squeezed into one room while the house was under construction, and my whole life felt like I was trying to pack ten pounds of flour in a five-pound sack. It was a two-hour drive to Johnson City, Tennessee, and I remember making it in one. "My shooting star," R.B. called me. In addition to all those professional obligations, I was also trying to be a good wife, mother, and daughter, care for a dozen players, and recruit.

I never could keep up with the lady. I can remember going on recruiting trips and we'd get on the plane and she'd pull out her briefcase and write recruiting letters. I'd say, "Can we talk for a minute?" And she'd say, "Okay, what do you want to talk about?" and keep writing. She was the queen of multitasking. I don't know how she did it, how her brain stored all that info. She had just boundless energy, boundless.

— MICKIE DEMOSS

The Lady Vols were not only recognized; we were apparently chic. Famed photographer Annie Leibovitz came to Knoxville and took our portraits, which our players found hilarious, since they viewed me as profoundly unhip and culturally out of touch. Fashion consultants put me in blue Armani and moussed my hair, tickling the Meeks.

"Coach, you look great. Very *GQ*," Semeka said.

"What's *GQ*?" I asked.

She explained that it was a high-end magazine. A few days later I had another nice outfit on.

"Hey, Mique!" I said. "Does this look QT?"

"No!" the kids shouted, falling about in giggles.

But the result of all the tumult was that our team went into the '99 season in a strange emotional state. Returning to practice was a let-down — we wanted a shortcut straight to another national title. On the very first day of the new season, Chamique said, "Man, I can't wait to cut down nets this year." It was the wrong attitude, and our minds were on too many other things.

The long joyride came to an end against Duke in the '99 NCAA regional final in Greensboro. "Why isn't this easier?" the looks on our faces said. By the end of the game, our bench was like the front row at a funeral. The final score was 69–63 in favor of Duke; there would be no four-peat. "I'm sorry," Kellie said, when she came to the bench, in tears. "I can't believe it."

Chamique almost fell into my arms. "Coach Summitt, I was so awful," she cried. She took a seat on the bench and draped a towel over her head. I kneeled next to her. "You have to take that towel off your head," I said. "You handled all that success, and now you have to handle failure. You've got to handle losing. We're all here to help you."

All these events led me to think carefully about how I defined success as we entered a new decade in 2000. As usual after a season-ending loss, I stayed in my pajamas the entire next day. But at around four P.M., I finally roused myself. I took a walk, and threw a ball with my son, and shook myself out of my mood.

When you win as much as we did, you start to think you should win every year, and that's just wrong. The three-peat had tricked us into doing the one thing I promised I'd never do: measure success purely on championships. It was my twenty-fifth year as a coach, and if there was one thing I'd learned in that quarter century, it was that losing was a far more common experience than winning.

The coming years would constantly remind me of that. Eight seasons would go by between the three-peat and our next national championship. Eight Aprils, passing in icy showers and shards of sunlight, annual spring sojourns in the NCAA tournament, blurs of action in indistinguishable domes in midsized host cities. We spent Easters as vagabond worshippers in strange churches. I shouted my way from arena to arena, until my throat felt raked in gravel and I carried the perpetual scent of eucalyptus drops on my breath, trying to soothe it.

Kids came in and went out, turning like leaves. Four years seemed like a long time, until it suddenly felt fleeting. Spring always became another fall, and we moved on.

There were impasses and negotiations with players who were changing, becoming more sophisticated and argumentative. They wanted more from the game than self-esteem, with the WNBA offering star players salaries approaching $100,000. They were in some ways more reticent, harder to reach, more attached to their electronics, less easily impressed. They didn't always get my down-home farm analogies, and I found myself stretching to communicate, in ways that didn't come as naturally to me.

Some of them were smarter than me — like Kara Lawson. She was a brilliant, self-possessed, cool-handed guard from Virginia who would lead us to NCAA Final Fours in three of her four years. She turned down Duke and Stanford to come to Tennessee, where she carried a 4.0 in finance, and required an explanation for everything we did. I had to constantly keep my wits about me in dealing with her. As a freshman she didn't feel watching tape was an efficient use of her valuable and highly focused time. "I don't see why we have to do it," she said.

"Let me ask you this," I said. "If you take a math test, when you get the test back, don't you look to see what problems you missed?"

"Coach, I don't *miss* problems on math tests."

"Well, you're gonna watch tape anyway," I said, laughing.

There was a constant undertow from spectators and media to treat those years as failures when we didn't win championships. It was easy for them to say we failed, but it was *my* livelihood and life, and I knew what went into it. Sometimes it was true that not hanging a banner was a disappointment — and sometimes it was the furthest thing from true. Sometimes it was heroic.

Michelle Snow taught us all something about handling loss. She was a six-foot-five center from Pensacola who reminded me of a giant baby bird; we even nicknamed her "Snowbird." She was utterly unique; God only made one of her, an elegant, long, unfolding player whose reach when fully extended was seven foot ten, with a lot of pieces to organize.

I'd never come across such conflicting strengths and weaknesses. Snow could press five hundred pounds with her long legs, but when it came to the upper body, she couldn't do a single push-up. She couldn't gain weight, either. I told her she was on a diet of "see-food": everything she could see, she was supposed to eat. She and Tyler bonded over sweets, and on road trips he would seek out her room and dive into her stash.

One evening someone asked me, "Where's Tyler?" I heard myself answer:

"He's in bed with Michelle Snow, watching cartoons."

But she was a shy and burdened young woman, who would sit apart in the locker room with her head down and her earphones on. It was all I could do to get her to look up. "No one will take you serious when you won't even look 'em in the face," I said. Her makeup was gentle, thoughtful, and sometimes blank. "Snow!" I'd yell, and her head would swivel toward me like a baby dinosaur, looking for a leaf to chew. "I think you need to major in psychology," I said. "Because I can't figure you out. Maybe you can figure yourself out." She took me up on it and got her degree in psychology.

> I told her, I said, "Psychology taught me a lot about you."
> — MICHELLE SNOW

It turned out that Michelle had deeper issues than basketball; she had life-and-death ones: her mother, Rosa, was dying of systemic lupus erythematosus, but she had kept it secret from us because she didn't want any excuses. Imagine carrying that to practice every day? When the rest of our players thought about where to eat, Snow thought about her mother's latest blood test and worried about being a surrogate parent to her four younger brothers and sisters. The things that were so important to the rest of us just weren't as important to Snow.

At the end of the 2001 season, Snow's junior year, we were upset in the Sweet 16 by an underdog team from Xavier, brilliantly coached by a young woman named Melanie Balcomb who eventually became a dear friend of mine. When we got back to Knoxville, Snow went missing. I spent the day in my pajamas, as usual, and late in the day I tried to call her to check on her. There was no answer. I started asking around, and one of the kids said, "Maybe she's at work." I was baffled.

"Snow has a job?" I said.

As soon as the season ended, she had taken shifts in a store at one of the malls to make extra money to send home to her family. I was in my pajamas chewing my lip over basketball, and Snow was at work trying to help her mother.

> I didn't tell her because I didn't want her sympathy.
>
> — MICHELLE SNOW

Never again would I look at a blank face and assume that I had the whole picture. I became a little more flexible and searching with kids.

I struggled constantly with how much slack to cut Snow. She was not a player that I could break down and build up again — because if you broke her down, she might just stay broken. How do you demand all-out commitment from someone when it's obvious she has more important commitments elsewhere? What was the right balance? How do you motivate someone who knows that a ball game is not the most important thing in life — and has her priorities in exactly the right order?

But Snow didn't want special treatment. I dogged her throughout her career, about her stance in the post, her weight; I forced her to take public speaking classes. "Snow!" I'd holler. "You're stronger than you *think* you are!" She didn't want my sympathy as much as she needed me to be a guardian of the right principles, and of her future, which was the greater form of love. Even when she stared back with that blank mask, I knew she was counting on me not to waver. As time went on, players were usually thankful for my firmness, and I had to trust Michelle would be too.

"You may not like me now, but you will love me later," I said.

She was right.

— MICHELLE SNOW

As a senior in '02, Snow carried us back to the NCAA Final Four and solidified her WNBA draft status. She went in the first round to the four-time champion Houston Comets, signing a big enough contract to pay for private nursing for Rosa, which was her real ambition. With Snow, the lessons weren't about championships. They were about carrying on, how to live with a shadow, and they were lessons I would need to employ myself in the years ahead.

Our losses weren't always about ourselves, or what we did on the court. Some years we just weren't quite as great as the team we faced: from 2000 to 2006 we went to five Final Fours and reached three championship games, losing each time to the team whose turn it was to dominate a decade, UConn. There was no beating them, but we sure liked trying. I have a proud image from the '03 final against them: Gwen Jackson rose to the backboard like a drowning swimmer fighting for her last breath, to cut it to 71–68 with twenty-one seconds left, before we finally bowed.

The expectations from the three-peat continued to haunt us: the record book tells me that in 2001 we went 31-3 — and didn't win. In 2002 we went 29-5 — and didn't win. In 2003 we went 33-5 — and again didn't win. At some point during those seasons an anonymous note appeared in my mailbox. It told me the game had passed me by and suggested I needed to quit. I'd never gotten hate mail, and it stung. I had just turned fifty.

Was I past it? Certainly not, though I had

to admit there were times when our players thought my expressions were quaint. I would holler, "Defense is not where you keep the cows!" The kids would stare at me, mystified.

> She used to make all these farm references and we didn't know what the heck she was talking about. Anytime she went into farm mode, I was like, I don't understand. One day she tried to compare herding sheep to closing out.
>
> — KARA LAWSON

The suggestion that I was tired or slowing only incensed me, and I set out to prove I had more energy than ever. I practiced our team for three hours at a stretch — my mantra was, "Let's go one more time." Kara Lawson depended on her legs for her shot, and she came to me to complain she was tired. It was the one thing sure to get no sympathy from me.

"Pat, I'm feeling run-down," she said.

I just gave her the stare.

"Maybe you need to get on a multivitamin," I said.

"You're kidding."

"No. Maybe you've got iron-poor blood."

There were exits and entrances, and some

of them were beloved colleagues. In 2002, Al Brown left us, and I replaced him with Nikki Caldwell, whose relationship with us had evolved from player to friend to protégée: she was a commanding sideline presence, with a husky bass voice and piercing gaze, who brought a fresh shot of urgent ambition. In 2003, Mickie became the head coach at Kentucky, where she would turn a last-place team into a twenty-game winner. We missed her badly, but in 2004, we replaced her with the preternaturally energetic Dean Lockwood.

We had injuries — six great players tore their anterior cruciate ligaments, the bane of my existence, in that period. "Loree Moore's the one player we can't lose," I said to Tyler. She was the best point guard in the country in '04, before she blew her knee on a steal and fast break against Duke.

The '04 team is lodged in a compartment of my heart for their sheer surprisingness, and staunch refusal to quit against long odds. How could I remember such players as anything but champions: Ashley Robinson, a willowy Texan with a funny gait on her surgically repaired ACL-damaged knee, her leg never quite straight; Tasha Butts, a Georgian of such steadfast leadership that everyone on the sideline would climb a mast in a hurricane for her.

"BUTTS!" I'd thunder at her, and she would bat her eyes at me and say calmly as a lamb, "Ma'am?"

Their run in the NCAA tournament was the damnedest thing I ever experienced: they won three straight games by 2 points in the final seconds to make it to the championship. They did it on pure fight: Ashley, fouling out of a game and hurling her warm-up into the stands in a fury. Tasha, slapping away a hand check so emphatically you could hear the *whap.* Against LSU in the Final Four in New Orleans, Shyra Ely snatching a steal and flinging it to LaToya Davis for a layup with two seconds to go, to explode the arena.

But there was a price for all that fight, work, and stress. Ten minutes after the final buzzer in the LSU game, I stood in a back hallway of the New Orleans arena with my hand to my chest. I was drenched with sweat and wrung out, my heart beating like a hummingbird.

"I can't breathe," I said, gasping.

"I guess not," said a reporter. "After that finish, I can't either."

"No," I said. "I mean it. I can't catch my breath."

I tried to inhale, but my heart would not

stop skipping. I sat down, and gradually my heart rate slowed, and I regained my breath. A team physician examined me and announced that I was having palpitations, and while it was nothing to be overly concerned about, I should have some tests.

A day later, we ran out of miracle finishes: the Lady Vols lost in the NCAA final to Diana Taurasi and UConn, 70–61. It was our eleventh championship game appearance, a new collegiate record. We headed back to Knoxville with the knowledge that we couldn't have done more.

At home, I was strapped to a heart monitor for a couple of days. The diagnosis was arrhythmia, an irregular beat — apparently one part of my heart raced ahead of itself. Imagine that, I thought, wryly. I was put on medication, a beta-blocker, to slow the rhythm.

It took me aback: I always imagined that I was in control of my heart, that its beat was rock steady. Years earlier, I had participated in a study for some Vanderbilt medical researchers, who wired coaches with heart monitors. I had the highest sustained heart rate in the group — except when the game was on the line. Under pressure, I was able to calm myself so effectively that my heart rate actually slowed.

For the first time, I felt stress had gotten the better of me. The doctors explained arrhythmia was nothing extraordinary; lots of people got it as they grew older. But in retrospect, it was the beginning of the long, gradual overall decline of my health.

It's not clear to me how much personal unhappiness contributed to the encroachment of illness. I just know that there was a cascade of grief, followed by a series of ailments. If I'd lived a life of perfect happiness and constant leisure, would I still have gotten sick? Was my health just an unfortunate genetic twist? Or did the load of overwork and sorrows begin to wear away at me?

The first blow was the loss of my father. Throughout '05 I watched him slip away, debilitated by a series of strokes. He and my mother came to Knoxville for long stretches so I could help care for them, and for days he would sit in a recliner, unable to move. He lost control of his bodily functions, and to his mortification and fury I would have to clean him up.

"I want to die," that towering man said, weeping.

"Don't say that."

"I can't believe my own daughter has to wipe my butt."

"Well, Daddy, I guess you wiped my butt a few times when I was little," I said. "Didn't you?"

His shoulders started shaking with silent laughter.

"I guess I did."

"How many times?" I asked.

"A few."

"That's right. A few."

He was so infirm he missed a landmark victory that spring: on March 22, 2005, we broke the all-time NCAA Division I record for coaching victories when we beat Purdue in the second round of the NCAA tournament for our 880th win. In a surprise ceremony after the game, the university rewarded me for writing our name in the history books by writing my name on the court. The floor of Thompson-Boling Arena would henceforth be known as *The Summitt*, a gesture that brought me to tears.

What made me cry was the thought of how many young feet had run up and down that court to create such a mark, for which I got the credit. "When I retire, I won't be sitting in a rocking chair looking at trophies," I told the press that night. "I hope I'll be on the phone talking to former players or sitting around chatting with them."

It was the highlight to an otherwise devastating year. We started that season with thirteen scholarship players, but by the end of it we had just nine, after a sickening epidemic of injuries. We had the finest recruiting class in the country, a half-dozen players nicknamed "the Six Pack," led by the magnificent six-foot-four prodigy Candace Parker of Naperville, Illinois. Four of them arrived with sore knees. Candace and a svelte in-state prospect named Alex Fuller both required surgery almost immediately and would have to sit out the year.

We still managed to make it to the Final Four in Indianapolis, carried by a couple of determined leaders in Shyra Ely and Shanna Zolman, who were native Indianans. But they did just about all they could do in getting us there. In the semifinal we built a 16-point lead against Michigan State, then surrendered it. We collapsed, mentally and physically, and lost 68–64.

Five months later, in October, my father died. He was a forbidding, unsmiling man, but he had buried warmth and I loved him. I made it home to Henrietta in time to spend about twenty minutes with him before he passed, long enough to hold his hand and tell him what was in my heart, how thankful I was for all he gave me.

The funeral was at Mt. Carmel United

Methodist Church, where I had been married, and it was filled to overflowing with people he had loaned money to or carried on his books. The pastor had to open the doors to adjoining rooms to accommodate the overflow, and there were more people packed in the back, standing on tiptoe trying to hear the eulogies.

"Your father loaned me thirty dollars and it started my life," one man said. "I told him I couldn't pay him back, and he said he didn't care."

Mrs. Mavis Gupton told about helping out in Head's Store many years earlier. One day an older lady came into the store and said, "Mr. Richard, I really need to borrow a hundred dollars." Daddy pulled out his old leather wallet and handed the lady a hundred dollars. She said, "Thank you, Mr. Richard. I promise I'll pay you back as soon as I can." When she left, Daddy turned around, looked at Mavis, and said, "Who was that woman?"

As R.B. and Tyler and I drove home, I talked to my son about his grandfather. I wanted him to remember how hardworking yet generous he was. "This day should be a celebration of what a good man he was," I said. "Funerals shouldn't be so much about mourning and sorrow. If you ever speak at a funeral, it needs to be a celebration. And that's what mine better be. A celebration."

But it was hard to follow my own advice and not mourn. My father had been an incalculably powerful presence for me, and I felt his absence. When you spend your whole life trying to please someone, and then they are gone, you don't know who to please anymore.

There were other sadnesses too — a seemingly unending stream of them. In the spring of 2004, Rosa Snow had died after her lengthy battle with lupus, news that devastated us. Holly and I drove to the funeral. Michelle didn't know we were coming; she was sitting in the front row with her family when we walked in, and when she saw us, she started choking with sobs. I just sat down with her, and put my arms around her, and held her for a long time. In August of 2005, there was another loss: one of my oldest friends in the business, LSU coach Sue Gunter, died at age sixty-six after a long battle with emphysema.

Raising my son sustained me. Tyler had grown from a little boy into a teenager, and he continued to haunt our locker room. I was concerned that all the privilege would spoil him: What other boy had a pass around his neck that said "All access" and could walk past ten security guards and sit wherever he wanted? Or knew Michael Jordan and Peyton Manning, and watched football games in skyboxes, and stayed in gigantic hotel suites? We had done so well financially that we now owned half the hillside behind the house, and I built him a basketball court and swimming pool, with a pool house stocked with arcade games.

Basketball gave him a counterbalance to all the indulgence. He hung out with our team managers and helped with their chores. One of them, a UT student named Adam Waller, became like a brother to him. There was an afternoon when they were roughhousing, and Tyler started punching on Adam. Adam looked at me and said, "What should I do?"

I said, "Punch him back."

When Tyler got cut from his sixth-grade basketball team, I decided it wasn't the worst thing that could have happened to him, because it kept him honest. I walked into the house, and he was sitting on his bed crying. He had a ball under each arm, and tears were running down his face.

"Tyler, what's wrong?"

He said, "I got cut."

My heart broke, and a voice in my own head said, *What coach in east Tennessee would cut* my *son*? But then the disciplinarian came out in me. I was pretty sure that a part of Tyler had thought he would make the team based on his name.

I said, "Well, do you think you worked hard enough?"

There was a pause, and he said, "No."

"Well, now you know what you got to do."

"Mom, will you help me?"

I said, "Son, I will *help* you. But I will *not* start your engine. You have to start your own engine every day. Do you understand?"

He nodded.

"I promise you, if you are willing to wear out the leather on both those basketballs, you'll make it."

Tyler will tell you it was a defining moment in his life. Getting cut changed him — it altered his habits, and his drive. I never had to motivate him again. So much of parenting was a matter of keeping your word, just as it was in coaching. I kept my word to Ty: his involvement in basketball came from his commitment and initiative, not mine. He learned to push himself.

She would never say, "Hey, let's go work out." I would always have to say, "Will you go shoot with me?" She would say, "Absolutely," and she'd be right there; she'd drop everything.

— TYLER SUMMITT

Initially, it was difficult for Tyler to take coaching from me. I didn't let him win so much as a game of PIG from me on the court. He wasn't exceptionally gifted; he had his father's physique with muscles all over, but he was more smart than athletic, and he had to work very fundamentally to become a good player.

"Get your eyes up."

"Okay."

"Get your EYES up!"

"Okay. Okay."

"Get your eyes UP!"

I could see the battle going on in his head. Rationally he knew I was one of the best coaches in the country; irrationally he couldn't stand for his mother to talk to him that way. After we were done shooting, I'd say sweetly, "What do you want for dinner? You want mashed potatoes or rice?" And he'd glare at me, like, "I'm so mad I can't speak right now."

I think I was getting mad because she was staying on me and I couldn't fix it quick enough for her, so I was mad at my own weakness, mad at her for staying on me, mad at the situation as a whole. She wouldn't so much yell at me, but she was very, very firm. She had my attention. There was no crowd, no referee, no horns buzzing, maybe some birds chirping, that's it. It was just me and her.

— TYLER SUMMITT

He began to outwork and outorganize his mother. He had a calendar with letter codes on each day: B for Bible, T for trash, S for sit-ups. At first when I watched film, he would play a video game or do kid stuff, but gradually he started paying attention and began to point things out.

And to argue. We were sitting together gazing at the screen when a ref called a walk on one of our players. "Yeah, she definitely walked," he said.

"No, she didn't," I said.

"Yeah, she took like three steps."

"No, she dribbled on the first step," I said. "Watch."

I backed it up and replayed it in slow motion.

"See that!" he said. "She walked!"

I didn't consciously set out to turn him into a coach, but I wanted him to study the game right if he was going to play it. When he watched film with our coaching staff, I'd pause and explain that just because the ball went in the net, it wasn't necessarily a good possession. I'd point out how a small detail, one player who set a poor screen, affected the overall flow and pattern.

At first, they were talking French. I mean, they were seeing eighteen things at once, and I was watching the ball go in like the rest of the fans in Thompson-Boling. I think once I realized they saw more, I wanted to see more. As time went on I tried to predict what she was doing. In those championship games I'd be, like, "She's about to take Michelle out." Or I'd think, "She's about to switch defenses." And sometimes she would.

— TYLER SUMMITT

He began to write notes for me. I'd go off to a road game, and when I came home, there would be a piece of paper waiting for me on the kitchen counter: "Point guards passed to corners too much, and ball got stuck down there. A lot of times, posts were late on help side."

Tyler eventually made the varsity and started at point guard as a sophomore for the Webb School, an elite private prep academy where a lot of kids had prominent last names. He also found that his own name came with a drawback. In his first game, no sooner did he take the floor for Webb than the whole cheering section for the opponent, West High, shouted in concert at him: "Mama's boy!"

Next time down the floor, he caught the ball, and here it came again. "Maaaama's boy!" It went on the whole game, a crescendo that only got louder, "MAMA'S BOY! MAMA'S BOY!" Ty kept his composure and managed to play well and came home bragging on himself.

"I didn't let it bother me, and I didn't have a single turnover," he said.

I felt I had finally done something basketball-wise that I could talk about. And she wouldn't let me. She listened to me and took it all in, and she said, "Tyler. You never blow your own horn. You let others blow it for you."
— TYLER SUMMITT

But I would rue my concern that Tyler's life was too easy, that he needed to learn to deal with problems. He would have more than enough of those at the end of that year, when he became a child of divorce. At the age of fifteen, Tyler found himself the man of the house and a caretaker, when his mother took to her bed and couldn't get up.

My marriage fell apart on the eve of the 2006 NCAA tournament, literally. It was a Sunday night in March, and I was up late cooking because the following day I was hosting a party: the NCAA brackets would be announced and every year the team gathered at my house for a big meal with homemade ice cream, while we learned our tournament draw together. Feeding everyone helped calm my nerves. Also a camera crew from ESPN was due at the house to film us live for a network show.

I put the ice cream in the freezer and cleaned the kitchen. R.B. had gone down early because he wasn't feeling well. I went into our semi-darkened room, and as I got ready for bed, I heard a buzz from his cell phone, indicating a text message. I wasn't in the habit of checking his cell, but he had left it lying on the bathroom counter. I glanced at it wondering who would text him at that hour. I picked it up and looked at it. After a sickened and stunned moment, I threw the phone across the room as hard as I could, hoping to destroy it the way I felt destroyed.

R.B. and I were awake for the rest of the night. I was white-hot with rage, and heartbroken at the same time. After twenty-seven years, I was at least smart enough to accept that all unions are compromised, and no mate is perfect, and we'd had our share of problems. But I thought we were working through them together. I was blindsided — and I'd never recover from the feeling of sudden alienation.

My career was tumultuous and could devour my energy, and at times he made it clear he needed more attention — there were a couple of Final Fours that were memorably tense weeks in our marital history. I was gone for days at a time, and R.B.'s responsibility as president of his family's bank meant he couldn't always come with me. But we'd nevertheless managed to travel the world together through basketball — to Australia, England, Italy, Alaska. Perhaps I should have been concerned when earlier that season we had gone to a Thanksgiving tournament in the Caribbean and, for the first time in our marriage, he hadn't come with us for the holiday. He said he had too much to do at the bank.

I thought I had worked hard at nurturing our home life, cooking every night, being the supportive wife at annual banking functions. I didn't think my job was an issue in our marriage — but I was always slightly afraid it could be, that he would tilt toward resenting all that came with it, the constant presence of other people in our lives, the separations and distractions. I knew we were attempting a highly difficult balance — and for the longest time, I thought we'd succeeded. But in the space of a single night, I questioned every assumption between us.

In the morning R.B. left for work, and I got Tyler off to school. My sister, Linda, arrived — I had called her. She found me with the covers over my head, and she crawled into bed with me.

The ESPN trucks pulled up and began unloading their cameras and lights at our pool house. Somehow, I got through that day, cooked for and fed more than fifty people, including the local media, and appeared on national television. For better or worse, I'd always had the ability to draw shutters over my personal feelings and keep operating, in the same way I was able to slow my heart rate down. With ESPN at the house, there was no time to dwell on the painful questions: *Can I restore a damaged relationship? Can he stay here? Can I stay here? Do I stay in a broken marriage for a child?*

I mostly held myself together, but not entirely. The NCAA committee gave us a nightmare regional matchup with Rutgers and North Carolina, a "bracket of death" as everyone called it. I was exhausted and distraught under my skin, and for the first time in my life, I didn't have it in me to put on a gracious public display. When an ESPN announcer asked me on live television how I felt about our tournament draw, I replied angrily that the committee had slapped us in the face. Everyone was shocked at my tone. Under the circumstances, I thought it was an essay in self-control.

Later that night after all the people and TV trucks had gone, I went into Tyler's room and sat down with my son for the most difficult conversation of my life. I explained that his father and I were separating. "It's just going to be you and me," I said. "And you and I are going to be okay."

R.B. came in — I had asked him to stay away during the TV show — and I left the room so R.B. and Tyler could talk. "You can explain this to your son," I said.

The next day, with a wedge in my heart, I dressed and went into the office. I called

Holly, Nikki, and Dean in for a meeting and broke down as I told them what had happened. I didn't know how I was going to get through the tournament, and I'd have to rely on them heavily, I said. They seemed almost as affected as I was.

Yes, there had always been a lot of demands on her, but she was one who tried to get home and cook every night, and make sure R.B. and Ty were included in every aspect of the program. It was almost like she was trying to show us, yes, you can have this unbelievable career and be in this profession, and, yes, you can have a family and be successful too. But then it was, "Can you?" You know?

— NIKKI CALDWELL

The staff took as much off me as they could, but we didn't stand a chance in the tournament. It had been a difficult season, quite apart from my personal problems. Candace Parker was tentative after two knee surgeries and suffering her own anguish because her parents were divorcing. Our wonderful, heedlessly slashing guard Alexis Hornbuckle broke her wrist diving for a loose ball. And our sophomore point guard Sa'de Wiley-Gatewood, a player on whom I'd lavished care, had transferred out at Christmas because she couldn't play "her game." As I'd always said, "Tennessee's not right for everyone — and not everyone's right for Tennessee."

We got through Rutgers in the Sweet 16 thanks to 29 points from our senior Shanna Zolman. But our players were out of sorts and sensed that something was wrong. Shanna asked Tyler, "Hey, where's your dad?" Ty just looked away and didn't answer. But that didn't fool Candace, who recognized what was happening from her own experience and gravitated to Tyler. They became confidants and spent the trip wandering the hotel lobby together whispering, comparing notes on parental breakups, a strange-looking pair, Candace a slender stalk at six four and Tyler looking mannish and boyish at the same time in his oversized baggy sweats.

North Carolina crushed us in the next round. It was one of Sylvia's best teams ever, starring a blistering guard named Ivory Latta, and they finished us off, 75–63. It was a terrible ending for Shanna, who set three Tennessee shooting records for her career but walked away feeling discontented and that I'd been both harsh and distant with her. She didn't understand my behavior, and I couldn't blame her. We parted with a rift.

I gave Sylvia Hatchell a hug and wished her well. Later that night, Sylvia said to her husband, "Sammy, something is wrong with Pat. She wasn't right. She didn't have her normal fight."

With the tournament over, I had no choice but to go home to an empty house and think about my marriage. I believed in and honored the institution, and R.B. had been an essential source of unconditional love for me. For all our problems, I'd been deeply content and always felt our worst day together was better than being apart. Especially early on, he treated me as if he had found a rare gem, and I had a string of diamonds on my wrist to remind me of that. He was a southern charm boy with a way with gestures. After every big win in a tournament, there were long-stemmed roses. Our relationship had given me a confidence, sureness. But now it seemed he wanted all the advantages of being married to me, but none of the disadvantages. I was brokenhearted, and bitterly angry, and something cut off inside me.

She can be pretty uncoachable in some areas. It's my life's greatest failure to not

be able to figure things out, and to fix it. I fell in love with her and never quit. We had something very special. I never claimed to be perfect. I did well for so long, and when I messed up, I didn't meet her standards.
— R.B. Summitt

As R.B. and I walked through the difficult situation, we struggled not to put Tyler in the middle, and to keep it private, but rumors were racing all over town. Someone anonymously called the local ABC affiliate and said, "You need to look into the breakup of Pat and R.B.'s marriage." As if it was a scandal. A local writer for the Associated Press called our media relations director, Debby Jennings, and inquired about our status. She tartly replied, "If you'd like to ask Pat that question yourself, I will be glad to have her call you back." Never mind, the reply came. It was a relief when summer came, and Tyler and I left town for a vacation in the Destin, Florida, area where we had a condominium on the beach. I stared at the blue water and tried to sort out my feelings with my oldest, closest friends.

While I was there, I also had to face the fact that something had gone badly wrong with me physically. For weeks, I had been feeling a pervasive achiness. Initially I thought it was lingering soreness and trauma from a terrible fall I'd taken when I was out walking our Labradors. But now I found myself almost immobilized by pain, so stiff I could barely move.

I quit eating, lost weight, went to bed. I felt like something was gnawing my joints from the inside out. Tyler would run hot baths of Epsom salts for me, filling a tub and trying to find the right relieving temperature. I could barely dress myself; Tyler had to pull my socks on for me. "You're my rock," I told him.

My longtime physician, Dr. Amy Bentley, found the answer: I had rheumatoid arthritis, the systemic autoimmune disease that put my grandmother in a wheelchair. It was incurable: for the rest of my life I'd have chronically inflamed joints, though medication could help control it. With the answer came some relief; a rheumatologist put me on a couple of different therapies, and the pain ebbed. But my body never returned to normalcy.

My emotional state remained tender too. I second-guessed myself a lot during that time. For all the control, intuitiveness, and direction I had on the basketball court, I beat myself up for not having the same control and insight into my personal life. I felt like I was living in a bad country music song.

Going back to work was the best medicine. A combination of anti-inflammatories, cold packs, and hot pads helped get me moving again; at practice I looked like a NASCAR pit stop on the sideline as our trainers worked to change the ice bags I wore on my knees under my sweats. But there wasn't a day that being in the gym with our players didn't lift me up and loosen my limbs. For a few hours every afternoon, it was a relief to be immersed in their young and simple worlds.

> She never got tired of it, she loved everything about it. . . . I remember when it was tough on us at home with the divorce, and she would be, like, "Okay, it's time for practice." And that was it, whether we were crying or sad, as soon as she looked at the clock and it was time for practice, it was like Wonder Woman.
> — TYLER SUMMITT

I couldn't help but feel reanimated by how promising our team was. As a coach you know when you can check off enough boxes to contend for a championship, whether there are enough scorers, defenders, re-bounders, and decision makers to make a deep run. In 2007, we had all of them, and after years of bedeviling injuries, we were finally whole and healthy.

Above all we had Candace Parker, the best player in a generation, who was finally healed and confident enough for her talent to flower. She was built like a green young tree, supple and strong. She was virtually ambidextrous, almost as good with her left hand as her right, and she could dunk with ease. She had a light, creative touch around the basket, but if you pushed her away from it, she would loft deadly fallaway jumpers, and she could handle and pass the ball like a guard.

Everyone in the country wanted Candace, but fortunately, I had a head start: I had unwittingly been nice to her when she was a little girl. Back in our heyday with the Meeks, we went to Chicago to play DePaul, and after the game I stepped into the bleachers to speak to Tamika Catchings's father, Harvey. A gentleman from another row leaned over and tapped me on the shoulder and said, "Do you mind taking a picture with my daughter?" I turned around and saw a thirteen-year-old girl, thin as a bamboo reed.

She looked over and said in this big southern accent, "I'm gonna have to take you home and fatten you up."

— CANDACE PARKER

When we met again as coach and recruit, we had an immediate bond — but by then every coach in the country was chasing her. A particularly overaggressive one from another conference swooped in and began campaigning hard, not just in her own favor, but against us, messing with Candace's head by mudslinging.

Things had gotten a little ugly. Stories were told, and strings were being pulled every which way. "You don't want to be a part of that program." Different things like that. Negative recruiting, I guess; that's what Pat called it. She never did it. She always talked about the positives of the University of Tennessee. She never really discussed other schools; because she said it didn't matter, she was selling me on Tennessee.

— CANDACE PARKER

I was well aware that we were being slimed. Holly and I flew to Naperville, Illinois, to visit Candace at home with her parents and make our last pitch. We sat down on their couch, and I said, "Holly, get me a glass of water, will you?"

Candace's mother, Sara, said, "Let me get that for you."

I said, "No, no, Holly will get it."

Holly came back to the sofa with two glasses of water and set them down on the table. I turned to Candace. "People can mess with your head," I said. "Can't they?"

"Yeah," she said.

I pushed a glass of water in front of her. "This is your mind," I said. "It's clear, right?"

Then I reached in my pocket for an Alka-Seltzer tablet and dropped it in the glass. It began bubbling.

"And this is what people are trying to do to your mind."

The water clouded up. It boiled and fizzled, getting murkier and murkier.

I pushed the second glass of water toward Candace. It was still and transparent.

"This is what Tennessee is," I said. "We're clear. And we're very clear with you. Don't let other people put stuff in it."

That was it; that was our pitch. Sold.

But then Candace arrived at Tennessee on a bad knee. She came to our first team meeting with a limp, and we immediately ordered her to sit out and scheduled an

MRI. "We don't play at Tennessee on swollen knees," our medical director told her. The MRI showed that she needed articulate cartilage surgery. When she found out, she burst into tears, and so did I. Not only was Candace hurt, she was away from home for the first time and her parents, Larry and Sara, had just separated.

Holly and I were at her bedside along with her mother when Candace woke up from surgery. She had dreamed she was playing basketball while she was under the anesthesia, and her first words were, "We won."

Holly smiled and said, "Did I hit the game winner?"

Candace murmured, "No. I did."

Hopefully, it was an omen.

With Candace healthy, the trick was to build a cohesive team that wouldn't resent her large presence and star quality. She was an attention magnet, but we had other great players, who probably wondered if there were enough basketballs to go around. Alexis Hornbuckle of Charleston, West Virginia, was our detonator, a guard with coiled springs for legs who seemed to cause a separation on the scoreboard every time she took the floor. We called her "Bucky" or "Lex." Sidney Spencer was a long, silky forward with a three-point shot so reliable it was almost unfair, and we called her "Sidville," because she could be sort of spacey and in her own world. Alex Fuller was a slim, elegant forward who was skilled in every aspect of the game.

We had two junior college transfers: Alberta Auguste of Marrero, Louisiana, was a wavy-limbed five-foot-eleven quick-stepper, and Shannon Bobbitt, a New York–bred point guard who originally committed to Rutgers but needed a year in junior college to shore up her grades. Shannon was just five foot two, but she had grown up in Harlem playing street ball with guys and had an uncanny ability to take apart a defense.

I'd never had a player more appreciative of a scholarship than Shannon. She was from a family of eight kids who grew up worried about food and shelter; her mother supported them with her job for the New York City Board of Education, while her father was on disability. Shannon was dazzled by the richness of our program; even her sweat socks were "the nicest socks I've ever had," she said. She exhausted herself on the practice court to "pay you back for the risk you took on me," she told me. She was supremely coachable, sponged instruction, and did exactly what I asked her to. "I'd adopt you if I could," I told her.

Nicky Anosike was a combination of strength and strong-mindedness. She was another New Yorker, a sculpted six-foot-four, 210-pound center with a pile of tightly woven braids and a centered, resolute quality that made her teammates vote her the person they would most like to have at their side in a dark alley. Her mother, Ngozi, was a Nigerian immigrant who had arrived in this country in 1977 with a sixth-grade education and raised eight children single-handedly in a Staten Island project. Ngozi was a remarkable success story; she had worked as a housekeeper while she put herself through high school, and by the time I began recruiting Nicky in 2003 she had just gotten her nursing degree.

Nicky didn't want me to come to their tiny apartment, because she was embarrassed by it and thought I'd judge her. She had no clue that I'd lived in a cabin with no water or electricity; she just saw my good suit and the diamond rings.

I was so embarrassed about where I was from. I didn't see the part of Pat that grew up on a farm and had to work to get where she was. I saw this immaculate woman always on ESPN and this huge celebrity. I didn't want her to see what I was struggling with. What if I invite her over and she sees the mice? Or she sees the cockroaches, or she sees eight kids in a small apartment? Or she sees I don't have a bed? What will she think of me? Will she still want me?

— NICKY ANOSIKE

I wanted Nicky, and here's why. She would pay any price to succeed, and her work ethic set the tone for our entire team. When I ran them ragged, and Alberta Auguste wailed, "Oh, help me, Jesus!," and players were bent double gasping that they were tired, I heard Nicky's voice.

"We're not tired," she said. "My mother's tired. This isn't what tired is."

Right then, I knew we were in business.

But there was one issue we had to solve: Nicky and Candace couldn't stand each other. They clashed like plaid and stripes, and no amount of circling up and campfire conversation could hide that fact. There were days in practice when they would barely exchange a glance.

The problem was that they were so different, yet equally competitive. Candace made everything look natural and smooth; Nicky was all work and power. Candace was our best offensive player, Nicky our best defender. I decided the tension between them wasn't all bad, if I could find a way to channel it.

I threw them into what Nikki Caldwell liked to call "the pit." Summoning a long-ago lesson from my experience in the Olympic Trials, I matched them up against each other in a one-on-one drill, then stood back and let them go at it. I had a feeling they would each learn a lesson. It was like an old movie where two monsters fight: Nicky would smack down Candace, but then Candace would school Nicky. Candace prided herself on winning every drill. Well, guess who won — Nicky. Defense had carried the day, as I suspected it might. Candace couldn't stand it — she hated to lose at anything, and she was beside herself. She stormed back and forth for a minute, and then she came running over to me.

She said, "We have to go again."

Nicky put the ball on her hip and said, "Coach, we're not playing again. I already won."

"No, no, no," Candace said.

"IT'S OVER!" Nicky said.

I was delighted. I said, "No, let's play again."

They went back on the court, Nicky fuming. Part of the drill was that they got to call their own fouls, an honor system. Nicky had trouble finishing around the basket, but if she didn't make the bucket, she was good at drawing fouls. She missed a layup, and she called a foul. Next possession, same thing: "Yep, you fouled me again," she said. Candace was boiling. The third time Nicky called a foul, Candace started screaming.

"I didn't even touch you, you're just calling fouls 'cause you can't score, you such a PUNK!"

Nicky screamed back, "I'm not a punk, I already WON!"

By now they were crowding each other and I had to step in and try to break them up, two very salty six-foot-four and six-foot-five bodies. The other coaches came running in, and we finally got them separated. Nicky said: "Pat, you could've gotten hurt."

I loved it. In those few minutes, Candace played better D, and Nicky was more efficient offensively, and you could see that they were pulling the best out of each other. Moreover, in an odd way, it made them trust. Each of them taught the other a lesson about her value, and when we were in a tight game and needed a score, or a stop, they would know who to go to.

Those are the situations Pat put us in, and

it wasn't done accidentally. She loves confrontation and likes to create that environment, because not only is she entertained by it, but it interests her to see what people are made of and what you have inside of you.

— NICKY ANOSIKE

We still had some issues to work out before we jelled. Too many of our players relied on their sizable gifts instead of each other and weren't quite willing to do all the dirty work. I stacked the deck against them every way I could think of in practice. We installed something Dean called "the persistence drill," which tested their stamina: they had to make consecutive full-court layups for two straight minutes — and if they missed, start over. On the defensive end, they had to make seven straight defensive stops before they could get off the floor.

But perhaps nothing was as effective as what Nicky Anosike did just before the NCAA tournament. She called a player-only meeting and presented each of them with a contract she had written up. She thought her teammates talked a better game than they played, and she understood that there was something about signing your name that resonated with people.

"I'm a woman of my word," she told the team. "My word is the one thing I have. I'm sick of people talking. Sign this contract, and if you aren't doing this on the court, you answer to me."

The word for that is *ownership.* Nicky took ownership, and we turned into beasts in the NCAA tournament. We ripped through Ole Miss in the regional final, 98–62, when Bobbitt scored our first 10 points by draining treys, and Candace went off for 24 points, 14 rebounds, and several blocked shots, which earned her the ultimate compliment from Nicky, who said, "I respect what you did tonight." That sealed the deal. Nikki Caldwell observed, "There's a language players speak when they're getting ready to win something big. And I'm hearing it."

We needed every bit of their togetherness in the Final Four in Cleveland, where we met the team that had our number recently, North Carolina. It was another nightmare game: Candace was double-teamed and got in foul trouble, and no one could knock down a shot. The Tar Heels, led by their comet of a guard, Ivory Latta, were up by 12 with just 8:18 to go, 48–36.

Time-out. I felt like I'd been in this game my whole life. Down by double digits, a short clock, and kids giving off a smell of desperation with their sweat, needing me to breathe life into their competitive lungs. They were hurting, concerned — there was a little bit of doubt; are we going under? I wasn't having it, wasn't having any of it.

I opened my mouth, and something close to a roar came out. "We are not losing this ball game!" I hollered. "We have come too far and worked too hard. We're not *leaving* here without a championship!" I reminded them of their persistence drills. "Can you make seven straight stops?" I asked. They nodded. That was what it would take. "Steal and score! Seven straight stops!"

> I just remember Pat was adamant; we are not losing this game. She made sure everybody heard her. You could see it in her eyes, hear it in her voice; you could see it in how she was standing.
> — NIKKI CALDWELL

On the next seven trips down the floor, here's what they did: they forced six steals. Trying to get past Alexis Hornbuckle was like trying to run through a windmill. It was a total shutout — Carolina scored exactly 2 points over the last eight minutes, on free throws. They never got another decent shot. We won, 56–50.

Two nights later we met Rutgers and won our first national championship in eight years, 59–46. "It's been way too long," Candace said. "And I'm tired of going into Thompson-Boling Arena and playing on the Summitt and not looking up and seeing a banner that has all our names written all over it."

Everyone always wanted to know how each championship felt, what defined and separated it. This one felt like a soft rain of confetti. It felt like an embrace with my son — who was now taller than me. It felt like a flying kiss on the cheek from Candace, who sailed around the arena like she had wings. It was my seventh title — but it was a first for our players, and as I celebrated it with them, it felt like newness. It was wonderful to feel something other than pain, and it made me young hearted again. As my old friend Steve Spurrier had said to me on my fiftieth birthday, "You and I both know why we do this. We do it so we don't ever have to grow up." And it was true.

I'd had a lot to prove that season: that I could live alone, that I could raise my son and run our household without a husband in it, that I could rebuild my life as a single woman, that I could fight off the arthritis and keep working and winning. I no longer felt so stiff and heartsore. I felt I was finally moving forward, and life could be good again, even joyful.

That summer, I made two important decisions about the quality of my life. After a year of separation, I decided to end my marriage. R.B. was a good person, a loving father, and we'd had a lot of good years. But I couldn't reconcile. I filed for divorce.

I also reached the decision that my professional life would be better without UConn in it. I canceled our annual series, the most controversial act of my career, and one for which I'd be heavily criticized, especially by people from Connecticut. Everyone should know that as of this writing, Geno and I have recovered our friendship — and I do regard it as friendship — and I want it to stay that way. We are in the best place we've ever been. My version of what happened is simply that, my version, as I experienced it.

Believe it or not, it had almost nothing to do with the rivalry itself. The fact is, relationships between coaches are rarely ruined by what happens on the court — we all know what goes around comes around, and that it's an inherently humbling game. Relationships between coaches are ruined *off* the court. It's what happens before and after, in the handshake line and most especially in recruiting, that poisons relationships. And that's what happened to Geno and me.

For the better part of thirteen years, Geno and I got along well. Though we were competitive, we felt a bond, a shared sense that we elevated the game to a very rare air.

One year there was a snow emergency in Hartford, with fourteen inches on the ground, and the governor of the state told everyone to stay off the roads. When we got to the Civic Center, fourteen thousand people were there, and the governor was sitting in the first row. It was a game played at a level that no one else in women's basketball could play at, for the longest time. . . . We knew that game ultimately was going to determine what kind of year we had. How will you compete in that game? That's how you will measure your team. That game was how I knew whether we had the heart for winning a championship. And regardless of what ended up coming out of that, the personalities, in the end the competitive spirit that both teams displayed on those game days is something that will never be duplicated.
— GENO AURIEMMA

On the court it was pure class, future Hall of Famers on both sides knocking down epic shots. Off the court we were amiable, and complimentary, even teasing. In the fall of 1998 after *Reach for the Summit* hit the bestseller list, I went to Hartford for a book signing. Geno sent a huge bouquet of flowers to the store, with a funny note. "Congratulations. I hope your next visit is not nearly so successful," he wrote. When we got a fish tank in our offices at Tennessee and two of the fish tried to devour each other, I named them Pat and Geno. I'd walk into the office and check the tank and ask our secretaries cheerfully, "Did Pat eat Geno yet?"

After we got killed by UConn in the 2002 NCAA Final Four, 79–56, I visited their locker room to tell them how superb I thought they were — their senior class of Sue Bird, Swin Cash, and Asjha Jones equaled anything the Meeks had ever done. "You guys are everything the game should be," I said. "You're one of the best teams I've ever seen, and you need to go on and win the whole thing."

Geno and I chatted regularly at functions, and when an issue arose in women's basketball, such as how to promote the game, we thought alike. We were allies when it came to the issue of pay. There were occasions when we shared contractual details so that the other could win a raise from their university. "I think I can help you," I remember Geno saying.

For all of that, Geno and I didn't socialize much; in all the years we competed, we had dinner just once, whereas I shared meals with other coaches regularly. Perhaps we should have done more of that and gotten to know the sides that people closest to us saw: the good parent, the funny cocktail companion, the generous colleague who helped younger coaches get their starts and inspired loyalty in staffs. We knew those sides existed, because people told us about them. But I'm not sure we ever met in the way we should have.

Then a couple of elbows got thrown. Geno always liked to make barbed remarks, but it seemed to me that from 2000 on, they had an ungenerous edge. Oddly, the more success UConn had, the more Geno seemed to resent Tennessee. In the summer of 2001, there was a bafflingly rude encounter when we were at different tables in the same restaurant, and he made me so uncomfortable by shouting my name derisively that I left the premises.

One evening during a coaching function

in New York, he said to Mickie, "You know, you're pretty funny. We could be friends if you weren't with Tennessee." Mickie was bewildered. We'd always been friendly with our rivals; some of our best friends had handed us painful losses: Sue Gunter at LSU, Jody Conradt at Texas, Sylvia Hatchell at North Carolina, Leon Barmore at Louisiana Tech, Tara VanDerveer at Stanford, and Melanie Balcomb at Xavier and then Vanderbilt.

After our traumatic upset loss to Xavier, someone faxed me a note scribbled in what looked like Geno's handwriting. "I predicted Tennessee would lose to Xavier, and I also predicted Pat would blame her team instead of herself," it read. I faxed it to Geno. "What's this about?" I wrote. He never replied. When I became great friends with Villanova coach Harry Perretta, who was an old friend of Geno's, he told the press that Harry "left me for an older woman" and made off-color jokes about us sitting in a hot tub together. I shot back. "I agree Geno is jealous," I said. "You could also put paranoid in there."

Geno felt elbows from us, too. I learned later that he believed Al Brown was discourteous to him in the handshake line. And when UConn was upset by Notre Dame in the 2001 NCAA Final Four, some of our staff had chanted, ungraciously, "Who let the dogs out!," and apparently he heard about it.

It got to the point where I took it up with him one summer when we wound up at the same all-star tournament. "It's a choice to play you," I said. If the ugliness continued, "I'll cancel the series." He looked shocked and said, hurriedly, "Well, that wouldn't be good for anybody." There was a temporary truce. When we met in the championship game at the 2004 NCAA Final Four in New Orleans, he leaned over during a pregame handshake and said, "Listen. Don't let anyone tell you I don't respect you. I've always respected you."

All of this should have been filed away as two coaches with competitive egos being thin-skinned. The problem was, it formed the backdrop of hard feelings for what happened next. Recruiting is the most difficult part of the game, and no coach likes it. Resentments arise when you can't just go out on a court and settle matters with a ball and a scoreboard.

I've seen it a thousand times: relationships in this profession destroyed over recruiting. Not in games — it doesn't matter if someone beats you on the court. But if they feel taken advantage of in recruiting, that's when things deteriorate and aren't so chummy. In a game if there are fouls, each side gets two free throws. Recruiting is where the battlegrounds are tougher, because the rules of engagement get real gray at times.

— MICKIE DeMoss

I didn't do gray. I only did black and white. I believed I had a special responsibility to follow the rules closely, because whatever a coach at the top of the game did, every other coach in the country was going to do twice as aggressively. Over the course of about a year, I became increasingly upset with a couple of UConn's tactics in recruiting. I didn't itemize my complaints publicly then, and I'm not going to now. I went through the appropriate channels and that's how it will stay. I made my concerns known to UConn through our athletic director, Joan Cronan, and the Southeastern Conference. UConn responded that they saw nothing wrong with what they were doing. I made my concerns known again. Same response.

I was finished. I didn't see any other choice. "I'm not putting up with this anymore," I told my staff. I met with Joan and our university president, Dr. John Petersen, and outlined my reasons for wanting to discontinue the series: the lack of response from UConn and the personal negativity convinced me it was no longer in our best interest. I thought we needed to send a message that we didn't want a game that wasn't played in the right spirit. The administration agreed, and we declined to renew the series.

A few nights later, my home phone rang. It was Geno. In retrospect, that was the moment when friendship and alliance should have prevailed. Each of us should have said, "Let's talk this through and solve this. What are your concerns?" But we had long passed the point of being able to talk that way. Instead it was hostile and defensive from the start. Geno made an opening remark.

"Geno, you and I both know we aren't playing by the same rules," I said.

The conversation only lasted a minute or so more. It mainly consisted of him saying that he hoped to see us in the NCAA tournament, so "I can kick your ass." But we never played again.

In the years since, the anger and suspicion have dissipated, replaced by the original bond. Shortly before I announced my diagnosis, a note came in the mail. It was from Geno, saying he'd heard I had health issues, and he was thinking about me. Shortly after I went public, I formed the Pat Summitt Foundation to fight Alzheimer's, with the help of my friend Danielle Donehew, an associate commissioner of the Big East Conference. Danielle asked Geno if he wanted to be the first contributor to it. He wrote out a check on the spot — for $10,000.

We're competitors and we have a lot of respect, and for anyone to expect more than that when there's so much at stake when we meet on court, it's just unrealistic. The average person out there wants to make it this blood feud. I'm thinking, Come on, it's still just basketball. You've got two competitive, strong-willed people, and some of it was blown out of proportion. And in the end, it came down to: the games were the games and that was that, and it's over, and life is life.

— GENO AURIEMMA

I still believe my decision was the right one, for me. I was more at peace without UConn on our schedule; I had enough battles between divorce, ill health, and single parenting, and I didn't need the constant skirmishing UConn had come to represent. I had a sharp sense that I had paid my dues, been a good ambassador for the game, and now I was on the downhill side of my career.

I also knew we had a great chance to win another title — if I could convince our team not to rest on their laurels, which they were in danger of doing. I had coached teams that got complacent and recognized all the signs.

I had some techniques for dealing with it, making them less self-satisfied.

I benched Candace Parker. Twice. The first time was at Stanford, when she disobeyed my instruction to deny the middle — you'd think they would learn by now. "You either stick to it, or you won't play," I told her. We were trailing — I didn't care, it was the principle of the thing. Besides which, a part of me thought, *Let's see what we do without her.* We lost in overtime, 73–69.

The second benching came in Chicago against number fifteen DePaul, just after the New Year. It was Candace's hometown and her whole family came, as did her fiancé, Shelden Williams, who stayed in our hotel. Two nights before the game, Candace missed curfew because she was visiting

Shelden's room. She didn't blow it by much — just twenty minutes or so. Still, the entire team knew she hadn't made bed check, and we had to constantly guard against the suspicion that Candace got special treatment because she was a star.

She left me no choice. I had to bench her. I hated to do it to her family, but I told Candace, "If it's good for everyone else, it's good for you." Lex and Nicky were our captains and I went to them. "I think I have to bench her for the whole game," I said. They argued that was too harsh and suggested I bench her for the first half, which was what I was hoping they'd say.

It ended up working in our favor, because it taught us that we could play without Candace if we had to. Alex Fuller, one of our most unsung but reliable players, came off the bench for a career-high 19 points, and Nicky chipped in 12, while Candace stood next to me on the sideline chewing on her jersey in frustration.

I did everything I could to unsettle them, plagued by a sense that they were too pleased with themselves. One afternoon when they arrived at practice, there were no balls in sight. I said, "You know what? Here's what we're going to do. I want you to climb the stairs to the very top of this arena. You guys don't understand what people go through to come here and watch you play. No team in the country has the support you have, and you take it for granted. So I want you to walk to the top and sit there and *reflect* on what it takes to get here, and the amount of money people pay to see you play. Sit up there and discuss what you're going to do different. Because this isn't about you."

At times you cringed, because you'd want to say, "It ain't perfect but it's pretty good, Pat." But she would just want to go in and shake it up. She'd take that snow globe and shake it and watch the snowflakes fall. Because her instincts were telling her, "Hey, we can't let 'em get too comfortable."
— DEAN LOCKWOOD

All these events combined to give us the edginess we needed for the NCAA tournament — in which nothing was comfortable. We drew the most hard-nosed and hot-handed team in the country for our regional final, Texas A&M. Early in the first half, Candace went for a steal — and came out of a scrum for the ball grabbing at her left shoulder. Her arm drooped weirdly, dangling like a limp fire hose. I knew on sight exactly what it was — she had dislocated her shoulder.

I knew because I had done the same thing two weeks earlier, fighting off a raccoon. Sitting on the rail of my back deck, it had surprised me, hissing and about to attack my Labrador, Sally. The dog tensed — and then let out a bay as the raccoon was about to spring. I said, "Sally, no!," and without even thinking I stepped forward and gave the raccoon a forearm shiver, knocking it off the rail and into the undergrowth below. I hit it so hard I yanked my shoulder out of joint. Now I was the one baying, in pain, as my arm fell to my side. I grabbed at my shoulder and staggered back inside and woke Tyler up so he could pop my arm back into place. The story got around and made it into the local paper, and I was practically pelted with fake raccoons. People sent them in the mail, left them on my desk, put pictures of them on my refrigerator.

Jenny Moshak, our longtime head of sports medicine, took Candace to the locker room and popped the shoulder back into place and put a brace on her. Candace was clearly favoring her arm, but she dug in and played through the pain. The Aggies led us by five, with 6:17 to play. We could have folded — instead, other players rose up, led by Lex Hornbuckle, who launched a three-pointer from 40 feet that blew through the net to give us some breathing room, and somehow we got out of there with the win, 53–45.

We went to Tampa for what would be the last NCAA Final Four of my career, though I hardly knew it at the time. All I knew was that we had to face LSU, our Southeastern Conference rival, coached by one of the savviest men in the game, Van Chancellor, and led by one of the few players who could meet Candace Parker eye to eye, a giant six-foot-five eagle named Sylvia Fowles.

Everything we tried to do, they checkmated. We were up by just 22–19 at the half, the lowest halftime score in NCAA Final Four history. Nobody could gain an edge. Until, with 7.1 seconds left, it was LSU ahead by a point, 46–45.

Time-out.

Candace was being smothered and struggling. Of all people, she went to Nicky Anosike for help; that was how far they had come. "Nicky, I need you to talk me through this," she said.

"Listen to me," Nicky said. "It doesn't matter what happened the rest of this game. It matters what happens here and now. *This* is what people are going to be talking about.

What happens in the next few seconds."

Over on the sideline, my old friend Tara VanDerveer was watching closely. Just two hours earlier, her Stanford team, led by a luminous star named Candice Wiggins, had beaten UConn to make it into the title game. Whoever prevailed over the next seven seconds would be her opponent. At the moment it looked like LSU. But Tara turned to her assistant coaches.

"You watch," she said. "Pat's going to pull another rabbit out of the hat."

But I wasn't the one who performed the magic trick. If I haven't talked enough about our staff, what happened next should illustrate how valuable they were all those years. During every time-out, I briefly huddled with them and sought ideas. Sometimes I drove them crazy: I wanted their stimulation, wheels turning, everyone feeding me ideas, but I was just as likely to sift through their suggestions and then discard them, saying, "Here's what I'm going to do."

But in this instance, I seized on an idea from Nikki Caldwell, who a week later would become a head coach in her own right at UCLA. "Have Candace bring the ball up," she said urgently. It was totally counterintuitive: Candace was our go-to player, on whom we counted when we needed a score. If Candace brought the ball up the court, that meant she'd have to pass it off. It meant someone else would take the last shot of the game. It meant that if we lost, everyone in the country would want to know why we hadn't gone to the best player in the game. I nodded. It was a high-stakes decision. But I loved being the trigger puller. *Loved* it.

I went into the huddle — and made the last critical call I would ever make in an NCAA Final Four. I looked at Lex, who would be our inbounder. "Get the ball in to Candace," I said. I turned to Candace. "They will converge on you. Find the open player." They all nodded and took their places.

What happened next is a credit to the culture of a program in which players are taught to commit, to play all out, to attend to every detail no matter how seemingly unimportant, to never go through the motions, no matter how routine seeming, to finish with as much energy as they started with.

Everything happened just as we predicted. Lex inbounded to Candace, who took four giant dribbles up the court. The clock ticked 7 . . . 6 . . . 5. The LSU defenders collapsed on her — drawn to her like iron filings to a magnet. Candace kept her eyes up the court . . . and rifled a pass to Nicky under the LSU basket. Nicky went up — an LSU defender swatted at her. The shot ticked off the rim. Nicky had missed. The clock ticked 4 . . . 3 . . .

Out of nowhere Lex came flying in like Batman. She had gone scoreless all game. But after inbounding the ball she had sprinted hard and trailed Nicky to the basket. She hurled herself into the air over Nicky's back and caught the ball up around the backboard. She hung there for a moment — and then kissed it softly off the glass. It fell through the net for the game winner, to send us into the national championship game. Lex Hornbuckle had started the play behind the baseline on the opposite end of the court — she was the last player to set foot on the floor. Yet she had beaten the defense to the basket and scored the game winner.

Pandemonium.

Two days later, we defeated Stanford for our eighth national championship, 64–48, and I stood under another soft, dense rain of confetti. Had I known I'd never see another Final Four as a competitor, I might have taken more careful note of my thoughts. All I remember is feeling blaze-eyed with euphoria, and yet snow-blinded by all the colorful paper that drifted around me. Those fluttering bits of brightness seemed so reflective of the countless inspired moments our players had given me, a great torrent of victories. More than three decades of potent emotions seemed to be cascading down on my head all at once. Up on the rim of the arena, a huge rainbow-lit LED display read "And then there was Tennessee."

I felt full of wistful, appreciative love for our seniors, whom I would miss badly. Candace Parker was simply the most gifted player I ever laid hands on. Lex Hornbuckle and Shannon Bobbitt would live in my memory as two of the greatest difference makers we ever had, and Nicky Anosike's combination of leadership and scholarship was matchless; she would be named NCAA Woman of the Year. That spring, they would all graduate with the highest cumulative grade point average we ever had, and our entire starting five would be drafted by the WNBA. The strangest outcome of all: Candace and Nicky would become the closest of friends. I was inexpressibly proud of all of them.

Not too long after we returned to Knoxville, Dean told me that he wanted to fix me up. He had met the man for me, he said. He had stopped at a gas station late one night to fill up his car. He stuck the nozzle into the tank, and he noticed a guy one pump over, looking at him weirdly. The guy was a rough character, long hair, tattoos, missing a tooth, with a grimy baseball cap.

Cap Guy goes, "Hey! You're that man-fella, aren't you, that works with the Lady Vols?"

Dean, disconcerted, said, "Yeah. That's me."

"You work every day with Coach Summitt. You see her every day, doncha?"

Dean surreptitiously checked out the guy's car, trying to assess the situation. It had a gun rack. He said carefully, "Yes, I do."

The guy handed him a card, with his name and phone number on it.

"You give her this," he said. "That's my kinda woman right there. Any woman gonna square off with a raccoon, that's my kinda woman. I wanna meet her."

Can we talk about your faith?

I'd like to do that.

What were you taught growing up?

Well, we just went to a very small country church. It was simple. We were taught to love the Lord.

Do you think God is with you in this?

I do.

Do you believe this happened to you for a reason?

Yes. I understand it. But I don't always like it. I know I got a big battle ahead. I'm going to outlive the life expectancy.

Do you believe when you do die, you'll be reunited with the people you love? Like Richard?

I don't know what form it will take. How do

you wrap your mind around that? I don't think I'm afraid to die.

You seem to have peace.
 You make it what you can. And then you move on.

— September 23, 2012, on the phone late at night, sixteen months after diagnosis

11
PATIENT

What I hated most about the Alzheimer's diagnosis was all the "can'ts" that came with it. Can't cure it. Can't reverse it. So many people told me about all the things an Alzheimer's patient eventually can't do. Can't work. Can't drive. Can't travel. I seemed to be surrounded by negativity, by fear, and by stigma.

Almost nobody talked to me about the things I can do.

There was only one "can't" I would accept regarding the illness. "I can't change it," I told Tyler. "But I can try to do something about it."

I was determined to make a list of the cans: I can continue to work for as long as possible — I refuse to stay at home and rot away. I can resist the pressure to retire and disappear. I can decline to be afraid, or self-conscious. I can try to be an example: it's easy to *tell* people how things are done; real teachers *show* people how things are done.

I can joke about it.

"I've forgotten I have it," I told Tyler.

I can fight.

I'd always told our players that attitude is a choice. "It is what it is," I said, "but it will become what you make of it." I'd prepared my whole adult professional life for this sort of battle. If this wasn't what I had been teaching young women over three and a half decades, under the guise of basketball, then I'd had no purpose at all. None.

The fact is, by the time I was diagnosed, I had been working with Alzheimer's quite well for some time. Three more Aprils had passed since we'd won our 2008 title. The afterglow of the championship wore off quickly: in '09, we replaced the Parker-Anosike crowd almost entirely with freshmen, and I couldn't grow them up fast enough to avoid an upset loss to Ball State in the first round of the NCAA tournament. But since then they had matured beautifully, with back-to-back seasons of 32-3 and 34-3. We had won just about everything in our sights; the only gap in our résumé was a Final Four. Whatever the signs of Alzheimer's, and whenever they manifested, they hadn't prevented us from running up a 66-6 record over two seasons.

I arrived at a decision: I wanted to meet the disease as assertively as I'd met every other challenge in my life. With Tyler's help, I sought treatment from my neurologist, Dr. John Dougherty, head of the Memory Clinic at the University of Tennessee's Cole Neuroscience Center, who put me on the standard Alzheimer's medications Aricept and Namenda. But Tyler also began to research cutting-edge clinics where I could get second opinions and explore emerging therapies and clinical trials.

Next, I had to inform the Tennessee administration, and I had to go public. I will be frank: the prospect of telling the world I had Alzheimer's made me flinch. All my vanity, and my competitive instincts as a coach, recoiled from the idea. *People will use it against me,* a voice in my head whispered. But another voice told me, *You have to face the truth.*

In the third week of August 2011, Tyler called our longtime friend and attorney Robert B. Barnett of the Washington, D.C., law firm Williams & Connolly to tell him what we'd learned at Mayo. Bob flew to Knoxville for a meeting. I'm sure he assumed he was coming to negotiate my retirement package.

I surprised him. I told Bob I didn't believe

the disease was severe enough yet to warrant retirement. "I'd like to coach two more years," I said. I feared resigning abruptly would harm the program that was such a labor of love for me and betray the players I'd recruited. Although I was having symptoms, I believed I could still do two critical things: teach and lead.

But Bob looked grim. Given the progressive nature of Alzheimer's, he thought it likely university administration officials would ask me to retire. I needed to prepare myself to walk away on my own terms.

I nodded and said something noncommittal. Then I got up from the couch and went into my bedroom and lay down in the dark and wept. It was a blow. I wanted to fight — and they might not let me.

At that moment, I had to confront the fact that Alzheimer's wasn't the kind of opponent over which I could declare a triumph. A victory in this case wasn't going to be a banner-raising affair. After thirty-eight years, all that I had built was being wrested away from me like a repossession in the night. Alzheimer's had walked into my home and taken over. It stood in the corner like a dim shade, giving all the orders and making decisions for me, while I sat there, saying, "But . . ."

I'd always been the decider, the trigger puller. But victory in this case was simply maintaining some say over my life. It was going to be a matter of smaller, day-to-day conquests over helplessness, and purposelessness. It was a siege, a one-step-up-and-two-steps-back affair. It was about buying time.

A few minutes later, Tyler came in. After I'd left the room, Tyler and Bob had continued to talk, and they arrived at a possible solution. Bob would propose that I remain as head coach, but with a redistribution of some of my duties to the assistants, who could take on the things I was struggling to do, like play calling. It was worth a try, but it would depend on whether or not Tennessee's administrators still saw me as having some value and abilities.

That afternoon, Tyler, Bob, and I met with UT chancellor Jimmy Cheek and Joan Cronan. Bob had his lawyer's body armor on and was prepared to battle on my behalf. But as Chancellor Cheek and Joan listened to my disclosure and heard the word *Alzheimer's,* tears streamed down their faces. Chancellor Cheek said, "You are now and will always be our coach, for as long as you're able. As long as you want to be part of the Tennessee family, there will be a place for you." He gave me the blessing to continue, as did Joan. They understood we would be in uncharted waters. Joan said, "But think about the difference you've made and can make going forward." Their attitude was that the experiment was well worth it. Tyler and I then left, and Bob sat down with the university counsel, Catherine Mizell, and Chancellor Cheek to iron out the details of reworking my contract.

It was a remarkable vote of confidence, and a relieving one. It also didn't surprise me; UT's administrators had been generous to me since I was twenty-two years old. Whether it was Andy Holt coming to a game with a sack of ham sandwiches, or Dr. Joe Johnson making me the highest-paid coach in the sport, or Dr. Cheek and Joan reaching a steadying hand out in the face of a mortal diagnosis, I'd had their unwavering support. There weren't many female professionals who could count on such benevolence from their employers. I could. But I couldn't help thinking about other Alzheimer's patients who wanted to keep working, but no one would fashion a role for them, because of the perception that the disease renders you instantly useless. Maybe I could change that perception — maybe that was how I was supposed to redefine victory.

Three days after meeting with the chancellor, I went public with my diagnosis and broke the news to our team. As soon as I shut the doors to a conference room and turned to face our players, a videotaped statement was released to the media. On the exterior, I looked composed as I made that simple though stunning announcement. But truthfully, it was a day of stomach-knotting fear and pressure. How would our players take it? Would they rebel at being coached by someone with a mind-wasting illness? What would the public think? I fought to be word perfect, because even the smallest trip over a word might make listeners say, "There it is, the disease. She can't do it."

It was time to circle up. Our players crowded around the table, so long and leggy they dwarfed their chairs and had to hunch over to rest their elbows on the table. I gazed at our five seniors and knew they had questions; they had seen signs of the disease trespassing on our program but had been too respectful to ask what was wrong with me, bless them. They included: Vicki Baugh, a soft-eyed six-foot-four center from Sacramento, California, who went at the basket like a javelin, until she blew her knee in the '08 title game against Stanford and needed multiple surgeries; Briana Bass, a selfless five-foot-two guard from Indianapolis with a face like an angel; Glory "Glo" Johnson, a razor-minded six-foot-three forward from Knoxville with booster rockets for legs; Alicia "A-Town" Manning, a grinning, sunny six-foot-one all-purpose player from Atlanta; and Shekinna "Strick" Stricklen, our versatile six-foot-two guard from Morrilton, Arkansas, with an ambling stride, so sweetly easygoing that I teased her she looked like she'd rather be fishing by a pond.

Many of them had noticed that I had issues with my memory, I began. "I went to the Mayo Clinic to get checked out," I said. "I have early-onset dementia, Alzheimer's type."

There was an audible gasp. A junior named Taber Spani, an archer-like shooter from Lee's Summit, Missouri, started to weep. All around the room chins were trembling. If I didn't get a grip on their emotions, they would dissolve. I didn't want that. I stared back at them stoically, hoping they would follow my lead.

"Listen up," I said. "This is not a pity party. Hear me? We're not going to cry over this. I'm still your coach."

They sat up a little straighter and stopped crying.

With a diagnosis like this you don't quit living, I explained. You keep going. We were going to reorganize the staff, but our principles would be the same, and so would our aim. The best thing they could do for me, I said, was "to cut down nets." "I'm not going to forget your names," I added. Then I went for a laugh. "And I'm certainly not going to forget to yell at you." That did it — they broke up into laughter. With that we dissolved the meeting, and I instantly felt better for having told them. There were no more questions or gray areas, no more big mysteries. We had clarity.

"We've got your back, Pat," Vicki Baugh said.

Next, I moved to the phones and began getting in touch with our recruits and their parents to explain the situation. To our astonishment, not a single one of them reneged that day. They all maintained their commitments to Tennessee.

I went home immensely relieved, and as thoroughly exhausted as I'd ever been. I was in strange new territory now. Alzheimer's was an unpredictable disease: What if my health declined rapidly? What if I subjected the team to embarrassment, or our players felt shortchanged, or the season became more about me than them?

I would need a lot of help to get through the coming months. But I had it. At my flank was my son, who had grown into a man of incredible strength and substance. Tyler Summitt was only twenty-one, but in the past few weeks he had engineered my trip to the Mayo Clinic, consulted with doctors and arranged for my treatment, assumed control of the family finances, brought himself up to speed on my legal affairs, and fought for me to keep my job. He had done all this while managing to work out like a fiend as a walk-on member of the Tennessee men's basketball team and staying on track to graduate in just three years cum laude with a degree in communications.

If anyone was uniquely positioned to make this experiment work, I was. Alongside me was the most stable, deeply experienced staff in the country: Holly had been with me for twenty-eight years, and Dean for another seven, though I'd known him for twenty. Daedra Charles was in charge of player development, and our director of basketball operations, Kathy Harston, had spent two decades at Texas as an assistant coach under Hall of Famer Jody Conradt. Our sports medicine director, Jenny Moshak, had been with us for twenty years, and our strength coach, Heather Mason, for nine.

Also, Mickie DeMoss was back. In 2010, I called her to ask if she would rejoin our staff. I'd missed her humor and advice every day of the seven years since she'd been away, and something told me I needed her to lean on. I didn't consciously know something was wrong with me at that point, but I didn't feel as strong as I once had.

"I want you to come back to Tennessee," I said.

Mickie had made a success at Kentucky, but then had suffered a case of burnout and taken some time off before migrating to Texas. I knew she missed us as much as we missed her.

"Come on, Mickie," I said. "Let's finish out our careers together."

Mickie heard a note in my voice that said, "I need you." She didn't hesitate to accept the job — but in the back of her mind she was a little concerned. She thought, *When has Pat ever needed help?* Shortly after Mickie came back to Knoxville, she felt twinges of uneasy recognition. Her mother, Wilma, had suffered from dementia, and it had started with the same tiny glitches that I had.

Now that Mickie knew my diagnosis, she felt she was in exactly the right place. She understood how much person was left underneath the symptoms, because she had walked Wilma through her illness. Once, Mickie, Holly, and I went to visit Wilma in the assisted living facility where she spent the last years of her life. Early one morning we all tiptoed into her room, trying not to make too much noise. But Wilma was awake, and when she saw us, she threw back the covers and popped up. She was fully clothed, down to a pair of red tennis shoes, and her purse.

"I'm ready to go," she said brightly. "Where are we going?"

Exactly my attitude.

I was ready to go too: I wanted to go back to a Final Four, and I thought we had a pretty good crack at it, if I could keep my health issue at bay and it didn't become a weight on our team or our staff. In addition to five seniors, we had some blazingly talented underclassmen. Ariel Massengale, of Bolingbroke, Illinois, was a five-six point guard who made great decisions and had a stocky, durable, bumper-car style of play. Cierra Burdick of Charlotte, North Carolina, was an exuberant six-foot-two forward with big hands and feet who could knock down shots from all over the court, and six-three center Isabelle Harrison played like there was an electric current running through her. Then there was our blindingly fast sophomore guard Meighan "Speedy" Simmons from Cibolo, Texas, and an antic, baby-voiced junior guard from Clarksville, Tennessee, Kamiko Williams.

Our team was rangy, athletic, and I liked the look of them. As Dean said, "We're very impressive getting off the bus or walking through airports."

On October 24, 2011, I made my first major public appearance since announcing my diagnosis, at the annual SEC media day in Birmingham to kick off the season. A wall of cameras and mikes awaited me, and the tension was heightened by the fact that just before I entered the room, I learned that ESPN was going live, because a rumor had gotten around that I was there to announce my retirement.

But I loved talking with the press; I'd been unself-conscious with them throughout my career. Holly was with me for moral support, and I also had the good wishes of my fellow coaches from around the SEC, all of whom had called or sent notes asking what they could do to help me through the day. I strolled through the throng and took a seat with Holly, surrounded by a horseshoe of klieg lights.

"I'm not ready to retire," I declared. "I've heard that one rolled out today. I may be old as dirt when I'm still trying to win games."

The questions began to fly, and for the next half an hour I fielded them as sharply as I could, conscious that what I put on display could change how people saw the disease.

Did the disease make me feel slower? "I don't think it's something that's slowing me down," I shot back. "I think if anything, it's revving me up."

What was my goal? "We need to cut down nets," I declared. "I'd be disappointed if we didn't."

Out of the blue, someone said I was known for my cooking — what did I still like to cook? The question was so out of context it took me aback, and I felt a telltale vagueness and uncertainty; had I understood it right? I peered into the lights and paused for a just a beat too long. Holly jumped in. "Mexican corn," she said. By then I'd caught up. "Jalapeño corn," I corrected.

There were more questions, probing my state of mind. I discussed our freshmen and their energy and praised Vicki Baugh for her leadership. Someone kiddingly asked if I still knew how to yell at the officials.

"Trust me, I remember the refs," I said, to laughter.

When I got home that night, I rewarded myself with a glass of cabernet. "You deserve a glass of wine tonight," Mickie said.

"Don't worry, I'm about to pour my second one," I said.

Workouts began, and with them, a new routine. My closest friends circled up to help me establish a regimen to fight the disease. Billie Moore came from California and Esther Hubbard drove in from Kentucky, and they installed themselves in the guest rooms.

Billie read up on anecdotal reports that coconut oil in large doses could slow Alzheimer's, and I began drinking protein shakes full of it every morning. I was less enthusiastic about Billie's insistence that I get on a Mediterranean diet, which did not include my preferred food groups: filet mignon and cabernet. She coached me like I was a student again, trying to make the Olympic team. "I want to save every single brain cell," she said. At dinner I sipped ice water and chewed salmon and vegetables.

Tyler, my nurse anesthetist friend Mary Margaret Carter, and my invaluable assistant Katie Wynn sorted through the hundreds of offers and suggestions I received, ranging from the eyebrow raising (the disease was caused by my dental fillings) to the frightening (had I tried electroshock therapy?). They zeroed in on the most helpful contacts and made appointments for two additional consultations, one at Brigham and Women's Hospital in Boston, and another at the Banner Alzheimer's Institute in Phoenix, Arizona. They turned over every stone.

On the morning of our season opener against Pepperdine, we all sat around doing puzzles, which had taken over the house. My iPad was loaded with brainteasers, and I also had books of Sudoku and word finders. We were all obsessed. Esther worked a "cryptograph" in the daily paper, while Billie did a crossword. Esther and Billie had completely different methods: Billie was a pen person, Esther a pencil person. Billie wouldn't fill in a box unless she was absolutely certain of the answer, whereas Esther freely scribbled.

"That's a guess," Billie said.

"No, it's a deduction," Esther answered.

I watched them argue back and forth, my head turning like I was following a Ping-Pong ball.

Billie asked, "What's a five-letter word for 'fast.' "

"Hasty," Esther said.

"That could be right," Billie said.

"It *is* right," Esther said. "Put it down.

"No, it's a guess."

That was how I spent my afternoon; I might as well have taken an SAT exam. Finally it was time for pregame, my first official contest coaching with Alzheimer's. When I walked into the locker room, Holly had already written the players' instructions up on the board. Once, it had been my job. I stared at it. "Is that Holly's handwriting?" I asked.

Yes, Mickie answered. "It can't be," I said. "Someone must have helped her." Holly had famously sloppy writing, but her new duties as a clipboard holder were bringing out the executive in her. We had settled on what felt like comfortable, defined roles: Mickie and I worked on the offense, while Dean and Holly handled the defense. Holly was the play caller during games. My job was to serve as the big gun, the disciplinarian.

Pepperdine was a veteran team and fourth in the country in steals, and while we led by 13 at the half, it wasn't pretty. The coaches started to retire to our separate anteroom to discuss it, but at the last second I swerved to the front of the locker room to address the players.

"Why are we turning the ball over?" I asked. "What is it?" No answer. But I suspected I knew the reason. "Are we overanxious?" Heads nodded. The kids probably felt as on display as I did. They settled down in the second half and ignited for an 18–0 run and blew the game open.

It was a good beginning to a season that we knew would have its bumps and pockets of turbulence. Our team and staff continually had to adapt to the circumstances that went with my diagnosis. I couldn't scout like I used to, so the workload of analyzing film had to be redistributed. I had to be occasionally absent for medical consultations, and there was the constant scrutinizing spotlight from the media.

But in general, things went on normally, as they always had. That's not to say we didn't have crises that season, but they were the usual ones — our seniors' motivation occasionally flagged as they contemplated life after college, and our freshmen struggled with the physical workload and hit a wall. But I was proud that no one ever used my diagnosis as an excuse or explanation for anything that happened. Our kids treated Alzheimer's like an uninvited guest — and ignored him.

In mid-November, Mary Margaret and I flew to Boston, where I spent part of an afternoon with Dr. Reisa Sperling, the head of Alzheimer's research and clinical trials at Brigham and Women's. She was a small tousle-headed woman in a tiny office dominated by stacks of papers. Deep down, I'd clung to the hope that maybe it was a terrible mistake, that my tests had been misinterpreted. But Dr. Sperling showed me an MRI of my brain and said, "I wish I could tell you something different." What it showed, unfortunately, was a classic case of Alzheimer's.

But Dr. Sperling did have some encouragement for me. She put an image of my brain on her computer screen. Green was bad, and orange was good, she said. The colors on the screen reflected glucose levels, which showed blood distribution in my brain. There, in the middle, was a small Crest-colored blob, the plaque buildup. But all around it was a beautiful vibrant orange, Tennessee's color. It showed that far more of my brain was healthy than not.

Dr. Sperling talked to me about the state of various clinical trials, but just as interesting was her advice on how to battle the disease in a nonpharmaceutical way. Heavy exercise showed a beneficial effect, she said. Puzzles were good too, but there was a danger of retreating into them, burying your head in them. Interact, she encouraged. Talk, work, laugh. Get out in the world. In a word, live.

It was reassuring to know that my instincts for how to deal with the disease met with the best medical opinion — and the advice to keep living came at a time when life expectancy was on my mind. In early December, *Sports Illustrated* named me co–Sportsman of the Year with the great Mike Krzyzewski of Duke. It was a rare tribute for a woman, given *SI*'s famously male-dominated outlook, and Kathy Harston urged me to give the following acceptance speech: "I was so honored when *SI* called and wanted to photograph me. Because I just knew I had finally made it into the Swimsuit Issue." Kathy even got ahold of an issue and superimposed my head over a swimsuit model reclining on her stomach in a thong. I laughed until I almost fell down.

The *Sports Illustrated* story by their senior

writer Alex Wolff was a glowing compliment, and I read it with immodest pleasure, until I arrived at a sidebar about Alzheimer's. A sentence jumped out at me: "the average life expectancy" for Alzheimer's was eight to ten years from diagnosis. The sentence hit me hard, right in the stomach. I suppose I had heard the figure before, but there was something about seeing it in type that leveled me. That night, I had a meltdown. Michelle Marciniak called to check in, and I burst into tears on the phone. It had been a bad week, I said; things seemed fuzzy, and I didn't feel right, and the idea of a death sentence weighed on me. It was one of those nights when optimism deserted me.

But the next morning I did what I'd always been taught to do by my father: I went back to work and made myself useful. The players took my mind off my health issues. We embarked on a road trip to New York to play DePaul and Rutgers. Our young point guard Massengale was out with a dislocated finger, and Meighan Simmons was in a shooting slump. I worked with Meighan on her form — she was "dipping" the ball, yanking it low instead of going straight into her release. It felt good to straighten her out, help her.

The Lady Vols hit New York hard, and my

mood lifted. We power shopped at Macy's in the heart of Christmas traffic, and ate Italian and listened to Mickie stretch tales. One was a riff about going into Victoria's Secret and having her personal dimensions announced over the store loudspeaker. Dean Lockwood took a turn: he had an uncanny ability to remember whole lengths of movie dialogue, and he loved to do the well scene from *Silence of the Lambs.* "It takes the lotion from the basket and puts it on its skin," he intoned. Mickie, Holly, and I indulged in our favorite sport, teasing him for his bachelordom. "Dean keeps his running shoes on," I said.

It was an encouraging trip — we beat DePaul handily and then made a big comeback against Rutgers after trailing by 11 points in the second half. Afterward, Vivian gave me a huge hug, and told the press graciously, "They're playing in Pat's image. It's a tribute to her."

A day later we flew out to California for a two-game swing against UCLA and Stanford, and between contests I met up with Billie for a day trip to the Banner Alzheimer's Institute in Phoenix, for yet another consultation. At first I was reluctant to go — "What else are they going to tell me?" I asked. But I won't ever question the value of a third opinion again.

Banner is a nonprofit, outpatient care and research facility devoted exclusively to Alzheimer's, and its goal is to think and act boldly. It's run by Dr. Eric Reiman and Dr. Pierre Tariot, whose mission is "to end Alzheimer's disease before another generation is lost." They emphasize innovation and "immediately applying discovery to patients" — meaning that if something seems to help, they do it, and don't hem and haw. From the moment I set foot on the premises, I loved them. They believed that "hope and help are possible now" when it came to Alzheimer's, and they were talking my language.

I spent a half day with them and left with new recommendations to think about. What impressed me most was their combination of optimism and specificity, their willingness to address my personal goals and professional challenges in dealing with Alzheimer's, rather than to make cookie-cutter pronouncements. They recommended that I get further neuropsychological testing to discern the individual pattern of strengths and weaknesses in my brain. "We're going to give you a scouting report of the opponent," Dr. Tariot said. "And we're going to give you a game plan."

Some of their recommendations were basic. There was a possible connection between Alzheimer's and vitamin B_{12} deficiency, so they suggested I get supplemental shots, which no one had mentioned before. They suggested that I drink loads of water — if Alzheimer's is an autoimmune disorder, then hydrating would help. They proposed that I think about my brain as an athlete: I should train for optimum performance. Sometimes my circuits would work, and sometimes they wouldn't — what circumstances were most conducive to them working? They recommended that I concentrate for ninety minutes at a time, and then take ninety minutes off, with periodic naps. Rest was as good as medication, they said.

Some of the advice was startling. I asked about the effect of stress: they responded that a certain amount of stress was actually *good* for people. Challenge, pressure, releases chemicals that sharpen the senses and invigorate us, helps us perform more efficiently, and actually improves the memory. Far from being something I needed to eliminate, some stress could stimulate me. But I had to be careful and not overdo it. The greater enemy was sloth, inactivity.

We also discussed emerging treatments; but I eventually decided against participating in any clinical trials, primarily because my arthritis regimen conflicted with some of the medications. We agreed that I would continue to explore and consider other treatments. I wanted to think "aggressively," I said.

What I liked best about the people at Banner was that they talked about working with Alzheimer's — working around it, working despite it, working against it. Dr. Tariot had seen a range of professionals stricken with the disease who continued to do what they loved — including doctors, dentists, lawyers, and CEOs of large companies — gradually refining their roles to accommodate the effects. Just because I might have to throttle back on some of my responsibilities, he suggested, didn't mean I had to throttle back on everything. There was a whole range of possibilities, and one size didn't fit all.

"When you got arthritis, you had to change some things, right?" he asked.

I said, "Of course."

"You adapted."

"Yes, I did."

"This is the same. You can adapt to it."

He said, "You are still Pat. You've got a new normal, you have a chronic illness, but it doesn't mean you have to curl up in a ball and die. It does not need to be the social kiss of death. You have new weak-nesses but also many strengths you can capitalize on."

This is a very slowly progressive condition, and people progress at different rates; it's not like something is going to happen overnight. In her case she invited total candor about the pros and cons of her high-profile, high-pressure role, and we were able to talk about positives and negatives of that. There's a whole spectrum, and it's interesting because professional organizations and corporations are beginning to have to come to terms with this. When does a trial lawyer with mild Alzheimer's have to have his or her competency called into question, and why? Or a doctor? These are real issues.

— DR. PIERRE TARIOT

I left Banner feeling more optimistic than at any time since I'd been diagnosed. I had a game plan, and I had a team.

Unfortunately, I didn't capitalize on my strengths in our next game — and neither did anyone else. I caught up with our team at our hotel just off the Stanford campus, and our staff headed to dinner at a small restaurant just down the block. Mickie had on a new pair of boots, and as we walked, one of her shoelaces came untied. She glanced down and decided she would deal with it when we got to the restaurant. But about thirty feet from the front door, I accidentally stepped on the shoelace — and Mickie went sprawling. She fractured her right arm and wound up in a cast.

It was just the latest injury to our staff; a few weeks earlier, Holly had fractured her hand when the heel of her shoe caught as she was stepping off the plane after the media day in Birmingham. She was in a cast too. The next day we went over to Stanford's Maples Pavilion for practice, and Tara VanDerveer and her staff wandered out to the floor to greet us.

"What happened to you?" Tara said to Mickie.

"I got hit by a bus," Mickie said.

"You need to stay away from us," Holly said. "Summitt's the only one in good shape."

We were in no condition for a fight; Stanford killed us that night, 97–80. It was the start of a terrible stretch in which our season appeared to be going down the drain. On January 12, 2012, we went to Kentucky and lost by a single point, 61–60, on a last-second shot when we got bitten by our lack of enthusiasm for defense, a chronic problem with our team for four years.

A week later LSU came to town led by Nikki Caldwell, who had become a superb head coach and also, to our collective joy, was pregnant and due in March. As I hugged her, I couldn't help but think back to my own radiance when I was pregnant. Nikki strolled into Thompson-Boling looking gorgeously self-satisfied, and everybody gathered around and patted her stomach. We studied whether she was carrying the baby low or high and discussed whether it would be a girl or a boy. Girl, we decided. That night there was a baby shower at a local hotel, and her team came in to say hello, a bunch of gangly-armed kids with lighted-up expressions when they looked at their coach, whom they clearly loved. One of them did a dead-on impression of Caldwell for us: she stalked around and then folded her arms and blasted the kids with her intense gaze and said, "Don't PUT something on my board you can't back up!"

I surveyed apprehensively how big and athletic LSU looked — and dreaded having to play them the next day. "Pool party at my house," I told them. "No curfew."

I was right; the next day was no fun at all. Nikki's coaching style was very much like ours, with an emphasis on physical defense, and it was a stalemate of a game that left both teams absolutely battered. Somehow, we won, 65–56, but in the locker room I heard one of the kids say, "I feel like I've been in a prizefight."

The Lady Vols were bruised and beat up. Shekinna, never the most energetic of players, was hobbling and sore. Taber was not practicing full court because of lingering knee pain. Glory had tape all over her shoulder. And Vicki was wearing a brace on her twice-repaired knee. They limped as bad as me. In the next game, Notre Dame killed us, 72–44.

Everything I feared about trying to coach with illness seemed to be coming true. We went to Vanderbilt and got crushed by the always-sharp Melanie Balcomb's team, 93–79. The worst part was, we were tied with twelve minutes to go, only to give up 40 points in twelve minutes. Forty.

I was sick as a dog — and not just because of the game. Mickie had come down with a terrible stomach ailment and passed it on to me. That morning I wasn't sure I could make it to the sideline, but Jenny Moshak gave me something that calmed my insides. I sat on the bench pale and trembling, and I don't remember much about the day, except making it home to Knoxville, just in time to go into my darkened bedroom and begin throwing up again.

A day later, a columnist for the Nashville paper said I looked disoriented on the sideline, that I wasn't the same coach I had been, and that it was time for me to step down because my health was affecting the Lady Vols.

I was aware that cameras were homing in on me, and that observers wanted my old demeanor back, the spirited bench coach, twitchy, exercised, up and down out of my chair. I also knew that any sign of vulnerability would be blamed on Alzheimer's. I didn't care; I had surrendered my vanity when I decided to coach with an illness. I was more engaged than they realized — and I wasn't quite sure what they expected. I didn't see things as well as I used to, which was why I turned the play calling over to Holly. I was trying to conserve my energy and manage my stress, and the arthritis made it hard to move around. Acting like a madwoman just wasn't a realistic performance anymore.

But I was still the big gun in the locker room. The players responded when I mustered my voice and told them what needed to be done with my old adamant, contagious certainty. We were at a juncture where things could go either way. On February 13, Kentucky came to Thompson-Boling for a rematch, with our entire season on the line. We badly needed a defeat of a ranked team to position ourselves for a postseason run. Dean gave a great, sharp pregame talk. "We've been uneven and we've had our ups and downs," he said. "But there is one thing I know. All we got is in this room. Look at the person next to you."

The kids all turned their heads. "That's what we got," he said. "Each other."

Now I stepped to the front of the room. There was no point in dodging the subject. Instead of avoiding it, I decided to go right at it.

"Y'all, we got to have this one," I said. "It's a must win."

The kids nodded. "Last time it was their turn," I said. "One-point loss, on their floor. But now we're at home — and we're not losing. Guess what. It's OUR TURN!"

That sent them out the door flying. Meighan hit two huge threes and blocked a shot, Stricklen made a stunning spin move in the lane, and Vicki Baugh leaped up around the rim like she was on a pogo stick.

We beat 'em by 40.

We were back in the national conversation

and had rescued our self-respect, and we were starting to look like a traditional Tennessee team again. Our problems weren't solved by a long shot, but we were headed back in the right direction.

We won two games in Mississippi to climb back into first place in the Southeastern Conference. It was a relief to us all — except for young Isabelle Harrison, who started crying on the bench because she wasn't getting enough playing time. Izzy was a beautiful young talent who ached to be great, but she was playing behind Glory Johnson and Vicki Baugh, experienced seniors and WNBA draft prospects. She was impatient to get on the court to the point of tears.

I sympathized, but the coach in me couldn't afford to show it. Izzy hadn't cried when Notre Dame slaughtered us, because she got to play a lot in that one. But she was in tears when we beat Ole Miss? Unacceptable. After consulting with Holly, Mickie, and Dean, I stalked into the locker room. "Are you sick?" I demanded. "What's the matter with you?" She sobbed something about not getting to play.

"If you don't quit crying right now, it'll be a lot more than one game you don't play in."

But the next afternoon I sat down with Izzy for a quiet talk and explained that court time had to be earned with maturity and consistency. Part of the reason for our streakiness was that our team had some lingering immaturity; even our seniors had a childish streak trapped in their big bodies. They carried around stuffed animals as good luck charms, and they named them. Ariel clutched a bear named "Kaiden." There was a lion cub named "Leo." Glory carted around a large, limp monkey that she named "Ralph." Ralph? College women, with stuffed toys. I rolled my eyes, but I couldn't help laughing. They drove our staff to cross-eyed distraction, but they were tremendously entertaining, and I adored them — in a funny way.

At a team breakfast in Mississippi, they argued over whether or not they were "grown." It was a debate that had raged all season, thanks to Daedra, who liked to scold them by saying, "You think you're grown, but you're not." Harston contributed by taking the players' side and whipped them into a frenzy.

"How many of you pay taxes, raise your hands?" Daedra asked at breakfast.

No hands went up. "See. You're not grown."

Harston jumped in to defend them.

"How many of you worked summer camp and got W-2s?"

Hands went up. "You're grown," Harston announced.

"No, they ain't!" Daedra came back. "They're not grown until they have a car and a house payment."

"How many of you have cars?" Harston asked.

Hands went up. "You're grown," she announced.

Daedra shot back, "How many of your mamas and daddies pay your insurance?"

By now things were getting loud; kids were whooping and hollering and banging their silverware on the table, insisting they were grown. Harston kept ratcheting it up and getting sillier.

"How many of you eat your steak medium rare?" Harston demanded.

Hands went up.

"You're grown," Harston announced.

Daedra said, "How many of you *don't* think you're grown?"

Ariel's hand went up. Ariel still let her mother do her hair.

A-Town's hand went partly up. Glory gasped. "A-Town! You're a senior! You *have* to be grown."

Harston said, "Okay, here's the deal. You're grown if the coaches don't have to yell at you one more time this season, 'You need to GROW UP!' "

All of a sudden there was dead silence. Shekinna shrank back in her chair. The coaches erupted in laughter.

They never made anything easy. But in the final home game of the season, we started our five seniors, and they walloped Florida 75–59. We sensed that our team had turned an emotional corner, and after talking with them, we decided to go with the all-senior lineup the rest of the way. I wanted to let them play it out.

As we approached the postseason, the tension drained away from me. I felt thoughtful, clear, and completely in the moment, which was where I wanted to be. I knew that I had a decision to make about whether to stay on as head coach after the season, which had been visibly hard on our staff. Holly was working so frantically on the bench that she'd sweat until her blond hair turned dark with moisture. Mickie had ongoing problems with her stomach. Harston had a theory about that. "Mickie needs to learn that chips and salsa are not a fiber," she said. But I didn't want to consciously address the question yet, for fear of distracting or torpedoing our team. I wanted all of us to get through the tournament without that pressure, to enjoy it without thinking about the future.

I walked through those last few games full of emotion, in a good way. I was suffused with a heightened sense of love for the game, the glorious action, the magnificent shapes of the players flying through the air, and the steadfast friends who stood beside me on the sideline. Our team gathered itself and gave me one more climb up a ladder to cut down nets. We swept through the Southeastern Conference tournament with our best three games of the year, mowing down Vanderbilt, South Carolina, and LSU in that order.

Holly texted Nikki Caldwell on the night before the SEC title game. "I hope your water breaks," she wrote.

Nikki texted back: "It already did and I have a little point guard ready to go."

After the trophy and net cutting, I climbed back down the ladder with a piece of silk net in my hand and made my way to the locker room, where I told our kids what was in my heart. It had been a long season, with seven losses, but I wanted them to understand that they could never disappoint me. They were my perpetual remedy, and my cure. "You are one of my favorite teams ever," I said. They jumped around and screamed with joy like they'd just won the lottery.

Two days later we went back into the gym to get ready for the NCAA tournament, and we heard that Nikki's baby had been born: little Justice Caldwell had come into the world. Her mother carried her around much as Tyler had been carried as a newborn; Justice attended her first practice when she was just a few days old. It was an inexpressibly sweet turn of the generational wheel.

The NCAA tournament was full of bookend moments like that for me. When the brackets were announced, of all schools, we drew UT-Martin for our first-round opponent. "Isn't that precious?" I said to our coaches. A handful of my Chi O friends drove to Chicago to see us play, including my old teammate Esther Hubbard, who teased me by telling everybody, "I had to stay on her ass. All she wanted to do was shoot."

"That's why we won," I said.

Dean gave our kids a motto for staying focused on one game at a time in the tournament: "If you chase two rabbits, you won't catch one." It was an old proverb that, given their love of stuffed animals, spoke to them. We blew Martin out, 72–49, and steadily worked our way deeper into the tournament. We defeated DePaul, 63–48, to get to the Sweet 16. We moved on to Des Moines, Iowa, where we dispatched Kansas, 84–73.

"Good win," Holly said. "Caught a rabbit."

"Got the dinner," Glory said, clapping.

"Silly rabbit," Kamiko said.

But there was no rabbit waiting for us in the Elite Eight; there was a competitive monster: Baylor, coached by my former point guard on the '84 Olympic team, Kim Mulkey. Baylor was undefeated thanks to the marvelous coaching job Kim did with her six-foot-eight prodigy, Brittney Griner, who was having a Player of the Year season. I sat with Holly and we devised the only game plan that made any sense: we'd attack them from the outside, with four players on the perimeter to try to stretch them out. It was our only chance against "the Griner Factor," as I called it.

Our kids never backed down, but to beat them we needed to make a bunch of rainbows from the outside, and instead we were cold shooting. We went 1 for 9 from the three-point line in the first half and trailed by 15. We could never make it up. I felt helpless — as helpless as I had the last time I'd faced a player so big, in Uljana Semjonova and the Soviets in the '76 Olympics.

Final score: 77–58. I had no profound last words for our team in the locker room, just affectionate ones. With everyone in the room sobbing, I told them to get their heads up and look at me. It was hard to make eye contact because they had huge tears rolling down their faces, but they lifted their heads. I told them I loved them and was proud of the way they took the court and battled.

"Think about the *good* things that happened, and what's to come," I urged them.

There were so many emotions in the room that it made me quake, and my voice trembled as I spoke. "I'll never forget you," I said.

Holly and the players then left to go to the press conference, and I walked into a small coaches' room off the main locker room. I sat down with Tyler. He rubbed my back and shoulders like he always did after a loss, ever since he was a little boy. "It was the Griner Factor," I told him. "She was just too much. We just couldn't get past them."

It was a defeat, yes. But then you ask yourself, Were we really the best team? And you say no. Or sometimes yes. You beat yourself up a little. You always think there was something else you could have done, or should have done, for the players. You don't think it's them. You think it's you.

I sat there, wishing I could have helped them more. It was a long and lonely half hour, waiting for them to finish with the press. Fortunately, at that moment a wonderful reporter from the *New York Times* named Jere Longman came into our locker room. Jere's father had suffered from Alzheimer's, and he asked to speak to me personally, not as a reporter. I gratefully motioned him into the room; his request touched me. Jere was just going to say a word or two and shake my hand, but it turned into more than that. I invited him to sit down, and we chatted for a moment, and then Jere spoke of his father and began to cry. I put my arms around him, and that finally brought me to tears too. Jere and I consoled each other, and I was grateful for that moment with him, and for the company.

But then I dried my tears. I was sad it was over, but I didn't want to be unduly so. The game had been so good to me, and to be too disconsolate would have been . . . ungrateful. When I looked back on it I wouldn't remember the losses, but rather the laughter like streamers, and the curative companionship of those kids.

Every ending is a potential point of renewal. It's over, and you start again, an endless cycle of seasons. We flew back to Knoxville that night, and I walked back in the house and tossed my keys on the counter, and patted my dogs. Then I went to the wine rack and pulled out a bottle of my favorite Caymus cabernet. I lifted a glass, and thought about Uljana Semjonova, and myself when I was young, at my original starting point.

My short-term factual memory can be like water; events are a brief disturbance on the surface and then it closes back up again, as if nothing ever touched it. But it's a strange fact that my long-term memory remains strong, perhaps because it recorded events when my mind was unaffected. My emotional memory is intact too, perhaps because feelings are recorded and stored in a different place than facts. The things that happened deeper in the past, and deeper in the breast, are still there for me, under the water.

I won 1,098 games, and eight national championships, and coached in four different decades. But what I see are not the numbers. I see their faces.

"Pat should get a tattoo!" The kids laughed. "What kind should she get?"

"A heart. She should get a heart."

Little did they know. They are the tattoos.

On the Saturday before Easter, Tyler and I drove to Henrietta to see my mother, who at eighty-six still cooks every holiday meal for our family. Ty was at the wheel, and he had his mother's touch on the gas pedal. We got pulled over for speeding. The officer came to the window on my side of the car. When he saw who it was, he said, "Well, I'm not giving you a ticket. I just want to know how you're doing. Furthermore, I want to know if you're coming back next year."

"Oh, I'll be back," I said.

But I wouldn't be back as head coach. During that drive, Tyler and I finally had the talk that I had been tamping down in my subconscious while we competed in the tournament: my role needed to change. I'd always said that no player was bigger than the program, and the same held true for me. I didn't want to be bigger than Tennessee. While continuing to work was good for me, the Lady Vols weren't my personal health clinic.

What made it easier to reach a decision

was the secure knowledge that I could pass on the job to someone I loved, Holly Warlick. A full year earlier, just weeks after I received the final confirmation of my diagnosis, Holly and I spent some vacation time together down in Destin, Florida. We ran our dogs on the beach and talked about the Alzheimer's, and Holly told me she hoped to be my successor. I told her then I would support her. While former players are like daughters and it's impossible to name a favorite, Holly's loyalty and devotion to Tennessee were unmatched and made her the right choice, as did her resilient, low-ego temperament. A few years earlier she had turned down a head coaching job at Clemson to stay with us, and working in my shadow wouldn't bother her.

But the lingering issue for me was the word *retirement.* I didn't want to retire, I told Tyler; I thought I still had strengths and insights to contribute. "I don't want some meaningless office and title with nothing to do," I said. The prospect of just sitting around was unacceptable. What was most important to me, I said, was to be able to still connect with players and to remain involved with basketball. Ty asked if it wouldn't embarrass me to be with the team in a smaller capacity. I said, "Absolutely not."

Ty quietly began to look into the possibility of handing my coaching duties over to Holly while I took on another role that allowed me to still be an adviser to the team. Our friend Bob Barnett flew to Knoxville and once again met with Chancellor Cheek, Joan Cronan, and other university administrators, who, as always, treated me with surpassing generosity and consideration. They fashioned a new job for me: I could become "head coach emeritus," continue as an active staffer in a variety of capacities, working with players on everything from motivation to academic issues. NCAA rules would limit some of my activities, but I could observe practices, participate in the locker room on game days, and recruit on campus.

It was an almost ideal outcome. I wasn't stepping down; I was stepping aside, and it gave me the latitude and flexibility to mentor players as much as my health would allow. Bob came up with a wonderful phrase for it. "Retirement with a small r," he said.

We scheduled a press conference for the morning of April 19, 2012, at which I would officially pass the torch to Holly. As I got dressed that morning, Holly called. "I'm going to need you," she said. "I can't do this without you." I told her, "I will be there for you." After we hung up, I pulled on a chalk gray pin-striped suit and got my game face on as I rehearsed my prepared statement. Camera crews were coming in from all over the country — ESPN and CNN were going live — and it was suggested that I not make any unrehearsed remarks. But I balked. "I want to take questions," I told Tyler firmly.

I put my lipstick on, shrugged into my jacket, and slipped a whistle into my pocket. The house was full of close friends, and we all struggled not to cry. LaTina failed completely. I didn't want to lose control of my emotions in the press conference, but I couldn't make any promises. *I'll play that one by ear,* I told myself.

I drove to Thompson-Boling Arena and went to the locker room, where our team and staff had gathered. Our players had mixed waves of emotions, I knew: reluctant to let me go, but thrilled for Holly.

Izzy Harrison said, "I just want to know you'll still be here."

"I'm still gonna be here — and y'all may not like it," I said, to laughter.

The press conference was a spectacular, upbeat success. It was impossible to feel gloomy when at my side younger people were beaming. Holly was about to start her own career as a head coach, and I wanted this day to be a celebration for her. I stood up and pulled the whistle from my pocket, hung it around her neck, and embraced her.

Then I sat back down next to my son, who was also beaming, because a day earlier he had received a piece of extraordinary news that made me swell with pride. At the age of just twenty-one, Tyler had been offered a job as an assistant women's basketball coach at Marquette University, after dazzling head coach Terri Mitchell during a job interview. I urged him to accept, though it meant Tyler would move to Milwaukee. I wanted him to have the same passion and deep satisfaction that I had enjoyed for so many years, and the knowledge that he was embarking on his career was a huge consolation for the end of mine.

There can be strength in surrender — and I felt it that day. I said, "It's never a good time, but you have to find the time that you think is the right time, and that is now." I fielded several questions from the press without a mishap. When I finally stepped down from the podium, I felt proud, and sure of myself. I was rewarded when *Sports Illustrated* described my attitude that morning as "wicked sharp, funny, and self-deprecating."

I didn't regret the decision to coach publicly with Alzheimer's. Far from it — I hoped the audience might see the disease in a new light: as something that could be managed, lived with in a purposeful way. The great stigma of it was in thinking that it robbed us of all dignity and value. Sometimes, I thought, we strip people of their capacities faster than the disease itself does. But now that my retirement "with a small r" was announced, I felt relieved. No longer did I have to worry about other people's expectations regarding my illness. If nothing else, maybe I could live this thing out the way I wanted to.

The decision to step aside was made immeasurably easier by the good people at the Banner Institute, whose attitudes and advice I had borrowed heavily from. Tyler and I spent long hours on the phone with Dr. Tariot talking through the transition. It was Dr. Tariot who urged us to think in terms of "a strategy for gradually adapting your role," rather than an abrupt giving up. He has led numerous other professionals through the delicate transition from a hands-on CEO to the next stage, candidly yet positively. "You have broad shoulders," he said to me at one point, "and you can make this transition with a systematic game plan that plays to your strengths."

I believe we did that. The day after my "retirement with a small r" press conference, I put my sweats and sneakers back on and went back to practice with the Lady Vols. As of this writing, I've missed only two workouts. Holly tells me I don't have to show up every single day, especially at the six A.M. sessions, but I tell her, "I don't want to be a sissy." My office is three doors down from Holly, who has moved into my old one. She says it's too big for her, and she keeps a Pat Summitt bobble-head on her shelf to help fill it up. She also tells me, "I don't care what disease you have, I'm going to pick that brain for as long as I can." But she doesn't need much help from me; she is thoroughly equipped for the job and has assembled a first-rate staff that includes Dean Lockwood and Jolette Law, a longtime friend of ours who worked for Vivian Stringer and served as a head coach at Illinois. But best of all, at her right hand is Kyra Elzy, who has grown into one of the most impressive young assistants in the game, sure to be a head coach herself one day.

Our team is young, but on the rise. Holly's motto for them is "Same heart, same pride, same fight," which I love. The kids, who include my last recruiting class, tell me they want to represent everything Tennessee has ever been about: hard work, defense, rebounding, and doing all the little things right.

"We want to be throwback players," Taber Spani tells me.

To which I reply, grinning, "You better be careful what you wish for."

How to sum it up? Perhaps with the realization that makes me happiest: my Tennessee legacy is not some flat, dry record on a piece of paper, but a beautiful tree with living branches.

It's a legacy that feels constantly renewed, every time I see a former player. They come back to stay the night with me, and we reminisce, and the best part is when we meet as adults, and we settle old issues. Shanna Zolman and I reconciled when she came back to Knoxville in the midst of her own divorce. She spent a few months in the pool house, and every morning we walked together. One evening she said, "Coach, everybody asks me what you mean to me, and what it was like to play for you. And I've never told you to your face how much I love and respect you, and what you did for me. You are my second mother."

It meant the world to me, because there was always that doubt, when things were hard with players, that I had broken down more than built up. To this day, not all of them felt wonderful about their experience at Tennessee. But Mickie always says, "If they all loved it, we were doing something wrong." It was supposed to be an elite, demanding environment, and it wasn't right for everybody. But it was right for the 161 players who wore the orange, and the real legacy wasn't the victories, but knowing that they were made of something stronger when they left.

> When you think you can't give any more, she's pushing you to give twice as much — and you don't think you have anything more to give. You feel like she's asking you to be this perfect person, and you just don't feel like that's going to happen. And then you realize, my gosh, she got you there. She got you to that point, better than you thought you would be.
>
> — KELLIE JOLLY

Not long after I was diagnosed, I heard the following story from Abby Conklin, who after graduating in 1997 had become a coach and then a graphic artist out in San Francisco. Although I always cared about Abby, we'd never been extremely close, but she came back to visit after she learned I had Alzheimer's. For all the years and distance, we understood each other.

In the summer of 2011, Abby was dealing with a medical crisis of her own. First, her father, Harlo, collapsed with a heart attack and had to be resuscitated with chest compressions. He was still recovering from quadruple bypass surgery when her mother was diagnosed with colon cancer. Abby went home to Indiana to spend time with them. As she walked through the door, she saw a home health care nurse changing her mother's colostomy bag.

At about midnight that night, when Abby was alone with her parents, the bag tore. Her mother called out to her, "The damn bag's leaking." Her father stalked around the room upset almost to the point of panic.

"I'll change it," Abby said. "It'll be okay."

"You don't know how."

Inside Abby was reeling. She had never changed so much as a baby's diaper, and she wasn't sure she could face it. But Abby said she heard a voice in her head that sounded like mine. It said, "Abby! Are you gonna let a bag scare you? You can do this."

And so my moment of truth came and I had to deal with this bag of crap. And the whole time I'm thinking, You're a Lady Vol, you rise to the occasion. And I just think had I not been a Lady Vol, with all that training, I couldn't have gotten through it. And my mom said to me, "I knew you would figure it out."

— ABBY CONKLIN

Stories like that suggest that I chose the right line of work.

People often ask what I'm proudest of in my career. The answer is easy: I'm proudest of them. I'm proud that our former players get teased that they're like a cult, because you can recognize them from the way they carry themselves and walk, with their heads high, their shoulders back. I'm proud that so many shy, nonaggressive girls left our program assertive women, with an air of confidence and self-respect. Shelley Sexton Collier's husband once teased her that at player reunions, "You all stand up straighter when Pat comes in the room." Shelley just stared at him and shot back, "So do you."

You either learn to be that way, or you are

already that way, or you just quit and leave, or don't come in the first place. It was no secret that's how she is, those are the expectations, and if you aren't made of what it takes to be part of the Lady Vols program, you don't last. She wasn't willing to just pamper somebody along. She would try to develop you, but she wasn't going to compromise what she wanted the personality of that program to be.

— Jill Rankin Schneider

I'm proud that for thirty-eight years we graduated 100 percent of our players. Don't get me wrong, we are very proud of the championships — they got more difficult every year to win, and we treasure them — but one thing we could do from year to year without fail was to make sure that we were about an education first, and basketball second. Our graduation rate was no accident; it was well planned and we did it with purpose and with a will; there were times when we literally picked kids up in our cars and hauled them back to campus.

Her attention to the value of education was right up front; it wasn't third or fourth or fifth. And it was there from the get-go. A lot of coaches don't do that — not many.

I'd hate to make the list.

— LIN DUNN

I'm proud that for thirty-eight years we did our best never to cut corners or to sacrifice principles. I'm proud that we stood the test of time, and that appreciation grew in our players, once they graduated, for how we went about our business, and that they understood that we were hard on them because we wanted them to be *more.*

For many of them it might have been the very first time that someone had been absolutely unrelenting in holding them to incredibly high standards. And that can be very uncomfortable, even excruciating, if it hasn't happened to you before.

— DEAN LOCKWOOD

I'm proud that we grew the game of women's basketball from an intramural played in pinafores into a sport played on national television, in domes, in front of sellout crowds of twenty-five thousand. I'm proud that even after all the years, we still did things we didn't have to do: be generous to our competitors, help younger coaches, stand and talk to fans, sign autographs, grant open access to our program.

I'm proud of the intense loyalty among

our former players, seventy-four of whom became teachers or coaches in their own right. I'm proud that our players always come back to visit Tennessee, that my home is a place they return to when things are difficult in their lives, when they're injured or struggling personally, and that we're glued together by so much trust and affection.

> This is the culture and atmosphere she has created. Two summers ago it was myself and Mickie and Pat on the road recruiting at a summer tournament, and there are a lot of Lady Vols in coaching, and we all got together and she had taken us all to dinner. I was driving, and I said, "Coach, you always pay for us, and you don't have to do that. Thank you." She leaned up and she said, "One thing I want you all to do for me is always pay it forward. The best gift you can ever give me is to keep the Tennessee Lady Vols sisterhood and legacy when I am dead and gone." This was before her diagnosis.
> — KYRA ELZY

But for all that, the Lady Vols sisterhood will forgive me when I say that there is one thing I am prouder of than all else, than the eight titles, 1,098 victories, lifetime achievements, medals, halls of fame, all-Americans, Olympic teams, and graduation rates.

My greatest achievement is my son. He is the greenest and most beautiful branch on the Summitt coaching tree. Let me describe him to you: He is six foot one and shaped, if I may say, like one of those beautiful statues I once saw at the Parthenon. He has a shelf of reddish-blond hair and steady, deep blue eyes, and his default disposition is set on thoughtfulness. He is devout, with an iron self-control, and determined.

He is also, as it turns out, talented. In the summer of 2011, I watched him coach a summer league team of thirteen- and fourteen-year-old boys and realized he had something. "Good job," I said to him afterward, "and tell your guys to stay off the sideline on the press break."

In the spring of 2012, as I was deciding to retire, Tyler coached a team of seventeen-and-under girls to a club league championship. But on the day of a critical playoff game, he found himself in the following predicament: he had just five available players, because the rest of the team was off taking college entrance exams.

Ty had a firm policy that his players had to arrive an hour before game time, and if they were late, they were benched for the first two minutes of the game. That day, one of his star players, young Brianna Tate, walked in fifteen minutes late. Ty just ignored her, got his clipboard, and called the team into the huddle. He began to draw.

"This is a diamond and one," he said. Then he erased the one player outside the diamond.

"Now this is a diamond," he said. "Bri's sitting on the bench to start the game."

They stared at him, openmouthed. When the teams took the court, the ref looked at Ty, as if to say, "Where's your other player?" Pretty soon everyone in the gym was staring at him, including the opposing coach.

The ref said, "Uh, I'm waiting on you."

Ty said, "I'm ready."

The ref looked at Ty and he looked at Brianna on the bench, and he said, "Ohhh. Okaaaaay."

He threw the jump ball and Ty sat there for two minutes watching his kids play four-on-five. It felt like two years. Finally he put Brianna in the game — and she fouled out. He finished the game like he started it, with four players — and won by six points.

That's my boy.

If Tyler has a single pronounced quality, it's serenity. It comes from his faith, which we had never talked about much, until the diagnosis. Although we went to church regularly together since he was a little boy, we'd never discussed the subject as adults. I discovered that my son's mind is focused firmly on what really matters, and that has helped him lead us through the ordeal of the past two years.

Tyler and I accept my diagnosis with the sure knowledge that none of us have a perfect life here on earth. Whether it's managing arthritis, losing a parent, breaking a marriage, dislocating a shoulder, or being diagnosed with Alzheimer's, we're not here to be completely satisfied. Nor are we in command — not even of our own bodies. We borrow, we don't own. I know that everything I've been given came as gifts from God, and he has a way of reminding us, "This is my work."

God's plan is a mystery to me. I just know that I was given certain work to do, and I know that the world is a creation masterpiece in which he doesn't play one note or use one color. It's not all primary chords — there are sharps and flats. Where I am concerned, he is playing on the black keys, and I'm resigned to that.

Twice a month, I pay a visit to Dr. Dougherty in the neurology department at the

University of Tennessee Medical Center, to have my memory and blood tested. The idea is to track my progress, or decline, depending on what the case may be.

The routine is always the same. LaTina and I drive to the hospital and take a winding, circuitous backdoor route to neurology, for the sake of privacy. Once there, I sit in a small room in a reclining chair while my friendly nurse Ruth wraps a piece of elastic around my arm and takes my blood, and we tease each other.

"Y'all just love stickin' me, don't you?"

"We do. We draw straws."

Then Dr. Dougherty arrives to examine me. All my doctors remain concerned about the rheumatoid medication, which conflicts with the Alzheimer's drugs. They would like to draw me off it, but when they do, the arthritis flares up until I'm almost bedridden. He examines my hands, which tend to swell.

"No shortness of breath?" he asks.

"No. Except when you come in here."

"Your hands are a little cold."

"Cold hands, warm heart."

Then the fun begins. Dr. Dougherty's son Andrew, a nice young neuropathologist, draws up a chair, and for the next twenty minutes he quizzes me from a clipboard.

The questions test my memory function, problem-solving skills, and mental reactions. Every now and then he poses a trick question — something so ludicrous I assume the idea is to test whether I know an absurdity when I hear it. To see if I'm still in my right mind. Those questions tick me off.

Andrew shows me a clock with no numbers. "Can you point to where the six would be on a clock? Where the twelve is? The three? The nine?"

I point.

"Now I'm going to say three words and I want you to repeat them. Police, house, stamp."

"Police, house, stamp."

"Great. Now I'd like you to name as many animals as you can think of."

"Dog, cat, horse. Pig. How many more do I need?"

"Just a few."

"Mule."

"What about the water. What's in the water?"

Blank.

"Do you know what year you're in?"

"Yep, 2012."

"Name the months."

"September, October, November . . ."

"What day is it?"

"Wednesday."

"What about the month?"

Pause.

"June."

"Okay, we are finished with that one."

"Hallelujah."

"Can you copy this cube for me?"

I draw a cube.

"Perfect. Repeat these words: face, velvet, church, daisy, and red."

"Face velvet church daisy and red."

"Great. Okay, subtract 7 from 100."

"This is the one I don't like."

"Repeat the following: 'I only know that John is the one to help today.' "

"I only know that John is the one to help today."

"Perfect. 'The cat always hid under the couch when dogs were in the room.' "

" 'The cat always hid when the dogs were under the couch.' No, that's not it."

"How are a train and a bike similar?"

"You ride 'em."

"What about a watch and a ruler."

"A watch tells time and a ruler tells inches."

"Do you remember any of those words we repeated earlier?"

"Face, velvet . . ."

Pause.

"I'll give you a hint, it's a color and it starts with an r, and it's Alabama's school color."

"Crimson Tide! Red."

"These are just for fun. Can you tell me how many camels are in California?"

Now, what did he take me for? If there was even one camel in California, it had no business being there. Camels. I mean, what kind of question is that?

He showed me an empty square. "If this was a football field . . ."

I stopped him. "I don't play football," I said. "You need to change that to a basketball court."

"Okay, it's a basketball court. If someone threw your keys on it, where would you look? Show me with a pen."

I drew a jump circle and started diagramming. "I'd start at center court," I said. "And if not there, I'd start working the corners."

"How would a boat and a bicycle be alike?"

"Travel."

"An orange and a banana?"

"Fruit."

"What state are we currently in?"

"Tennessee."

"What place are we in?"

"UT Hospital."

"Do you know what floor we are on?"

"Heavens no."

"Can you spell *world*?"

"W-o-r-l-d."

"Okay, can you spell it backwards."

"Awwww. I knew that was coming. D . . . o . . . w . . . r . . . l."

"What about those three objects we talked about before."

"Honestly? I forgot about them."

"Write a sentence for me, any sentence."

Last came a series of questions about my emotional state. These are the questions that test my attitude. I'm told that apathy, depression, and a sense of worthlessness can go with Alzheimer's. I've had my moments with all those — what person with the diagnosis wouldn't? But as of this writing, I've always found my way through the dark and back into the light.

"Are you satisfied with life?"

"Yes."

"Do you feel a drop in interest?"

"No."

"Do you often get bored?"

"No."

"Are you in good spirits most of the time?"

"Yes."

"Are you afraid something bad is going to happen?"

"No."

"Do you worry about the future?"

"No."

"Do you feel you have more problems than most people?"

"No."

"Do you get downhearted or blue?"

"No."

"Do you worry a lot about the past?"

"No."

"Do you get upset over little things?"

"No."

"Do you feel your situation is helpless?"

"No."

I don't feel helpless, and I don't feel hopeless. Why? Because the truth is, nothing is certain with Alzheimer's, and everything is possible. I know that dementia is highly unpredictable and has a wide range. I know that at the moment I still have a good quality of life. I know that the people at Mayo, and Brigham and Women's, and the Banner Institute are working daily on a cure. I'm interested to see where a combination of faith and science will take me.

Above all, I know that Alzheimer's has brought me to a point that I was going to arrive at someday anyway. With or without this diagnosis, I was going to experience diminishment. We all do. It's our fate.

No, I can't size up a court of ten players anymore, see the clock out of one eye and the shifting schemes of opposing players with the other, and order up a countermove by hollering "Five!" or "Motion!"

But I can suggest that people with mild to moderate stages of dementia have far more abilities than incapacities. I can suggest that just because certain circuits of memory or swiftness of synapses may fail, thought and awareness and consciousness do not.

I can prove that just because Alzheimer's might prevent my mind from working the way it used to, and sometimes my tongue arrives at a roadblock and I can't find a word, that doesn't mean I've lost my feelings, or the primal urge to express them.

I can make myself useful, keep working in some capacity every day for as long as I'm able. Someday, I suppose I'll give up, and sit in the rocking chair. But I'll probably be rocking fast, because I don't know what I'll do without a job.

I can write a book. As of this writing — the fall of 2012 — my memory is still sound enough. Which is not to deny that, despite my best effort, I've felt serious effects of the disease. Some days it's as though my mind is buried in a cloud bank. Other days the cloud recedes. There are places in these pages where friends had to take over the storytelling.

But what better way to kick a memory-wasting disease in the teeth — to keep my mind sharp and my heart engaged and my life in perspective — than with a memoir?

Shortly before Tyler left home to begin his own adult life, he planted a vegetable garden for me. It's on a ridge just by the house, overlooking the Little River. Every morning I walk my dogs to the top of our property, where you can see just around the bend of the river toward the Smoky Mountains. On the clear days you can gaze far into the distance, four ghostly ridges away. Standing there, I know something with a certainty. God doesn't take things away to be cruel. He takes things away to make room for other things. He takes things away to lighten us. He takes things away so we can fly.

WHERE SOME OF
THEM ARE NOW

NICKY ANOSIKE graduated in May of 2008 with a triple major in political science, legal studies, and sociology. She won a Boyd McWhorter postgraduate scholarship award, the highest honor an athlete in the Southeastern Conference can win, volunteered at East Tennessee Children's Hospital, and qualified for the Teach for America program, with the intention of going into education. However, based on her performance in the NCAA tournament, she was a second-round draft choice of the Minnesota Lynx of the WNBA and made the league's All Rookie team in her first season. In February of 2012, she was traded to the Los Angeles Sparks, where she plays alongside her close friend Candace Parker.

DIANE BRADY is a high school math teacher.

NIYA BUTTS got her bachelor's degree in social work with a minor in psychology from Tennessee in 1999, and she obtained her master's degree in education from Tennessee Tech in 2002. After understudying with Mickie DeMoss at Kentucky for five years, where she was promoted to associate head coach in 2007, Niya was named head coach at the University of Arizona in 2008. She took over a team that had won just twelve games; in 2011, her Wildcats won twenty-one.

TASHA BUTTS graduated from Tennessee with a major in sports management and a minor in business in 2004. After a brief career in the WNBA, she returned to Tennessee as a graduate assistant, then joined Nikki Caldwell's staff at UCLA and LSU, where she is widely regarded as one of the fastest-rising young talents in coaching.

NIKKI CALDWELL, in just three seasons as head coach at UCLA, built a 71-25 record and finished runner-up in the Pac-10 twice to Final Four teams from Stanford. In 2011, she moved to LSU, where she went 23-10 in her first season, at the conclusion of which her first child, Justice, was born.

TAMIKA CATCHINGS went on to win championships at every level of her career. She is the winner of two Olympic gold medals, was the 2011 WNBA Most Valuable Player of the Year, and led the Indiana Fever to the 2012 WNBA championship. She is also the founder of Catch the Stars, a foundation that seeks to promote literacy, fitness, and mentoring for youth.

DAEDRA CHARLES-FURLOW played basketball professionally overseas in Italy, Japan, Turkey, and France from 1991 to 1996 and was the eighth overall pick by the Los Angeles Sparks in the 1997 WNBA draft. She was also a member of three USA national teams. From 2003 to 2006, Daedra was an assistant coach at the University of Detroit Mercy, before moving to Auburn University, and then Tennessee, where she became director of character development in 2010 while also battling breast cancer. In 2012, she was named head coach at Knoxville's West High School. She has a son, Anthonee.

BECKY CLARK received her doctorate in psychology and counsels abuse victims as a clinical social worker in New York. In 2005, Becky revealed to us that her deafness was a result of being beaten as a child by an alcoholic stepfather. She came back to Knoxville for a fund-raiser for victims of child abuse and went public with her experiences. In addition to her work as a child advocate, she runs marathons.

SHELLEY SEXTON COLLIER is the assistant athletic director and head women's basketball coach at the Webb School in Knoxville, where she has won two state championships. She lives in Knoxville and is the mother of four "nice" girls. Almost every morning, Shelley comes to my house and we power walk together.

ABBY CONKLIN recently got an advanced degree in graphic design and opened her own San Francisco graphic art and signage firm, A52, named after her Tennessee jersey number. Abby also received her master's in organization and leadership from the University of San Francisco and spent a decade as a high school and collegiate basketball coach before making her career change to graphic art.

KYRA ELZY received her bachelor's degree in psychology in 1999 and a master's degree in cultural studies in education in 2001.

After finishing her superb playing career and earning her degrees with consistent dean's list performances, Kyra entered the coaching profession. As an assistant at Kentucky, she was considered one of the top recruiters in the nation and helped UK advance to three consecutive NCAA tournaments, including two NCAA Elite Eight appearances, in 2010 and 2012. In the fall of 2012, she returned to Tennessee as Holly Warlick's associate head coach.

BRIDGETTE GORDON, following her graduation, played professionally in Italy, where she was a perennial All-Star and won seven Italian championships and two European Cups (1994 and 1996), before returning home for a two-year stint with the WNBA's Sacramento Monarchs. She also won an Olympic gold medal. After retirement, she became a college basketball coach. She is currently an assistant at Wichita State under former Lady Vol Jody Adams.

KELLIE JOLLY HARPER became head coach at Western Carolina in 2004 at the age of just twenty-six. In 2009, she was named head coach at North Carolina State University, where she promptly won twenty games.

PAT HATMAKER is a captain of security at Oak Ridge National Laboratory.

DEBRA HAWHEE is a professor of English at Penn State University and a historian of rhetoric. She was named a 2011–2012 Resident Scholar of Penn State's Institute for the Arts and Humanities.

CHAMIQUE HOLDSCLAW was the WNBA Rookie of the Year following her graduation from Tennessee in 1999. She has waged a valiant battle against depression throughout her career. In 2012, she wrote an autobiography, *Breaking Through: Beating the Odds Shot After Shot,* in which she documented her struggles with mental illness, including a suicide attempt. She is currently a mental health advocate for Active Minds, a group that counsels college students who find themselves in emotional trouble.

ALEXIS HORNBUCKLE was drafted fourth overall by the Detroit Shock in 2008, and in her first WNBA game, she set a franchise record with seven steals while playing just nineteen minutes. She became the first player to win an NCAA title and a WNBA title in the same season. She currently plays for the Phoenix Mercury.

646

KARA LAWSON won a WNBA championship with the Sacramento Monarchs in 2005, and in 2008 won a gold medal at the 2008 Olympics in Beijing, China. She currently plays for the Connecticut Sun. In addition, she is regarded as one of the brightest young announcing stars on ESPN. On January 12, 2007, she became the first woman to work as a nationwide broadcast analyst for an NBA game.

MICHELLE MARCINIAK is a nationally recognized young entrepreneur, cofounder of Sheex, a luxury line of bedding and sleepwear.

CANDACE PARKER became the first WNBA player to win both the Rookie of the Year and the Most Valuable Player awards in the same season for the Los Angeles Sparks in 2008. She missed the first eight games of the 2009 WNBA season after giving birth to her daughter, Lailaa Williams. She has won two straight gold medals with the USA Olympic team.

JILL RANKIN SCHNEIDER is a member of the Women's Basketball Hall of Fame and a nationally recognized high school basketball coach in Texas. In 2012, she coached the

USA women's under-17 team to a world championship.

JOY SCRUGGS is a faculty member and basketball coach at Emory and Henry College.

VONDA WARD was the world heavyweight women's boxing champion in 2002 and 2003. She retired with a record of 22-1 with seventeen knockouts. She is a personal trainer in Cleveland.

HOLLY WARLICK, after serving as either a player or an assistant for 949 of Tennessee's NCAA-record 1,098 wins and all eight NCAA championships, became Tennessee's head coach in 2012. In addition, Warlick teamed up with former Lady Vols player and assistant Nikki Caldwell, the current head coach at LSU, to establish the Champions for a Cause Foundation, which sponsors a long-haul motorcycle ride dedicated to raising funds and awareness for a cure for breast cancer. They have raised and donated more than $125,000.

■ ■ ■ ■

APPENDIX

■ ■ ■ ■

Pat Summitt Coaching Record
Season by Season

Season	Team	W-L	Postseason
1974–75	Tennessee	16-8	4th, state
1975–76	Tennessee	16-11	2nd, state
1976–77	Tennessee	28-5	AIAW Final Four
1977–78	Tennessee	27-4	AIAW tourney
1978–79	Tennessee	30-9	AIAW Final Four
1979–80	Tennessee	33-5	AIAW Final
1980–81	Tennessee	25-6	AIAW Final
1981–82	Tennessee	22-10	NCAA Final Four
1982–83	Tennessee	25-8	NCAA Regional
1983–84	Tennessee	23-10	NCAA Final
1984–85	Tennessee	22-10	NCAA Regional
1985–86	Tennessee	24-10	NCAA Final Four
1986–87	Tennessee	28-6	NCAA Champion
1987–88	Tennessee	31-3	NCAA Final Four
1988–89	Tennessee	35-2	NCAA Champion
1989–90	Tennessee	27-6	NCAA Regional
1990–91	Tennessee	30-5	NCAA Champion
1991–92	Tennessee	28-3	NCAA Regional
1992–93	Tennessee	29-3	NCAA Regional
1993–94	Tennessee	31-2	NCAA Regional
1994–95	Tennessee	34-3	NCAA Final
1995–96	Tennessee	32-4	NCAA Champion
1996–97	Tennessee	29-10	NCAA Champion
1997–98	Tennessee	39-0	NCAA Champion
1998–99	Tennessee	31-3	NCAA Regional
1999–2000	Tennessee	33-4	NCAA Final
2000–01	Tennessee	31-3	NCAA Regional
2001–02	Tennessee	29-5	NCAA Final Four
2002–03	Tennessee	33-5	NCAA Final
2003–04	Tennessee	31-4	NCAA Final
2004–05	Tennessee	30-5	NCAA Final Four

Season	Team	W-L	Postseason
2005–06	Tennessee	31-5	NCAA Regional
2006–07	Tennessee	34-3	NCAA Champion
2007–08	Tennessee	36-2	NCAA Champion
2008–09	Tennessee	22-11	NCAA 1st round
2009–10	Tennessee	32-3	NCAA Regional
2010–11	Tennessee	34-3	NCAA Regional
2011–12	Tennessee	27-9	NCAA Regional

TOTAL (38 years): 1,098-208 (.840)

RECORDS AND MILESTONES

- 1,098 wins, most in NCAA Division I college basketball history by any coach, man or woman
- Eight-time NCAA champion — 1987, '89, '91, '96, '97, '98, 2007, and '08 — most in women's basketball
- Holds a 112-23 career record in NCAA tournament games
- Seven-time NCAA Coach of the Year — 1983, '87, '89, '94, '95, '98, 2004
- 36 consecutive seasons with 20-plus wins
- Gold medal winner as coach of 1984 U.S. Olympic team
- Silver medal winner as a player (cocaptain) on 1976 U.S. Olympic team
- Graduated from University of Tennessee at Martin in 1974, leaving as the school's all-time leading scorer with 1,045 points
- Inducted into five halls of fame — Nai-

651

smith Basketball Hall of Fame, Women's Basketball Hall of Fame, Women's Sports Foundation Hall of Fame, Tennessee Sports Hall of Fame, and Tennessee Women's Hall of Fame

- Most seasons coached in NCAA/AIAW play without a losing record (38, lost more than nine games in a season only six times and more than ten games in a season only twice)
- Most consecutive NCAA/AIAW postseason appearances (38, never missed a tournament)
- Most number one seeds in NCAA Division I postseason play (20)
- Most wins as an NCAA/AIAW Division I basketball head coach (1,098; in second place is Mike Krzyzewski with 927 wins)
- Most wins in NCAA postseason play (112)
- Most NCAA Final Four appearances (18, six more than John Wooden, who holds the men's records)
- Most NCAA/AIAW championship game appearances (15)
- Most 20-win seasons in NCAA/AIAW play (36, all consecutive seasons)
- Most 30-win seasons in NCAA/AIAW play (20)

HONORS

2000 Named the Naismith
     Basketball Coach of the
     Century
2008 ESPY Award for Best Coach
     of the Year; award
     encompasses all sports, col-
     lege and professional
2009 Named to *Sporting News*'s list
     of the 50 greatest coaches of
     all time (MLB, NBA, NFL,
     NHL, college basketball,
     and college football)
2011 Named *Sports Illustrated*'s
     Sportsman of the Year
     (shared with Duke
     University men's basketball
     coach Mike Krzyzewski)
2012 Awarded the 2012
     Presidential Medal of
     Freedom by President
     Barack Obama; Arthur Ashe
     Courage Award, ESPYs

ALL-TIME TENNESSEE LADY VOLS
UNDER COACH PAT HEAD SUMMITT

Jody Adams.... 1989–1993
Nicky Anosike.... 2004–2008
Alberta Auguste.... 2006–2008
Lauren Avant.... 2010–2011

Suzanne Barbre.... 1974–1978
Briana Bass.... 2008–2012
Vicki Baugh.... 2007–2012
Angie Bjorklund.... 2007–2011
Shannon Bobbitt.... 2006–2008
Cindy Boggs.... 1974–1975
Fonda Bondurant.... 1975–1977
Sherry Bostic.... 1984-1986
Nancy Bowman.... 1972–1975
Gina Bozeman.... 1981
Diane Brady.... 1973–1975
Alyssa Brewer.... 2008–2011
Cindy Brogdon.... 1977–1979
Cierra Burdick.... 2011–present
Niya Butts.... 1996–2000
Tasha Butts.... 2000–2004
Kelley Cain.... 2007–2011
Nikki Caldwell.... 1990–1994
Sonya Cannon.... 1981–1985
Abby Canon.... 2004–2005
Amanda Canon.... 1998–2002
Tamara Carver.... 1990–1991
Kelli Casteel.... 1988–1992
Tamika Catchings.... 1997–2001
Lesia Cecil.... 1985–1986
Daedra Charles.... 1988–1991
Becky Clark.... 1979–1980
Regina Clark.... 1988–1992
Kristen "Ace" Clement.... 1997–2001
Susan Clower.... 1978–1982

Lynne Collins.... 1980–1984
Shelia Collins.... 1981–1985
Abby Conklin.... 1993–1997
Pam Cook.... 1982–1983
Elizabeth Curry.... 2006–2007
Bev Curtis.... 1979
Latina Davis.... 1992–1996
LaToya Davis.... 2000–2004
Susie Davis.... 1976–1979
Freda DeLozier.... 1975
Rochone Dilligard.... 1991–1994
Gail Dobson.... 1971–1975
Sybil Dosty.... 2004–2005
Faith Dupress.... 2009–2010
Kris Durham.... 1987–1989
Sarah Edwards.... 1998–2001
Tonya Edwards.... 1986–1990
Cindy Ely.... 1977–1981
Shyra Ely.... 2001–2005
Kyra Elzy.... 1996–2001
Peggy Evans.... 1990–1993
Sherri Fancher.... 1976–1979
Tye'sha Fluker.... 2002–2005
Susan Foulds.... 1979–1981
Valerie Freeman.... 1983–1985
Sheila Frost.... 1985–1989
Alex Fuller.... 2004–2009
Amy Gamble.... 1983–1984
Marci Garner.... 1974–1976
Teresa Geter.... 1997–1999

Bridgette Gordon.... 1985–1989
Liza Graves.... 1975–1978
Amber Gray.... 2008–2012
Kathie Greene.... 1975–1976
Misty Greene.... 1995–1998
Debbie Groover.... 1977–1981
Aubrey Guastalli.... 2004–2005
Tanya Haave.... 1980–1984
Leanne Hance.... 1977–1978
Jerilynn Harper.... 1978–1979
Isabelle Harrison.... 2011–present
Lisa Harrison.... 1989–1993
Pat Hatmaker.... 1980–1984
Debbie Hawhee.... 1988–1992
Dena Head.... 1988–1992
Lea Henry.... 1979–1983
Chamique Holdsclaw.... 1995–1999
Alexis Hornbuckle.... 2004–2008
Karla Horton.... 1984–1987
Brittany Jackson.... 2001–2005
Gwen Jackson.... 1999–2003
Marlene Jeter.... 1990–1992
Dana Johnson.... 1991–1995
Glory Johnson.... 2008–2012
Michelle Johnson.... 1993–1995
Tiffani Johnson.... 1994–1997
Kellie Jolly.... 1995–1999
Janice Koehler.... 1974–1976
Tammy Larkey.... 1981–1983
Kara Lawson.... 1999–2003

Brynae Laxton.... 1995–1998
Cheryl Littlejohn.... 1983–1987
Alicia Manning.... 2008–2012
Michelle Marciniak.... 1993–1996
Pam Marr.... 1982–1986
Dawn Marsh.... 1984–1988
Ariel Massengale.... 2011–present
Melissa McCray.... 1985–1989
Nikki McCray.... 1991–1995
Courtney McDaniel.... 2000–2004
April McDivitt.... 1999–2002
Carla McGhee.... 1986–1990
Lisa McGill.... 1976–1979
Cait McMahan.... 2006–2009
Laurie Milligan.... 1994–1998
Nicci Moats.... 2006–2007
Zandra Montgomery.... 1977–1979
Loree Moore.... 2001–2005
Pearl Moore.... 1987–1990
Tasheika Morris.... 1990–2000
Karen Morton.... 1982–1983
Lindsey Moss.... 2005–2006
Sabrina Mott.... 1986–1987
Michelle Munoz.... 2001–2002
Cindy Noble.... 1978–1981
Kathy O'Neil.... 1976–1980
Mary Ostrowski.... 1980–1984
Candace Parker.... 2004–2008
Jane Pemberton.... 1975–1976
Shalon Pillow.... 1998–2002

Semeka Randall.... 1997–2001
Jill Rankin.... 1979–1980
Linda Ray.... 1981–1985
Dominique Redding.... 2003–2007
Emily Roberts.... 1976–1977
Patricia Roberts.... 1976–1977
Ashley Robinson.... 2000–2004
Debbie Scott.... 1988–1990
Joy Scruggs.... 1971–1975
Jan Seay.... 1977–1978
Shelley Sexton.... 1983–1987
Meighan Simmons.... 2010–present
Sydney Smallbone.... 2007–2011
Kim Smallwood.... 1995–1996
Melissa Smith.... 1989–1990
Tanika Smith.... 1993–1995
Michelle Snow.... 1998–2002
Kristie Snyder.... 1983–1984
Taber Spani.... 2009–present
Sydney Spencer.... 2003–2007
Kathy Spinks.... 1984–1988
LaShonda Stephens.... 1996–2000
Shekinna Stricklen.... 2008–2012
Sue Thomas.... 1974–1977
Pashen Thompson.... 1993–1997
Mina Todd.... 1980–1981
Paula Towns.... 1980–1984
Gay Townson.... 1986–1987
Jennifer Tuggle.... 1984–1988
Vonda Ward.... 1991–1995

Holly Warlick.... 1976–1980
Jackie Watson.... 1974–1977
Lisa Webb.... 1983–1988
Sa'de Wiley-Gatewood.... 2004–2005
Kamiko Williams.... 2009–present
Tiffany Woosley.... 1991–1995
Shanna Zolman.... 2002–2006

ACKNOWLEDGMENTS

Writing a memoir with Alzheimer's disease is an unlikely undertaking. Fortunately, there was abundant documentary material to draw on, primarily three lengthy sets of interviews between the coauthors of this book. The first two took place in 1997 and 1998, the voluminous tapes and notes of which still exist. The third occurred during the season of 2011–2012, as I dealt with the diagnosis and the task of trying to coach with the disease.

No one sees one's life wholly, even under the best circumstances. I'm therefore grateful to all the family and friends who rounded out my memories with their own and reminded me of things I'd forgotten. My mother, Hazel; my sister, Linda; and my brothers, Tommy, Charles, and Kenneth, and their spouses helped me revisit my youth in Henrietta, Tennessee, and I thank them for that, and for their sustaining devotion to our family.

Many former Tennessee Lady Vols shared their recollections graciously, hilariously, and forgivingly. The omission of names or events is in no way reflective of their importance to me — if I included them all, this book would have numbered thousands of pages. I could write a separate chapter about each and every Lady Vol and care for them equally.

Tennessee's current and former coaches Mickie DeMoss, Holly Warlick, Nancy Darsch, Dean Lockwood, Nikki Caldwell, Carolyn Peck, Jane Albright, and Al Brown literally lived these pages. Their loyalty and friendship survived every high and low and would have been worth the journey without a single championship. Thanks also to Billie Moore, to Bill Wall, and to all those coaches who shaped me in some way, none more so than our opponents, especially Jody Conradt, Vivian Stringer, Leon Barmore, Tara VanDerveer, Melanie Balcomb, Kim Mulkey, Joe Ciampi, Sharon Fanning, Nell Fortner, Sonja Hogg, Andy Landers, Theresa Grentz, Debbie Ryan, Gail Goestenkors, Carol Ross, and Wendy Larry. I wish Kay Yow and Sue Gunter were here to thank. I'm especially grateful to those who were kind enough to share their thoughts in formal interviews for the book: Marynell Meadors, Lin Dunn, Sylvia Rhyne Hatchell, and Geno Auriemma.

I owe the administrators and faculty at the University of Tennessee past and present, in particular my longtime friend Joan Cronan, four decades' worth of affection and gratitude. I owe the same to all those on our support staff: the many people who worked in operations, academic support, sports medicine, and strength and training, who contributed so much to our success for so little credit. Kathy Harston in particular made it possible for me to continue working these last couple of years. To the donors who supported us through the years, I can only express my profound thank-you by saying, "Look what you built."

Deepest thanks go to my old pal Jane Brown Clark for her many stories and pictures. And to the sisters of the Chi Omega house, particularly Esther Stubblefield Hubbard, Carla Witherington, and Mary Margaret Carter, for their longstanding friendship and steadfastness.

To all the doctors who have cared for me, consulted with me, and aided me, thanks to you I'm still standing.

Without the institutional memory, crack research, and devoted efforts of Debby

Jennings, there would simply be no book. The same is true of the invaluable personal assistance of Katie Wynn and LaTina Haynes. During the writing of it, my friends Adam Waller and Danielle Donehew not only managed to help with some of these pages but also launched the Pat Summitt Foundation.

I am indebted to Tina Constable of Crown for her belief in this undertaking, and to Mauro DiPreta for his superb editing, and his care and patience in seeing it onto the page, and to Jessica Wallin for her help with anything and everything. I'm also thankful for the support and friendship of Esther Newberg of ICM on the project, as well as Tammy Blake, David Drake, and Meredith McGinnis at Crown.

Almost twenty years ago I began getting letters from a guy named Robert B. Barnett of Williams & Connolly, urging me to write a book. Under Bob's guidance I've written three. More important, his protective counsel guided me through the last two difficult years and pointed me toward the future.

Above all, thanks to my son, Tyler, my rock.

ABOUT THE AUTHORS

Pat Summitt became the head coach of women's basketball at the University of Tennessee in 1974 and has won more national championships than any coach except the legendary John Wooden. She is the first coach in NCAA history to reach 1,000 wins. She lives in Tennessee, where she is head coach emeritus of the Tennessee Lady Vols.

Sally Jenkins is the author or coauthor of nine books, including the #1 *New York Times* bestseller *It's Not About the Bike; The Real All Americans: The Team That Changed a Game, a People, a Nation;* and *The State of Jones.* Her work has been featured in *Vanity Fair, GQ,* and *Sports Illustrated,* and she has been a staff writer for the *Washington Post* for more than two decades. A native of Texas, Jenkins graduated from Stanford and lives in Sag Harbor, New York.